"Easily the most comprehensive and readable
most disgraceful episodes in American history . . . tells of officials
who ignored the hard evidence that there was no evidence that
Japanese Americans were disloyal . . . who nevertheless cooperated
in putting their fellow Americans in concentration camps."—
Congressional Affairs Press

"Excellent. A work of high merit and genuine originality which goes
well beyond the considerable literature on the subject. . . . The
phrase in the subtitle, "the untold story," is not a publisher's blurb
but the truth. It is a remarkable tribute to [Weglyn's] tenacity and
intelligence that she has unearthed documents that a series of
trained scholars and reporters overlooked."—**William Peterson,
author of *Japanese Americans***

"A heartbreaking chronicle of man's inhumanity to man . . . meticu-
lously documented and well written . . . should win a Pulitzer or
National Book Award."—**George Morgenstern, author of
*Pearl Harbor***

"Overwhelming in its evidence . . . the mountain of evidence about
the unconstitutional and repressive policies . . . sting and burn . . .
the sense of overkill is with the reader."—*Minneapolis Tribune*

"The first book to crack the governing interpretative perspective on
the internment years and establish, in the process, a supplanting one
that the new wave of writers on the subject will be writing within
. . . sound research, compelling and penetrating writing."—**Arthur
Hansen, California State University, Fullerton**

"The first and only Asian American work to actually effect a change
in Japanese American character and history. . . . *Years of Infamy* got
Japanese America up for chasing redress by recovering what was lost
and restoring what was abandoned. No book, no work of science,
literature, or art has had such an immediate and palpable effect on
Japanese American behavior and history."—**Frank Chin, author of
*The Chickencoop Chinaman and The Year of the Dragon***

"One of the most significant publications of this decade—not merely
to Japanese Americans but to all Americans. This significance will be
recognized more and more as the years go by."—**Dr. Clifford Uyede,
National Japanese American Historical Society**

Yesterday, December 7, 1941—a date which will live in infamy—the United States of America was suddenly and deliberately attacked by naval and air forces of the Empire of Japan.

—Franklin D. Roosevelt, War Message to Congress,
December 8, 1941

August 1999

To my good friend Frank

— Dave Lips

Years of Infamy was awarded the Anisfield-Wolf Award in Race Relations in 1976 by judges Oscar Handlin, Gwendolyn Brooks, and Ashley Montagu.

YEARS OF INFAMY

The Untold Story of America's Concentration Camps

Updated Edition

Michi Nishiura Weglyn

With an Introduction by James A. Michener

University of Washington Press

Seattle and London

Library of Congress Cataloging-in-Publication Data
Weglyn, Michi, 1926–
  Years of infamy : the untold story of America's concentration camps /
Michi Nishiura Weglyn : with an introduction by James A. Michener. —
Updated ed.
     p.   cm.
  Includes bibliographical references and index.
  ISBN 0–295–97484–2 (alk. paper)
  1. Japanese Americans—Evacuation and relocation, 1942–1945.
2. World War, 1939–1945—Concentration camps—United States.
3. World War, 1939–1945—Personal narratives, American. I. Title
D769.8.A6W43   1996   95–453374
940.53'1503956073—dc20   CIP

Cover photo of Manzanar monument by Boku Kodama

DEDICATED
TO
WAYNE M. COLLINS

Who Did More to Correct a Democracy's Mistake
Than Any Other One Person

Wayne Collins
(San Francisco Chronicle)

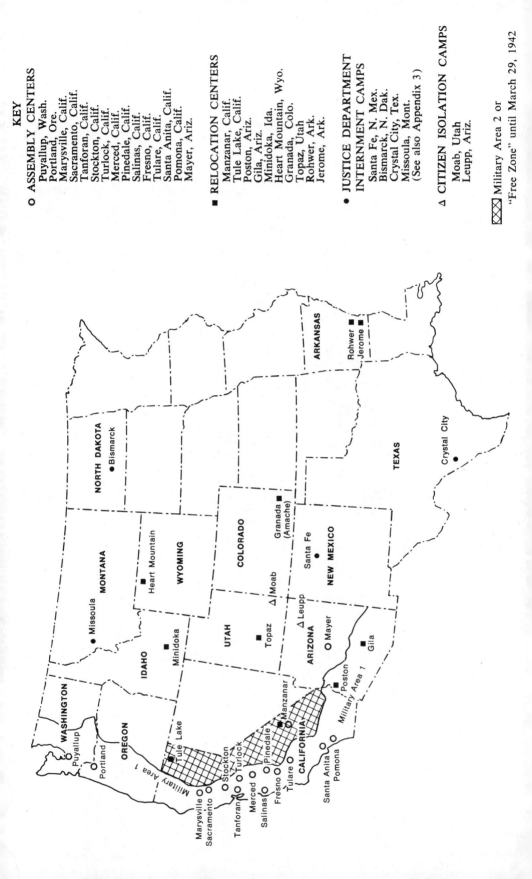

KEY

○ ASSEMBLY CENTERS
Puyallup, Wash.
Portland, Ore.
Marysville, Calif.
Sacramento, Calif.
Tanforan, Calif.
Stockton, Calif.
Turlock, Calif.
Merced, Calif.
Pinedale, Calif.
Salinas, Calif.
Fresno, Calif.
Tulare, Calif.
Santa Anita, Calif.
Pomona, Calif.
Mayer, Ariz.

■ RELOCATION CENTERS
Manzanar, Calif.
Tule Lake, Calif.
Poston, Ariz.
Gila, Ariz.
Minidoka, Ida.
Heart Mountain, Wyo.
Granada, Colo.
Topaz, Utah
Rohwer, Ark.
Jerome, Ark.

● JUSTICE DEPARTMENT
INTERNMENT CAMPS
Santa Fe, N. Mex.
Bismarck, N. Dak.
Crystal City, Tex.
Missoula, Mont.
(See also Appendix 3)

△ CITIZEN ISOLATION CAMPS
Moab, Utah
Leupp, Ariz.

⊠ Military Area 2 or
"Free Zone" until March 29, 1942

Most of the 110,000 persons removed for reasons of "national security" were school-age children, infants and young adults not yet of voting age. *(National Archives)*

The sick were not exempt from the roundup and removal, except critically ill individuals who were left behind in institutions. *(National Archives)*

The first order of business in the detention centers after checking into a one-room "apartment" was to improvise mattresses for family members. *(National Archives)*

Evacuees in the relocation centers took on tasks essential to the camps' maintenance. The rate of pay for most was sixteen dollars per month. *(National Archives)*

Toilets and showers were left unpartitioned. Only after vigorous protests from church groups were partitions (without doors) put up in the women's latrines. *(Courtesy of Estelle Ishigo)*

Farewell ceremonies in Honolulu. In Hawaii, where wholesale internment was not carried out, thousands upon thousands gratefully and enthusiastically volunteered for the all-Nisei Combat Team. *(United Press International)*

The Manzanar Project jail was a prison within a prison located in the police station, the locale of the December 6 riot. It was a steel cell block which accommodated four persons. *(University Research Library, UCLA)*

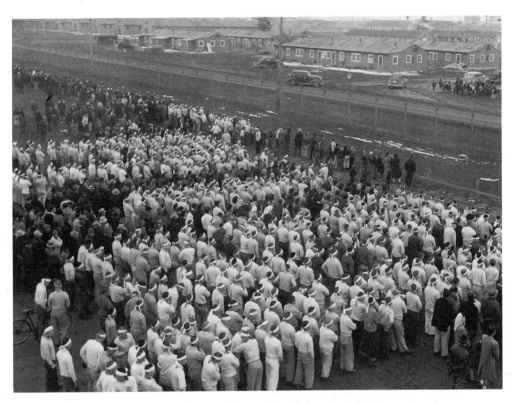

After Tule Lake was converted into a Segregation Center, discontent and antagonism were more openly aired by extremists and their sympathizers. A group is shown standing opposite the administration area in preparation for a mass demonstration. *(National Archives)*

As the once-compliant turned defiant and attempted to pressure others, early morning raids and removals to FBI camps were instituted by the Border Patrol. *(National Archives)*

DATE **DEC 1 1943**
p.

Inspiration by Short-Wave

Tokio Radio Directed 'Riot' at Tule Lake, Costello Says

By United Press

Rep. Costello (D., Calif.) said today there was evidence that recent disturbances at the Tule Lake, Calif., Segregation Center were "inspired" by the Jap government and touched off by short-wave messages from Tokio to pro-Japanese internees.

Costello, chairman of a Dies sub-committee investigating the disorders, said the inquiry had indicated the riots were inspired by Tokio "to make the American Government look bad," and that the committee had reports that leaders of the outbreaks were in radio contact with Tokio.

He said residents in the camp area reported that Jap language broadcasts interfered with their reception of long-wave programs immediately preceding the disturbances, and that explanations offered by spokesmen for the internees were "unsatisfactory."

After the Army moved in troops, he said, the interference was no longer heard. The FBI is investigating reports that at least two short-wave sending sets were located in the Tule Lake area, he declared.

The chairman said it was his opinion that Dillon Myer, War Relocation Authority director, should be replaced by a "man better qualified to establish and enforce discipline." He had no candidate but believed the job could best be filled by a "retired Army officer with administrative experience."

He also suggested that the internal security structure of the War Relocation centers be reorganized and Jap police supplanted by white police. He disagreed with a suggestion by Rep. Engle (D., Calif.) that the Tule Lake camp should be placed under military control.

From OF 4245-G
Tule Lake,
FDR Library

DATE **NOV 9- 1943**
p.

THERE is just one word to describe the situation which is being uncovered by investigations of the Jap mutiny in the Tule Lake (Calif.) segregation center. That is "ROTTEN." Former employes at the camp have told a California senate committee that WHITE EMPLOYES OF THE CAMP WERE UNDER INSTRUCTIONS FROM THE WAR RELOCATION ADMINISTRATION NOT TO GIVE ORDERS TO JAP INTERNEES BUT TO MERELY "MAKE SUGGESTIONS." And after the riot a week ago, a former camp official testified, employes were told by WRA Director Myer, "if you can't take it, get out."

Apparently, this camp where ENEMY JAPS are interned, has been RUN BY THE JAPS INSTEAD OF BY AN AGENCY OF THE UNITED STATES GOVERNMENT. Either the WRA is a "Jap-loving" outfit or its policies are dictated by "Jap-lovers." It would be interesting to know what American victims of Jap atrocities in the southwest Pacific would say about the way the WRA has been coddling enemy Japs in this country.

A few days ago, the Seattle Star quoted WRA Director Myer as saying the postwar problem of handling the Japs in this country is no problem at all because "we can, within three generations, assimilate them." THE ONLY WAY THE JAPS IN THIS COUNTRY COULD BE "ASSIMILATED" IS THRU INTERMARRIAGE WITH WHITE AMERICANS. IS THAT WHAT MYER IS ADVOCATING? DOES HE WANT TO MIX YELLOW AND WHITE BLOOD?

Chronicle (IR)
San Francisco, Calif.

DATE NOV 6 - 1943
p.

Army Should Keep Control, Warren Says

SACRAMENTO, Nov. 5 (AP)—Presence of many thousand Japanese in California including "so many of those admittedly American - hating Japs" in the Tulelake Relocation Center constitutes a "positive" danger to the State, and a threat to the war effort, Governor Warren told a press conference today.

He declared the United States Army should take permanent charge of the relocation center and disclosed that he had urged the military to take action last Tuesday after reaching the conclusion "that the Federal authorities had not been telling the truth about the conditions there."

Times-Herald (I)
Washington, D. C.

DATE NOV 1 4 1943
p.

Chandler Asks Jap Rioters Be Transferred to Aleutians

Senator Albert B. Chandler (D.) of Kentucky, of the Senate Military Affairs Committee, said yesterday that disloyal Jap rioters in western internment camps should be transferred to special quarters in the Aleutian Islands.

Chandler, who headed an investigationg of the Japanese camps a year ago, warned that trouble would result from the "coddling" of prisoners by the War Relocation Authority under Director Dillon S. Myer.

"These disloyal Japanese have no place at all in the American way of life," Chandler said. "I am convinced that they came here only to make trouble

"Now the safety and decent treatment of American prisoners in Japanese hands will be held over o . heads and complaints will be made on the slightest pretext by the Japanese government.

"We should immediately prepare to move Japs who rioted at the Tule Lake Camp in California to quarters in the Aleutian Islands."

Chandler said an Aleutian cantonment could be built at relatively little cost and effort. Japs sent there would be completely free to do as they pleased and yet could cause no harm to this country, he asserted.

"If the Army had been put in chage of these camps, as we suggested, these recent riots would never have occurred," Chandler continued. "I think Mr. Myer now has a clear idea of what our committee meant when it urged the change." Myer. head of the whole Relocation Authority, was held a prisoner in the Tule Lake camp for several hours by Jap rioters.

Chandler was bitter in denunciation of the "kid glove" type of handling Jap internees. He specifically referred to women workers in some Western camps who reportedly have invited internees to their homes for meals.

Oregonian (IR)
Portland, Oregon

DATE
P. NOV 5 1943

The Army Writes the Sequel

With tanks, tommy guns, rifles and bayonets the army moved into the Tulelake segregation center, where Jap chauvinists had disregarded the civilian authorities and created a situation pregnant with dread. Now that the army is there, and in full control, it would seem that we have no cause for further apprehension. And the army itself deserves praise for the cool military method with which it handled a highly inflammable emergency, quelling the disorder without firing a shot. Had that camp been an American camp in Japan, and had Japanese soldiers been summoned to abate a similar uprising, the ground would have been drenched with blood. The Jap, as a soldier, revels in the slaughter of unarmed human targets.

Sun (I)
Chicago, Ill.

DATE NOV 1 5 1943
p.

The Axis on the Air

Tokyo Makes Most Of Tulelake Riots

By Harold Ettlinger.

TOKYO propagandists, as had been predicted in this column, have lost no time in making capital of the disturbances at the camp for Japanese internees at Tulelake, Calif.

Broadcasts on the subject have been beamed to Asia and South America as well as this country, some of them praising the internees and others condemning the American authorities.

An English language broadcast to this country said that the internees had been "living up to the true spirit of the Japanese" and that the riots were "another instance of American brutality."

The Spanish language broadcast said that the "news had caused great indignation to the Japanese people," while French-speaking audiences in Asia were told that the Japanese at Tulelake had "refused to work for the American war effort" and that the American authorities "finally took recourse to machine guns and tanks in order to force these defenseless Japanese to work." That version of the disturbances was a fanciful one which did not agree at all with the facts as reported to official government investigators.

Authoritarian tactics employed by security personnel served to make "martyrs" of victims and increased agitation within the Segregation Center. (*Smuggled photos courtesy of Wayne M. Collins*)

An upsurge of Japanese consciousness occurred in their isolation from American life; by a reawakening of pride in their cultural heritage, a sense of dignity and self-respect was restored. *(By permission from* Impounded People, *Edward H. Spicer, et al., Tucson: University of Arizona, © 1969)*

Even in Tule Lake, where anti-American feelings ran high, the President's death was mourned by the general camp population and special services were held in Franklin D. Roosevelt's memory. *(National Archives)*

Subjected to influences which caused them to renounce their American citizenship, thousands sought to recover their birthright after awakening from their delirium. Here, hundreds of Tulean Nisei and Kibei targeted for deportation wait patiently in line for mitigation hearings. (*National Archives*)

The Asian American contingent, Vietnam Peace March (November 15, 1969) in San Francisco. Along with other ethnic minorities in the U.S., once-quiet Japanese Americans have turned vocal. The progenies of former camp inmates vow "never again!" *(By permission of Raymond Y. Okamura, © 1976)*

JOHN J. McCLOY IN "CONVERSATIONS WITH ERIC SEVAREID" (CBS-TV, JUNE 25, 1975)

SEVAREID: Some people known as political liberals had something to do with that [expulsion to inland camps]. You were involved in that to some degree at least.

McCLOY: Hm-hmm, hm-hmm . . . yes.

SEVAREID: And I wondered why on earth was it done that way?

McCLOY: Well . . . in the first place, the Japanese had attacked Pearl Harbor, and they— the shock that that created was a shock that I think that very few people now realize . . . unless they were there on the ground, and . . . the Yellow Menace concept that pretty well pervaded the thinking on the West Coast. But at any rate, after Pearl Harbor there was this enormous shock, and there was— there was this— appeals coming immediately from the Commanding General out there. What was his name?

SEVAREID: DeWitt?

McCLOY: DeWitt, General DeWitt . . . and there was this somewhat— this— this hysterical situation. He didn't know then whether the Japs— Japanese were going to attack the West Coast or whether they weren't. . . . They did send a submarine over there. . . . One of the things that we don't realize was occurring then . . . the barn burnings that were starting in that valley where the Japanese were. . . . And the local situation was getting out of hand, and it was— you had to protect a lot of the Japanese people. At any rate, Mr. Roosevelt was called— was in on it, and he was in favor of it. And then we had to move a hundred thousand people, or whatever it was.

SEVAREID: Well, that should be done by normal police methods.

McCLOY: Well, yes, but it was— it— it was— the barn burnings were— were getting beyond it. . . . We don't know that we can control this situation if it gets much worse. . . . But the decision was a civilian decision. It wasn't an Army decision. But the only fellows that could carry it out were the Army. . . . So, I was sort of told off to do this, and I went out there and spent a lot of time on it. I do think the thing was rather benign in the way it was carried out. Later on, I spent a lot of time trying to get them . . . compensation for the—

SEVAREID: They lost so much.

McCLOY: . . . Overnight they were kicked out.

SEVAREID: People just ripped them off.

McCLOY: . . . And they weren't adequately compensated.

On June 21, 1984, McCloy testified before the Commission on Wartime Relocation and Internment of Civilians regarding the Pearl Harbor attack: "I was the chief, the highest civilian official in the War Department on that day . . . I had been reading MAGIC to some extent because I had been cleared for it. . . . I was perfectly convinced that that Sunday morning, something was going to happen in the Pacific. . . . I came in that morning with these premonitions." Interestingly, barn burnings may have taken place when internees returned to coastal homes but *not prior to their exclusion.* McCloy ended up strongly opposing redress to his dying day.

Preface

In the wake of the wartime panic which followed the Japanese attack on Pearl Harbor, 110,000 Japanese Americans *. residing along the West Coast of America were driven from home and society and banished to desert wastes.

As a teen-age participant in this mass exodus I, like others, went along into confinement, trusting that our revered President in his great wisdom and discernment had found that the measure was in the best interest of our country. With profound remorse, I believed, as did numerous Japanese Americans, that somehow the stain of dishonor we collectively felt for the treachery of Pearl Harbor must be eradicated, however great the sacrifice, however little we were responsible for it. In our immaturity and naïveté, many of us who were American citizens—two-thirds of the total—believed that this, under the circumstances, was the only way to prove our loyalty to a country which we loved with the same depth of feeling that children in Japan were then being brought up to love their proud island nation.

In an inexplicable spirit of atonement and with great sadness, we went with our parents to concentration camps.

Twenty-five years later, curiosity led me into exhuming documents of this extraordinary chapter in our history, which had seen the shattering of so many hearths, lives, careers—of so many hopes and dreams. Among once impounded papers, I came face to face with facts, some that left me greatly pained. A quarter of a century later, at a time when angry charges of government duplicity and "credibility gaps" were being hurled at heads of state, the gaps of the evacuation era appeared more like chasms.

Persuaded that the enormity of a bygone injustice has been only partially perceived, I have taken upon myself the task of piecing together

* Although 110,000 individuals were involved in the West Coast evacuation, 120,000 persons of Japanese ancestry eventually came under WRA custody. This included 1,275 institutionalized individuals transferred to the centers, 1,118 citizens and aliens evacuated from Hawaii, 219 voluntary residents, and 5,981 who were born in the camps. WRA Statistics Section.

what might be called the "forgotten"—or ignored—parts of the tapestry of those years. This I have done not to awaken disquieting memories or arouse negative feelings, but because of a clear responsibility I feel for those whose honor was so wrongly impugned, many of whom died without vindication.

More significantly, I hope this uniquely American story will serve as a reminder to all those who cherish their liberties of the very fragility of their rights against the exploding passions of their more numerous fellow citizens, and as a warning that they who say that it can never happen again are probably wrong.

New York City   MICHI NISHIURA WEGLYN

NOTE TO THE 1996 EDITION

This edition of *Years of Infamy* contains information not found in the original. The author has not attempted a systematic revision or update, but has added: the transcript of a conversation between John J. McCloy and Eric Sevareid (p. 20); statements by George S. Patton, Jr., and Karl R. Bendetson (aka Bendetsen) (p. 182); an excerpt from a memo to the State Department from Assistant Secretary of State Breckinridge Long (p. 184); a memo concerning Curtis Munson's "confidential mission" (p. 194); Mrs. Curtis Munson's comment to the author (p. 194); a brief update on the Japanese American quest for redress (pp. 281-82); a supplement to the Notes regarding landmark legal victories (p. 326); information on microfilmed documents (p. 326); and a supplement to the Bibliography (pp. 341-42).

Acknowledgments

In the preparation of this volume, I have become indebted to scores of people who have contributed to it, directly and indirectly, by their courtesy in answering queries by mail, granting interviews, providing me with leads and contacts, in criticizing portions of the manuscript, in sending me books, pamphlets, clippings, and documents from their own evacuation files and libraries. To all, I give sincere thanks.

None has contributed with more constancy than Edison Uno, Lecturer in Asian American Studies at San Francisco State University, who has been a source of unfailing support, encouragement, and inspiration. I recall that, years back, a request for contributions of evacuation reminiscences directed to readers of the *Pacific Citizen* brought only one response: It was from Edison Uno, challenging the credentials of a "Weglyn" presuming to write about a matter of such deep concern to the Japanese community on the basis of such a query. The letter had been accompanied by a bulging envelope filled with faded old newspaper clippings, pamphlets, and a bibliography of the internment years, with a pointed suggestion that the matter be properly researched.

I hope that, as a fellow Nisei, I have not failed him.

A sincere debt of gratitude is owed Dr. William Petersen, Robert Lazarus Professor of Social Demography, Ohio State University, for invaluable editorial criticism and suggestions made available to me after a reading of an earlier draft of the manuscript. It was my singular good fortune to have the distinguished Senior Editor of the *Yomiuri Shimbun,* Mr. Tatsugi Ogane, bring Dr. Petersen's strongly positive critique of *Years of Infamy* to public attention, which led to its Japanese-language publication by the Political Public Relations Center, Tokyo.

Earlier drafts of this book (or portions thereof) were read by a number of persons whose criticisms, suggestions, and insights have been extremely helpful. I am indebted to Richard Marshall and Betty Voigt Marshall for their ever-dependable counsel and vigorous support; to Mrs. Yvonne Cannon for helpful editorial suggestions on my first draft; to Paul G. Robertson for a careful scrutiny of the chapter on the isolation centers; to Harry Honda for perusing the section dealing with evacuee claims and for responding, without failure, to query after query through the years; to Karl Yoneda for some vigorous criticisms which were helpful and constructive; to Grant Ujifusa for a perceptive analysis which, I hope, has resulted in the strengthening of certain chapters; to Mrs. Mary Naka-hiro Karasawa, whose contributions have gone beyond providing advice and encouragement; to Fairley Muehleck for her expert and invaluable editorial assistance; to Merrill Pollack for his unfailing enthusiasm and encouragement.

Special and grateful acknowledgment is made to Mrs. Yone Stafford, who made available to me a whole library of books—some of them eye-openers—and for being a constant inspiration for all who seek after truth. And to Mrs. Mabel Sheldon Williams, lovingly remembered by countless Japanese Americans who knew her in Gila, I pay special tribute for having profoundly influenced my camp and postcamp years.

And for making the publication of this book in the English language possible, I am deeply mindful of my indebtedness to Mr. Howard Cady of William Morrow for the deep personal interest he has taken in the project; and I feel singularly privileged to have the warm support and invaluable assistance of my editor, Susanne Williams Howard, and others of Morrow's very capable staff. I wish to express my gratitude, also, for the strong moral backing given the project by the distinguished former National Secretary and long-time Washington Representative of the Japanese American Citizens League, Mike M. Masaoka, and by JACL's current National Executive Director, David Ushio, and others in the organization who have encouraged the publication of *Years of Infamy*. Among these, I make special mention of the Executive Director of the New York JACL Chapter, Ruby Yoshino Schaar, for her most energetic support, and to Bill Hosokawa, Associate Editor of *The Denver Post,* whose astute editorial suggestions after a reading of one of the final rewrites proved exceedingly helpful.

And deep-felt appreciation goes to my husband, Walter Weglyn, without whose never-failing encouragement and vital contributions the entire project might have been abandoned years ago.

Contents

26

Introduction

For the past thirty-three years I have been involved, one way or another, with moral problems relating to the 1942 evacuation of Japanese American residents on our West Coast and their imprisonment in camps. As a devoted American and one who volunteered to fight against Japan in World War II, I have striven to construct a justification for this curious, unjust and unconstitutional behavior. The following facts seem relevant.

Prior to December 7, 1941, our military personnel, including even commanders who should have known better, believed that Japanese soldiers, sailors and airmen were inferior. The incredibly successful Japanese attack on Pearl Harbor, requiring as it did superior planning, coordination and execution, shocked our leaders and prepared them psychologically to consider all Japanese inscrutable enemies. One way to save face was to explain the disaster at Pearl Harbor as the result of espionage by Japanese living in Hawaii and along our West Coast.

After Pearl Harbor our political leaders faced terribly difficult decisions. Our nation had suffered its worst defeat in history, of a magnitude that could have proved fatal, yet the general public had to be denied knowledge of how extensive our losses were. I held a fairly responsible position within the Navy in Washington and was privy to many secret documents, but even military people like me were not allowed to know the vast extent of our defeat. When, belatedly, I did learn, I was appalled both at the size of our losses and at the efficient manner in which these losses had been kept secret.

It was very tempting, in such circumstances, for the President, his military leaders and most of his Cabinet to utilize any psychological weapon that fell into their hands. If animosity and hatred could be directed against all Japanese, whether in Japan or in the United States, the war might be more vigorously pursued. This may seem like a fallacious argument today; it did not during the disastrous days of January and February 1942 when the fate of our nation swung in the balance.

Finally, our population had for many years been subjected to a propaganda barrage calculated to prove that Japan posed a mortal threat to us in the Pacific (possibly true), and that all Japanese residing within the United States were disloyal and sure to engage in sabotage should war ever erupt between Japan and the United States (totally untrue). We had been taught to hate and many did.

Those were the justifications—shabby, ignorant, malicious and fraught with danger to ourselves—which underlay the decision to throw all persons of Japanese ancestry on the West Coast into prison camps. When the order was promulgated in 1942 I doubted the validity of the arguments on which it was based. During the years I fought Japanese and studied their characteristics, I doubted the propaganda even more. When I lived in postwar Japan and observed the nation intimately, I knew the propaganda to be false. And in recent years when I have watched the emergence of modern Japan as one of our strongest allies, I have thought back on the prewar propaganda and realized how positively ridiculous it was. But consider the enormous follies our nation committed under the last of such false thinking.

1. The Army was authorized and encouraged to formulate repressive civilian policies which the Department of Justice knew to be unconstitutional, and then to enforce them illegally.

2. Monomaniacal Army personnel like General John L. DeWitt and Colonel Karl Bendetsen were handed authority to make arbitrary decisions affecting the lives of hundreds of thousands of civilians, thus scarring the reputation of our nation.

3. Great to-do was made of the fact that Japanese immigrants born in Japan but living for decades in the United States had refused to take out American citizenship—sure proof of their continued allegiance to the Emperor—but no mention was made of the American law which forbade them to become citizens. It is absolutely correct to argue that none of the older Japanese had taken out citizenship; there was no possible way they could have done so.

4. On the West Coast 110,000 Japanese Americans who could hardly have disrupted the war effort were interned, primarily because Caucasian citizens in the area sought econ   revenge. But in frontline Hawaii, where 150,000 Japanese Americans might have constituted a danger, had they been subversive as charged, there was no evacuation because the islands' industrial leaders realized that they could not operate their industries if deprived of their Japanese labor force.

5. In this time of great crisis, the United States decided for

humane and sensible reasons not to intern German or Italian nationals who might be living in the States, unless they had given overt cause to be suspected of being enemy agents. But at the same time our government decided to intern all Japanese Americans on the West Coast, regardless of their behavior; of those interned some 73 percent were American citizens, born in this country and entitled to the full protection of our laws. These citizens were imprisoned for no reason other than their race.

6. These grave injustices were perpetrated in spite of the fact that our government had in its possession proof that not one Japanese American, citizen or not, had engaged in espionage, not one had committed any act of sabotage.

This was a bleak period in the history of American freedom. A few isolated voices tried to protest—some clergymen, some scholars, some members of the government, a surprising number of military personnel who knew the Japanese Americans and understood the true situation—but our nation was bent upon revenge. The long years of propaganda were bearing fruit, and we struck out blindly, stupidly, to our eternal discredit.

It is frightening to remember the names of those well-intentioned Americans who participated in this hysteria and who engineered acts of terror against Japanese holding full American citizenship: John J. McCloy, Henry Stimson, Abe Fortas, Milton Eisenhower, Hugo Black. Some even went so far as to spell out that their illegal acts must apply to Japanese alone, and never to Italians or Germans, even though the latter might be citizens of enemy nations.

The performance of two national leaders in this crisis has always fascinated me. Colonel Frank Knox, the Secretary of Navy, was a Republican brought into the Roosevelt Cabinet to demonstrate that our wartime government transcended partisan politics. In his early years, prior to becoming publisher of the *Chicago Daily News,* he had been general manager of the Hearst press while it was conducting its crusades against the yellow peril. Understandably, he became the most blatant voice in the administration calling for the imprisonment of all Japanese Americans. On December 15, 1941, less than two weeks after Pearl Harbor, he told the nation's major wire services: "I think the most effective Fifth Column work of the entire war was done in Hawaii, with the possible exception of Norway." When he said this he already knew that no single shred of evidence had been found to prove even one case of espionage.

On February 23, 1942, he submitted an urgent memorandum to President Roosevelt recommending that every Japanese on Oahu (the most populous Hawaiian island, containing Honolulu and Pearl Harbor) be interned. To justify such action he said, "Our forces in Oahu are practically operating now in what is, in effect, enemy country—

that is all of their defense of the islands is now carried out in the presence of a population predominantly with enemy sympathies and affiliations." To repeat, he had in his hands at this time reports proving exactly the contrary.

And on March 24, 1942, he submitted a letter to a congressional committee saying that the naval disaster at Pearl Harbor was due primarily to espionage and sabotage on the part of Japanese Americans long resident on Oahu as seemingly ordinary citizens but who were in reality spies serving Japan:

> There was a considerable amount of evidence of subversive activity on the part of the Japanese prior to the attack. This consisted of providing the enemy with the most exact possible kind of information as an aid to them in locating their objectives, and also creating a great deal of confusion in the air following the attack by the use of radio sets which successfully prevented the commander in chief of the fleet from determining in what direction the attackers had withdrawn and in locating the position of the covering fleet including the carriers. . . .

There has never been even the slightest proof of such allegations, and Secretary Knox knew this.

I worked in Washington for the Navy and had numerous opportunities to observe the Secretary. He was needed in the Cabinet to provide Republican ballast and he probably served other useful purposes, but I found him a pompous, simplistic business operator most of whose utterances were as bombastic and foolish as the statements he issued to justify the imprisonment of Japanese American civilians.

But the most fascinating behavior was that of Earl Warren, then Attorney General of California, who acted in an unconscionable manner, apparently foreseeing that if he gained local popularity by inflammatory acts against the Japanese he stood a good chance of being elected governor later on.

There were three stages in the Warren performance. First he testified vigorously that Japanese farmers had willfully and with malign purpose "infiltrated themselves into every strategic spot in our coastal and valley counties." (He proved this accusation by designating any place that Japanese Americans had settled as strategic.) He then promulgated one of the most extraordinary legal theories ever foisted upon the American public: since not a single Japanese American had so far committed any disloyal act, this was proof that they intended doing so in the future. He went on to state as fact that "there is more potential danger among the group of Japanese who were born in this country than from alien Japanese who were born in Japan."

Finally, when the government began to release certain internees of rectitude so impeccable that to keep them in camp was preposterous, Governor Warren protested that every citizen thus released was a potential saboteur and must be kept out of California.

The only reason I comment on Warren's behavior—which was no worse than that of other leaders—was that in his later life, when he must have recognized the cruel folly of his wartime behavior, he became a stalwart defender of individual freedoms, a crusader for social justice, and one of our greatest Supreme Court justices. The Japanese evacuation was his graduate course in humanity; he flunked but later on remembered the problem and its just solutions.

Curiously, he never alluded publicly to his wartime folly, even though the Japanese American community repeatedly asked him to recant. On the other hand, when Tom Clark resigned from the Supreme Court in 1966 he did purge his conscience, confessing that while Attorney General of the United States he had shared the national guilt regarding the Japanese American internments: "I have made a lot of mistakes in my life . . . One is my part in the evacuation of the Japanese from California . . . Although I argued the case, I am amazed that the Supreme Court ever approved it."

The crucial point is this. Our leaders, having used unconstitutional means to treat our Japanese American citizens as they did in 1942, were half-inured to such treatment of any minority, anywhere, so that later on when Admiral William Leahy submitted his infamous recommendation that the United States do nothing about providing refuge for Jews being slaughtered in Hitlerian Germany, lest our Allies be incommoded, President Roosevelt was able to adopt the recommendation as logical.

Two remarkable facts must be pointed out. Our internment camps were not allowed to become hell holes of starvation or death; many concerned Americans, military and civilian, saw to it that this did not happen, and in their hard, persistent work helped salvage our national honor.

And the stoic heroism with which the impounded Japanese Americans behaved after their lives had been torn asunder and their property stolen from them must always remain a miracle of American history. The majesty of character they displayed then and the freedom from malice they exhibit now should make us all humble. Mrs. Weglyn, who in this book codifies and substantiates this remarkable episode in our national history, has served the nation well, for this is a story that deserved telling.

JAMES A. MICHENER

27 August 1975
Pipersville, Pennsylvania

You may think that the Constitution is your security—it is nothing but a piece of paper. You may think that the statutes are your security—they are nothing but words in a book. You may think that elaborate mechanism of government is your security—it is nothing at all, unless you have sound and uncorrupted public opinion to give life to your Constitution, to give vitality to your statutes, to make efficient your government machinery.

—CHIEF JUSTICE CHARLES EVANS HUGHES

(1)
The Secret Munson Report

One important difference between the situation in Hawaii and the mainland is that if all the Japanese on the mainland were actively disloyal they could be corraled or destroyed within a very short time.

—CURTIS B. MUNSON, November 7, 1941

I

By fall of 1941, war with Japan appeared imminent. For well over a year, coded messages going in and out of Tokyo had been intercepted and decoded by Washington cryptoanalysts. With relations between Tokyo and Washington rapidly deteriorating, a desperate sense of national urgency was evidenced in messages to Ambassador Nomura, then carrying on negotiations in the nation's capital. On July 25, Japan had seized south French Indo-China. The activation the following day of the Morgenthau-Stimson plan, calling for the complete cessation of trade with Japan and the freezing of her assets in America—Great Britain and the Netherlands following suit—had resulted in the strangulation and near collapse of the island economy.

By late September, Tokyo's coded messages included demands for data concerning the Pacific Fleet stationed at Pearl Harbor. Of great implication for U. S. Army and Naval Intelligence was the September 24 dispatch directed to Consul Nagao Kita in Honolulu:

HENCEFORTH, WE WOULD LIKE TO HAVE YOU MAKE REPORTS CONCERNING VESSELS ALONG THE FOLLOWING LINES IN SO FAR AS POSSIBLE:

1. THE WATERS OF PEARL HARBOR ARE TO BE DIVIDED ROUGHLY INTO FIVE SUB-AREAS. WE HAVE NO OBJECTION TO YOUR ABBREVIATING AS MUCH AS YOU LIKE. AREA A. WATERS BETWEEN FORD ISLAND AND THE ARSENAL. AREA B. WATERS ADJACENT TO THE ISLAND SOUTH

AND WEST OF FORD ISLAND. THIS AREA IS ON THE OPPOSITE SIDE OF
THE ISLAND FROM AREA A. AREA C. EAST LOCH. AREA D. MIDDLE LOCH.
AREA E. WEST LOCH AND THE COMMUNICATING WATER ROUTES.
   2. WITH REGARD TO WARSHIPS AND AIRCRAFT CARRIERS WE
WOULD LIKE TO HAVE YOU REPORT ON THOSE AT ANCHOR (THESE
ARE NOT SO IMPORTANT), TIED UP AT WHARVES, BUOYS, AND IN
DOCK. DESIGNATE TYPES AND CLASSES BRIEFLY. IF POSSIBLE, WE
WOULD LIKE TO HAVE YOU MAKE MENTION OF THE FACT WHEN THERE
ARE TWO OR MORE VESSELS ALONGSIDE THE SAME WHARF.[1]

With all signs pointing to a rapid approach of war and the
Hawaiian naval outpost the probable target,[2] a highly secret intelligence-gathering was immediately ordered by the President.[3] Man-
dated with *pro forma* investigative powers as a Special Representative
of the State Department was one Curtis B. Munson.[4] His mission: to
get as precise a picture as possible of the degree of loyalty to be found
among residents of Japanese descent, both on the West Coast of the
United States and in Hawaii.

Carried out in the month of October and the first weeks of
November, Munson's investigation resulted in a twenty-five-page report
of uncommon significance, especially as it served to corroborate data
representing more than a decade of prodigious snooping and spying
by the various U.S. intelligence services, both domestic and military.
*It certified a remarkable, even extraordinary degree of loyalty among
this generally suspect ethnic group.*

Yet, for reasons that still remain obscured, this highest level
"double-checking" and confirmation of favorable intelligence consensus—that *"there is no Japanese problem"*—was to become one of
the war's best kept secrets. Not until after the cessation of hostilities,
when the report of the secret survey was introduced in evidence in the
Pearl Harbor hearings of 1946, did facts shattering all justification
for the wartime suppression of the Japanese minority come to light.

What is more remarkable, perhaps, is that to this very day, the
unusual significance of these findings has been strangely subdued.

Evidence would indicate that the Munson Report was shared
only by the State, War, and Navy departments; yet, paradoxically,
Cordell Hull, Henry L. Stimson, and Frank Knox, who then headed
up these Cabinet posts, were to end up being the most determined
proponents of evacuation. Researchers and historians have repeatedly
—and with justification—leveled an accusatory finger at Stimson's
War Department cohorts as being the Administration's most industrious evacuation advocates. The question naturally arises: Were aides
of the Secretary kept in the dark regarding the "bill of health" given
the vast majority of the Japanese American population?

On February 5, 1942, a week before the go-ahead decision for
the evacuation was handed down, Stimson informed the Chief Execu-

tive in a letter sent along with the President's personal copy of the Munson Report: "In response to your memorandum of November 8 [see Appendix 10], the Department gave careful study and consideration to the matters reported by Mr. C. B. Munson in his memorandum covering the Japanese situation on the West Coast." This meant that the General Staff had had fully three months to study, circulate, review, and analyze the contents of the report before it was returned to the President.[5]

Owing to the wartime concealment of this important document, few, if any, realized how totally distorted was the known truth in pro-internment hysterics emanating from the military, with the exception of those in naval intelligence and the FBI, whose surveillance of the Japanese minority over the years had been exhaustive. Both services, to their credit, are on record as having opposed the President's decision for evacuation.[6]

To the average American the evacuation tragedy, well shrouded as it remains in tidied-up historical orthodoxy and in the mythology spawned by the "total-war" frenzy, remains no more than a curious aberration in American history. Only during the civil rights turbulence of the sixties, when personal liberties of unpopular minorities were once again in jeopardy, was interest sharply rekindled in this blurred-out episode in America's past. A generation of the nation's youth, who had grown up knowing nothing or little of so colossal a national scandal as American-style concentration camps, suddenly demanded to know what it was that had happened. Noticed also was an upsurge of interest among the "Sansei" (the children of the second-generation "Nisei"), some of whom had been born in these camps, who now wanted to be told everything that their parents and grandparents, the "Issei," had tried so hard to forget.[7]

Yet the enormity of this incredible governmental hoax cannot begin to be fathomed without taking into consideration the definitive loyalty findings of Curtis B. Munson, especially in relation to the rationale that in 1942 "justified" the sending of some 110,000 men, women, and children to concentration camps: namely, that an "unknown" number of Japanese Americans presented a potential threat of dire fifth-column peril to the national security, that it would be difficult to sort out the dangerous ones in so short a time, so to play it safe all should be locked up.

II

Behind it all was a half century of focusing anti-Asian hates on the Japanese minority by West Coast pressure groups resentful of them as being hyperefficient competitors. An inordinate amount of regional anxiety had also accompanied Japan's rapid rise to power.

Years of media-abetted conditioning to the possibility of war, invasion, and conquest by waves and waves of fanatic, Emperor-worshiping yellow men—invariably aided by harmless-seeming Japanese gardeners and fisherfolk who were really spies and saboteurs in disguise—had evoked a latent paranoia as the news from the Pacific in the early weeks of the war brought only reports of cataclysmic Allied defeats.

In 1941, the number of Japanese Americans living in the continental United States totaled 127,000. Over 112,000 of them lived in the three Pacific Coast states of Oregon, Washington, and California. Of this group, nearly 80 percent of the total (93,000) resided in the state of California alone.

In the hyperactive minds of longtime residents of California, where antipathy toward Asians was the most intense, the very nature of the Pearl Harbor attack provided ample—and prophetic—proof of inherent Japanese treachery. As the Imperial Army chalked up success after success on the far-flung Pacific front, and as rumors of prowling enemy submarines proliferated wildly, the West Coast atmosphere became charged with a panicky fear of impending invasion and a profound suspicion that Japanese Americans in their midst were organized for coordinated subversive activity. For the myriad anti-Oriental forces and influential agriculturists who had long cast their covetous eyes over the coastal webwork of rich Japanese-owned land, a superb opportunity had thus become theirs for the long-sought expulsion of an unwanted minority.[8]

By enlisting the support of civic leaders, politicians, and their powerful mass-media allies, with special emphasis on those important in the military, the tide of tolerance which had surprisingly followed the news of attack was reversed by what soon appeared like a tidal wave of cries for evacuation. In the more inflammatory journals, the switch-over from tolerance to mistrust had been as simple as juxtaposing news of the bestial, despised enemy with that of "Japs" in their own backyards. The public became totally confused in their hatred.

Because little was known about the minority which had long kept itself withdrawn from the larger community in fear of rebuff, it was possible to make the public believe anything. The stereotype of the Oriental of supercunning and sly intent was rekindled and exploited in such a manner that Chinese Americans and other Asians began wearing "I am a Chinese" buttons in fear of being assaulted and spat upon. The tactics used in manipulating public fears were hardly different from those used to achieve the cutoff in Chinese immigration in 1882 and in bringing a halt to all Japanese immigration in 1924.

Significant for those maximizing this once-in-a-lifetime opportunity was that although the Japanese minority comprised only a minuscule 1 percent of the state's population, they were a group well on their way to controlling one-half of the commercial truck crops in California. Centuries-old agricultural skills which the Japanese brought over with them enabled Issei farmers not only to turn out an improved quality of farm produce but also to bring down prices. The retail distribution of fruits and vegetables in the heavily populated Southern California area was already a firmly entrenched monopoly of Japanese Americans.

And it was in the name of the citizen Nisei that much of the rich growing acreage belonged to the immigrants.

Like the Chinese before them, the immigrant Japanese were denied the right to become American citizens. Because they lacked this right of naturalization, they could not own land. Even the leasing of land was limited by a 1913 land law to three years. But the Issei found ways to get around such laws devised to drive Orientals away from California, the most popular of which was for the Issei to purchase property in the name of their citizen offspring.

It was a common practice among the Issei to snatch up strips of marginal unwanted land which were cheap: swamplands, barren desert areas that Caucasians disdained to invest their labor in. Often it included land bordering dangerously close to high-tension wires, dams, and railroad tracks. The extraordinary drive and morale of these hard-working, frugal Issei who could turn parched wastelands, even marshes, into lush growing fields—usually with help from the entire family—became legendary. In the course of the years, notably during periods of economic crisis, a hue and cry arose of "unfair competition" and accusations that "the Japs have taken over the best land!"

Then, with the wild tales of resident Japanese perfidy that Pearl Harbor unleashed, rumors flew back and forth that Issei landowners had settled in stealth and with diabolical intent near vital installations. Their purpose: a "second Pearl Harbor." At the Tolan Committee hearings, then ostensibly weighing the pros and cons of evacuation, impressive documentation was unfurled by the top law officer of California, Attorney General Earl Warren (later to become the Chief Justice of the U. S. Supreme Court), purporting to support his theory of a possible insurrection in the making: that, with malice afterthought, Japanese Americans had "infiltrated themselves into every strategic spot in our coastal and valley counties." Substantiation of this county-by-county penetration read, in part, as follows:

Alameda County
Japs adjacent to new Livermore Military Airport.
Japs adjacent to Southern Pacific and Western Pacific Railroads.
Japs in vicinity of Oakland Airport.
Japs in vicinity to Holt Caterpillar Tractor Co., San Leandro. . . .

San Diego County

Thirty miles of open coast broken by small water courses with a Jap
on every water course.

Thirty miles of main railroad and highway easily blocked by slides,
etc., with Japs throughout their entire length. . . .

Japs adjacent to all dams supplying water to San Diego and vicinity. . . .

Japs adjacent to all power lines supplying the city of San Diego and
vicinity.[9]

There was no possible way of separating the loyal from the disloyal, insisted the Attorney General: ". . . when we are dealing with
the Caucasian race we have methods that will test the loyalty of them
. . . But when we deal with the Japanese we are in an entirely different field and we cannot form any opinion that we believe to be
sound." Warren urged speedy removal.

Unfortunately for the Nisei and Issei, it was an election year. The
tide of "public opinion"—the ferocity of the clamor, at least—indicated total unconditional removal, citizen or not. And all politicians
were falling in line.

In a desperate last-ditch effort to halt the mass uprooting, Nisei
leaders proposed the formation of a volunteer suicide battalion, with
parents as hostages to insure their good behavior. Just one opportunity
to demonstrate the depth of Nisei integrity, implored Mike Masaoka,
the mystic mainspring behind the audacious proposal. How else could
they disprove Attorney General Warren's outrageous assertion that
"there is more potential danger among the group of Japanese who
were born in this country than from the alien Japanese who were
born in Japan"?

Though Masaoka's brash proposal was summarily rejected at the
time, it would later be reconsidered and implemented by the military,
notwithstanding their initial insistence that America did not believe in
the concept of hostages or of a segregated battalion—except, of
course, for blacks.

Being one of the outstanding members of the xenophobic brother-
hood of the "Native Sons of the Golden West" and not having access
to Munson's intelligence summation, Attorney General Warren may
have been merely vociferating some widely held concepts of suprema-
cist groups as he readied himself for the gubernatorial race in the
fall. But the Army, which did have the facts, went on to interpret the
surprising lack of disloyal activity among the Japanese minority as
proof positive of intended treachery: "The very fact that no sabotage
has taken place to date is a disturbing and confirming indication that
such action will be taken."

Because the decision for concentrating the Japanese American
population was one made in total isolation from the American people,

the justifications given for it were often conflicting, varying from authority to authority. Humanitarian groups and civil libertarians who sharply protested the stamping out of due process were assured that it was merely a "protective custody" measure deemed necessary to shelter "these admirable people" from mob action. Yet when violence and intimidation were encountered by families who attempted voluntarily to relocate themselves in the "Free Zone" of California (the eastern half) and in intermountain areas of the American interior, not one move was made by federal authorities to help stem the harassment and vigilantism so that an orderly resettlement might have been made possible. The proven failure of this voluntary movement, halted by a military freezing order on March 27, 1942, was given as one more justification why "drastic measures" were called for. The Nisei who pleaded to be allowed to remain free, and Caucasian friends who attempted to aid them, were reduced to helplessness, since Washington and the military insisted they had knowledge of certain facts not known to the average person, that only the authorities were equipped to know what was best for the "Japanese."

To explore such facts not then known to the U. S. citizenry, indeed, to cut through the morass of long-nurtured, still-persisting myths, is therefore the primary objective of this chapter.

III

Apart from occasional brief references to the Munson Report in works of scholarly research, the eye-opening loyalty findings of Curtis B. Munson have yet to receive merited exposure in the pages of history. As it is a document which brings into better perspective the often grievously misunderstood and misinterpreted 1942 federal action, its more pertinent passages have been excerpted for examination in the pages which follow. For readers interested in studying the report in its entirety, a reprint of the document may be found in the Pearl Harbor hearings of the 79th Congress, 1st session. The original copy of the report may be found at the Franklin D. Roosevelt Library, Hyde Park, New York. A duplicate copy may be found in the files of the Assistant Secretary of War, National Archives.

A far greater portion of the allotted investigatory time had been spent by Curtis Munson in probing the West Coast Issei and Nisei; for the three naval districts (11th, 12th, and 13th) covered in Munson's coastal survey encompassed the full length of the West Coast—Southern California, Northern California, Washington, and Oregon. The report on the findings of the Special Investigator began as follows:

JAPANESE ON THE WEST COAST
Ground Covered

In reporting on the Japanese "problem" on the West Coast the facts are, on the whole, fairly clear and opinion toward the problem exceedingly uniform. . . . Your reporter spent about a week each in the 11th, 12th, and 13th Naval Districts with the full cooperation of the Naval and Army Intelligence and the FBI. Some mention should also be made of the assistance rendered from time to time by the British Intelligence. Our Navy has done by far the most work on this problem, having given it intense consideration for the last ten or fifteen years. . . .

Opinions of the various services were obtained, also of business, employees, universities, fellow white workers, students, fish packers, lettuce packers, farmers, religious groups, etc. The opinion expressed with minor differences was uniform. Select Japanese in all groups were sampled. To mix indiscriminately with the Japanese was not considered advisable chiefly because the opinions of many local white Americans who had made this their life work for the last fifteen years were available . . .

In other words, long before the bombs began to fall on Pearl Harbor, efficient counterintelligence activity along the West Coast of the United States had resulted in all necessary loyalty-disloyalty information on Japanese Americans being evaluated, correlated, and catalogued—an impressive amount of amassed data representing more than a decade's worth of surveillance and intelligence-gathering. What is equally impressive is that this vast accumulation of military and domestic intelligence estimates (including opinions of private organizations, individuals, and informers) was, "with minor differences," in the estimation of the presidential sleuth, "exceedingly uniform."

Yet, with amazing aplomb, the Army, whose own intelligence service had been an integral part of the investigative teamwork, was to maintain baldly throughout that the loyalties of this group were "unknown" and that "time was of the essence." If the time factor had, indeed, been so critical as to prevent holding hearings to separate the loyal from the disloyal, it is curious that some eleven months were to elapse before the last of such men, women, and children constituting a special menace were removed from restricted areas.

For the benefit of executive officers deficient in knowledge of the "Japanese background," historical and sociological background data "as [they have] a bearing on the question" were then briefly summarized by Munson. "No estimate of the elements characteristic of the Japanese is complete without a word about 'giri,'" explained the Special Investigator, displaying a keen power of observation for a nonspecialist working under obvious pressure:

There is no accurate English word for "giri." The nearest approach to an understanding of the term is our word "obligation," which is very inadequate and altogether too weak. Favors or kindnesses done to a Japanese are never forgotten but are stored up in memory and in due time an adequate quid pro quo must be rendered in return. . . . "Giri" is the great political tool. To understand "giri" is to understand the Japanese.

Individuals aware of this ingrained character trait of the Japanese were even then attempting to convince the President that the strategy of tact and civility would prove more constructive than threats, sanctions, and affronts to Japan's pride. Among such individuals concerned for peace was the eminent theologian E. Stanley Jones, who sought repeatedly in the months preceding the attack to convince the President that if America were to revoke its punitive protectionist stance and accord discretionary treatment to a "have-not" nation vexed by problems of an exploding population, Japan would not only doubly reciprocate but also might possibly end up as an ally.

Severely damaging then to the Nisei was the habit of being lumped as "Japanese," or the pejorative "Japs," which also meant "the enemy." Munson was careful to point out to policy makers that "in the United States there are four divisions of Japanese to be considered." A brief definition of each followed:

1. The ISSEI—First generation Japanese. Entire cultural background Japanese. Probably loyal romantically to Japan. They must be considered, however, as other races. They have made this their home. They have brought up children here, their wealth accumulated by hard labor is here, and many would have become American citizens had they been allowed to do so. [The ineligibility of Orientals to acquire citizenship through naturalization had been determined by a Supreme Court decision: *Ozawa v. U.S.*, 260 U.S. 178(1922).] They are for the most part simple people. Their age group is largely 55 to 65, fairly old for a hard-working Japanese.

2. The NISEI—Second generation who have received their whole education in the United States and usually, in spite of discrimination against them and a certain amount of insults accumulated through the years from irresponsible elements, show a pathetic eagerness to be Americans. They are in constant conflict with the orthodox, well disciplined family life of their elders. Age group—1 to 30 years.

3. The KIBEI—This is an important division of the NISEI. This is the term used by the Japanese to signify those American born Japanese who received part or all of their education in Japan. In any consideration of the KIBEI they should be again divided into two classes, i.e. those who received their education in Japan from childhood to about 17 years of age and those who received their early formative education in the United States and returned to Japan for four or five years Japanese education. The Kibei are considered the most dangerous element and closer to the Issei with special reference to those who received their early education in Japan. It must be noted,

however, that many of those who visited Japan subsequent to their early American education come back with added loyalty to the United States. In fact it is a saying that all a Nisei needs is a trip to Japan to make a loyal American out of him. The American educated Japanese is a boor in Japan and treated as a foreigner . . .

4. The SANSEI—The Third [sic] generation Japanese is a baby and may be disregarded for the purpose of our survey.

One of the gross absurdities of the evacuation was that a preponderance of those herded into wartime exile represented babes-in-arms, school-age children, youths not yet of voting age, and an exhausted army of elderly men and women hardly capable of rushing about carrying on subversion. The average age of the Nisei was eighteen. The Issei's average age hovered around sixty.

The Nisei generation, the American-born and -educated, had appeared relatively late on the scene, for only after years of saving up from his meager earnings did the early male immigrant send back to Japan for a bride. "Between these first and second generations there was often a whole generation missing," notes sociologist William Petersen in a January 9, 1966, *New York Times Magazine* article, "for many of the issei married so late in life that in age they might have been their children's grandparents." Owing largely to this generational chasm which separated the Issei from their fledgling offspring, the Nisei suffered not only from a serious communication gap —neither group speaking the other's language with any facility—but from the severe demands of an ancestral culture totally alien to the Americanizing influence of the classroom: a culture which emphasized strict conformity as opposed to individuality, duty more than rights.

The Kibei, the return-to-America Nisei, were an extreme product of this paradox. Some 8,000 of these native-born Americans had received three or more years of schooling in prewar Japan, often a desperate and sacrificial move on the part of parents at a time when even the highest level of educational preparation could not break down white employment barriers on the West Coast. Severe maladjustment problems were usually the lot of the Kibei on their return to a Caucasian-dominated society, causing some to withdraw into a shell of timidity. Ostracized not only by whites but also by their more Americanized peers as being too "Japanesey," the Kibei (often the older brothers and sisters in the family) suffered in angry isolation, feeling contemptuous of the Nisei as being a callow, culturally deprived generation whose "kowtowing" to whites they found distasteful. Marched into concentration camps before many had had a chance to readjust to the culture shock, and where the Kibei were subjected to stricter security surveillance, the more strident camp firebrands and disruptive deviants were inevitably to emerge from this group of misfits.

The factor of ethnicity, or "racial guilt" for the crime of adhering to old world cultural patterns, had been another of the bizarre arguments advanced by the military in justification for the preventive detention of a minority. In the words of Colonel Karl Bendetsen, the Army architect-to-be of the racial uprooting, it was highly suspect that Japanese Americans were then part of a "national group almost wholly unassimilated and which had preserved in large measure to itself its customs and traditions." In the event of a Japanese invasion, he determined, the Issei and Nisei would hardly be able to "withstand the ties of race."

And for Secretary of War Stimson, mere racial identification with the fiendish Asiatic foe, whose military might had been woefully miscalculated, was cause enough to have little confidence in the American-born Nisei: "Their racial characteristics are such that we cannot understand or trust even the citizen Japanese." [10]

In striking contradiction to such insinuations and untruths fabricated of prejudice, a far kindlier assessment of Issei and Nisei acculturation, aspirations, and value priorities had been documented for the President in the weeks prior to the outbreak of hostilities. Munson's prewar assessment had been strongly positive; his commendation of the Nisei was glowing:

> Their family life is disciplined and honorable. The children are obedient and the girls virtuous. . . .
>
> There are still Japanese in the United States who will tie dynamite around their waist and make a human bomb out of themselves. We grant this, but today they are few. Many things indicate that very many joints in the Japanese set-up show age, and many elements are not what they used to be. The weakest from a Japanese standpoint are the Nisei. They are universally estimated from 90 to 98 percent loyal to the United States if the Japanese-educated element of the Kibei is excluded. The Nisei are pathetically eager to show this loyalty. They are not Japanese in culture. They are foreigners to Japan. Though American citizens they are not accepted by Americans, largely because they look differently [sic] and can be easily recognized. The Japanese American Citizens League should be encouraged, the while an eye is kept open, to see that Tokio does not get its finger in this pie—which it has in a few cases attempted to do. The loyal Nisei hardly knows where to turn. Some gesture of protection or wholehearted acceptance of this group would go a long way to swinging them away from any last romantic hankering after old Japan. They are not oriental or mysterious, they are very American and are of a proud, self-respecting race suffering from a little inferiority complex and a lack of contact with the white boys they went to school with. They are eager for this contact and to work alongside them.

Noting the "degrees to which Americans were willing to believe almost anything about the Japanese," Professor Roger Daniels (*Con-*

centration Camps USA: Holt, Rinehart and Winston) wonders whether Munson's apocryphal reference to the fanatic-minded Japanese "who will tie dynamite around their waist and make a human bomb out of themselves" might not have contributed to alarming the President.

In 1941, the Japanese American Citizens League (JACL) was still a politically unsophisticated neophyte organization preoccupied with the problems of how to better the status of their own minority in the United States; most Nisei were not yet old enough to belong to it. In an eagerness to gain white approbation, and moved by the deep and unselfish ideals of the Republic, the League had early taken the route of superpatriotism, leading in time to a near-systematic disavowal of things Japanese. This marked compulsion on the part of the minority's youth generation to demonstrate an extraordinary allegiance may have accounted for the excellent bill of health given the Nisei, generally, and the Investigator's positive recommendation to policy makers: "the Japanese American Citizens League should be encouraged." Which military and civilian authorities proceeded to do to such a discriminatory degree that the manifest partiality shown JACL leaders in the stressful removal and adjustment period was to later become the fundamental cause of intracamp ferment.

Contradicting widely held assumptions to the contrary, Munson's following assessment of the immigrant group reveals the personal esteem in which many Issei had been held as individuals, even in the face of mounting prewar feelings:

> The Issei, or first generation, is considerably weakened in their loyalty to Japan by the fact that they have chosen to make this their home and have brought up their children here. They expect to die here. They are quite fearful of being put in a concentration camp. Many would take out American citizenship if allowed to do so. The haste of this report does not allow us to go into this more fully. The Issei have to break with their religion, their god and Emperor, their family, their ancestors and their after-life in order to be loyal to the United States. They are also still legally Japanese. Yet they do break, and send their boys off to the Army with pride and tears. They are good neighbors. They are old men fifty-five to sixty-five, for the most part simple and dignified. Roughly they were Japanese lower middle class, about analogous to the pilgrim fathers.

A strong factor in the Issei's ability to adapt to their inhospitable environment was that most of the immigrants had come from the lower rung of the social and economic ladder of their highly class-conscious homeland, thus were inured to inequalities in rights. Their self-effacing, uncritical admiration of America despite obvious repudiation was something "short of miraculous," recalls the Reverend Daisuke Kitagawa, an Episcopal priest from Japan who had worked among them in the less populous Pacific Northwest, where a lesser degree of discrimination was experienced than in California.

The Issei's admiration of, and ever-increasing attachment to, their adopted land was profoundly reinforced as the Nisei began to be inducted into the Army under the Selective Service Act of 1939, Father Dai notes discerningly:

> When he saw his son standing proudly in a U. S. Army uniform, he knew that he had been wedded to the United States for all these years, even though there had been many in-laws, as it were, who mistreated him. . . . At that moment the Issei was in a frame of mind that would easily have led him to fight the Japanese forces, should they invade the Pacific Coast. Emotionally it would have been an extremely painful thing for him to do, but he would have done it just the same, for he saw quite clearly that it was the only thing for him to do as one who had been "wedded" to the United States. The traditional Japanese ethic, when faithfully adhered to, would not only justify, but more positively demand, his taking the side of the United States.[11]

The Nisei "show a pathetic eagerness to be Americans," had been Munson's perceptive summation, and it was an apt one; for it described the state of mind of a substantial majority of draft-age Japanese Americans then pridefully answering their nation's call to arms as a heaven-sent opportunity to prove that, first and foremost, they were Americans—that their love and loyalty were for the Stars and Stripes.

The report continued: "Now that we have roughly given a background and a description of the Japanese elements in the United States, the question naturally arises—what will these people do in case of a war between the United States and Japan?" In other words, could Japanese Americans be trusted to withstand the ties of "blood" and "race" in the ultimate test of loyalty, of being pitted against their own kind? Would there be the *banzai* uprisings, the espionage and sabotage long prophesied and propagandized by anti-Oriental hate exploiters? "As interview after interview piled up," reported Investigator Munson, "those bringing in results began to call it the same old tune."

> The story was all the same. There is no Japanese "problem" on the Coast. There will be no armed uprising of Japanese. There will undoubtedly be some sabotage financed by Japan and executed largely by imported agents . . . In each Naval District there are about 250 to 300 suspects under surveillance. It is easy to get on the suspect list, merely a speech in favor of Japan at some banquet being sufficient to land one there. The Intelligence Services are generous with the title of suspect and are taking no chances. Privately, they believe that only 50 or 60 in each district can be classed as really dangerous. The Japanese are hampered as saboteurs because of their easily recognized

physical appearance. It will be hard for them to get near anything to blow up *if it is guarded.* There is far more danger from Communists and people of the Bridges type on the Coast than there is from Japanese. The Japanese here is almost exclusively a farmer, a fisherman or a small businessman. He has no entree to plants or intricate machinery.

Despite the restrained intelligence estimate that "only 50 or 60 in each district can be classed as really dangerous," the ferocity of the sneak attack which followed provided apparent justification for a ruthless sweep for suspects, made possible by the blanket authority given the Attorney General by Presidential Proclamation No. 2525, of December 7, 1941. Over 5,000 Issei and Nisei were pulled in by the FBI, most of whom were subsequently released after interrogation or examination before Alien Enemy hearing boards. Over 2,000 Issei suspects bore the anguish of having businesses and careers destroyed, reputations defiled in being shipped to distant Department of Justice detention camps for an indefinite stay.

Herbert V. Nicholson, a former Quaker missionary to Japan who then headed up a Japanese American congregation in Los Angeles, recalls the haphazardness of the indiscriminate pickups—that the FBI, with the help of law enforcement officers:

> . . . picked up anybody that was the head of anything. The same thing they did when Lenin and the Communists took over in Russia. . . . Anybody that was a *cho*—that means "head"—he was picked up. Heads of prefectural organizations were picked up. Just because we come from the same country, we get together occasionally, see, and just have a social time and talk about our friends back in Japan. But everybody that was head of anything was picked up, which was a crazy thing. . . . Because of public opinion and pressure, others were picked up later for all sorts of things. Buddhist priests and Japanese language schoolteachers were all picked up later . . . because of public opinion, they picked up more and more.[12]

Since it was assumed that years of social and legislative slights had hopelessly estranged the Japanese American minority, little did authorities then realize that with all their zealotry, not one instance of subversion or sabotage would ever be uncovered among the Issei, or a single case involving the Nisei. James Rowe, Jr., then second-in-command at the Justice Department as the Assistant Attorney General (today a prominent Washington attorney) recently admitted with candor that "we picked up too many . . . some of this stuff they were charged on was as silly as hell." [13]

The four-week probe of the West Coast "problem" had ended up putting the Nisei entirely in the clear. Munson was positive the enemy would look elsewhere for agents: "Japan will commit some sabotage largely depending on imported Japanese as they are afraid of and do not trust the Nisei."

There will be no wholehearted response from Japanese in the United States. They may get some helpers from certain Kibei. They will be in a position to pick up information on troop, supply and ship movements from local Japanese. . . . [Another salient passage that may have alarmed the President.]

For the most part the local Japanese are loyal to the United States or, at worst, hope that by remaining quiet they can avoid concentration camps or irresponsible mobs. We do not believe that they would be at the least any more disloyal than any other racial group in the United States with whom we went to war. Those being here are on a spot and they *know it.*

IV

A total of nine days were spent by the Special Investigator in Honolulu. As had been done in the Pacific Coast probe of the Japanese minority, an independent check was made with "the full cooperation of Army and Navy Intelligence and the FBI" on intelligence estimates of each agency, culled from years of accumulated surveillance data. Munson's assessment of the Hawaiian-Japanese problem began as follows:

The concensus of opinion is that there will be no racial uprising of the Japanese in Honolulu. The first generation, as on the Coast, are ideologically and culturally closest to Japan. Though many of them speak no English, or at best only pigeon-English, it is considered that the big bulk of them will be loyal. . . . The second generation is estimated as approximately ninety-eight percent loyal. However, with the large Japanese population in the Hawaiian Islands, giving this the best interpretation possible, it would mean that fifteen hundred were disloyal. However, the F.B.I. state that there are about four hundred suspects, and the F.B.I.'s private estimate is that only fifty or sixty of these are sinister. . . .

Following the Pearl Harbor assault, 980 suspects from the Hawaiian-Japanese community were to be pulled in by authorities and penned up at the Hawaiian Detention Center before their removal to mainland Justice Department camps. It is worth noting that the Honolulu-based FBI appears to have exercised far more restraint than its West Coast counterparts, considering that twice as many mainland Issei were to end up in Justice's custody.

A marked difference between the kind of discrimination being practiced on the Islands as compared to that on the mainland caught the attention of the Special Investigator. On the West Coast, there was no mistaking that racial attitudes were at the root of the animosity against the Issei and Nisei: "there are plenty of 'Okies' to call the Japanese a 'Yellow-belly,' when economically and by education the Japanese may not only be their equal but their superior." On the other hand, discrimination as practiced in Hawaii (where the Japanese "fit in" because "the bulk are dark-skinned of one kind or another") struck Munson as being based more on one's financial standing—on whether one fitted in on a social and economic basis.

> The result of this is that the Hawaiian Japanese does not suffer from the same inferiority complex or feel the same mistrust of the whites that he does on the mainland. While it is seldom on the mainland that you find even a college-educated Japanese-American citizen who talks to you wholly openly until you have gained his confidence, this is far from the case in Hawaii. Many young Japanese there are fully as open and frank and at ease with a white as white boys are. In a word, Hawaii is more of a melting pot because there are more brown skins to melt—Japanese, Hawaiian, Chinese and Filipino. It is interesting to note that there has been absolutely no bad feeling between the Japanese and the Chinese in the islands due to the Japanese-Chinese war. Why should they be any worse toward us?

More than a few Nisei and Kibei detained by Hawaiian authorities were to end up, with family members, in mainland "relocation centers," where the breezy outspokenness of Hawaiian youths and their uninhibited tendency to be openly resentful of insult was to come as a shock and special vexation to administrators—accustomed, as they were, to the docile, more taciturn mainland Nisei.

However marked the difference in personality makeup, the compelling need to demonstrate love of country and loyalty to the flag was a character trait shared in common by both the Hawaiian and mainland Nisei, or one might gather as much by their positive attitude toward Army enlistment—no doubt a moral imperative—"country before self"—passed on to them by their duty-conscious parents. Noted the Investigator:

> Due to the preponderance of Japanese in the population of the Islands, a much greater proportion of Japanese have been called to the draft than on the mainland. As on the mainland they are inclined to enlist before being drafted. The Army is extremely high in its praise of them as recruits. . . . They are beginning to feel that they are going to get a square deal and some of them are really almost pathetically exuberant.

Postwar statistics were to dramatize this remarkable *esprit de corps* more tellingly. A higher percentage of Americans of Japanese ancestry ended up serving in the U. S. Army during World War II than any other racial group, divided almost equally between the mainland Nisei (13,528) and those in Hawaii (12,250). "The final count of Hawaiian war casualties revealed that 80 percent of those killed and 88 percent of those wounded throughout the war were of Japanese descent," states Andrew Lind, writing in *Hawaii's Japanese.*

V

Los Angeles, California: December 20, 1941 (or some two weeks *after* the Pearl Harbor attack).

Munson offered no comments or post-mortems on the "surprise" attack which finally came—in obvious anticipation of which he had warned Washington from his Hawaiian vantage point in the early part of November: *"The best consensus of opinion seemed to agree that martial law should be proclaimed now in Hawaii."*

From his post-Pearl (December 20) Los Angeles vantage point, Munson volunteered some strong private opinions on a fast-developing situation which augured no good for the Coastal Japanese.

> We desire respectfully to call attention to a statement of the Secretary of the Navy evidently made to some reporter on his return to Washington after the Pearl Harbor attack as printed in the *Los Angeles Times* of December 18 . . . We quote, "I think the most effective Fifth Column work of the entire war was done in Hawaii with the possible exception of Norway," Secretary of the Navy Knox said. . . . Fifth Column activities, such as in Norway, impugns [sic] the loyalty of a certain large proportion of a population. Your observer still doubts that this was the case in Honolulu. . . .
>
> Some reaction of an undesirable nature is already apparent on the West Coast due to this statement of the Secretary's. In Honolulu your observer noted that the seagoing Navy was inclined to consider everybody with slant eyes bad. This thought stems from two sources: self-interest, largely in the economic field, and in the Navy usually from pure lack of knowledge and the good old "eat 'em up alive" school. It is not the measured judgment of 98% of the intelligence services or the knowing citizenry either on the mainland or in Honolulu. . . .

Knox's allegations of foul play were providing the opening wedge for racist forces to begin reactivating slumbering anti-Oriental prejudices along the Pacific Coast. Subsequently, the climate was to take an abrupt turn toward intolerance, notably when the Roberts Commission Report on the attack, released on January 25, 1942, reinforced the misleading impression that the aid of resident traitors had been received by the spy operation then centered in the Japanese Consulate: ". . . some were consular agents and others were persons having no open relations with the Japanese foreign service." Yet Washington was to remain remarkably silent about it. By the time official denials reached the mainland public, the developing fear hysteria had become irreversible.

Even as Munson sought to set the record straight, the President and his Cabinet had agreed, as early as December 19, 1941, to concentrate all aliens of Japanese ancestry on an island other than Oahu.[14] Navy Secretary Knox doubted that the measure went far enough and sought, from the outset, to convince the President that citizens, too, should be included. In a memorandum of February 26, a supremely confident President assured Knox that there would be no problem in removing "most of the Japanese": "I do not worry about the constitutional question, first because of my recent order [West Coast evacuation], second because Hawaii is under martial law. The whole matter is one of immediate and present war emergency. I think you and Stimson can agree and then go ahead and do it as a military project."[15]

Had the island roundup involved only aliens, as originally agreed upon, the Hawaiian evacuation might have proceeded swiftly, without hindrance. Approximately 20,000 aliens and 98,000 citizens then lived on the island of Oahu, the Japanese minority then making up one-third of the total island population. The small Issei population might have been readily replaced by an equivalent work force.

But because of Knox's stubborn insistence on a large-scale evacuation, which would have involved some 100,000 Nisei and Issei (recommended by the Joint Chiefs of Staff on March 11, 1942, and approved by the President on March 13, 1942),[16] the project was to end up becoming unwieldy and unworkable, especially since the Joint Chiefs of Staff ruled on removal to the mainland "utilizing empty ships returning to the west coast" at a time when shipping facilities were being taxed to their utmost.

The Hawaiian evacuation, to begin with the removal of 20,000 of "the most dangerous" aliens and citizens, was vigorously opposed —later thwarted—by island Army and Navy authorities closer to the problem as being too costly, logistically complex, and self-defeating. As Munson had prophetically forewarned in his pre-Pearl Harbor report, "it would simply mean that the Islands would lose their vital labor supply by so doing, and in addition to that we would have to feed them . . . it is essential that they should be kept loyal."

Accordingly—and paradoxically—it had become a veritable military necessity for authorities to retain, not detain, Hawaii's Japanese population in a battle zone thousands of miles closer to the enemy mainland than the jittery state of California and to do everything possible to encourage their loyalty so that all would stay at their tasks.

It was in sharp contrast to the policy pursued on the West Coast in reference to a people then posing an increasing threat to the prosperity of native farmers and merchants though still an infinitesimal percentage of the population—thus expendable, both politically and economically. Should the "Japanese" on the mainland "prove actively disloyal *they could be corralled or destroyed within a very short time,"* the Special Investigator, in his prewar assessment, had dramatically punctuated this expendability.

But on the basis of the highly favorable impression he had gained during the hurried survey, Munson was moved to submit to the President his own well-considered recommendations with the reassurance: "Your reporter, fully believing that his reports are still good after the attack, makes the following observations about handling the Japanese 'problem' on the West Coast."

A. The loyal Japanese citizens should be encouraged by a statement from high government authority and public attitude toward them outlined.

B. Their offers of assistance should be accepted through such agencies as:

1. Civilian Defense
2. Red Cross
3. U.S.O., etc., etc.

This assistance should not be merely monetary, nor should it even be limited to physical voluntary work in segregated Nisei units. The Nisei should work with and among white persons, and be made to feel he is welcome on a basis of equality.

C. An alien property custodian should be appointed to supervise Issei (first generation-alien) businesses, *but* encouraging Nisei (second generation-American citizen) to take over.

D. Accept investigated Nisei as workers in defense industries such as shipbuilding plants, aircraft plants, etc.

E. Put *responsibility* for behavior of Issei and Nisei on the leaders of Nisei groups such as the Japanese American Citizens League.

F. Put the *responsibility* for production of food (vegetables, fish, etc.) on Nisei leaders.

In essence, Munson's power-to-the-Nisei policy was to involve federal control:

In case we have not made it apparent, the aim of this report is that all Japanese Nationals in the continental United States and property owned and operated by them within the country be immediately placed under absolute Federal control. The aim of this will be to squeeze control from the hands of the Japanese Nationals into the hands of the loyal Nisei who are American citizens. . . . It is the aim that the Nisei should police themselves, and as a result police their parents.

Munson's suggested course of governmental action, which would have catapulted the Nisei into a position of leadership and control, might have proved sound had both the Issei and Nisei been permitted to remain at liberty as in Hawaii. But the power-to-the Nisei policy was to become the root cause of resentment and conflict, when imposed behind barbed wire, in abortively speeding up the process whereby the still fledgling Nisei were taken out from under the control of elders, a generation to whom they owed unlimited deference and obedience.

Regrettably ignored was Munson's strong recommendation that the public's attitude toward the minority be positively led with a reassuring statement by the "President or Vice President, or at least [someone] almost as high"—as was the adopted policy in Hawaii, where the newly appointed Military Governor acted swiftly to squelch fifth-column rumors while assuring justice and equitable treatment to aliens and citizens alike, if they would remain loyal.

But on the U. S. mainland, where other pressing considerations apparently outweighed justice for so inconsequential a minority, fear and fiction were allowed to luxuriate as part of the total war propaganda. And for reasons that defy easy explanation, Secretary of the Navy Knox was to further crucify a powerless minority by reporting to the Tolan Committee in a letter of March 24, 1942:

> . . . There was a considerable amount of evidence of subversive activity on the part of the Japanese prior to the attack. This consisted of providing the enemy with the most exact possible kind of information as an aid to them in locating their objectives, and also creating a great deal of confusion in the air following the attack by the use of radio sets which successfully prevented the commander in chief of the fleet from determining in what direction the attackers had withdrawn and in locating the position of the covering fleet, including the carriers. . . .[17]

It can only be assumed that Knox's tissue of fallacies impugning the fidelity of the resident Japanese was meant merely to divert, to take political "heat" off himself and the Administration for the unspeakable humiliation that Pearl Harbor represented. By the convenient redirection of public rage, a nation on the verge of disunity and disaster was finally—and purposefully—united as one.

The actions of Knox and the wartime suppression of the Munson papers, like the more familiar Pentagon Papers, once again make evident how executive officers of the Republic are able to mislead public opinion by keeping hidden facts which are precisely the opposite of what the public is told—information vital to the opinions they hold.

In the case of Japanese Americans, data regarding their character and integrity were positive and "exceedingly uniform," the facts clear cut. But as once observed by Nobel Peace Prize recipient Sir Norman Angell: "Men, particularly in political matter, are not guided by the facts but by their opinions about the facts." Under the guise of an emergency and pretended threats to the national security, the citizenry was denied the known facts, public opinion skillfully manipulated, and a cruel and massive governmental hoax enacted. According to one of the foremost authorities on constitutional law, Dr. Eugene V. Rostow: "One hundred thousand persons were sent to concentration camps on a record which wouldn't support a conviction for stealing a dog."

(2)
Hostages

I'm for catching every Japanese in America, Alaska, and Hawaii now and putting them in concentration camps . . . Damn them! Let's get rid of them now!

—CONGRESSMAN JOHN RANKIN,
Congressional Record, December 15, 1941

I

Since much of Munson's documentation for the President reads more like a tribute to those of Japanese ancestry than a need for locking them up, the question remains: Had the President, having perceived the racist character of the American public, deliberately acquiesced to the clearly punitive action knowing it would be rousingly effective for the flagging home-front morale?

Or could factors other than political expedience, perhaps a more critical wartime exigency, have entered into and inspired the sudden decision calling for mass action—made as it was at a time when the Allied cause in the Pacific was plummeting, one reversal following another in seemingly endless succession?

A bit of personal conjecture: Shocked and mortified by the unexpected skill and tenacity of the foe (as the Administration might have been), with America's very survival in jeopardy, what could better insure the more considerate treatment of American captives, the unknown thousands then being trapped daily in the islands and territories falling to the enemy like dominoes, than a substantial *hostage reserve?* And would not a readily available *reprisal reserve* prove crucial should America's war fortune continue to crumble: should the scare propaganda of "imminent invasion" become an actual, living nightmare of rampaging hordes of yellow "barbarians" overrunning and making "free fire zones" of American villages and hamlets—looting, raping, murdering, slaughtering . . .

In an earlier crisis situation which had exacerbated U. S.-Japan relations to the near-breaking point, the very sagacity of such a contingency plan had been forthrightly brought to the attention of the President by Congressman John D. Dingell of Michigan. On August 18, 1941, months before the outbreak of hostilities, the Congressman had hastened to advise the President:

> Reports contained in the Press indicate that Japan has barred the departure of one hundred American citizens and it is indicated that the detention is in reprisal for the freezing of Japanese assets in the United States of America.
>
> I want to suggest without encroaching upon the privilege of the Executive or without infringing upon the privileges of the State Department that if it is the intention of Japan to enter into a reprisal contest that we remind Nippon that unless assurances are received that Japan will facilitate and permit the voluntary departure of this group of one hundred Americans within forty-eight hours, the Government of the United States will cause the forceful detention or imprisonment in a concentration camp of ten thousand alien Japanese in Hawaii; the ratio of Japanese hostages held by America being one hundred for every American detained by the Mikado's Government.
>
> It would be well to further remind Japan that there are perhaps one hundred fifty thousand additional alien Japanese in the United States who will be held in a reprisal reserve whose status will depend upon Japan's next aggressive move. I feel that the United States is in an ideal position to accept Japan's challenge.
>
> God bless you, Mr. President.[1]

Within two months after the crippling blow dealt by the Japanese at Pearl Harbor, a fast-deteriorating situation in the soon untenable Philippine campaign moved Stimson to call for threats of reprisals on Japanese nationals in America "to insure proper treatment" of U. S. citizens trapped in enemy territory. On February 5, the very day when mass evacuation-internment plans began to be drawn up and formalized within the War Department,[2] Stimson wrote Hull:

> General MacArthur has reported in a radiogram, a copy of which is enclosed, that American and British civilians in areas of the Philippines occupied by the Japanese are being subjected to extremely harsh treatment. The unnecessary harsh and rigid measures imposed, in sharp contrast to the moderate treatment of metropolitan Filipinos, are unquestionably designed to discredit the white race.
>
> I request that you strongly protest this unjustified treatment of civilians, and suggest that you present a threat of reprisals against the many Japanese nationals now enjoying negligible restrictions in the

United States, to insure proper treatment of our nationals in the Philippines.[3]

If a reprisal reserve urgency had indeed precipitated the sudden decision for internment, the emphasis, as the tide of the war reversed itself, switched to the buildup of a "barter reserve": one sizable enough to allow for the earliest possible repatriation of American detainees, even at the price of a disproportionate number of Japanese nationals in exchange. Behind this willingness on the part of the State Department *to give more than they expected back* may have lurked profound concern that unless meaningful concessions were to be made in the matter of POW exchanges, the whole procedure would get mired in resistance and inertia to the jeopardy of thousands subject to terrible suffering in enemy prison camps.

As revealed in a letter from the Secretary of the Navy to President Roosevelt, the Secretary of State, in Knox's estimate, was being overly disconcerted by the belief that German authorities intended to hold on indefinitely to American detainees "as hostages for captured Germans whom we might prosecute under the war criminal procedure."[4] A similar alarmist concern may have been entertained by Secretary of State Hull as to the intent of Japanese authorities.

The use of the Nisei as part and parcel of this human barter was not totally ruled out in the realm of official thinking. By curious circumstance, such intent on the part of U. S. authorities became starkly evident in the latter part of 1942 and early 1943, when numerous Nisei, to their shocked indignation, were informed by Colonel Karl Bendetsen in a form letter: "Certain Japanese persons are currently being considered for repatriation [expatriation] to Japan. You and those members of your family listed above, are being so considered."[5]

II

The removals in the United States were only a part of forced uprootings which occurred almost simultaneously in Alaska, Canada, Mexico, Central America, parts of South America, and the Caribbean island of Haiti and the Dominican Republic.

Canada's decision to round up and remove its tiny (23,000) West Coast minority, 75 percent of whom were citizens of Canada, preceded America's by about a month and may have had a decisive influence on the War Department's decision to proceed similarly (see p. 290, fn. 4); but, in many ways, discriminatory measures imposed on the Canadian Japanese were more arbitrary and severe. An order of January 14, 1942, calling for the removal of all enemy alien males over sixteen years of age from the area west of the Cascade Mountains resulted in men being separated from women in the initial stage of the evacuation. But a follow-up decree of February 27 demanded total evacuation, citizens as well as aliens, most of whom were removed to work camps and mining "ghost towns" in mountain valleys of the Canadian interior. Property and possessions not disposed of were quickly confiscated and sold off at public auctions since evacuees were expected to assume some of the internment expenses from the proceeds. Canadian Japanese were not permitted to return to British Columbia and their home communities until March 1949, seven years after the evacuation.[6]

Of the 151 Alaskan Japanese plucked from their homes and life pursuits under color of Executive Order 9066, around fifty were seal- and whale-hunting half-Indians and half-Eskimos (*one-half* "Japanese blood" was the criterion in Alaska), some of whom were to associate with Japanese for the first time in the camps. Except for a "few fortunate ones with second-generation fathers," [7] families were left fatherless since male nationals suffered mass indiscriminate internment in various Justice Department detention centers. Most ended up in the camp maintained exclusively for Japanese alien detainees in Lordsburg, New Mexico. Remaining family members were airlifted to the state of Washington (following a short initial stay at Fort Richardson, Alaska) and penned up temporarily in the Puyallup Assembly Center near Seattle. In the mass Japanese American exodus out of the prohibited military area during the summer of 1942, the evacuees from Alaska wound up in the relocation center of Minidoka in Idaho.

In Mexico, the Japanese residing in small settlements near the American border and coastal areas (along a sixty-two-mile zone) were forced to liquidate their property and move inland, some to "clearing houses" and resettlement camps, a number of them to concentration camps in Perote, Puebla, and Vera Cruz.

Even less selectivity was exercised in the case of the Japanese then scattered throughout the Central American republics. Many were simply "picked up" by reason of their "hostile origin" and handed over to U. S. authorities, who, in turn, arranged for their transportation by sea or air to the U. S. mainland.

Such gunpoint "relocations" to American concentration camps became quite commonplace on the South American continent in the days and months following the Pearl Harbor attack. The reason: Considerable pressure had been applied by the U. S. State Department on various republics of the Western Hemisphere to impound, with the option of handing over to American authorities for care and custody, persons who might be considered "potentially dangerous" to hemispheric security, with special emphasis on the Japanese. More than a month before the war's outbreak, plans for this unusual wartime action began to take shape. On October 20, 1941, U. S.

Ambassador to Panama Edwin C. Wilson informed Under Secretary of State Sumner Welles:

> My strictly confidential despatch No. 300 of October 20, 1941, for the Secretary and Under Secretary, transmits memoranda of my conversations with the Foreign Minister regarding the question of internment of Japanese in the event that we suddenly find ourselves at war with Japan.
>
> The attitude of the Panamanian Government is thoroughly cooperative. The final memorandum sets out the points approved by the Panamanian Cabinet for dealing with this matter. Briefly, their thought is this: Immediately following action by the United States to intern Japanese in the United States, Panama would arrest Japanese on Panamanian territory and intern them on Taboga Island. They would be guarded by Panamanian guards and would have the status of Panamanian interns. *All expenses and costs of internment and guarding to be paid by the United States.* The United States Government would agree to hold Panama harmless against any claims which might arise as a result of internment.
>
> I believe it essential that you instruct me by telegraph at once to assure the Foreign Minister that the points which he set out to cover this matter meet the approval of our Government.[8] [Italics mine.]

Funds which would be immediately needed, as in the construction of a prison camp which would serve as a staging area for transshipments to U. S. detention facilities, were to be provided by the Commanding General of the Caribbean Defense Command.[9] And from Chief of Staff General George Marshall came the suggestion that a more liberal interpretation of persons to be detained be considered. On October 28, 1941, he wrote Under Secretary Welles:

> It is gratifying to know that Panama is prepared to intern Japanese aliens immediately following similar action by the United States.
>
> I suggest, however, that the agreement be enlarged to provide for internment by the Panamanian Government of all persons believed dangerous, who are regarded by the United States as enemy aliens, under similar conditions.[10]

Similarly encouraged to undermine in advance any possibility of Japanese sabotage, subversion, or fifth-column treachery was Panama's neighbor republic of Costa Rica. On December 8, 1941, upon America's declaration of war on Japan, the U. S. Legation in Costa Rica wired the State Department: . . . ORDERS FOR INTERNMENT OF ALL JAPANESE IN COSTA RICA HAVE BEEN ISSUED.[11]

At a Conference of Foreign Ministers of the American Republics held in Rio de Janeiro in January 1942, a special inter-American agency (the Emergency Committee for Political Defense) to coordinate hemispheric security measures was organized, with headquarters subsequently established in Montevideo. The Emergency Committee adopted, without delay, a resolution which had been drafted by the U. S. Department of Justice in conjunction with the Department of State which stressed the need for prompt preventive detention of dangerous Axis nationals and for the "deportation of such persons to another American republic for detention when adequate local detention facilities are lacking." [12] States interested in the collaborative effort were assured that not only detention accommodations but also shipping facilities would be provided by the United States "at its own expense." [13] The State Department offered an additional incentive: It would include any of the official and civilian nationals of the participating republics in whatever exchange arrangements the U. S. would subsequently make with Axis powers.

More than a dozen American states cooperated. Among them: Bolivia, Colombia, Costa Rica, the Dominican Republic, Ecuador, El Salvador, Guatemala, Haiti, Honduras, Mexico, Nicaragua, Panama, Peru, and Venezuela.[14] Three states, Brazil, Uruguay, and Paraguay, instituted their own detention programs (Paraguay, for one, promptly arrested the two Japanese residing within her borders). Since Argentina and Chile held back breaking off diplomatic relations with the Axis powers until much later, both nations took no part in the hemispheric imprisonments.

In time, the State Department was able to claim that "the belligerent republics of the Caribbean area have sent us subversive aliens without limitation concerning their disposition"; but four republics—Venezuela, Colombia, Ecuador, and Mexico—exacted "explicit guarantees" before turning over internees.[15] Panama liberally granted the U. S. "full freedom to negotiate with Japan and agrees to the use of Japanese internees . . . for exchange of any non-official citizen of an American belligerent country." [16]

The concept of hemispheric removals had its origin in the State Department, but responsibility for the success of the operation was shared by the Departments of War, Navy, and Justice.[17] With the safety of the Panama Canal a veritable life-or-death matter after the near annihilation of the Pacific Fleet, it appears that all concerned acted on the conviction that the threat to continental security was so grave as to outweigh the momentary misuse of executive, military, and judicial power.

As a direct result of the hemispheric nations' agreement to "cooperate jointly for their mutual protection," over two thousand deportees of Japanese ancestry were to swell the already impressive U. S. barter reserve by ending up in scattered mainland detention camps, whose existence was virtually unknown then to the American public (see Appendix 3). Though the deportees were legally in State

Department custody, the custodial program for them was supervised by the Immigration and Naturalization Service of the U. S. Justice Department.

III

As for persons of Japanese ancestry residing in the democratic republic of Peru, racial antagonism fed by resentment of the foreign element as being exceedingly successful economic competitors had more to do with the Peruvian Government's spirited cooperation than its concern for the defense of the Hemisphere. The steady economic encroachment of the resident Japanese and their alleged imperviousness to assimilation had aroused increasing nativist hostility; and anti-Japanese legislation and restrictive ordinances of the West Coast type had been copied through the years, culminating with the revocation, by executive action, of citizenship rights of Nisei possessing dual citizenship. Racial feelings against the Japanese minority, abetted by the press, had burst into occasional mob action even before the Pearl Harbor attack. And much of the blame for the cut-off of Japanese immigration in 1936 had been attributed to the "social unrest" stirred up by the unwanted minority because, in the words of Foreign Minister Ulloa, "their conditions and methods of working have produced pernicious competition for the Peruvian workers and businessmen."

Accordingly, 80 percent of the Latin-American deportees of Japanese ancestry was to be contributed by the government of Peru, an enthusiasm stimulated not only by the opportunity presented to expropriate property and business (Law No. 9586 of April 10 authorized seizure of Axis property) but also to rid the realm of an undesirable element. On July 20, 1942, Henry Norweb, the U. S. Ambassador to Peru, informed the State Department of President Manuel Prado's manifest fervor in this regard:

> The second matter in which the President [Prado] is very much interested is the possibility of getting rid of the Japanese in Peru. He would like to settle this problem permanently, which means that he is thinking in terms of repatriating thousands of Japanese. He asked Colonel Lord to let him know about the prospects of additional shipping facilities from the United States. In any arrangement that might be made for internment of Japanese in the States, Peru would like to be sure that these Japanese would not be returned to Peru later on. The President's goal apparently is the substantial elimination of the Japanese colony in Peru.[18]

Pressure in the name of "mutual protection" had obviously paid off. Only three months earlier, a dispatch from the American Embassy in Lima had underscored the gravity of the subversion potential inherent in the Peruvian Japanese, "whose strength and ability have, in the past, been vastly underestimated and whose fanatic spirit has neither been understood nor taken seriously. . . . there appears to be little realization of the actual danger and a reluctance on the part of the Government to take positive measures." Recommendations from the Legation included the removal of key Japanese leaders, the encouragement of "propaganda intended to call attention of the Peruvians to the Japanese dangers," and suggestion that covert assistance might even be rendered by U. S. authorities: "Ways may be found to provide . . . material without of course permitting the source to become known as the Embassy." [19]

In light of such concerns among Embassy officials of the Lima Legation, the Peruvian President's unexpected eagerness to cooperate to the fullest came as a welcome turn of events and as an instant go-ahead for the core of U. S. advisers to assist in widening the scope of Peruvian expulsions. An intradepartmental State Department memo noted ways in which the operation might be expedited:

> President Prado has officially stated his willingness to have this deportation program carried through. . . . The suggestion that Japanese be removed from strategic areas should be followed and this should be carried on by *well-paid* police; even if this necessitates a loan from this government. All police charged with supervision of Japanese should be well paid. [Legation had warned that Peruvian law officers "are susceptible to Japanese bribes . . . their alertness cannot be depended upon."] The suggestion that Japanese be expelled whether they are naturalized Peruvians or not might be met by a denaturalization law.[20]

Arrests were made in swift, silent raids by the Peruvian police, who first confined detainees in local jails, then turned them over to the custody of U. S. military authorities. Then began the strange odyssey which would take them northward to the United States mainland: "We were taken to the port of Callao and embarked on an American transport under strict guard and with machine gun pointed at us by American soldiers." [21] As it was found that immunity from deportation could be "bought" by a generous bribe unless the removal was swiftly expedited, Army Air Transport planes were used in a number of cases involving the "extremely dangerous," usually the wealthier and influential Peruvian Japanese considered high-priority trade bait. After a short stopover in the Panama-based internment camp used as a staging area, deportees were shipped on to various Department of Justice detention centers in the States, after landing at a Gulf Coast or West Coast port.

More fortunate prisoners enjoyed reunion with family members at the Crystal City Internment Camp in Texas, the only "family camp" operated by the Justice Department where detainees were dealt with as "prisoners of war." Even the voluntary prisoners. The latter were mostly women and children. A total of 1,094 of them, officially designated as "voluntary detainees," answered the State Department's "invitation" to place themselves in war-duration voluntary incarceration with the 1,024 men who had been seized and spirited to the mainland by the U. S. military.

The question of whether the reunion program had been undertaken as a direct means of swelling the U. S. barter stockpile or whether the entire procedure represented a "humanitarian" concession on the part of the State and Justice departments is a matter still shrouded in mystery.[22]

By late October of 1942, fears concerning hemispheric security had greatly diminished. A pounding U. S. counteroffensive in the Solomons had finally begun to check the thrust of the Japanese juggernaut in the Pacific. And with the mass transportation of the coastal subnation to the inland camps nearing completion, Hull hastened to advise the President of what, to the Secretary of State, were still overriding reasons why there should be no letup in the hemispheric removals—at least of "all the Japanese . . . for internment in the United States."

> There are in China 3,300 American citizens who desire to return to the United States. Many of them are substantial persons who have represented important American business and commercial interests and a large number of missionaries. They are scattered all through that part of China occupied by the Japanese. Some of them are at liberty, some of them are in concentration camps, and some of them have limited liberty, but all of them subject to momentary cruel and harsh treatment by their oppressors. Under our agreement with Japan which is still operating, we will be able to remove these people. It will take two more trips of the *Gripsholm* to do so. In exchange for them we will have to send out Japanese in the same quantity. . . .
>
> In addition, there are 3,000 non-resident American citizens in the Philippines. We have no agreement for their exchange but it has been intimated that Japan might consider an exchange of them. It would be very gratifying if we could obtain those people from Japanese control and return them to the United States. But to do so we would have to exchange Japanese for them. That would take two more round trips of the *Gripsholm*.
>
> Still, in addition, there are 700 civilians interned in Japan proper captured at Guam and Wake. It is probable that we might arrange for their return. But in order to obtain them we would have to release Japanese. . . .
>
> With the foregoing as a predicate, I propose the following course of action:
>
> . . . Continue our exchange agreement with the Japanese until the Americans are out of China, Japan and the Philippines—so far as possible. . . .

Continue our efforts to remove all the Japanese from these American Republic countries for internment in the United States.

Continue our efforts to remove from South and Central America all the dangerous Germans and Italians still there, together with their families . . .[23] [Reparagraphed by author]

In the Secretary of State's recommended course of action, the precise wording of the directive is significant: Note the qualifying prerequisite, *dangerous,* in reference to hostages-to-be of German and Italian nationalities. In Hull's implied suggestion of more discriminating treatment of non-Oriental Axis nationals, while calling for wholesale removal—dangerous or harmless—of "all the Japanese," evidence again lies tellingly exposed of racial bias then lurking in high and rarefied places in the nation's capital.

IV

By early 1943, the Justice Department, in its custodial role in the hemispheric operation, had become greatly alarmed at the number of internees being sent up. Worse, it had come to its attention that many being held under the Alien Enemies Act were not enemy Japanese but Peruvian nationals, thus aliens of a friendly nation; and that little or no evidence supported the Peruvian Government's contention that their deportees were dangerous. "Some of the cases seem to be mistakes," Attorney General Biddle wrote the Secretary of State on January 11, 1943.[24]

Biddle insisted on more conclusive proof that the deportees were in fact "the dangerous leaders among the Japanese population in Peru," and he proposed sending his own representative to Peru and other donor nations to help sort out the people to be sent up. Since barter negotiations between Washington and Tokyo had then come to a standstill, Biddle balked at going along with the indiscriminate internment of bodies being sent up in ever-growing number from Peru, insisting that his department had merely agreed to "expediting *temporary* custody" pending repatriation.

The State Department's primary concern was that the competence and sincerity of the donor states would be impugned if Biddle were to challenge the veracity of their criterion of "dangerousness." But the State Department finally gave in, and Raymond W. Ickes (of the Central and South American division of the Alien Enemy Control unit) of the Justice Department was permitted to make on-the-spot reviews of all pending deportee cases. Ickes found little evidence anywhere to support the claims of the participating republics that individuals being held—or targeted—for deportation were "in any true sense of the word security subjects." On turning down the deportation from Venezuela of thirty Japanese, he advised the U. S. Legation in Caracas:

> This is the very thing that we have to guard against, particularly in the case of Peru, where attempts have been made to send job lots of Japanese to the States merely because the Peruvians wanted their businesses and not because there was any adverse evidence against them.[25]

All deportations to the United States thereafter ceased.

With the coming of peace, the once felicitous relationship between the U. S. and Peru suffered another setback. While the State Department proceeded to return various ex-hostages to their respective homelands, the government of Peru refused to allow reentry in the case of Japanese. Only a few select citizens were permitted readmission, mostly native-Peruvian wives and Peruvian-citizen children.

The Justice Department thereupon pressed ahead with an extraordinary piece of injustice on the onetime kidnapees no longer needed to ransom off U. S. detainees. With certain hierarchal changes in the Department (FDR's death on April 12, 1945, had resulted in Tom Clark, a Truman appointee, becoming Attorney General on September 27, 1945), all were scheduled for removal to Japan despite vigorous protest that a sizable number of them had no ties in a country many had never visited; wives and children of many were in fact still living in Peru.[26] The grounds for the second "deportation" of the Peruvian kidnapees was that they lacked proper credentials: they had entered the U. S. illegally, without visas and without passports.[27]

From despair arising from their prolonged detention without the possibility of return to their homeland or release, a contingent of some 1,700 Peruvian Japanese (700 men and their dependents) allowed themselves, between November 1945 and February 1946,[28] to be "voluntarily" unloaded on Japan. Many had acquiesced to this drastic federal action in the belief that reunion with families left behind in Peru could not otherwise be achieved.

Awaiting a similarly grim fate were 365 remaining Peruvian rejects, whose desperate plight came to the attention of Wayne Collins, a San Francisco attorney then conducting a one-man war against the Justice Department in trying to extricate thousands of Nisei caught in their "renunciation trap" (see Chapter 12), another one of the extreme consequences of the evacuation tragedy.

To abort U. S. plans to "dump" this residual Peruvian group on a defeated, war-pulverized enemy hardly able to care for its own starving masses, Collins filed two test proceedings in habeas corpus on June 25, 1946, in a U. S. District Court in San Francisco after the Immigration Department contended that suspension of deportation on a like basis as Caucasians was not permitted, and a subsequent appeal directly to the Attorney General and the President came to no avail.[29] With the removal program brought, by court action, to a forced halt, the detainees were placed in "relaxed internment"— many of them at Seabrook Farms, New Jersey, the well-known frozen food processing plant where the labor of German POWs had been utilized during the war years, and where evacuee groups from many camps were given employment.

Collins, with the aid of the Northern California office of the American Civil Liberties Union, also sought to bring to public attention what both contended was a "legalized kidnaping" program masterminded by the State Department and sanctioned by the nation's chief guardian of decency and legality, the Attorney General, whose office and the State Department now disclaimed any responsibility for the plight of the unfortunate people.

Interior Secretary Harold Ickes (father of Raymond W. Ickes), the only high-level officer of the FDR Administration to speak out in criticism of the State and Justice departments' highly clandestine proceedings, took issue with Attorney General Clark, then seeking the U. S. Vice-Presidency spot by paying glowing homage to the nation's democratic ideals of human rights and individual liberty. This did not sit well with former Cabinet officer Ickes, who knew, through and through, the wartime injustices perpetrated on the Issei and Nisei throughout the Western Hemisphere, which, even then, were being perpetuated by Attorney General Clark's zealous pursuance of postwar deportations of "disloyals" and scores of defenseless aliens under arbitrary classification as "dangerous." [30]

Ickes was sharply outspoken:

What the country demands from the Attorney General is less self-serving lip-service and more action. . . .

The Attorney General, in the fashion of the Russian Secret Police, maintains a top-secret list of individuals and organizations supposed to be subversive or disloyal. What are the criteria for judging whether a person is disloyal? . . .

I cannot begin . . . even to call the role of our maimed, mutilated, and missing civil liberties, but the United States, more than two years after the war, is holding in internment some 293 naturalized Peruvians of Japanese descent, who were taken by force by our State and Justice Departments from their homes in Peru.[31]

The resolution of the Peruvian-Japanese dilemma was to take years of unprecedented legal maneuvering on the part of lawyer Collins to untangle the mess in which so many charged with not one specifiable offense found themselves—their lives often mangled beyond repair through the prolonged splitting of families.

Changes in U. S. laws eventually enabled the Peruvian Japanese to apply for suspension of deportation if it could be shown that deportation to Japan would result in serious economic hardship and if "continued residence" in the United States of at least ten years could be proved—with years spent in various concentration camps counting also as "residence."

Peru finally permitted reentry of the deportees in the mid-1950s, but less than one hundred returned. By then the job of reconstructing their lives had begun elsewhere.

Three hundred of the 365 rescued by Collins chose to remain in the United States. An impressive number became American citizens under the amended U. S. naturalization law of 1952, which finally gave immigrants of Asian ancestry the right to become Americans.[32]

(3)
"So the Army Could Handle the Japs"

Has the Gestapo come to America? Have we not risen in righteous anger at Hitler's mistreatment of the Jews? Then, is it not incongruous that citizen Americans of Japanese descent should be similarly mistreated and persecuted?

—JAMES M. OMURA,
Testimony before Tolan Committee Hearings, February 1942

I

The wartime incarceration of Japanese Americans has been characterized by historian James J. Martin as "a breach of the Bill of Rights on a scale so large as to beggar the sum total of all such violations from the beginnings of the United States down to that time." It was this veritable descent to despotism which Francis Biddle, an eminent "practicing liberal," was obliged to defend as national policy in his position as FDR's wartime Attorney General.

According to his former aide, James Rowe, Jr., Biddle's "only failure," and one that was to burden his soul to his dying day, was the part he reluctantly played in this mass repression through his failure to deal more firmly with the then august Secretary of War and with his willful college-mate-turned-President, both of whom were of the opinion that the "Japanese problem" was strictly a military one—that Biddle and the Justice Department were not to intrude upon their sovereignty.

Though constitutional bounds had been flagrantly overstepped by the Attorney General's office in its wholesale seizure of Issei suspects against whom there had been little or no evidence of wrongdoing, and despite the increasingly harsh security measures being imposed on Japanese residents under the prodding of the War Department, the wrath of West Coast pressure groups was relentlessly concentrated on Biddle for what they derided as "pussyfooting"—his unwillingness to negate the rights of citizens.

"A great many West Coast people distrust the Japanese [and] various special interests would welcome their removal from good farm land and the elimination of their competition," the Attorney General wrote the President on February 17, 1942, to assert for the record what he plainly believed were racist and economic motivations behind all the public and political proevacuation hysterics. Biddle, moreover, made a last-ditch try at slowing down at least the large-scale, and hurried, removals which he suspected were under Army consideration —over and beyond the stepped-up activities of his own department, then busily engaged in removing enemy aliens from around strategically important areas recommended by the military. Though pleading conciliatorily that "there is no dispute between the War, Navy and Justice Departments," the Attorney General called the President's attention to the "legal limits" of his own department's authority and the fact that "under the Constitution, 60,000 of these Japanese are American citizens."

Biddle then lashed out in severe criticism of journalists who, he felt, were "acting with dangerous irresponsibility" (he compared their inciting utterances to "shouting FIRE! in a crowded theater") in arousing sentiment for speedy arbitrary action on the ground that an enemy attack and concerted sabotage were imminent. "My last advice from the War Department is that there is no evidence of imminent attack and from the F.B.I. that there is no evidence of planned sabotage," [1] Biddle assured the President.

Had the Attorney General vigorously lashed out against the obvious un-Americanism of singling out for especially cruel treatment a colored minority, the President, in turn, might conceivably have had to face up to his nobler libertarian instincts. But Biddle, like the President—though championing the rights of downtrodden minorities abroad—lacked the driving, down-reaching commitment against racism within America's own borders, and the opportunity to assert the very principles for which Americans were then fighting and dying was lost. "Only a great outcry of protest on the highest moral grounds would have stopped the drift toward evacuation," declares James MacGregor Burns in *Roosevelt: The Soldier of Freedom,* "and Biddle was neither temperamentally nor politically capable of it."

With sadness and regret, the Attorney General was to recall in his postwar memoirs:

American citizens of Japanese origin were not even handled like aliens of the other enemy nationalities—Germans and Italians—on a selective basis, but as untouchables, a group who could not be trusted and had to be shut up only because they were of Japanese descent. . . .
Their constitutional rights were the same as those of the men

who were responsible for the program: President Roosevelt, Secretary of War Stimson, and the Assistant Secretary of War, John J. McCloy [later High Commissioner to Germany and World Bank president], Lieutenant General John L. DeWitt, commanding officer of the Pacific Coast area, and Colonel Karl Robin Bendetsen of the General Staff, who was brought into the Provost Marshal's office in Washington from a successful law practice on the West Coast, where a strong anti-Japanese prejudice prevailed.[2]

It was the West Coast-born, Stanford-educated Karl R. Bendetsen who catapulted himself into veritable immortality by coming up with the legally—and constitutionally—airtight plan enabling the incarceration en masse of the citizen Nisei without too obvious an appearance of discrimination.[3] Bendetsen's achievement was considerable in that it wrested the entire "Japanese problem" away from Justice, enabling Army advocates of drastic action to rid themselves of the irksome "constitutional conscience" represented by Biddle, with public opinion fully on their side.

The Bendetsen formula, which earned its architect an immediate promotion, later one of the nation's highest military decorations, was simple but sweepingly effective. It involved the following:

the issuance of an Executive Order which would authorize the Secretary of War to designate "military areas" from which all persons who did not have permission to enter and remain to be excluded as a "military necessity"

the designation of military areas (as per General DeWitt)

the immediate evacuation from these areas of all persons lacking licenses to reenter or remain.[4]

The Army stratagem, which makes no mention of the "Japanese" for whom it was intended, was to become the basis of the now famed Executive Order 9066, issued by the President on February 19, 1942, also under the authorship of Bendetsen. It enabled the military, in absence of martial law, to immediately circumvent the constitutional safeguards of over 70,000 American citizens and to treat the Nisei like aliens. Although the order theoretically affected German and Italian nationals, more of whom lived in the restricted area than Japanese Americans, all considered suspect were given individual hearings and very few were interned.

By virtue of coming up with the adroit proposal, Bendetsen thereafter soared to instant national prominence. The thirty-five-year-old Major, who had been promoted to Lieutenant Colonel on February 4, 1942, was tendered another promotion within a remarkable ten-day period: to the position of full Colonel (on February 14), in order that he might personally supervise the execution of the presidential mandate.

"We will not under any threat, or in face of any danger, sur-

70

render the guarantees of liberty our forefathers framed for us in the Bill of Rights," the President had loftily proclaimed after the United States entry into the war. But that was before the grim days and weeks of spirit-shattering reverses in the Pacific War; before Bendetsen's remarkable blueprint made simple and expedient a procedure which would undoubtedly be a rousing morale booster for the public at large—a public then in desperate need to give vent to their frustrations, to lash out at the nearest, most visible target.

II

The decision for collective evacuation and internment was made on February 11, 1942, a veritable "Pearl Harbor" for the Nisei, many of whom had felt reasonably confident that those of greater wisdom and charity in Washington would ultimately reject the regional clamor of bigots and self-serving greed interests. Even as the Attorney General was putting the finishing touches to a *Collier's* article eulogizing the Administration's determination that it would be "wiser and more humane to hold only those who were dangerous to our safety, or who might become so . . . America is too big and generous, too open of heart and hand, to allow petty persecutions," other forces were at work. Biddle's personal recollection of events, as recorded in his memoirs, also points to the eleventh of February as the day of betrayal for the Nisei and Issei—the day when the President figuratively tossed the Munson certification of loyalty into the trash heap.

Apparently the War Department's course of action had been tentatively charted by Mr. McCloy and Colonel Bendetsen in the first ten days of February. General DeWitt's final recommendation to evacuate was completed on February 13, and forwarded to Washington with a covering letter the next day. Mr. Stimson and Mr. McCloy did not, however, wait for this report, which contained the "finding" on which their "military necessity" argument to the President was based, but obtained their authority before the recommendation was received. On February 11 the President told the War Department to prepare a plan for wholesale evacuation, specifically including citizens. . . . After the conference the Assistant Secretary reported to Bendetsen: "We have *carte blanche* to do what we want to as far as the President is concerned." [5]

The wartime diary of Secretary of War Stimson provides additional insight into the tenor of high-level thinking at that critical moment for the Nisei in America. When the question of evacuating American citizens was forthrightly put to the President (Stimson diary entry for February 11), he "fortunately found that he [the President] was very vigorous about it."

In this amazingly private conduct of affairs on the part of the

Secretary of War and the President, not only Biddle but also Congress had been by-passed. The impatient exclusion demands of the West Coast congressional delegation calling for the "immediate evacuation of all persons of Japanese lineage" thus landed on the President's desk two days *after* such a plan had already been set in motion.

Once the Attorney General had decided not to oppose the evacuation further, however, the drastic wartime forfeiture of constitutional principles was far less troubling to Biddle at the time than his postwar memoirs would indicate. Biddle capitulated without a murmur to the Army grab of power for removing citizens as well as aliens and, in fact, had given the draft of Executive Order 9066 a quick once-over prior to its submission to the President.[6] And on February 20—the day after Executive Order 9066 had been promulgated—a memorandum reassuring the President and the military of their wartime powers and immunities was sent to the White House by Biddle. A covering letter explained: "I thought that you might have questions asked you with reference to the Order at a press conference and that this memorandum would therefore, be convenient." It read:

> This authority gives very broad powers to the Secretary of War and the Military Commanders. These powers are broad enough to permit them to exclude any particular individual from military areas. They could also evacuate groups of persons based on a reasonable classification. The order is not limited to aliens but includes citizens so that it can be exercised with respect to Japanese, irrespective of their citizenship.
>
> The decision of safety of the nation in time of war is necessarily for the Military authorities. Authority over the movement of persons, whether citizens or non-citizens, may be exercised in time of war. . . .
>
> The President is authorized in acting under his general war powers without further legislation. The exercise of the power can meet the specific situation and, of course, cannot be considered as any punitive measure against any particular nationalities. It is rather a precautionary measure to protect the national safety. It is not based on any legal theory but on the facts [sic] that the unrestricted movement of certain racial classes, whether American citizens or aliens, in specified defense areas may lead to serious disturbances. These disturbances cannot be controlled by police protection and have the threat of injury to our war effort. A condition and not a theory confronts the nation.[7]

On the same day that Biddle informed the President of the sweeping extension of his war powers by virtue of Order 9066, which also passed on near-carte-blanche power to the military, Secretary of War Stimson designated General John L. DeWitt to be the military commander who would carry out the evacuation. On March 11, DeWitt, in turn, designated Colonel Karl Robin Bendetsen as Director of the Wartime Civil Control Administration (established as a "Civilian Affairs" branch of the Western Defense Command), to supervise the actual removal and roundup of the evacuees under the terms of Executive Order 9066.

Though there was little likelihood of opposition to the grim surgical removal of a minority about to be precipitated, Army lawyers took special care to obtain the implied sanction of Congress before issuing the exclusion orders. Public Law No. 503 (77th Congress), which made it a federal offense to violate any and all restrictions issued by a military commander in a "military area" (under authority of Executive Order 9066), and which provided for enforcement in the federal courts, passed both houses of Congress on March 19 by unanimous voice vote. It was signed into law by the President on March 21, 1942.

The only lawmaker in Congress to take issue with the legislation intended to ratify and give legal clout to Executive Order 9066 was Senator Robert Taft of Ohio. Taft objected specifically to the wording of the measure, calling it "probably the sloppiest criminal law I have ever read or seen anywhere." It was not that Taft opposed the intent of the legislation: "I do not want to object, because I understand the pressing character of this kind of legislation for the Pacific coast today." But with apparent concern that the penal sanctions provided for could perversely affect persons other than those for whom it was intended, Taft recommended that the measure be "redrafted in some kind of legal form, instead of in the form of a military order." [8]

Many lawmakers may have been led to believe that the anticipated Army restrictions and removals, and the penalties provided under Public Law No. 503, would affect only noncitizens since Senator Robert Reynolds, who had been requested by Stimson to introduce the bill in the Senate, had done so describing the emergency measure "to deal with the peril" as one dealing "primarily with the activities of aliens and alien enemies." Only once did the Senator mention that the act could apply to citizens.

In the House, Congressman Robert F. Rich asked if military zones were plainly marked "so that citizens of this country cannot get into them without their knowledge and then be penalized." Congressman Andrew J. May, who had introduced the measure in the House, replied that "citizens of this country will never be questioned about them, as a matter of fact. This is intended for a particular situation about which the gentleman knows." (All relocation centers were in time designated as "military areas.")

Though Public Law 503 passed both houses overwhelmingly, Congress had not gone so far as to expressly authorize the impending mass exclusion; but in the failure of the nation's lawmakers to repudiate, even question, the clearly totalitarian aspects of a law which gave unbridled "teeth" to the military, Congress had unwittingly placed itself in the role of accomplice.

III

That Roosevelt himself had been motivated by racial bias in authorizing the evacuation is a fact inadvertently laid bare in a letter left by the troubled Attorney General, who had never ceased to entertain the gravest doubts about the legality of this highly authoritarian move on the part of the President. The circumstance which prompted Biddle's letter was the sharply intensified conflict between Justice and the War Department—one which had had its origin in the "Japanese problem," once the exclusive province of Justice. Biddle, who at the time of the evacuation had been new to the Cabinet, was now stubbornly standing his ground, unwilling to bow to the whims of the Secretary of War, of whom he had once stood in awe.

Following the West Coast evacuation, Biddle's disinclination to prosecute a number of cases involving Germans and Italians against whom exclusion orders had been issued by military commanders of the Eastern, Western, and Southern commands had become exceedingly irksome to the military; and on March 31, 1943, Secretary of War Stimson importuned the President:

> The Attorney General should not be permitted to thwart the military commanders. . . . I request that you direct the Attorney General to enforce these orders in accordance with the provisions of Public Law 503 . . .[9]

Biddle's acid response to this continued Army "pushing" is singularly revealing. On April 17, he wrote the President:

> I have your memorandum of April 7th, suggesting that I talk to the Secretary of War about these cases. I shall, of course, be glad to do so, and so informed him sometime ago. Conferences have already been going on for several months; and I have talked personally to McCloy (and others) for several hours.
>
> The Secretary's letter [Stimson to FDR] misses the points at issue, which are:
> 1. Whatever the military do, as Attorney General I should decide what criminal cases to bring and what not to bring. *I shall not institute criminal proceedings on exclusion orders which seem to me unconstitutional.*
> 2. You signed the original Executive Order permitting the exclusions *so the Army could handle the Japs. It was never intended to apply to Italians and Germans.* Your order was based on "protection against espionage and against sabotage." There is absolutely no evidence in the case of ADRIANO, who has been a leading citizen

of San Francisco for thirty years, that he ever had anything to do either with espionage or sabotage. He was merely pro-Mussolini before the war. He is harmless, and I understand is now living in the country outside of San Francisco.

3. KRAUS was connected before Pearl Harbor with German propaganda in this country. She turned state's evidence. The order of exclusion is so broad that I am of the opinion the courts would not sustain it. As I have said before to you, *such a decision might well throw doubt* on your powers as Commander in Chief. . . .[10] [Italics mine.]

In short, Roosevelt's Executive Order 9066—and the exclusioninternment program which grew out of it—represented nothing less than a rash, deliberate violation of the Constitution by the President himself, the Attorney General's letter suggesting that racism more than national security had motivated the decision.

As it turned out, decisions handed down by the lower courts (in cases involving Caucasians who refused to obey exclusion orders) varied widely. In one suit brought by Kenneth Alexander, an excludee from the Los Angeles area, the Ninth District Court of Appeals went on to declare on March 10, 1944, that orders excluding citizens from the military area were not orders legally but merely notices, that they "commanded nothing and prohibited nothing." [11] Biddle had had good reason to be emphatic in his recommendation to the President (memo of April 17) that no more prosecutory action be taken—until the nation's highest tribunal pass judgment on the "power to exclude the Japanese."

Yet, in what has been referred to as "the most suppressive opinion in the history of the Court," the Supreme Court of the United States was to go on in a case involving a Nisei who refused to submit to evacuation (*Korematsu v. U. S.* 323 U. S. 214 [1944])[12] to uphold the validity and constitutionality of such spurious orders against the strong dissenting opinions of three Justices: Owen J. Roberts, Robert H. Jackson, and Frank Murphy. Justice Roberts saw through the Bendetsen-devised strategy aimed only at those of Japanese ancestry as "a cleverly designed trap to accomplish the real purpose of military authority, which was to lock him [Korematsu] in a concentration camp." Justice Jackson: ". . . we may as well say that any military order will be constitutional and be done with it." Justice Murphy: "Being an obvious racial discrimination, the order deprives all those within its scope of equal protection of the laws as guaranteed by the Fifth Amendment."

Speaking for the majority, Justice Hugo Black was to reject as nonsense the charges of race prejudice: "Our task would be simple, our duty clear, were this a case involving the imprisonment of a loyal citizen in a concentration camp because of racial prejudice. . . .

To cast this case into outlines of racial prejudice, without reference to the real military dangers which were present, merely confuses the issue."

Clearly, the lofty judiciary, like Congress, was totally unaware of the Munson certification of loyalty then in careful wartime impoundment. By the High Court's majority decision (6–3) vindicating the mass forcible removals on the basis of a fictitious military necessity, the Supreme Court, the Congress, and the President had coalesced as "accomplices" in one of history's most remarkable legalizations of official illegality.

"Those who now most oppose our methods will ultimately adopt them." Hitler had given this prophetic warning.[13] In the Supreme Court's sanctification of this "legalization of racism," as bluntly charged by Justice Murphy in his *Korematsu* dissent, there was chilling irony. It was a decision to be cited repeatedly in defense of Nazi war criminals at the Nuremberg Tribunal.[14]

(4)
Outcasts

The watch-tower
Stands where
Escape is impossible.

—Senryu, by Tule Lake inmate

I

Repression was applied, one small step at a time. First came the roundup of suspect enemy aliens; the freezing of bank accounts, the seizure of contraband, the drastic limitation on travel, curfew, and other restrictive measures of increasing severity. Executive Order 9066, of February 19, 1942, then authorized the establishment of military areas and the exclusion therefrom of "any or all persons." A March 2 Army proclamation finally made clear that not only aliens but also the American-born of Japanese ancestry would be affected, the restricted military areas defined as the western halves of the Pacific Coast states, including the southern half of Arizona. Then in quick succession came the posters on telephone poles carrying the same terse notice: . . . ALL PERSONS OF JAPANESE ANCESTRY, BOTH ALIEN AND NONALIEN, WILL BE EVACUATED FROM THE ABOVE DESIGNATED AREA BY 12:00 O'CLOCK NOON . . .

The Army had not anticipated some of the resulting confusions. Among them: What was meant by "all Japanese persons"? Were these to include people of mixed blood, some of them mere infants abandoned in orphanages?

Taken aback by the Third Reich harshness of the Commandant presiding over the uprooting was the late Father Hugh T. Lavery of the Catholic Maryknoll Center in Los Angeles:

Colonel Bendetsen showed himself to be a little Hitler. I mentioned that we had an orphanage with children of Japanese ancestry, and that some of these children were half Japanese, others one-fourth or less. I asked which children should we send . . . Bendetsen said: "I am determined that if they have one drop of Japanese blood in them, they must go to camp."[1]

Upon registration at one of the sixty-four Civil Control stations established near centers of Japanese American concentration, individuals and families were turned overnight into numbers on tags. Instructions laid down by the Army were explicit and absolute: On an appointed time and date, evacuees were to assemble themselves voluntarily for internment with bedrolls and baggage, no more than could be carried by hand, properly tagged. A week to ten days was usually given for winding up their businesses.

The suddenness of the removal edict, and bureaucratic inertia in making provisions for the sale or safeguarding of property, precipitated a condition of utter chaos as evacuees sought frantically to dispose of their life accumulations in any way they knew how in hopes of salvaging what cash they could. Few dared to take advantage of governmental storage facilities offered "at the sole risk" of the evacuees. Widespread suspicion and mistrust, moreover, hampered the efforts of government agents who offered assistance in the transfer of land into Caucasian hands.

In the few days allowed the evacuees before their eviction, bargain hunters and junk dealers descended in hordes. The frightened and confused became easy prey to swindlers who threatened to "arrange" for the confiscation of their property if they would not agree to a forced sale at the pittance offered.

Some permitted hopefully trustworthy white friends to move into their homes as overseers—often rent-free—or to take over the care of their land, sometimes with a power of attorney mandate. There were many who turned over possessions for storage in local Japanese temples and churches, others who simply boarded them up in garages or vacant sheds belonging to kindly disposed neighbors. But pilfering and vandalism often began before they were hardly out of their homes. A postwar survey was to reveal that 80 percent of goods privately stored were "rifled, stolen or sold during absence."

For the majority of the Issei who had helped to make the California desert bloom, the rewards of a lifetime of zealous perseverance evaporated within a frenzied fortnight.

II

True to their cultural imperative of unquestioning obedience, the evacuees turned themselves in at the appointed time and place with such orderliness as to astound the Army. Only if one were tubercular, critically ill in the hospital, or hopelessly mad and institutionalized was one exempt from the roundup.[2]

A solitary Nisei was found in hiding and near starvation three weeks later. A page-one story in the *San Francisco News* of June 1, 1942, declared: "No Food Since May 9—Jap Found Hiding in Cellar."

Two Issei had chosen suicide to being evacuated. One had hanged himself because of a condition of uncontrollable trembling which he knew caused people to draw away from him. According to the statements of a friend, fear that he would bring shame and disgrace to his attractive sixteen-year-old daughter had driven him to the desperate act.

> To explain his actions, he left a concise note . . . In it he explained to the daughter why he had done such a thing, and he asked her to forgive him. . . . that if he went to camp, his beloved daughter would be ridiculed by thoughtless children and made miserable for something that was not her fault. He knew, he said, that she loved him, and that she wouldn't mind, but the mothers and fathers of the other children perhaps would not let her be friends with them, on account of her father. Her chances of marriage, in such a confined place, would be almost hopeless if his condition were generally known. In everything, he was thinking of her first and foremost. . . . He couldn't give her material things, he said, but maybe this last action of his would, in some way, help her achieve his dreams for her.
>
> This is just one personal tragedy in many, but that was the state of mind of many people during those trying days of evacuation . . . the hopelessness of these people was astounding. To them their world had come to an end, and they really felt they had nothing more to live for.[3]

Another Issei, Hideo Murata of Pismo Beach, was found with a bullet through his head, an Honorary Citizenship Certificate grasped in his hand. The testimonial, which had been bestowed on Murata at an Independence Day celebration the year before, read in part:

> Monterey County presents this testimony of heartfelt gratitude, of honor and respect for your loyal and splendid service to the country in the Great World War. Our flag was assaulted and you gallantly took up its defense.[4]

Otherwise, the evacuation proceeded "without mischance, with minimum hardship, and almost without incident," according to its coordinator, Colonel Karl Bendetsen. It had begun with the issuing, on March 24, of Exclusion Order No. 1 calling for the March 30 evacuation of Bainbridge Island near Seattle, Washington—about which an editorial writer of a Seattle paper was moved to comment:

If anything ever illustrated the repute of these United States as a melting pot of diverse races, it was the recent evacuation of Japanese residents, American and foreign-born, from the pleasant countryside of Bainbridge Island . . . The Japanese departed their homes cheerfully, knowing full well, most of them, that the measures was [sic] designed to help preserve the precious, kindly camaraderie among divergent races which is one of this country's great contributions to humanity.[5]

From the various evacuation depots, evacuees were transported by Army-commandeered trains or buses to assigned "reception centers," one of the several Army euphemisms for the initial camps of detention. Officially referred to as "assembly centers," twelve of these temporary detention compounds had been established within the state of California alone. Only one was located in the state of Oregon—at the Portland Livestock Pavilion. In the neighboring state of Washington, the Puyallup Assembly Center—or "Camp Harmony" —was the only camp setup for its Japanese American population. The smallest of all the assembly centers was the one erected in Mayer, Arizona, which accommodated 260 evacuees.

All centers (except the Arizona-based one) were still within the forbidden military zone (Zone A) and had been improvised within a remarkable twenty-eight-day period with such dispatch that the Japanese community had no idea of the concentrated activity taking place, some of it in their own backyards. Assurance was given by way of propaganda channels that these reception and assembly centers were by no means concentration camps and that the inmates were not prisoners.[6] But the sense of being debased human beings was inescapable for a people being guarded night and day by soldiers up in guard towers. As one Nisei put it: "This evacuation did not seem too unfair until we got right to the camp and were met by soldiers with guns and bayonets. Then I almost started screaming."

The assembly centers were under continual close supervision from both the Presidio and the War Department, but were administered by a WPA staff at a per diem cost per evacuee which varied from twenty-five cents in the Salinas Center to seventy-three cents at the Mayer Assembly Center. From the word "go," speed and economy had been overriding factors in the construction of these camps,[7] so building them on race tracks, fairgrounds, and livestock pavilions had substantially minimized the need for establishing electrical, water, and sewage systems. At the same time, stadiums, livestock stalls, and stables provided instant—though odoriferous—housing for thousands.

The shortage of critical building material also had much to do with the crudeness of the hastily thrown-up shacks which made up the balance of the housing. Obvious labor- and lumber-saving efforts at the Puyallup Assembly Center had resulted in near-windowless shacks resembling chicken coops, they had been built so low.

Generally, a bare room comprised a "family apartment," provided only with cots, blankets, and mattresses (often straw-filled sacks). The apartment's only fixture was a hanging light bulb. Each family unit was separated from the adjoining one by a thin dividing partition which, "for ventilation purpose," only went part way up.

Under a declared policy of the "preservation of the family unit," camp authorities tried to keep parents, grandparents, and the children together—all of them packed together, wherever possible, in a single room. In camps where housing facilities fell drastically short of the intake, couples with few children (or none at all) were often forced to double up with other couples.

> I was rather disappointed at the barracks which we evacuees were to live in. I thought at least each individual family would be assigned to a separate apartment. Instead, two or three families were crowded into a six beam apartment, offering no privacy. It didn't matter so much with the bachelors or the single girls if they slept in quarters together. But when two or three families were placed in one apartment to make the quota for the barrack, it was terrible.[8]

At the Tanforan (Race Track) Assembly Center, the lower grandstand area was converted into a mammoth dormitory which housed 400 bachelors, who, according to artist Mine Okubo, then documenting her camp experiences, "slept and snored, dressed and undressed, in one continuous performance."

Evacuees ate communally, showered communally, defecated communally. Again with an eye toward economy, no partitions had been built between toilets—a situation which everywhere gave rise to camp-wide cases of constipation. Protests from Caucasian church groups led, in time, to the building of partial dividing walls, but doors were never installed. Equally abhorred by the Issei, for whom scalding baths were a nightly fatigue-relieving ritual, were the Western-style showers, from which they usually walked away unsatisfied and shivering, for the hot water supply was never dependable.

In interior California camps, the hot summer sun beating down on paper-thin roofs turned living quarters into sizzling ovens, sometimes causing the floors to melt. Alan Taniguchi, whose family was assigned to a converted horse stable, recently recalled "falling on the cot and going to sleep and finding myself sleeping on the floor—the legs of the cot had penetrated the asphalt topping and sunk. The bed frame had ended up resting on the floor."

Notwithstanding concerned efforts of humanitarian groups, the Public Health Service could not be moved to condemn the stables as unfit for human habitation though the stench became oppressive in the summer heat, especially in stables which had been merely scraped out and no floors put in. At the largest of the assembly centers, the Santa Anita Race Track outside of Los Angeles, then housing over 18,000 evacuees, hospital records show that 75 percent of the ill-nesses came from the horse stalls.[9]

Insight into conditions prevailing at Tanforan, another well-known race track (located south of San Francisco in San Bruno), is provided by hospital notes recorded during the early days of the center intake:

Pregnancy cases—Dr. Fujita says there are many of them but she has had no time to contact them or get them registered for care . . .

Many cases of German measles are coming into camp as new evacuees arrive—It is almost uncontrollable. Doctor said she asked for an isolation building but none was given. Dr. Harrison of U. S. Public Health Service told the doctor "Well, they all have to get measles some time so let them get it."

Morale: Is high so far among young people but not among older ones. Older people who have poor memories, etc., get up at night and try to get out—Doctor says she has to bandage and sew up heads in the mornings of the old people who try to get thru the gates and have been struck on head by soldiers.[10]

During the first ten days of Tanforan, only one woman doctor attended the needs of thousands. Equipment and medicine were in short supply, and newborn babies slept in cardboard cartons. The report noted inadequacies in the mess hall diet:

Food No milk for any one over 5 years of age

Had eggs only once (1 egg each) in first ten days

No meat at all until 12th day when very small portions were served

NO BUTTER AT ALL

There is both white and brown bread served with meals

Coffee for breakfast, cocoa made with water completely is served for lunch, tea for dinner . . .

Anyone doing heavy or outdoor work states they are not getting nearly enough to eat and are hungry all the time. This includes the doc-tor . . .

In the early days of the Army-controlled assembly centers, camp fare consisted largely of canned goods: hash, pork and beans, canned weiners, beans of infinite variety. Conspicuous by their absence were the fresh fruits and vegetables which the Issei had once raised in succulent profusion. Following the mass dislocation of farm special-ists, prices had skyrocketed.

At the Santa Anita Assembly Center, some 800 Nisei who had patriotically volunteered to work on the Army's camouflage net-mak-ing project suddenly announced a sit-down strike, complaining, among other things, of weakness from an insufficiency of food. Hunger drove restless adolescents into invading neighboring mess halls, eventually bringing about the wearing of regulatory badges at mealtime. A teenager chronicled his personal escapades:

> One day I and some friends went to messhall One and saw on a table reserved for doctors and nurses a lot of lettuce and tomatoes, fresh. We just went wild and grabbed at it like animals. When it gets down here [the stomach] they can't get it back. It was the best treat I ever had. . . . One day we went to messhall Two and they had three kinds of beans with bread for lunch.[11]

Mess halls in most of these centers served thousands. One thus learned to eat rapidly in deference to the multitude waiting patiently in lines which stretched endlessly. With little else to look forward to, food assumed a place of supreme importance for the young and old, and the queuing up which began well before the meal hour turned into an accepted ritual of camp life. In the driving rain and mud, in whipping sandstorms and under the blistering midday sun, the line leading to food was always doggedly held. Observed a Nisei:

> In a camp, it can be said that food, above all things, is the center and the pleasure of life. It's natural to want to eat something good. I cannot help thinking about the old men standing with plates in their hands. Residents in America for forty or fifty years, they pursued gigantic dreams and crossed an expansive ocean to America to live. The soil they tilled was a mother to them, and their life was regulated by the sun. They were people who had worked with all they had, until on their foreheads wave-like furrows were harrowed. Everytime I see these oldsters with resigned, peaceful expressions meekly eating what is offered them, I feel my eyes become warm.[12]

III

Life behind these bleak detention pens, however, was not all deprivation and Dostoevskian gloom. The Issei who had relentlessly driven themselves without thought of self were now enjoying their first real vacation. If losses had been heart-rending, there were others who had suffered incalculably more. There was consolation in misery being mutually shared; there was the balm of newfound friendship. Mothers and grandmothers inured to dawn-to-dusk drudgery were, all of a sudden, ladies of leisure, no longer confronted by the day-to-day struggle for survival. For many, there was an all-pervasive feeling of relief in not being continually rebuffed and humiliated by the larger society, in suddenly feeling equal—if only to one another.

> In my heart I secretly welcomed the evacuation because it was a total escape from the world I knew. Even when the men took me away to the tarpapered barracks I felt for the first time in my life a com-

plete sense of relief. The struggle against a life which seemed so futile and desperate was ended.[13]

Before long, dainty patches of flowers broke the virgin sod. Serenely tasteful Japanese-style rock gardens began to transform cheerless barrack fronts under the loving ministration of earnest ubiquitous landscape artists. Needed articles of furniture were ingeniously hand-crafted, and drab interiors underwent colorful "Sears Roebuck" transformations. One saw everywhere a remarkable yearning for beauty and neatness assert itself even in temporary refuge.

A strong sense of community was also evidenced among a people to whom indolence was foreign. However little the remuneration ("salaries," when they finally came through, amounted to around five cents an hour), many volunteered their services as recreational directors, doctors, dentists, mess hall workers, garbage collectors, stenographers, clerks, block wardens, sign painters, reporters, and sketchers on the camp newsletter. Informal grade school classes were organized so youngsters would not be entirely deprived of an education; hobby groups were begun for adults. But meetings, classes, or lectures could not be conducted in the Japanese language (unless by a Caucasian), and all books written in Japanese, except religious ones, were confiscated.

In this caged-in government-made ghetto without privacy or permanence, the adolescent Nisei also experienced their first exhilarating sense of release—from the severe parental restraint placed upon them. Until their camp experience, such phenomena as youth gangs and social workers, for example, were virtually unheard of in Japanese communities. In the free-and-easy contacts now available to the army of teen-agers involved, the carefully inculcated discipline, the traditional solidarity of the Japanese family and its extremely rigorous moral code all underwent a steady weakening.

IV

While order was gradually being established in the assembly centers, work crews under the supervision of Army engineers were toiling at a feverish pace to meet the near-impossible governmental deadline on relocation camps in the far interior. While most of these sprawling encampments were located on hot desert acres or on drought-parched flatlands, two of the relocation projects (Rohwer and Jerome) were taking shape on swampland areas in distant Arkansas.

Again, with scant regard for the elderly in fragile health, rough-hewn wooden barracks—the flimsy "theater-of-operations" kind meant for the temporary housing of robust fighting men—had been speedily hammered together, providing only the minimum protection from the elements. Though lined on the inside with plasterboard and almost totally wrapped with an overlay of black tarpaper, they afforded far from adequate protection against the icy wintry blast that swept through the warped floor boards in such northerly centers of relocation as Heart Mountain, Minidoka, Topaz, and Tule Lake, where the mercury dipped, on occasion, to a numbing minus 30 degrees in the winter.

A degree of uniformity existed in the physical makeup of all the centers. A bare room measuring 20 feet by 24 feet was again referred to as a "family apartment"; each accommodated a family of five to eight members; barrack end-rooms measuring 16 feet by 20 feet were set aside for smaller families. A barrack was made up of four to six such family units. Twelve to fourteen barracks, in turn, comprised a community grouping referred to as a "block." Each block housed from 250 to 300 residents and had its own mess hall, laundry room, latrines, and recreation hall.

The construction "is so very cheap that, frankly, if it stands up for the duration we are going to be lucky," testified Milton Eisenhower before a Senate appropriations committee, noting that the Arizona camps were in areas which could be "as high as 130 degrees in summertime." On March 18, 1942 (the same day that the War Relocation Authority was established by Executive Order 9102), the youngest brother of the famous wartime General had been appointed by the President to become the first National Director of the WRA, a nonmilitary agency.

Mindful that evacuees were capable of effecting soil improvements which would turn into postwar public assets, hitherto worthless parcels of real estate were purposely chosen for the WRA campsites [14]—an idea which had been pushed with vigorous persistence by one Thomas D. Campbell, a name lost to history despite the considerable impetus and direction he appears to have given the evolving program at the time. Campbell, an agricultural engineer and top expert on available private and federally owned farm lands,[15] saw in "the emergency" a tremendous opportunity for the wartime exploitation of Japanese American manpower and their farming wizardry. His ambitious, wide-ranging proposals for an expeditious solution to a "national problem" had momentarily caught the imagination of War Department officials, then in urgent need of such expertise. Campbell, in fact, had called for the colonization of the raw, unexploited Indian land which would later become the site of Poston.[16]

In a recent letter to the author, then Assistant War Secretary John J. McCloy commented: "I remember that Tom Campbell had a very provocative, energetic mind and I was disposed to take his ideas seriously." [17] Campbell believed that an "Army officer of rank must be in full charge." And that the first order of business was to gather up the West Coast minority in Army-established concentration camps with an eye to "the big movement" later: i.e., seeing to their orderly transfer, with the cooperation of other governmental agencies, to potentially self-supporting federal projects involving such activities as food production, land subjugation, soil conservation, irrigation, road building, etc., which he believed would be less costly than prison camps.

Campbell cautioned against having anyone of Japanese extraction left "near any factory, dock, warehouse, public utility, railroad, bridge or reservoir," and suggested that the "safest place for these people is in that part of the United States west of the Mississippi and east of the Rocky Mountains." [18] He envisioned the seasonal use of internees as migratory harvesters in sugar beets, cotton and perishable crops ("beet growers alone can use 25,000 men"), utilizing CCC camps as way stations or by the utilization of "trailers which can be moved from place to place." In his memorandum of February 25, 1942, to McCloy, Campbell called for a meeting of the Governors "of all Western States."

On March 11, Campbell met with President Roosevelt over dinner. A follow-up letter sent the following day to the President stressed once more:

> There are many and various projects between the Mississippi Valley and the Rocky Mountains, publicly and privately owned which have been abandoned or are in receivership, in poor financial condition, or partially used. . . .
>
> The various governors, who are opposing the movement, can be shown that, in addition to being a military necessity, it can become an asset. Land in Southern California has its high value today, to a great extent, as a result of the ability and industry of the Japanese. . . .[19]

Campbell's paranoiac misconception of the minority was typical of prevailing racial attitudes:

> We probably can place the men in camps or at gainful jobs, but how about the wives and children? It is better for us to err on the safe side and place many foreigners in camps, some of which foreigners may be loyal, than to be less careful and let just one remain free who might do great damage.[20]

Though Milton Eisenhower (whose advice and expertise as Land Use Coordinator with the Department of Agriculture was then also being sought) ended up being tapped for the unprecedented job which Campbell had described to the President as one in which "we can write a new chapter in the care and utilization of aliens and war prisoners," some of Thomas D. Campbell's proposals had been passed on to Eisenhower, for McCloy had been roundly impressed: "I think some of the ideas are excellent, and perhaps Campbell himself could be useful in this connection, but since the President has already appointed Mr. Eisenhower, who seems to me to be an excellent man, I think that Mr. Campbell could only be useful if Mr. Eisenhower desired his services." [21] Campbell, who operated 95,000 acres of Montana wheat and flax land, chose not to serve under Eisenhower and ended up in the Pentagon as a Colonel in the Army Air Force.

Yet doubtlessly on some of the barren, unexploited acreage to which Campbell had early called attention, barbed-wire-ringed communities bearing the following names took shape during the spring and summer of 1942:

Poston Relocation Center (Arizona)
Gila Relocation Center (Arizona)
Jerome Relocation Center (Arkansas)
Rohwer Relocation Center (Arkansas)
Topaz Relocation Center (Utah)
Granada Relocation Center (Colorado)
Heart Mountain Relocation Center (Wyoming)
Minidoka Relocation Center (Idaho)
Tule Lake Relocation Center (California)
Manzanar Relocation Center (California)

The switch-over of the Army-operated Owens Valley Reception Center (subsequently renamed "Manzanar") and the Colorado River Project (Poston) to WRA jurisdiction in June 1942 had resulted in ten "relocation centers" then in partial readiness for the mass deportation inland. Known only to high-level planners, at the time, this was to include the intake of around 15,000 from Hawaii "in family groups, from among the United States citizens of Japanese ancestry who may be considered as potentially dangerous to national security." There had been remarkably little agitation locally or on the mainland demanding such a move, and few people were aware of the one exception in this regard: the strong, steady proevacuation pressure emanating from the Western Defense Command. WRA National Director Dillon Myer would declare after the war: ". . . after the evacuation order was issued here on the mainland, he [Colonel Bendetsen] tried for weeks to get a large group of people evacuated from Hawaii with the idea, I am sure, of justifying their West Coast evacuation." [22]

V

Though under constant pressure from Washington to carry out the March 13, 1942, directive calling for wide-scale removal of Hawaii's Japanese community to U. S. mainland camps beginning with 15,000 to 20,000 of the "most dangerous," the Hawaiian Department made it crystal-clear on July 1, 1942, that it "does not want to arbitrarily select 15,000 Japanese," and that the "present situation was highly satisfactory." [23] For months the severe lack of shipping and transportation had precluded the sending in of troops, munitions, and replacement labor believed necessary before the movement could begin. Considered essential also was the prior evacuation of 20,000 wives and children of servicemen, for the possibility of a retaliatory enemy attack had to be considered.

What finally contravened to prevent removals on a massive scale were the legal difficulties which developed: ACLU action had forced, at once, the return of thirteen citizens earlier shipped off to mainland internment camps.[24] The legal setback portended annoying complications inherent "in placing American citizens, even of Japanese ancestry, in concentration camps"; and it led to a total recision of the March directive, which had called for the transfer to mainland camps of 100,000 Japanese Americans, both citizens and aliens.

The new Chiefs of Staff directive of July 15, 1942 (approved by the President on July 17), called for a vastly reduced withdrawal of no more than 15,000 individuals considered "potentially dangerous to national security." The directive specified that the evacuees be "in family groups, from among the United States citizens of Japanese ancestry" and that they were being sent to the mainland "for resettlement rather than internment." Individuals who constituted "a source of danger to our national security"—if citizens—were to be interned locally (under martial law) rather than be removed to mainland camps since "it has been found that this procedure is not feasible as through application for a writ of habeas corpus any United States citizen can obtain release from custody." [25]

But once again the authorized removal, still pressingly demanded by Secretary of Navy Knox and the President, never got off the ground. The number targeted for transplantation in mainland relocation centers dwindled precipitously—15,000 to 5,000, then to 1,500—with the factor of "dangerousness" eventually getting lost in the shuffle. To designate anyone as even *potentially* dangerous had become exceedingly difficult for the team of three G-2 officers responsible for selecting the individuals and families to be removed, as others in the island population were hard put to match the exemplary loyalty demonstration of the Hawaiian Japanese.

The hard-line Knox-FDR team nevertheless kept up its evacuation demands far into 1942 despite the near-total lack of political and economic pressure on the local level calling for such a move, and in dynamic opposition to recommendations of Hawaiian authorities who preferred to "treat the Japanese in Hawaii as citizens of an occupied country." [26] Following an on-the-spot assessment, even Secretary

McCloy joined local authorities in discouraging the called-for trans-plantation which could topple the island economy if undertaken with-out sending in an equivalent labor force of comparable skill and experience. Yet mindful of existing pressures, McCloy had put it squarely to General Emmons that "he had better work out some alternative evacuation plan . . . to satisfy the President and Mr. Knox." [27]

The Military Governor subsequently organized a "voluntary evacuation" for which a total of 1,037 evacuees were netted—912 of them citizens. Included in the group were Nisei suspects then being held in the Sand Island Concentration Camp, along with family members "persuaded" into accompanying them. (A conference permitted between internee and wife usually settled the matter.) Also fetched up in the net of "voluntary" exiles—generally individuals considered nonproductive and "a drain on the economy"—were wives and children of alien husbands and fathers who had been sent earlier to the mainland for internment (the "welfare group").[28]

Included, too, were individuals the island authorities considered "potentially dangerous" in Hawaii but harmless on the mainland: alien and citizen fishermen with knowledge of the waters; persons who had requested repatriation; a number of Kibei and released detainees under surveillance, all of whom (including accompanying family members) were considered to be harmless, but a group the military preferred not to have at large. As Colonel Fielding of G-2, Hawaiian Department, explained to General DeWitt and his aide over the trans-Pacific hotline, "the evacuation is merely a matter of relieving pressure . . . They really aren't dangerous and not bad at all." [29]

On the departure of the Hawaiian contingent, beginning in November 1942, Governor Emmons appealed to the public: "No stigma or suspicion should be attached to the individual."

Contrary to the mythology of decent and admirably restrained treatment of the Hawaiian Japanese built up over the years, the Hawaiian evacuation was a surrealistic tale of chicanery and duress, deplorable for its official use of mendacity to abrogate the rights of ordinary citizens blameless of wrongdoing. With slight variation, the curious experience recounted below was one shared by numerous evacuees from Hawaii who unsuspectingly ended up in the mosquito-infested, fenced-in muddy compounds of Jerome and Topaz.

> One day a Caucasian who talked fluent Japanese came into the [Sand Island] center and told them that they had good news for them. He said the citizens could evacuate to the mainland with their families and that they would be free over here. Before leaving the center they had to sign a statement that they would not sue the government for arrest or detention. On the ship coming over here, they were told that they were coming to the mainland where they would be free citizens

and would get employment. Most of them anticipated doing some farm work. Women and children were told that they would be united with their husbands who were interned on the mainland.

The relocation center was somewhat of a shock to the people in several respects. In the first place, the guard towers and the barbed wire fences did not seem consistent with their being free citizens. Furthermore, they found they were unable to engage in regular employment . . . Those who had expected to be re-united with their husbands or fathers were also disappointed. Furthermore, aliens and some of the citizens had their assets frozen in Hawaii. At the center they have found that they are spending their capital continuously in order to provide necessities . . .[30]

A theme widely exploited by U. S. propaganda channels, including the Army's own public relations setup, was that relocation centers were wartime "resettlement communities" and "havens of refuge," so it is little wonder that the public—and even those who ended up in them—were easily misled. Assembly center internees resentful of searchlights, machine-gun-manned watchtowers, and other repressive paraphernalia were generally reassured that it was all "a temporary measure," that their freedom would be largely restored to them after the move to civilian-controlled "permanent camps" in the hinterland.

VI

The midsummer of 1942 saw the activation of the second phase of the mass withdrawal. This involved the herding off daily of approximately 500 deportees from each of the assembly centers to unfinished barrack communities, some of them so geographically remote that the train trip sometimes took from four to five days.

Tubercular patients (hundreds were discovered during the uprooting) and their families were thoughtfully diverted from the Siberia-like winter clime of the more northerly camps of resettlement to the dry Arizona desert compound of Gila. Considered less suitable for individuals weakened by respiratory disfunction was Poston, the larger of the sprawling sun-baked Arizona stockades, which became known for its choking dust-storms of such merciless ferocity that they sometimes tore away roofs.

To travel-weary refugees, the spectacle of guard towers and gun-toting sentries in the middle of a vast, primitive expanse of nothingness came as a rude shock, especially to evacuees who had been assured in the assembly centers that the relocation centers were to be resettlement communities, not prison camps, and that the evacuees would be free to go to the neighboring villages to shop. Evacuees who, after their arrival, found themselves being caged in by degrees were hotly indignant; for at camps Minidoka and Heart Mountain, as had been the case in the early days of Manzanar, the construction of the spectacularly useless guard towers and fence began *after* the start of the intake. In the Idaho-based camp of Minidoka, feelings soared to a dangerous degree of intensity when residents discovered the fence to be electrified. The camp Community Analyst (one was assigned to each relocation center to analyze and interpret evacuee moods) [31] reported back to his Washington superiors:

> On November 12, the contractor became so incensed by the continual sabotage on the fence by the residents that an electric generator was hooked up and the fence charged. This was done without knowledge or consent of either Army or local WRA authorities. . . .
>
> The removal of portions of the fence early in April, 1943, was an occasion of deep satisfaction for the workers involved. It is reported that never on the project was a job attacked so willingly. It may be significant to note that the residents believe the fence in these areas to be permanently out. As one resident phrased it, "There will be revolution if the fence is put back again." This is exaggeration but illustrates the depth of feeling with respect to the fence. . . . The bitter feeling about the fence runs through the entire resident group from children in school to the oldest Issei. It crops out in school children's themes, in art work, in letters written by the residents. Everywhere the feeling is found that the fence has and will have a deep psychological effect on the younger people.
>
> Here in Minidoka, it is impossible to point out any practical value of the fence. True, there is a canal and there is danger of small children drowning. To defend the fence in this area on those grounds is to have the answer flung back: "Safety for children is fine, but it is a funny way to protect small children with barbed wire on which they can cut themselves." . . . The residents put it this way: "Who would want to go over the fence anyway? There are no Seattles or Portlands on the other side. Besides there are ticks and rattlesnakes all over the place." [32]

There was no mistaking, however, that internment—not refuge—was the intent and purpose of the military personnel charged with guarding a people who, in all too many fired-up minds, were somehow connected with the Pearl Harbor perfidy. It was therefore fortunate that authorities had early determined that troops be restricted to patrolling the outer perimeter and the gates because of attempts made by a few of them to seduce female evacuees. "The M.P.s are mostly Limited Service men, some of whom are not too intelligent," wrote back Jerome's Community Analyst to Washington, adding, "and they are trying to make their work appear dangerous and exciting." An alarming trigger-minded proclivity on the part of Army sentries had, indeed, come to light at Manzanar. A WRA investigation conducted in the summer of 1942 had revealed:

The guards have been instructed to shoot anyone who attempts to leave the Center without a permit, and who refuses to halt when ordered to do so. The guards are armed with guns that are effective at a range of up to 500 yards. I asked Lt. Buckner if a guard ordered a Japanese who was out of bounds to halt and the Jap did not do so, would the guard actually shoot him. Lt. Buckner's reply was that he only hoped the guard would bother to ask him to halt. He explained that the guards were finding guard service very monotonous, and that nothing would suit them better than to have a little excitement, such as shooting a Jap.

Sometime ago, a Japanese [Nisei] was shot for being outside of a Center. . . . The guard said that he ordered the Japanese to halt— that the Japanese started to run away from him, so he shot him. The Japanese was seriously injured, but recovered. He said that he was collecting scrap lumber to make shelves in his house, and that he did not hear the guard say halt. The guard's story does not appear to be accurate, inasmuch as the Japanese was wounded in the front and not in the back.[33]

In more vigilantly guarded assembly centers, children were instructed to stay within twenty feet of the fence since pot shots had been taken at a few who strayed, one child suffering a gunshot wound.[34] News of such incidents, however, was kept discreetly suppressed.

It was a bewildering, unreal world for youngsters. And for parents and elders, the problem of how best to explain to them that this is "still America" and why soldiers had to patrol about with rifles ("Mommy, who are they afraid of?") was a continuing dilemma which all parents of small children grappled with and devised solutions for in the best way they knew how. But however much the internees strove corporately to maintain a lofty image of America for the sake of a whole generation growing up behind stockades, little could be done to erase from impressionable minds the all too pervasive evidence that much of the treatment which cast them as separate and inferior people had to do with the color of their skin.

A Nisei mother once told me with tears in her eyes of her six-year-old son who insisted on her "taking him back to America." The little boy had been taken to Japan about two years ago but was so unhappy there that she was compelled to return to California with him. Soon afterwards they were evacuated to Santa Anita, and the little boy in the absence of his Caucasian playmates was convinced that he was still in Japan and kept on entreating his mother to "take him back to America." To reassure him that he was in America she took him to the information center in her district and pointed to the American flag but he could not be consoled because Charlie and Jimmie, his Caucasian playmates, were not there with him in camp.[35]

An oft-repeated ritual in relocation camp schools (where "Americanization" was constantly stressed, as demanded by congressional lawmakers in their unfailing patriotic zeal) was the salute to the flag followed by the singing of "My country, 'tis of thee, sweet land of liberty"—a ceremony Caucasian teachers found embarrassingly awkward if not cruelly poignant in the austere prison-camp setting. After a speaking visit of five of the far-flung citizen detention camps, the famous missionary to India and Methodist Bishop, E. Stanley Jones (who, with his spiritual colleague, Toyohiko Kagawa, had sought in vain to deter Japan and America from their collision course), wrote movingly in the *Christian Century* of November 24, 1943:

> Their spirits are unbroken. They took the pledge of allegiance to the flag in a high school assembly, and my voice broke as I joined with them in the promise of loyalty "to one nation, indivisible, with liberty and justice for all." "Liberty and justice for all"—how could they say it? But they did and they meant it. Their faith in democracy is intact. Their faith in God holds too, in spite of everything.

(5)
Reentry into America

War-duration "protective custody," the Army's declared course of action, was to undergo a sudden about-face as farmhands throughout the nation fled in droves for better-paying employment in defense industries. Only after the horde of West Coast farm specialists had been securely placed behind lock and key did a new hue and cry arise: "They should force those Japs to take this work!" To forestall deportations to the interior was the sudden counterpressure now faced by the Army.

Secretary of War Stimson alerted the President on July 7, 1942:

> Now Governor Olson has discovered that the harvesting season is coming for some of the California fruits and that it may be profitable for Californians to keep these Japanese huddled up in these assembly camps to be used cheaply on this harvesting.
>
> These assembly centers are merely improvised structures where there is considerable danger of overcrowding and epidemics. I do not think that he should be allowed to blow first hot and then cold without any reference to the safety or welfare of these unfortunate people . . . I suggest therefore that you keep this situation in mind in case the Governor approaches you on the subject.[1]

Governor Culbert L. Olson, a leading California liberal (then Chairman of the Northern California Committee on Fair Play for Citizens and Aliens of Japanese Ancestry), was a reflection of the hot-cold shifts in West Coast public attitudes following the Pearl Harbor attack. Within weeks, Olson had flip-flopped from his post-Pearl espousal of just and equitable treatment for the Japanese American minority to one which condoned the State Personnel Board's summary firing of hundreds of Nisei holding civil service jobs.

Olson, however, had not been for evacuating the state's 93,000 Japanese Americans entirely. Faced by the crashing realization that inundation of the state by blacks and Chicanos would be unavoidable if Japanese American manpower were to be totally replaced, the Governor had early sought a compromise measure which would keep the minority's adult male population conveniently concentrated in state-supervised work camps in inland rural areas so as not to disrupt the food supply.

At a February 2 meeting, General DeWitt, the Commanding General responsible for the safety and defense of the Western theater of operations, had agreed with the Governor to have the Japanese problem handled on a purely local basis as a measure which he hoped might relieve some of the mounting pressure for speedy arbitrary action by the military. For the publication of the Roberts Report in late January, linking the success of Japan's sneak attack to the activities of resident spies and saboteurs, had aroused anti-Japanese sentiment to a dangerous pitch of excitement.

The news of this sudden "weakening" on the part of DeWitt [2] had been received with considerable dismay among hard liners within the General Staff—notably the Provost Marshal General, Allen W. Gullion, and his departmental aides who were all for making short work of rounding up the Japanese population and putting them where they couldn't do much harm. In the opinion of Gullion's deputy, Colonel Archer L. Lerch, DeWitt's dovish acquiescence to a partial evacuation to rural work camps—a move the California Governor was hoping to engineer with the cooperation of "America-born Japanese leaders"—smacked "too much of the spirit of Rotary" and overlooked "the necessary cold-bloodedness of war." [3] Gullion, himself, was all for mandatory "internment east of the Sierra Nevadas of all the Issei" (including family members willing to go along), and he didn't think resettlement need be "an essential part of the plan." [4]

As it turned out, the acute vexation over the Olson-DeWitt agreement contributed to touching off within the War Deparment the formalization of plans for mass forceable detention.

It was at this point that Karl Bendetsen, the tough-minded young West Coast-raised lawyer whose brilliance in drawing up legal documents was to make him indispensable to the wartime detention program, quickly polished off the formula which would provide the legal basis for excluding citizens. As Bendetsen sized up the situation in a lengthy memorandum to General Gullion on February 4, detaining *only the Issei* on a compulsory basis "would accomplish little as a measure of safety" since they were mostly elderly:

The average age of the alien Japanese is upwards of sixty years. A great majority of the males are old and ill. The Nisei of second generation (citizen) Japanese has an average age of around thirty [nineteen] years. Most of these have been indoctrinated with the filial piety which characterizes that race. Their affections, if any, for the United States will not be stimulated by the wholesale removal of their parents from their several homes. On the contrary, it would be a natural and only human reaction if, as it is to be expected, the Nisei were incensed by such action and if even the loyal ones were persuaded to become disloyal. However, by far the vast majority of those who have studied the Oriental assert that a substantial majority of Nisei bear allegiance to Japan, are well controlled and disciplined by the enemy, and at the proper time will engage in organized sabotage, particularly should a raid along the Pacific Coast be attempted by the Japanese. . . .

It [mass evacuation] is undoubtedly the safest course to follow, that is to say as you cannot distinguish or penetrate the Oriental thinking and as you cannot tell which ones are loyal and which ones are not and it is, therefore, the easiest course (aside from the mechanical problem involved) to remove them all from the West Coast and place them in the Zone of Interior in uninhabited areas where they can do no harm under guard. . . . As a matter of fact, in the opinion of the undersigned, mass evacuation is a course which, if followed, will largely relieve the necessity for eternal vigilance. However, no one has justified fully the sheer military necessity for such action. It is the recommendation of the undersigned that the course described [the licensing theory as the legal basis for exclusion] be adopted as War Department policy and recommended to the President for accomplishment. . . .[5]

All of this meant that DeWitt's irresolute stance would have to be remedied. Assistant War Secretary McCloy, to whom Stimson had given direct charge of all matters relating to the West Coast problem, had lost little time in feeling out the West Coast Commander's attitude in regard to the General Staff's concern for an expeditious solution.

DeWitt's meeting with the California Governor had taken place on February 2, and it was on the following day that the General received a call from McCloy. In the course of the rambling conversation in which DeWitt expressed considerable satisfaction over what the California authorities were planning, McCloy—with reference to the evolving plan within the General Staff—indicated in a general way that "the War Department had taken a definite position in favor of a mass withdrawal" which would "include not only Japanese aliens but also Japanese citizens." But the Assistant War Secretary took special care to admonish the West Coast Commander to be publicly non-committal about the matter as "it might stimulate action if the mass withdrawal did not immediately ensue."

McCloy's acute concern was that the legality of the movement be assured: ". . . the best way to solve it, at least for the time being," as he saw it, "would be to establish limited restricted zones around airplane plants, the forts and the other important military installations, but do that merely on a military basis" and "to go a little slowly on it."

A concern to McCloy, also, was that the voluntariness of the plan to keep able-bodied Issei and Nisei penned up locally as a war-time source of labor supply, a procedure in which "we could be up against the question as to whether we could move the American citizen of Japanese race," was unreliable: "The bad ones, the ones that are foreign agents, that are sympathetic with Japan, will not volunteer, will they. . . . suppose he does not move?" McCloy was clearly in favor of the licensing concept being advocated by Bendetsen:

> You see, then we cover ourselves with the legal situation . . . be-cause in spite of the Constitution you can eliminate from any military reservation, or any place that is declared to be in substance a military reservation, anyone—any American citizen, and we could exclude everyone and then by a system of permits and licenses permitting those to come back into that area who were necessary to enable that area to function as a living community. Everyone but the Japs— [6]

For one who would bear the historical burden of having "pushed the button," DeWitt was surprisingly unenthusiastic. The General saw the idea of excluding "everyone" from "any place" designated to be a military reservation as a big headache administratively, especially in areas of dense population, for initially it would mean uprooting Italian and German nationals as well to maintain a semblance of legality. "You take, for example, the Embarcadero," he pointed out to McCloy, "it would be quite a job."

"But I think you might cut corners," McCloy had hastened to assure DeWitt, and he proceeded to explain how it might be done. The advantage of the permit system, as McCloy pointed out, was that "you can do that [expel the Nisei] on a military reservation without suspending writs of habeas corpus and without getting into very important legal complications . . ."

The General agreed to study the matter further, but he also suggested waiting for California authorities to firm up their plans, which he thought would require another ten days ("in view of the energetic steps that are now being taken"). McCloy was probably aware that the General, despite his moments of vacillation, could be counted on to come around to the War Department point of view in the end, as he often did. And indeed, once the Executive Order empowering the Commanding General "to handle the Japs" had been issued, DeWitt rose to the occasion and more than matched the enthusiasm of his civilian superiors. So much so that the West Coast Commander would end up being accused of having "far exceeded the President's intentions." [7]

As for the aborted Olson plan for a webwork of state-oriented resettlement projects, McCloy had been right about possible Nisei resistance. When the California Governor proposed to hastily assembled Nisei representatives that all males over eighteen years of age—exclusive of their families—evacuate themselves to segregated work camps 150 miles inland as a counter-fifth-column move and "as a sacrifice for your country," most of the delegates present summarily rejected the scheme, galled at the thought of being willy-nilly relegated to "slave labor camps" in repudiation of their right to equal protection under the law.

As it turned out, the concept of bringing "Japs" back on work leaves into the evacuated areas, or "combat zones," following the clearing of the coastal strip became a heated political issue, with Attorney General Earl Warren strongly opposed to it. It was then, on July 7, that Stimson had cued the President about "that patriot in California, Governor Olson . . . hatching up a new project" and had warned the Chief Executive of the "danger of overcrowding and epidemics" in keeping "these Japanese huddled up" for the purpose of saving California crops.

As had been anticipated, a wire from the Governor requesting the use of internee labor reached the White House almost immediately. Failing this, requested the Governor, could the importation of Mexican laborers be expedited? The President passed on the wire to the Department of Agriculture for a reply,[8] choosing not to get involved in what was fast turning into a political "hot potato" in California.

Thus, as a war emergency measure, the importation of laborers from Mexico was hurriedly instituted as tons of California produce began to rot in the fields. And though a program of work leaves within the state of Oregon had gotten slowly under way at the Portland Assembly Center in mid-May, 1942, it was much later that Nisei internees in California-based camps were allowed to accept agricultural employment, and then only if contracted for in other states.

II

Faced with the same numbing specter of crop spoilage and financial ruin were sugar beet farmers in the Rocky Mountain area at a time when the harvesting of beets was considered the hardest and lowest paid of farm work. Governors and Senators, who had fulminated with rage at the very idea of their respective states being made dumping grounds of California's "unwanted Japs," now fought frantically to get evacuees released to their communities—with the assurance, of course, that there be no postwar residue. Emotion-riddled communiqués ended up on the desk of the President and his White House aides:

WE HAVE EXHAUSTED EVERY MEANS AVAILABLE TO US TO GET SUGAR BEET ·FIELD LABOR . . . FINANCIAL RUIN FACE THE BEET GROWERS IN OUR AREA. WE REQUEST YOU STATE OUR CASE TO THE PRESIDENT IN EFFORT TO HAVE COMPANY OF US SOLDIERS DESIGNATED TO MONTANA BEET AREAS FOR GUARD AND PATROL DUTY FOR JAPANESE EVACUEES ALSO ASSURANCE THESE PEOPLE WILL BE MOVED FROM MONTANA AT END OF WAR IN ACCORDANCE WITH GOVERNOR'S RE-QUEST. . . . QUICK ACTION NECESSARY IF CROP IS TO BE SAVED.[9]

"The loss of this sugar beet crop will rest completely and solely upon the shoulders of the War Relocation Authority for their crass negligence in cutting red tape," cried growers as they hammered away at their Senators to get speedy action through White House intervention. Senator James Murray of Montana complained bitterly to the President's secretary, M. H. McIntyre:

Dear Mac: I have been trying to get a war relocation center established in Montana but nothing has been done. If Senator Wheeler had asked for it, probably he would have gotten it; but these agencies around here seem to pay no attention to my requests. . . . We have got all these Jap evacuees, but the Employment Service under McNutt has failed to get them out on the farms.[10]

Needs now outweighed prejudices, forcing open for the internees the sought-for wedge for an escape, a much earlier one than the Army had intended. After regulations had been instituted making it mandatory for farmers to pay prevailing wages, and after local and state officials agreed to assume full responsibility for maintaining law and order, work furloughs began to be urged on the Nisei. In the initial stage of the seasonal leave program, launched on July 20, 1942, applicants had to be citizens who had never lived or studied in Japan; the Kibei were categorically disqualified. But Nisei, by the thousands, answered the call for volunteers—women included—many of them college youths and professionals desperate to flee the claustrophobic camp environment.

Though freed of barbed wire and armed-guard surveillance, the Nisei remained in "constructive" custody of the military, liable to a maximum penalty of $5,000 fine or imprisonment for one year, or both, for violating furlough regulations based on provisions of Public Law 503; also "Civilian Restrictive Orders" were imposed over counties in which they worked.[11] Despite the risks involved and parental objections which had to be overcome, nearly 10,000 volunteers were out in the beet fields by mid-October, 1942.

At season's end, the Nisei were credited with having saved the sugar beet crops of Utah, Idaho, Montana, and Wyoming. And from once bigoted state functionaries, there were exuberant words of praise:

We can just as well face the facts. If it had not been for Japanese labor, much of the beet crop of Utah and Idaho would have been plowed up . . . These are industrious people who want work . . . Suggestions that relocation evacuees be put into concentration camps and paid $30 a month are ridiculous. We are fighting this war to end slavery wherever it exists." [12]

III

In the mass flight of farm workers to the cities, the farm crises had also spread to areas of intense southland heat. With the rural labor market dried up to a near crisp in south-central regions of Arizona, distressingly few workers could be rounded up to take on the meager-paying task of harvesting the state's long staple cotton crop.

Emergency plans for speeding troops to the Arizona cotton fields had been drawn up by War Department officials when it had suddenly dawned on them that by a simple expedient, captive labor in both the Poston and Gila relocation camps could be put to effective use. In a memorandum of March 1, 1943, Acting Secretary of War Robert P. Patterson informed the President: "In connection with the harvesting of the long staple cotton crop in Arizona, the Chairman of the War Manpower Commission has stated it would be very helpful if, by an alteration of the boundaries of the restricted area, we could make available Japanese labor. I have found it practicable to do this." [13]

The Nisei initially reacted with cynicism and indignation to this opportunistic redrawing of the boundaries. Intense intracamp controversy ensued as to whether they should cooperate, especially when it was learned that a detachment of MPs was being used to prevent escapes. But a considerable number eventually gave in to governmental appeals to their patriotism—with Japanese Americans, once again, helping to avert an agricultural disaster of national consequence. Daily, volunteers were trucked to the cotton fields to put in long exhausting hours on the burning desert floor.

Stinging repudiation, not praise, however, crowned the Nisei's efforts in behalf of Arizona farmers. With Poston and Gila then representing the third- and fourth-largest "cities" in Arizona, the state legislature acted swiftly against the possibility of potential spies and saboteurs being heedlessly let loose on rural communities. Local vested interests—farm lobbies, in particular—saw to it that they would never be placed in a position of competition with those whose proven capabilities in the agricultural area were such as to present a serious threat. Commercial transactions with persons of Japanese ancestry were, by law, virtually banned.

Until the legislation was declared unconstitutional by the State Supreme Court on December 13, 1943, longtime Japanese American residents of Arizona (around 600) then living outside the restricted military area were faced with virtual extinction, economically and otherwise. Under the maliciously devised anti-evacuee law, a hotel room, a meal, or even a loaf of bread could not be purchased without first publishing a public notice of such intent at least three times and filing a copy of such notice with the Secretary of State. In one case which came to public attention, the Standard Oil Company was fined $1,000 for selling $9.25 worth of gas to a Nisei.

Much of this carefully nurtured hostility spilled over into the neighboring state of Nevada, where a similar racist overreaction was noted, many shopkeepers refusing to "trade with the enemy." Project Director Merritt of the Manzanar Relocation Center alerted the head of the West Coast WRA office, Robert B. Cozzens:

> The weakest spot in our national relocation operations is, I believe, Reno, Nevada. This city is the point from which all departure from Manzanar is made to the East . . .
>
> During the last week we have had women with little children who have stayed in the railroad station at Reno for as long as 3 days and 2 nights without being able to get a bed or any food other than what could be bought from the lunch counter in the station.[14]

Receptivity varied greatly in other parts of the country. As a result of furlough workers' finding the Mormons of Utah to be a "gentler breed of Americans," Salt Lake City was to become one of the more favored cities to which evacuees gravitated. Yet, in the same state of Utah, there were counties which turned out to be hotbeds of vigilante-style intolerance, where "Let's go beat up some Japs" appeared to be a popular pastime with small-town hoodlums. An irate group of volunteers returned en masse to Manzanar with harrowing tales of near lynchings, of being bilked by unscrupulous employers, and other indignities endured.

A survey taken in the late fall of 1942 among Manzanar returnees showed only 2 to 3 percent expressing enthusiasm for outside relocation. Ten percent of furlough workers queried swore that they wouldn't go out again under any circumstance; a substantial majority had found the general public "not yet ready to accept an Oriental as a U.S. citizen."

> They guarded us like cattle on the trains; . . . They refused us admittance to the movies; we couldn't get a meal at the cafes. They had a sign: 'No Japs.' We had to spend a night in jail, there was no other place to go; the farmer tried to gyp us, broke our contract. The W.R.A. man, instead of representing us, stuck up for the farmer.[15]

Returnees were unanimous in their assessment that outside relocation was risky, perilous, and hardly to be recommended for evacuees lacking funds or the ability to speak English fluently—an admonition which drove fear into the Issei, the elderly and families with multiple dependents, the bulk of whom were beginning to feel more and more grateful for the emotional and physical security of their fenced-in island of safety. With wartime passions at a fever pitch and with no one knowing how long the war would last, few but the young with vigor and daring felt up to reestablishing themselves in unknown and untested parts of America.

Thus the turnabout policy of "indefinite leaves," beginning in the fall of 1942, which extended relocation privileges to anyone who could pass a stringent security clearance was, of necessity, accompanied by a WRA promotional campaign not only to mitigate evacuee fears but also to reeducate a paranoiac public to differentiate between the bitterly despised foes across the Pacific and fellow U. S. citizens.[16] Much of it was concentrated on tracking down prominent citizens in key relocation communities known to be staunch defenders of the Nisei's right to full acceptance as Americans. A host of church groups and sympathetic service organizations also became dedicated allies in the WRA's nationwide public relations and rehabilitation efforts.

With a grant of $25, a one-way ticket, and an admonition to "make yourself inconspicuous," the evacuee was proffered freedom if assured employment in some hopefully nonhostile community, and if the excruciatingly slow security clearance came through in time. The Japanese American Joint Board, made up of representatives from the WRA, the Provost Marshal General's office, and Army and Navy intelligence, had been established on January 20, 1943, to pass on each applicant's eligibility for departure, which was dependent on a staggering number of considerations.[17] Evacuees suspected of holding strong pro-Japanese sentiments were denied leave clearance. (See Appendix 11.)

Leaves were conditional and revocable, for the military had strongly opposed the WRA decision of October 1 to permit leaves on a more permanent basis. On October 5, 1942, DeWitt had written to McCloy:

> I am told by Colonel Bendetsen that you are sympathetic toward the development of a plan to determine whether an opportunity is now within reach for learning more about the Japanese as a people than is known at the present time. Further, it would be unfortunate in the highest degree if because of the turn of future events it became necessary only to gather them up again, once released.
>
> I cannot emphasize too strongly my feeling that the War Department must actively secure the agreement of War Relocation Authority in the retention of evacuees until the military aspects of these important questions can be answered through thorough study.[18]

Director Dillon Myer considered the continued pressure and interference from the Western Defense Command as "arbitrary" and "categorical"[19] and the repressive nature of the leave clearance procedure as the greatest deterrent to resettlement. Jobs and educational opportunities were repeatedly lost because of delays involved in the validation of an applicant's loyalty, and evacuees came to doubt the sincerity of the WRA's relocation efforts.

Undaunted, the WRA intensified its dispersal efforts by setting up a total of nine relocation field offices in principal Eastern and Midwestern cities to help develop job opportunities and to provide a prop for evacuees attempting to reestablish themselves. Again they relied heavily on the goodwill and cooperation of church and service groups, who contributed significantly to the relocation program by setting up hostel facilities which provided temporary refuge at low prices.

In larger Midwestern cities, such as Chicago, Detroit, Cleveland, St. Louis, Cincinnati, Milwaukee, and others where employment was plentiful, relocatees found the climate of acceptance surprisingly favorable. Recommended even then was the procedure of having a son or daughter venture forth first to check out community attitudes and pave the way in the crucial area of housing. For resettling whole families, acceptance was found to be better in urban rather than in rural communities, leaving the WRA faced with the unnerving problem of what to do with its large residue of horticulturists and fisherfolk, the disproportionate number of orchardists and farm specialists who had once tilled vast acreages, who regarded the idea of punching time clocks or going back to the category of stoop labor as distasteful. Included in this collection of "unrelocatables" were many single persons —the crop followers—usually old and in unsound health, dependency cases due to internment of the breadwinner, widows with small children unable to work.

So even when the policy of resettlement began to be aggressively encouraged in 1943 to cut camp expenditures while helping to solve the nation's employment problems, these remained a part of the majority population whose lives and family structure had been so cataclysmically disarranged that no other option was opened to them but to remain trapped.

(6)
"Dear Mr. President"

We were told these relocation camps were not for internment but for refuge. Has the W.R.A. really power to intern American citizens? Is it reasonable for Japanese-Americans to be interned and Germans and Italians, not? Is not the very essence of our democracy that we are made up of all races and colors?

We are all tied together by an *idea, democracy.* That is what all our boys are fighting and suffering for. If we cannot all stand before the law in equal liberty and freedom—to live our lives, regardless of race, creed or color—then *What Price Democracy?*

—MARION R. WEDDELL to President Roosevelt, December 23, 1943

I

"As you know, quite a little mail is being received by the President from liberal groups and kindhearted people protesting the evacuation," wrote WRA Director Milton Eisenhower to the President's secretary on May 15, 1942. "Much of it questions the military necessity of the program. . . . Since this Authority cannot appropriately speak on military questions, we have been forwarding it to the Assistant Secretary of War, John McCloy. May I suggest that such mail be sent directly to Mr. McCloy?" [1]

Against the din of nativist agitators exploiting racist fears, the democratic privilege of petitioning to the President was being used by fair-minded and concerned Americans for all it was worth, but to no avail for a luckless minority whose rights the President had decided should come "after victory, not before." [2]

"Could the President give, at least, a word of hope and encouragement, a spiritual uplift to those asked in so drastic a manner to prove their loyalty?" was another request occasionally received by the White House—more often than not from educators and classroom instructors familiar with the exemplary citizenship and often superior scholastic standing of the Nisei. From Bainbridge Island near Seattle came the plea of a high school teacher:

> Do you think the President . . . could find it suitable and wise, at a press conference or even in a fireside talk, to say a word of praise for the American citizens of Japanese descent, loyal and of good record who, because of the common peril and exigency, have endured and are enduring no little hardship? . . .
>
> I am sure that these people, in whom gratitude is a leading characteristic, will have "a happy thrill" if the President can find it in his great heart to give them a cheer.[3]

At a time when White House mail and public opinion polls reflected vigorous public support of executive policies,[4] the President left discreetly unsaid anything which might call attention to—or arouse unnecessary sympathy for—the exiled minority; especially when a near-total apathy on the part of congressional lawmakers indicated much more than tacit approval among a wide segment of the American public.

Yet, intermingled with reams of patriotic approbation which reached the President's attention, there was occasionally evidenced the heroism of the individual citizen holding steadfast to principle, as the following wire to the President gives mute testimony:

> NEXT THURSDAY NOON, JUNE 10TH, IMPORTANT LOCAL ORGANIZATION WILL VOTE ON RESOLUTION MEMORIALIZING CONGRESS TO IMMEDIATELY DEPORT ALL JAPANESE REGARDLESS OF WHETHER OR NOT THEY ARE AMERICAN CITIZENS. THIS HIGHLY UN-AMERICAN MOVE IS AGGRESSIVELY SUPPORTED BY THOSE AFFILIATED WITH AMERICAN LEGION, ASSOCIATED FARMERS, GRANGE AND OTHER BLOCS. LAST WEEK I SUCCEEDED IN DELAYING VOTE BUT I GREATLY NEED HELP AT NEXT THURSDAY'S MEETING. CAN YOU OR SOMEONE CLOSE TO YOU SEND ME A STRONG FAST WIRE COLLECT POINTING OUT INJUSTICE OF SUCH ACTION . . . YOUR HELP WILL BE MOST TIMELY AND GREATLY APPRECIATED, I ASSURE YOU.[5]

II

Outstanding among citizens determined to demonstrate that not all Americans agreed with the repressive policies being practiced in their name were individuals of uncommon moral vigor belonging to the Society of Friends. For the abiding love of humanity which these sterling Americans exemplified at an impressionable moment in their lives, the "Friends" (or Quakers, as they are more popularly known) are warmly remembered to this day by all Japanese Americans. Wherever there was a camp, the Quakers made their presence felt, many driving the long, hot miles to even the most out-of-sight concentration camps to bring gifts, camp needs, and the precious reassurance that there were white Americans who cared. From beginning to end the Quakers' busy concern in helping to alleviate the plight of the evacuees, always in ways that were direct and personal, did more to keep bitterness from making too deep an inroad than their smallness as a group might indicate.

It is worth noting that most of the few white Americans who took a stand against the policy of racial internment were pacifists, like the Quakers, and opposed America's participation in the war. Other groups committed to pacifism, such as the Mennonites, the Brethren, and the Fellowship of Reconciliation, joined in taking a collective stand against the evacuation in the manner of the Quakers. More than a few individuals from among these denominations ended up working in the camps as conscientious objectors.

Though a soft-spoken and gentle-mannered lot, the splendid Quakers did not mince words in their open criticism of the Army's raw abuse of power, a candor little appreciated by the military and one which hampered the group's early attempts to rescue and reestablish college and university students being held in assembly centers under Army jurisdiction. What particularly outraged Colonel Bendetsen was the forthright accusation of the Quakers that *the motives behind the wholesale evacuation were political rather than military and that the Army did what other groups had tried to effect for years.*[6]

In the initial stages of the uprooting, the patience of Army authorities was thus sorely tried by the presence of these busy, ubiquitous Quakers, who were quick to criticize, as in their condemnation of the stables and shacks as out-and-out firetraps; so it was not surprising that their attempts to gain admittance to these hurriedly thrown-up guarded enclaves which could hardly stand up to unfriendly scrutiny were actively discouraged. Keenly resented by authorities was a well-attended mass meeting which the Quakers quietly succeeded in arranging with potential college students at the Santa Anita Assembly Center, with the Army subsequently ruling that no such meetings or interviews with students would be allowed except in the presence of an Internal Security officer.[7] A student rescue group hurriedly activated on March 21, 1942, by leading West Coast educators with active support from the Quakers—the Student Relocation Council—was forbidden, moreover, from issuing press releases, except through the Wartime Civil Control Administration (WCCA), headed up by Colonel Bendetsen.[8]

When the government failed to respond to a humanitarian suggestion by Dr. Robert Gordon Sproul, President of the University of California (Berkeley), that federal scholarships be made available to deserving students whose higher education had been curtailed, it became apparent that a rescue group on a nationwide scale would have to be speedily organized to coordinate the transfer of thousands of

Nisei students to inland institutions. Even Governor Olson's appeal to the President for federal aid to students ("because the income of their families will be greatly reduced") had resulted in nothing more than presidential assurance that the "problem has been receiving serious consideration" and that cooperation would be forthcoming for whatever nongovernmental handling of the student transfer might be devised by "Mr. Eisenhower who is Administrator of the Japanese Relocation Authority." [9] Sidestepped was the question of federal subsidy. [10]

Under the initiative and leadership of Clarence E. Pickett, an outstanding Quaker leader to whom Milton Eisenhower had turned for help, a privately organized committee, the National Japanese American Student Relocation Council, was subsequently activated at a May 29, 1942, Chicago conference.

Pickett appointed Robert W. O'Brien, Assistant Dean of Arts and Sciences at the University of Washington, to head up this joint, wholly voluntary effort of eminent West and East Coast educators and churchmen whose use of their personal influence was to play an important part in prying open often reluctant academic doors to the deserving Nisei. [11] A student relocation scholarship fund was immediately established, with the money coming from church boards, service groups, foundations, and individual philanthropists across the nation. Numerous church groups also made it possible for the Nisei to attend colleges of their denomination, sometimes with the help of generous scholarships.

Considering the importance most relocation center residents attached to the cause of further education for their deserving youths, perhaps no single project did as much to restore the badly shattered faith of evacuees in their fellow white citizens than this rallying together of what they considered the decent segment of American society.

"It is my belief that the efforts we expend now will be repayed [sic] a thousandfold in the attitude of citizens of Japanese ancestry in years to come," wrote Robert Gordon Sproul to fellow administrators in a plea for a pulling together in a worthwhile cause. But not all university officials were as convinced that the Nisei were worth salvaging. A Princeton spokesman wanted nothing to do with "American-born Japanese students even though they may be in good standing and not under suspicion," at least, not at first; and more than a few institutions demanded FBI and G-2 clearance as part of the entrance requirements. [12] Regional and community hostility also had to be overcome: The furor sparked by the bitterness of anti-Japanese feelings was sometimes statewide. In both the Iowa and Arizona state legislatures, resolutions which would bar the Nisei's admittance to state-subsidized schools were introduced.

The transfer of students was frequently hampered more by the severity of Army and Navy restrictions than by that of local and institutional ones, with a stern clearance procedure being required of students attempting to enter schools located in the Eastern Defense Command. Though willing to take on the Nisei, numerous top institutions were, themselves, unable to obtain the needed clearance from the military because of classified war work being carried on, which then included more than 180 of the best schools. Clearance was frequently denied because of an institution's proximity to defense plants, railroad tracks, and other installations and areas considered vital to the national security, thus closed to Japanese Americans. Valuable scholarships and once-in-a-lifetime learning opportunities were jeopardized by delays over these and other absurd technicalities, many of them rooted in racial distrust.

As it turned out, not a cent of federal subsidy went toward the resettlement of students (except for train fare from camp to college campus), support which could have prevented many who fell short of being top scholars from having career aspirations curtailed. Student relocation assistance was generally limited to individuals in the top 10 percent of their high school graduating class.

Yet, the need to rekindle hope and confidence in youths who had lost all incentive proved to be more of a problem for the Student Relocation Council than turning down applicants. Successfully reenrolled students were oftentimes sent back into the camps on speaking missions to embolden others to follow in their footsteps. The "lose fight" attitude among students was largely due to the pervasive negativism of parents fearful for their children's safety; and with circumstances overwhelming the ability of families to meet even basic needs, there were many among them who staunchly maintained that not a cent of the fast-dwindling family savings should go toward a fancy education which would "get them nowhere anyway"—that the prime duty of the younger generation was to see that the family was first reestablished.

Still, it was not unusual to find parents, remarkably unswerving in their conviction that only through education and worthy accomplishments could the widened gap of prejudice and misunderstanding be narrowed, who encouraged their children to let nothing stand in the way of achieving a fine education, however much the strain and sacrifice to the family. According to one student:

My father is old, 78 years old, and I know he misses me. But as I left he strengthened me with these words: "I am old, someday you will hear that I am dying, perhaps while you are still in school. Forget about me. Make my dying days happy in the knowledge that you are studying and preparing yourself for service. My life is in the past, yours is in the future. Go and be of service to men.[13]

III

Some 2,500 Nisei students were in West Coast colleges and universities at the time of the evacuation. One of them was Harvey Itano (the same Harvey A. Itano, M.D., Ph.D., who recently received the Reverend Martin Luther King, Jr., Medical Achievement Award "for Outstanding Contributions in Research of Sickle Cell Anemia"), then a "straight A" premed student at the University of California. Itano had won top scholastic honors in his graduating class of 4,800 students but was prohibited from attending the commencement exercises and summarily placed in camp. At the commencement ceremonies, Dr. Robert Gordon Sproul regretfully announced: "The winner of the University Medal is not here today because his country has called him elsewhere."

Itano's plight and the rank injustice which the incident symbolized may well have triggered the following memorandum in the form of a ready-to-be-delivered presidential address. It had been penned by Dr. Monroe E. Deutsch, a colleague of Dr. Sproul—and an equally concerned cofighter in the interest of the Nisei—and speeded to a White House contact. The "ghosted" speech, representing one concerned citizen's attempt to place a few compassionate words in the mouth of the President, landed on the Chief Executive's desk with an appended memorandum written by a White House aide, parts of which read:

MEMORANDUM FOR THE PRESIDENT RE: Suggestion that you touch in a speech on the Japanese problem in this country

A friend of mine . . . has written me on behalf of President Sproul and Provost Deutsch of the University. They are gravely concerned over what is happening to the Japanese, particularly the students . . . My friend has asked me to bring the attached memo to your attention in hope that you might make use of some of the ideas in a radio talk at some time. It was written by Dr. Deutsch, Vice-President and Provost.[14]

May 27, 1942   Lauchlin Currie

Dr. Deutsch's thoughtfully prepared presidential radio talk read in part:

There are many things we must do to win the war; but in doing so, we must not abandon our American ideals. We must remember that the principle on which our nation rests forbids discrimination because of race, religion or ancestry. We are Americans all, united in a common cause, whatever our descent, our place of birth, our creed, our color. That is Americanism.

In this country are men and women from all parts of the world, yes, from Oriental lands too, from China, from India, from the Philippines—and from Japan. And their children are Americans—with as much right to the name American as any one of us.

I deeply regret the necessity which prompted the removal of the Japanese nationals and their children from the Pacific Coast area; it seemed a wise precaution, and so the Army asked that it be done. But remember that not a single one of those evacuated had been proved guilty of any crime—of any subversive act or sabotage. . . . the huge population transferred from the coastal strip was moved to free the rest of the people of that area from any possible anxiety. Indeed, the Japanese constitute a group in which crime has been almost non-existent and juvenile delinquency is practically unknown. . . . The Japanese and Japanese Americans have cooperated loyally in this move, which entailed hardship, much financial loss to them, and a removal from their homes and a severance of ties . . .

Authorities had undoubtedly assured Dr. Deutsch that the "relocation" to interior regions following the assembly center roundup phase was to be a simple dispersal into American communities.

Their residence in reception centers is intended to be but temporary, pending their migration to other parts of the country. And it is of this migration that I desire to speak tonight.

Remember that there should be absolutely no stigma upon them; on the contrary their cooperation deserves our approval and calls for our applause. . . . I call upon the people of the rest of the country to be ready to receive them with friendship and goodwill, to give them a chance to work among them and resume their relations with the life of our country. They are eager to be self-sustaining, and by far the greater part of them covet an opportunity to help win the war. . . .

This we have a right to demand of all Americans—that they treat men as men, not as descendants of one stock or another. "All men are created equal," we are proud to say . . . If we really believe these words—yes, for others as well as for ourselves—we will give our fellow Americans of Japanese ancestry a chance to come into our communities, to secure work and thus to reestablish their uprooted lives. This is a patriotic duty. . . .[15]

Had the revered and charismatic Chief of State—then at the pinnacle of prestige and power—chosen to express such humane sentiments as were spelled out by Provost Deutsch in the crucial days and months to follow, there is little doubt, given Roosevelt's genius for persuasive oratory, that public opinion could have been more positively led, with the added probability that the "migration" need not have ended up as so many wasted years of internment, wasted military might, wasted tax dollars expended on the likes of concentration camps.[16]

But for a nation then locked in mortal combat with an enemy whose "violence, fury, skill and might . . . exceeded anything we had been led to expect" (in the words of Winston Churchill), anything contributing to public confusion or controversy was obviously to be avoided, however drastic the momentary moral slippage. Editorial opinion in densely populated urban areas west of the Rockies reflected rousing approbation of the strong measures taken for the nation's safety. It was hardly the time for the President to attempt to de-brainwash a jittery public firmly sold on the idea that "a Jap's a Jap," inherently treacherous, and not to be trusted.

Of necessity, therefore, the President's war-duration policy, in regard to a minority whose rights for the sake of unity and final victory could very well wait, was silence.

(7)
Storm Warnings

I

Pacifist, outspoken Socialist crusader, and five times unsuccessful presidential candidate, Norman Thomas was the only personage of national stature to vehemently oppose the indiscriminate eradication of coastal Japanese American communities as "another proof of racial arrogance," characterizing the procedure as "a good deal like burning down Chicago to get rid of gangsters."[1] When the national office of the American Civil Liberties Union (which he had cofounded) timidly took the myopic position that the sweeping evacuation edict—given legitimacy by Order 9066—fell quite within the proper limits of the President's war powers, Thomas furiously denounced the Union's weak-kneed "dereliction of duty," adding: "What is perhaps as ominous as the evacuation of the Japanese is the general acceptance of this procedure by those who are proud to call themselves liberals."

The intensity of the intraorganizational dispute which ensued over this and other evacuation issues totally immobilized the usually intrepid champion of the rights of unpopular groups and minorities even as the wholesale roundup began. So protracted was the controversy that a permanent rift developed between the Northern California affiliate and the parent body (New York), then under the directorship of the eminent dean of civil libertarians, Roger Baldwin.

"The national office objected to our challenging the constitutionality of the evacuation," declares the longtime Executive Director of the San Francisco office, Ernest Besig, now retired. "All they wanted was that we should concern ourselves with the manner in which the evacuation was carried out. They felt that hearing boards should be established to determine which persons should be removed and which should be allowed to remain."[2] After a polling of the entire Northern

California membership by mail, Director Besig was to learn that even within his own ranks, the question of whether the ACLU should challenge evacuation orders had resulted in near half of those responding expressing opposition to the move.

Notwithstanding the lame support from the general membership of the group most sympathetic to Japanese Americans, few men worked as tirelessly as a wartime fighter for evacuee rights at a time when it was unpopular to be one than its Director, Ernest Besig, whose capsule comment after forty years of dedicated work with the San Francisco unit is that "power does corrupt whoever is in authority."

In the Rooseveltian era of avowed concern for the underdog, liberals and civil libertarians had been no exception. The stripping of a minority of their constitutional rights, indeed the entire evacuation-internment folly, was "engineered by liberals," asserts Professor William Petersen of Ohio State University. "Among the civilians one can hardly name a person, from the President down to local officials, who was not one." [3]

Historical orthodoxy also persists in treating the episode as an unfortunate regional phenomenon, as indeed the Administration hoped it would be interpreted,[4] and in placing the lion's share of the blame on the "West Coast," as though the state of California and others along the Pacific basin were to blame for the misdeeds of an administration in power; as though "public opinion" had literally forced the President into making the unfortunate decision. The reactionary tumult being orchestrated by West Coast special interest groups and politicians undoubtedly made the decision easier to make. But had it not been for the stunning indifference of the citizenry everywhere—the racist nature of society in general—the mass subjugation of a minority could not have been made possible.

As the roundup phase proceeded with not a murmur of protest from the hallowed halls of Congress, not a single student demonstration on any of the campuses of the nation's higher institutions of learning, Norman Thomas wrote despairingly in the *Christian Century* of July 29, 1942:

> In an experience of nearly three decades I have never found it harder to arouse the American public on any important issue than on this. Men and women who know nothing of the facts (except possibly the rose-colored version which appears in the public press) hotly deny that there are concentration camps. Apparently that is a term to be used only if the guards speak German and carry a whip as well as a rifle.[5]

Though decision makers within the military were far from fastidious in resorting to euphemisms in their conversations and official correspondence, the utterance of the term "concentration camp" was strenuously objected to by the WRA custodial staff within the barbed-wire-ringed compounds. So effectively brainwashed were the custodians, and their captives, that even today it is downright awkward for former residents of relocation centers, white or yellow, to refer to them as concentration camps.

Yet, by beclouding the extent of America's betrayal, the semantic obscuration had helped immeasurably to ease the hurt for evacuees who preferred not to face up to the truth of what their own country had done to them; and among fair-minded Americans, recognition of the basic moral issues involved dawned too late to do much good, owing to such propagandistic blur-outs on a national scale. The near absence of protest had enabled the Army to proceed swiftly, smoothly, and without a hitch.

Readers familiar with Carey McWilliams' eminently fair and compassionate treatment of the evacuee plight in *Prejudice: Symbol of Racial Intolerance* (Little, Brown, 1944) would be hard-pressed to believe that it was the same McWilliams who, as a high-ranking California governmental official, was then finding the whole "accomplishment" so breath-takingly impressive. "This may not be as exciting as bombing Japanese warships in the Coral Sea, but it must be credited as a major feat for the Army," McWilliams had rhapsodized in an on-the-spot report of the evacuation in *Harper's* magazine of September 1942.

Visiting the Pomona Assembly Center, McWilliams had been astonished at the sight of evacuees who in no way appeared to be Japanese but who had fallen within the evacuation order because of "Japanese blood, no matter how small the quantum" —also Koreans, Chinese, Mexicans, and Negroes swept into the camps by virtue of their being married to Japanese. On a tour of the posh playground of sportsmen, the Santa Anita race course converted into a detention camp for 18,000, McWilliams described it as being completely encircled by barbed wire, guarded by soldiers, with stalag-style searchlights playing over the barrack community at night. But the State Commissioner of Immigration and Housing protested, as others were then doing, that it would hardly be accurate to allude to Santa Anita as a "concentration camp." [6]

McWilliams' thinking was to undergo a profound change as he closely followed the progress of the internment program for the purpose of gathering research material for his book *Prejudice* (commissioned by the American Council of the Institute of Pacific Relations), the first in-depth study of why and how the evacuation hysteria developed and a work published at the height of the agitation to prevent the evacuees' return. The author is thoroughly persuaded, by then, that the camps are a blunder of the first magnitude and an insult to Amer-

ican concepts of democracy, and tries valiantly to engender sympathy
for the evacuees.

Before America's extraordinary wartime experiment was over,
there were to be many embarrassed "illiberal liberals" (a term coined
by Norman Thomas) writhing in tortured self-recrimination, realizing
all too late the folly of their war-born exuberance. Far and away the
most outspokenly remorseful among the conscience-stricken was the
nation's leading liberal (later Nuremberg Judge), Francis Biddle,
who, even as the highest court in the land went on to place its stamp
of approval on the federal action, lamented: "We should never have
moved the Japanese from their homes and their work. It was un-American, unconstitutional and un-Christian." [7]

Another key figure to regret his early racist excesses was Biddle's
aide, Tom Clark, who, as Coordinator of Alien Enemy Control, had
been dispatched to the coast to convince California officials that a full-
scale evacuation was unjustified; but the future Attorney General of
the United States quickly came under the spell of Earl Warren and
others who convinced him that it was impossible to determine who
could be trusted. "The choice of Clark under the circumstances was
not a fortunate one," Biddle has written in his postwar memoirs.

On his retirement in 1966 as an Associate Justice of the U. S.
Supreme Court, Tom Clark confessed publicly:

> I have made a lot of mistakes in my life . . . One is my part in the
> evacuation of the Japanese from California in 1942 . . . I don't think
> that served any purpose at all . . . We picked them up and put them
> in concentration camps. That's the truth of the matter. And as I look
> back on it—although at the time I argued the case—I am amazed that
> the Supreme Court ever approved it." [8]

On April 1, 1942, then WRA Chief Milton Eisenhower wrote
to Agriculture Secretary Claude Wickard: "I feel most deeply that
when the war is over . . . we as Americans are going to regret the
avoidable injustices that may have been done," leaving little doubt
that he, too, might be counted among the penitent. As the first appointed administrator of the War Relocation Authority, Eisenhower
had helped in the establishment of the camps and in the formulation of
WRA policies following a West Coast conference on March 25 with
General DeWitt. On June 15, 1942, only three months after he had
embraced the collaborationist role in this startling deviation from democratic procedure, Interior Secretary Ickes wrote FDR: "I have it
from several sources that Eisenhauer [sic] is sick of the job." [9]

Under the Rooseveltian banner of "liberty, decency, justice,"
Eisenhower had taken on the unique assignment in the midst of the
"total war" mobilization frenzy and had permitted WRA determination to be swayed by popular prejudice: ". . . public attitudes have

exerted a strong influence in shaping the program and charting its direction. In a democracy this is unquestionably sound and proper," the resigning WRA Director had maintained in his parting report to President Roosevelt.[10]

As the WRA National Director at a time when the "blind yearning for vengeance"—William Manchester's description of the national mood (*The Glory and the Dream*)—was at its peak, Eisenhower had concluded that the centers would have to be guarded camps, and that both the Issei and Nisei would have to be maintained in close confinement for their own safety. Such was the course of action Eisenhower had early prescribed for the evacuated people as a result of a highly acrimonious conference held in Salt Lake City on April 7, 1942, in which governors and official representatives of ten Western states vehemently expressed their opposition to any manner of evacuee resettlement, except under armed guard.

Despite early Army statements which had placed the evacuee wage scale in the $70- to $80-a-month bracket,[11] internment policy planners (who included Eisenhower, DeWitt, and McCloy) had buckled under vigorous public protest which insisted that no internee be paid more than the prevailing $21-a-month GI pay, bringing to pass a situation tantamount to creating a class of serfs in a free society since evacuees were accorded none of the fringe benefits enjoyed by servicemen. On resigning from his WRA position to join the Office of War Information in mid-June, 1942, Eisenhower sought to diplomatically urge the President to an increased measure of clemency by recommending, in his parting report, that he "issue a strong public statement in behalf of the loyal American citizens who are now bewildered and wonder what is in store for them"; also that the President "at the appropriate time . . . call for a more liberal wage policy . . ."

> If public opinion had permitted, it might have been preferable in many ways to pay WPA wages to members of the Work Corps and to provide their families with subsistence in addition. This would have been more in keeping with the spirit of the Geneva Convention. I sincerely hope that changing public attitudes will later on permit a change in this severe wage policy.[12]

Geneva Convention regulations stipulated that "work done for the State shall be paid for in accordance with the rates in force for soldiers of the national army doing the same work." But throughout the internment period, the evacuee wage scale remained unaltered, providing less than sixty cents a day, or $12 to $16 a month, to the vast majority of the employed. The work week in the centers then comprised forty-eight hours (or five days with a half day on Saturday). Although GI wages climbed to $50 a month, the $19-a-month professional pay (given doctors, surgeons, dentists, administrative aides, architects, and others of "exceptional skills") remained constant throughout the war years.

Under an "incentive plan" which allowed for increased pay for increased output, Axis prisoners held in U. S. prisoner of war camps fared considerably better than citizen evacuees. POWs were paid eighty cents for a normal day's work. However, earnings of up to $1.20 a day were possible for internees who were able to increase their productivity.[13]

Had the President acted upon the Eisenhower recommendations at that precise psychological moment in the evacuee experience, the mere gesture of concern might have helped to curb the ever-heightening feeling of disaffection and betrayal and prevented passive forbearance from shifting to angry militancy. A surprise relief shipment to inmates (of tea, soy sauce, soy bean paste, etc.; see Appendix 3) from the Japanese Government, for example, resulted in enhancing the feeling of nationals in camps everywhere that, unlike the Nisei, the Issei had not been forgotten by their mother country. But an otherwise preoccupied President chose not to bother with such remedial measures as had been urged by the resigning WRA Director, and those of immediate consequence to the evacuees were to end up being shelved for the duration.

Though most evacuees could not help but feel that their well-meaning President was being kept in the dark as to what was happening to them, White House files were already bulging with memos, letters, reports, on a project so unprecedented that no one but the Chief Executive could decide on some of the more important issues affecting their treatment. "The President might have been more sensitive to the situation if the evacuees had protested vigorously, had demonstrated, gone on strike, fought their guards," writes James MacGregor Burns in *Roosevelt: The Soldier of Freedom*.

> But they did not, at this time. The authorities were impressed by their almost cheerful determination to make the best of their lot; their resourcefulness in knocking together tables and benches for their ill-equipped rooms, their quick reconstruction of a semblance of community life through dances, sports, handicrafts, schools. But as the hot months of summer 1942 passed, the mood in some camps changed. The WRA did not live up to its earlier promises and expectations about wages, clothing, garden plots, jobs, and ordinary comforts. Tension rose among the inmates and between them and their Caucasian superiors.[14]

Besides the inmates' lack of privacy and creature comforts and the ever-present fear of not knowing what was going to happen to them, the prejudiced attitudes of some of the less educated members of the custodial staff added to the heightening of tension. Since the reasons for the camps were not at all clear, even to those working in an administrative capacity, there was a pervasive tendency to look down on their charges as an untrustworthy, sinister, and morally inferior lot by the very fact that their incarceration had been deemed necessary. Social analyst Alexander H. Leighton, then conducting a behavioral study of the camp population in Poston, noted:

> In spite of the fact that the FBI was doing a thorough job of security control there were government employees who thought vegetable cellars dug to conserve food because of the heat were caches for Japanese paratroops, who saw kitchen cooks as admirals in disguise and believed athletic teams were Japanese soldiers drilling. During the major strike there were people willing to swear they had seen men, machine guns and knives where none existed.[15]

Most of the ten WRA centers located in six states had been built on public land belonging to the Interior Department. Harold L. Ickes, a member of the President's Cabinet, then heading up the Department of Interior, was perhaps the most outspoken among those who made frequent reports to the President. "I am unwilling to believe that a better job in general could not have been done than has been done," remonstrated the Interior Secretary as he sought to arouse the President. "Neither do I believe that we can't do better from here out."

> Information that has come to me from several sources is to the effect that the situation in at least some of the Japanese internment camps is bad and is becoming worse rapidly. Native-born Japanese who first accepted with philosophical understanding the decision of their Government to round up and take far inland all of the Japanese along the Pacific Coast, regardless of their degree of loyalty, have pretty generally been disappointed with the treatment that they have been accorded. Even the minimum plans that had been formulated and announced with respect to them have been disregarded in large measure, or, at least, have not been carried out. The result has been the gradual turning of thousands of well-meaning and loyal Japanese into angry prisoners. I do not think that we can disregard, as of no official concern, the unnecessary creating of a hostile group right in our own territory consisting of people who are engendering a bitterness and hostility that bodes no good for the future.[16]

The incisively forthright letter, characteristic of the blunt-spoken Interior Secretary, was passed on to Milton Eisenhower for comment. (That Eisenhower was no longer heading up the WRA had apparently slipped the President's mind.) Heedless of the error, Eisenhower dutifully sent back to the President a prepared reply to the Ickes letter as coming from the Chief Executive, noting in a separate letter to the President that "it may be that you intend sending the enclosed letter to Mr. Dillon S. Myer, the Director of the War Relocation Authority."

In the same personal letter directed to the President, Eisenhower seized the opportunity "to offer a few comments on the Secretary's letter."

Unlike Dillon Myer, his successor, who frequently took to the air waves and the public forum in an effort to combat public prejudice with appeals to Americanism and social justice, Eisenhower had carefully refrained from publicly articulating his views on the camps during his brief tenure and afterward. For this reason, his attitude toward the mass action (until the recent publication of his memoirs, *The President Is Calling*) has been somewhat of a mystery, and at times, harsh "war criminal" charges have been leveled against him.[17]

Because of what is generally believed to be his insensate failure to bring the dismal facts behind the benign "protective custody" curtain to the attention of the President, the following excerpted comments from his letter to the President are significant:

> . . . My friends in the War Relocation Authority, like Secretary Ickes, are deeply distressed over the effects of the entire evacuation and relocation program upon the Japanese-Americans, particularly upon the young citizen group. Persons in this group find themselves living in an atmosphere for which their public school and democratic teachings have not prepared them. It is hard for them to escape a conviction that their plight is due more to racial discrimination, economic motivations, and wartime prejudices than to any real necessity from the military point of view for evacuation from the West Coast.
>
> Life in a relocation center cannot possibly be pleasant. The evacuees are surrounded by barbed wire fences under the eyes of armed military police. They have suffered heavily in property losses; they have lost their businesses and their means of support. The State Legislatures, Members of the Congress, and local groups, by their actions and statements bring home to them almost constantly that as a people they are not really welcome anywhere. States in which they are now located have enacted restrictive legislation forbidding permanent resettlement, for example. The American Legion, many local groups, and city councils have approved discriminatory resolutions, going so far in some instances as to advocate confiscation of their property. Bills have been introduced which would deprive them of citizenship. . . .
>
> Furthermore, in the opinion of the evacuees the Government may not be excused for not having attempted to distinguish between the loyal and the disloyal in carrying out the evacuation.
>
> Under such circumstances it would be amazing if extreme bitterness did not develop.
>
> The War Relocation Authority in developing its program must choose, as I see it, between emphasizing one of two plans. One is to build permanent relocation centers in which all evacuees may live and work for a small wage during the war. (The present wage is $16.00 a month.) The second alternative is to strike out vigorously in helping

the loyal become reabsorbed in normal American communities during the war period.

The War Relocation Authority has chosen to place major emphasis on the second alternative, in the hope that when the war is over only those people will be living in centers whose loyalty may be in doubt or who because of age or other reasons are unable to reestablish themselves. . . . The director of the Authority is striving to avoid, if possible, creation of a racial minority problem after the war which might result in something akin to Indian reservations. It is for these reasons primarily, I think, that he advocates the maximum individual relocation as against the maintenance of all ten relocation centers. . . .[18]

Following Eisenhower's resignation from the WRA in June of 1942, Dillon S. Myer (who, until his appointment to head the Authority, had served as an administrator in the Department of Agriculture) had fallen heir to what may well have been the toughest, most exasperating civilian job during the war, a job made more difficult by the lack of an established procedural guide and because complete WRA jurisdiction over the camps was not achieved until August 1942. By then the multiple bunglings of the Army, its working at cross-purposes with the Navy, the FBI, and the War Department, the frequent abrupt and arbitrary changes in the policies of these and other governmental agencies had served to exacerbate evacuee tension to the near-exploding point.

Nor had it helped matters for the incoming National Director that JACL activists in the camps were still being used as the government's liaison with the detainee population, an arrangement made conspicuous by their prestige jobs and ready access to privileged treatment.[19] This, while a paranoiac distrust of the Kibei worked to further alienate these marginal native-born citizens who sought solace in the disaffected Issei camp, a group keenly resentful of being categorically denied the right to hold office in the community government established in the centers. (A temporarily organized "self-government" was promptly outlawed in Manzanar, for example, when a large number of Issei were voted into office.)

In the cascading loss of prestige which the Issei had suffered since the assembly center days, when the best jobs had been grabbed up by the Nisei, an undercurrent of resentment began to percolate. There were innuendoes of the Nisei having plotted their overthrow, sly insinuations that the evacuation, itself, had been abetted by opportunists among them in hopes of appropriating Issei holdings. As frustrations mounted, rumors began to abound of corruption, self-seeking, and collusion, of Nisei informants still turning in names to the FBI and naval intelligence (see Appendix 4). A flurry of grudge assaults followed on individuals considered much too "chummy" with the *ketos* (the "hairy whites") and on others suspected of having co-operated with the intelligence agencies in making prewar loyalty assessments.

As first-echelon Issei leaders began to trickle back from FBI detention camps in late 1942 (1,700 victims against whom little or no incriminating evidence could be found were "paroled" to relocation centers), it became widespread knowledge that interned nationals could make their grievances known to the Japanese Government by availing themselves of the intercession of the Spanish Consul. Advised that the Consul would begin conducting inspection tours of all citizen detention camps, Myer quickly alerted all project directors:

> The Spanish Government is the protecting power for the Japanese interests in the U.S. . . . In this connection, you need to understand that *the U.S. does not consider that evacuees in the Relocation Centers have been interned.* . . . Basically, the Spanish representative is concerned with aliens, i.e. Japanese Nationals in this case. [Italics mine]
>
> Please bear in mind that the Japanese Government has recently evidenced a substantial amount of interest in the West Coast evacuation through diplomatic channels and has lodged some rather vigorous protests concerning various phases of the treatment of Japanese generally in the U.S.[20]

Until the return of their esteemed prewar community leaders, it had not occurred to the Issei group that protests could be made with any degree of success.[21] Bolstered by the renewed infusion of leadership, they initiated more resolute demands for changes. Farm workers began to organize, as did hospital workers and the Issei- and Kibei-dominated kitchen help, notably in Manzanar. In centers everywhere the Issei consolidated their power behind the block managers, who were mostly Issei or Kibei of high repute and who, though not considered an official part of the community government, wielded considerable influence because of the key role they played in attending to the needs and wishes of the people.

Better pay, more milk for children, and improved living conditions were high on the list of Issei priorities in all relocation centers. Heading a group of concerned Issei in Topaz, famous landscape painter Chiura Obata requested through the neutral power, on January 19, 1943, that "there be the quickest possible adjustment of all abnormal housing conditions, so that not more than one couple, and no single men and women, be housed together in the same room. This we ask on the basis of universal principles of health and morals."[22]

With the Issei's newfound leverage, the Nisei and their "self-government behind stockades" became more than ever the target for derision. The Nisei-dominated Community Council (each block was represented by one member) was ridiculed as "a baby's plaything," as something "to make the kids feel good"; for the function of Council members amounted to little more than acting in an advisory capacity to the camp director and seeing to it that rules and regulations handed down by Washington were enforced by the block managers, many of whom simply ignored the more disagreeable edicts. In neo-colonial fashion, the Project Director held the reins of power tightly, maintaining the absolute power of the veto over his youthful Council members. Until judicial commissions were established to try lawbreakers (not installed in Gila, for example, until 1944), project directors everywhere assumed the role of judge, jury, and prosecutor.[23] In times of crisis, the Nisei—unlike the Issei—had no one to intercede in their behalf.

> The Nisei have been laughing this off and stressing the fact that we are not prisoners of war, but now the Issei have the last laugh. It is going to make the work of keeping up Nisei morale much more difficult . . . Now every time things are not satisfactory to the Issei they will make their appeal. They do not have to depend upon Democracy for results any longer. . . . It's sort of a jolt, like your best friend is letting you down. I still say we are not prisoners of war even though it is a concentration camp.[24]

II

As the months wore on, resentment and unrest accentuated frictions and polarized the communities. In camp Manzanar, the atmosphere was especially charged with bitterness and contention, the mood ugly. For jammed together within its stiflingly cramped confines were those most victimized and embittered by the evacuation—the expellees from Terminal Island—and some of the topmost JACL patriots, steadfast in their unquenchable faith in American benevolence.

The presence of another combustible element, the *aka* or left-wingers of decidedly pro-Soviet leanings, added to the heightening of tension. On July 12, 1942, the Manzanar Citizens Federation was formed, a coalition between pro-America and pro-Communist patriots whose concerns coalesced in the matter of military service, with volunteering for a "second front" the overriding concern of the *aka* group.[25] In opposition to this alarming development, an underground obstructionist clique using a Black Dragon emblem and labeling itself the "Blood Brothers Organization" made its presence known to those suspected of being pro-WRA *inu* ("dogs" or stool pigeons) by a program of harassment and threats of violence.

On the side of the dissidents, and inciting increased ire against those who would clamor behind barbed wire for the opening up of

the armed forces, were insurgents like the Hawaiian-born World
War I veteran of strong convictions, Joe Kurihara, who had seen and
experienced more than "textbook democracy" on the mainland.
Kurihara had witnessed, for example, the cruel overnight ouster of
his Terminal Island friends:

> To pack and evacuate in forty-eight hours was an impossibility. See-
> ing mothers completely bewildered with children crying from want
> and peddlers taking advantage and offering prices next to robbery
> made me feel like murdering those responsible without the slightest
> compunction in my heart. . . . Having had absolute confidence in
> Democracy, I could not believe my very eyes what I had seen that
> day. America, the standard bearer of Democracy, had committed the
> most heinous crime in its history.[26]

A proud onetime patriot of intense dedication to democratic
precepts, Kurihara saw red at the tyrannical order, subsequently de-
creed, for wholesale evacuation. The "protective custody" argument
he angrily rejected as obvious deception: "The government could have
easily declared Martial Law to protect us." Convinced that a vigorous
protest movement within the Japanese community would bring the
government to its senses, Kurihara attended a JACL-sponsored meeting "with a firm determination to join the committee representing the
Nisei and carry the fight to the bitter end."

But, in Kurihara's words, the "goose was already cooked":
JACL leaders counseled nonresistance to the violence.

Kurihara was enraged. Having been brought up in the relative
racial harmony of Hawaii ("Let it be white, black, or yellow, we
were all treated alike"), Kurihara could not see that passivity and
quiescent accommodation were essential survival mechanisms for the
stateside Nisei. "These boys claiming to be the leaders of the Nisei
were a bunch of spineless Americans. Here I decided to fight them
and crush them in whatever camp I happened to find them. I vowed
that they would never again be permitted to disgrace the name of the
Nisei as long as I was about." [27]

In Manzanar, Kurihara found himself hemmed in with the self-
same leaders he had vowed to crush.

December 6, 1942. Violence exploded. The audacity of an outspoken Kibei heading up the Kitchen Workers Union in openly accus-
ing the Assistant Project Director of theft of sugar and meat may have
initiated the sequence of events which led to the savage violence.

The arrest of the tart-tongued, immensely popular Union spokesman, Harry Ueno, following a grudge assault on Fred Tayama, a
JACL leader suspected of being a government informer,[28] aroused
furious indignation within the community and charges of an administration "frame-up." The Kitchen Workers Union, which Ueno had

organized, was composed largely of anti-JACL, antiadministration Kibei and Issei. Many among them were Terminal Islanders who were violently antimanagement (believing the staff to be grafters par excellence) and caustic in their denunciation of individuals suspected of being collaborators. Most were convinced that unionist Ueno's brazen exposure of corrupt practices, and the investigation he was then pushing, were at the root of his being punitively confined in the county jail on the "outside," while two others picked up as suspects had been lodged in the center jail.

At an emotionally charged mass meeting, a "blacklist" was drawn up of a number of Nisei vilified as being "stool pigeons" and "traitors to our people," still cooperating with investigative agencies and the OWI; and Kurihara and four others were appointed as a committee of five to demand Ueno's unconditional return to Manzanar. The agitated mob of over a thousand then proceeded to the administration building, where the delegates made their demands to the Project Director.

To mollify the staggering intensity of the community reaction, Ueno was quickly returned to the project jail by order of camp director Merritt on the condition that there be no more mass meetings; also, that the committee of five would give assistance in apprehending the guilty. Kurihara's failure to abide by the first part of the agreement—of no more meetings—resulted that evening in a noisy mammoth rally of the more extremist element, whose long-pent-up thirst for revenge against fellow informers could no longer be contained, all of it exploding into a cry for immediate retribution and the rescue of Ueno from the center jail.

The administration, which had all public meetings infiltrated with "researchers," acted swiftly. The intended victims ("participating informants" and "outstanding pro-America leaders") and family members were quickly spirited to the safety of the military garrison as troops armed with submachine guns and rifles swarmed into the compound and surrounded the project jail.

Riled by their failure to find their intended blacklisted victims, the angry crowd surged in a frenzy toward the camp jail, running head-on into the barricade of waiting troops.

As for the ensuing sequence of events which ended in violence and bloodshed, a report submitted to Secretary of State Cordell Hull read, in part, as follows:

A line was drawn, beyond which the evacuees were instructed not to pass. The commander then talked to the crowd at length and asked the evacuees to disperse; they did not do so. There is some evidence that stones and sand were thrown at this time by evacuees in the crowd and that they were jeering and threatening the soldiers. After waiting some time, the commander decided that the crowd would not voluntarily disperse and ordered tear gas grenades thrown. The grenades caused considerable confusion and the crowd scattered in all directions. Some of the evacuees ran toward the soldiers. At this point three shotgun shots were fired by the soldiers into the crowd. About the same time a driverless truck was released by several evacuees and headed for the police station. It struck the corner of the station and ran into a Government truck. As it careened toward the soldiers a commissioned officer, who could not see that it was driverless, opened fire on it with a submachine gun.

The crowd dispersed immediately, and the injured were found lying on the ground.[29]

A somewhat divergent interpretation of what happened is provided by a transcript of Senator A. B. Chandler's inquiry into the Manzanar incident, conducted sometime after the event (on March 3, 1943), parts of which read:

Q. [Chandler] You used tear gas on the mob and when they kept on, you had to shoot?
A. [Captain Martyn L. Hall, commander of Military Police] Yes, sir.
Q. The tear gas didn't stop them, they came right on?
A. [Project Director Merritt] The wind was blowing and blew the tear gas away from the crowd.
Q. But it didn't stop them. Did they turn back when you began to shoot?
A. [Captain Hall] Yes, sir.
Q. [Chandler] Did the crowd break up immediately?
A. [Captain Hall] They went back and gathered in little knots and crowds and in some of the kitchens. We gassed them again in those places and they broke up.
Q. [Chandler] What armament have you?
A. [Captain Hall] We have four light machine guns
        two heavies
        eighty-nine shot guns
        twenty-one rifles (Enfield)
        twenty-one tommie guns [30]

The shots which ripped into the crowd had instantly killed one, mortally wounded another. An exact count of those wounded was not possible, for many had fled into hiding to nurse their wounds in private. The Manzanar hospital record listed the following known casualties:

One man was killed instantly, one injured by inhalation gas, nine injured by gun shots. Of the nine, two required major surgery—one involving resection of 14″ of small bowel; other, perforation of stomach. Other cases treated included compound fracture of femur and several gun shot wounds. Of nine cared for, one died from hemorrhage of lungs. Others recovering—majority were in critical condition.[31]

Immediately put under arrest were the committee of five, then conferring with the Project Director for the Kibei's release. "On December 7th a new committee of six persons were elected, but they were also arrested," Secretary of the Interior Ickes had advised the State Department.

For a period of two weeks, martial law was imposed upon surly residents welled up with anger and grief, most of whom refused to report for work. Services for the dead were held outside the fence for fear of touching off another uprising; and for some time thereafter the caste line was drawn more sharply than ever, and fear of evacuee reprisals persisted among administrators.[32]

The State Department and the WRA had nervously anticipated angry reaction from Tokyo. But in time the WRA reported with relief: ". . . it is really remarkable that there were no reverberations in Tokyo. The incident, which might well have been represented to Japanese governmental authorities as an attempt at mass murder, could easily have touched off a wave of unrestrained brutality at prisoner of war camps and detention stations throughout the Far East. Actually, however, the incident provoked no particular reaction from the Japanese authorities and apparently went almost unnoticed." [33]

Or so it was assumed. After the docking of the first detainee exchange ship, the Japanese Government sharply protested "these outrages on part of the United States Authorities" in which "unarmed civilian internees who offered no resistance were mercilessly killed and wounded. Japanese Government demand of United States Government . . . that they must bear responsibility for any and all consequences of these outrages." [34]

III

Kurihara and a total of fifteen others arrested and removed, including union organizer Ueno, went on to pay a heavy price for their alleged complicity. Though the collaborationist group which Kurihara had vowed to crush had been extralegally given their freedom to resettle on the outside (after a two-month stay in an abandoned CCC camp, the Cow Creek Camp, in Death Valley), all evacuee-appointed mediators who had sought to negotiate a settlement of differences were seized and removed to the nearest county jail. With the exception of Kurihara, all were Kibei, half of them—including Kurihara—college graduates.

A heavily guarded isolation camp for citizen "troublemakers" was subsequently established at another abandoned CCC camp near

Moab, Utah. Transferred to it on January 11, 1943, the 1,000-mile trip was made by Kurihara and others in a blacked-out truck guarded by seven MPs. Camp Moab, in no time, filled up with citizen dissidents from other relocation centers. There, in total isolation from the prying eyes of civilization ("we are situated in a mountain several hundred miles from a civilized town"), a pretense was made at solving a problem but humanity ignored.

The "crimes" of the inmates varied widely. There were young men accused of having instigated work stoppages; of having made bravado statements of disloyalty; of throwing jars of filth in apartments of informers; of making pin-ups of Japanese soldiers. Among them was a father of fifteen children, suffering from a chronic illness and a mental condition; also a boy, all alone in the country as his father had committed suicide in an internment camp, who had written a bitter essay which had fallen into the hands of authorities.

From the Canal Community in Gila, there was an embittered group of high-ranking officers of the *Seinen Kai* (Kibei cultural fraternity) "causing considerable agitation and unrest." And no wonder. Apart from the rude fact that the fraternity president was to have been married a few days after his summary banishment, an interdepartmental memo hints of a grave administrative blunder: ". . . a subsequent investigation revealed . . . that the Seinen Kai in Canal Community had no active affiliation with the Seinen Kai in the Butte Community." [35] Butte's *Seinen Kai* leadership—Canal (Camp 1) and Butte (Camp 2) comprised the Gila Relocation Center—had been earlier suppressed for their pro-Japanese tendencies and "indoctrination with Japanese culture." In more than a few relocation centers the climate was such that too strong an emotional attachment to the enemy's culture was considered tantamount to disloyalty to the United States—a bedeviling issue which came to a head during the loyalty registration, to be discussed in the following chapter.

Because of the often capricious and arbitrary manner in which citizen dissidents were seized and isolated, flagrant mistakes were made, such as the exiling of a perfectly innocent individual because his name happened to be similar to one turned in by an informer.[36] The discovery of such errors caused the keepers, themselves, to shudder; but with hardly an exception, authorities determined that there be no return of the victim to the center of "prior residence." Face-saving was not then the monopoly of Orientals, as moral and ethical values were exiled to darker recesses of official concern.

Arbitrary arrests peaked during the stormy loyalty registration and later at the reinstitution of Selective Service (January 1944), when even more rigorous "justice" was meted out, many youths ending up in federal penitentiaries for taking a stand for the restoration of basic human rights before they would take up arms for a freedom that neither they nor their parents enjoyed.[37] FBI files suddenly bulged with Japanese names. The long-held, lowest-in-the-nation crime rate was virtually demolished during the tumultuous war years since repression, hastily applied, was the joint WRA-FBI response to the slightest political misfeasance. The Chinese in America, who had endured grave courtroom injustices until China became a wartime ally, thereafter took over the honors of boasting the nation's lowest crime rate.

Powerless against a system which had cut them off from the more human world of relationships—of wives, parents, children, friends—the men sequestered in the Moab isolation pen lived a lonely life, with rigid dehumanized rules governing their every activity. Troops had orders to shoot to kill. Frustration occasionally erupted into fuming rampage, and stern justice was meted out to prisoners stigmatized as "aggravated troublemakers": "The four were moved out and now they are living in a different building. They are watched by soldiers equipped with fixed bayonets at meal time, in the shower room and at the lavatory." [38]

Mail was not only censored but file copies were also made so that headquarters and the intelligence services could keep better tab on all who corresponded with the men. The following intercepted letter, penned by one of the Manzanar sixteen, hints of the torment experienced by the Nisei, who, by a demeaning twist of circumstance, suffered especially pitiless treatment because, in most of the cases, they also fell in the category of Kibei.

. . . My four months life in here has been a mental strain I shall never forget. It will be the same with not only myself, but with any person in my predicament. The reality of this psychological struggle could only be experienced here and the true nature of it cannot be imagined.

The life here has been worse than a prisoner's life and if I go into minor details it will be too long . . . No definite charges for our internment have been issued and we don't know when we will be able to return . . . it will depend on Washington's orders.

In the event that our internment will be until after the war, there may be much bitter disillusionment brewing from this cruel camp life. Any person who has a soul shall shed a tear for these youths who go through such mental strain and suffering in their daily life.

At the present there are approximately forty youths interned here and individually they are normal and without a fault. They are not pro-Japanese nor are they radicals. You could take my word for this. The authorities have stamped our camp as a pro-Japanese Camp, but the true basic outlook of every individual is on the contrary. The camp is only a miniature model of all the various sufferings of life.[39]

[Edited by author]

By a peculiar morality of the time in regard to the "Japanese," the traditional presumption of innocence was conveniently transformed into a presumption of guilt. There were repeated promises from WRA headquarters of a speedy trial, but none materialized. Even when the innocence of the victims became apparent, it was cynically determined by Washington that the men should remain "separated"—the cruelest of punishment for a people bereft of everything, for whom family relationships were the only consolation left.

Driven to the limits of their endurance, they switched once fervent loyalties to pride in their *yamato damashii* ("spirit of the Japanese race") heritage, which enabled them to bear with a measure of dignity the abject humiliation imposed. Passive deference was replaced by intensified disaffection and the attitude: "It is better to die on your feet than to live on your knees."

In a burst of fury on hearing that the WRA "Review Board" had ruled that the Manzanar sixteen not be allowed to rejoin their families, a victim of the summary justice wrote back to his wife: "They are afraid to disclose the inside story of their stool pigeons . . . I shall be happy to die as a descendant of the Japanese race. I am quite satisfied even to get shot for not licking a white man's ass."

Despairing of ever obtaining an explanation of his long detainment without trial or charges, another Manzanar youth wrote back: "Sooner or later you will know the facts about us sixteen men. Here I am writing to you in tears before other reports are made to you . . ."

In camp Manzanar, the men banished to Moab were idealized as martyrs by a fired-up segment of the population who looked upon Tayama as a symbol of WRA repression and his beating as fully justified.[40] But in many of the centers, parents, families, and relatives of persecuted political dissenters ran into powerful social disapproval and ostracism by residents in whom respect for authority was strongly reinforced.

A highly guarded isolation camp surrounded by a manproof fence and guard towers was eventually installed on a desolate Navaho Indian Reservation near Leupp, Arizona, to which the Moab population was transferred on April 27, 1943. The subsequent appointment of Paul G. Robertson (replacing Raymond Best) as administrator of the Leupp Isolation Center came as a stroke of luck to inmates. Robertson, a man of humane persuasion, saw no reason why eighty inmates had to be guarded by 150 armed troops; nor could he fathom the need for subjecting the men to treatment so absurdly despotic. Robertson recently recalled: "The funny part of it is that most of the men sent there were not incorrigible at all . . . One fellow was brought down from Utah in a blacked out truck . . . I eventually allowed him to work outside the fence . . . he did my gardening, washed windows and stayed with my children on numerous occasions. He wasn't in the least bit dangerous."

Robertson still corresponds with a number of his former wards. One of them is George Yamashiro, who, until recently, was Chairman of the Board of Tokyo Railway Company. Robertson had personally spirited Yamashiro back to Gila, his "place of previous residence," long enough for him to get married. "I learned to like all of these fellows at the Leupp Center and had no real trouble with any of them. . . . They are truly a wonderful race of people. Anyone who has been associated with them for any length of time comes to think very highly of them." [41]

Robertson's glowing reports of his "incorrigibles" ("extremely cooperative with administration and work, by choice, from nine to ten hours per day, often spending the entire day Sunday in the carpenter shop") jogged a few consciences in Washington in respect to certain arbitrary practices, such as refusing the right to a trial or hearing before removal from the center, and denying the right of the accused to say good-bye to his family and friends. On June 5, 1943, an alarmed Dillon Myer issued the following alert to "all Field Assistant Directors and Project Directors":

> Under our present procedures we give a hearing before the Project Director or the Judicial Commission for every minor offense. Surely, therefore, we should give an evacuee a hearing before *convicting* him of being an aggravated and incorrigible trouble-maker and transferring him to the Leupp Center.[42]

The Leupp Hearing Board Committee in Washington (headed up by Elmer Rowalt, WRA Deputy Director, and including Dr. John Provinse, Chief of Community Services and Philip M. Glick, Solicitor) was responsible for the disposition of all citizen isolation cases, with final decisions requiring the approval of the National Director. Noting some of the procedural ineptitude coming to light, the Acting Solicitor, on August 14, confided in Solicitor Glick:

> —Many of the dockets are still incomplete. We still don't have dockets on many of the men sent to Leupp from Gila. It is inexcusable to permit this situation to continue indefinitely. We have had reports from several sources indicating that the Project Director at Leupp does not know why some of the men were sent there; that the men themselves don't know why they were sent there, and that requests for information go unanswered.
>
> —A definite time schedule should be established for reviewing the dockets of each person sent to Leupp. I understand that one Masuo Kanno was probably sent to Leupp as a case of mistaken identity. He has been there for five months. Nothing has as yet been done about it.
>
> —We should do something to check transfers to Leupp on the

basis of telephonic clearance. My only suggestion is that the Director or the Acting Director become more tough on their attitudes on this subject.

—Finally, I should like to see a reexamination made of the advisability of continuing the Leupp Center. I think it is an un-American institution, corresponds to and is premised on Gestapo methods. I don't like the idea of individuals being sent to Leupp without being told why they are being sent. If Leupp is to be continued as a center for troublemakers, I would like to see no one go to Leupp without going through the procedure of Administrative Instruction No. 85.[43]

Meanwhile, a letter from camp director Robertson of Leupp took exception to a series of sweeping official assumptions made on the frailest of factual data.

Confidential   Dillon S. Myer   August 18, 1943

Attention: Leupp Review Board

Dear Mr. Myer:

At the present time we have sixty-seven men at the Leupp Relocation Center. In reviewing the dockets of these evacuees, I was very much amazed at the lack of evidence which I had believed necessary to warrant a transfer to this center. Administrative Instruction #95 subsection IB states that persons should not be considered for Leupp who do not persistently interfere with effective administration or engage constantly in threats or beatings and then only when the administration attempts to control it, punish it and prevent it.

Of evacuees now at Leupp, at least according to their dockets, I fail to find but two cases involving other than a first offense and no indication of attempted correction. I cite for you the following cases:

George Eto [44] from Granada. George is a boy twenty years of age, timid and well behaved. He states that he has never been in trouble and that he had nothing to do with the organizing of the carpenters' strike at Granada. Of the sixty carpenters involved, he was the youngest. Due to the fact that he speaks English more fluently than the others, he was appointed spokesman. Since the majority of these carpenters were old issei, he was almost compelled to do their bidding. He states that when the negotiations were still in process he withdrew and asked to be assigned to some other division. He was of the opinion that the greatest reason for his transfer to Leupp was the fact that he had previously applied for repatriation to Japan. George asked to be put to work immediately upon his arrival at Leupp and has been a model boy during the time of residence here. No hearing, nor even an interview, was held for him at Granada . . .

Edward K. Mio and J. Tsuji formerly of Jerome are both thoroughly Japanese, but from reading their dockets I am unable to find any other reason for sending them to Leupp.

While I have no complaints against the boys forwarded to us from Manzanar, it occurs to me they were transferred to the Isolation Center as a result of information received from informers, and not because they are known to have a record as constant trouble makers. . . .[45]

The group of evacuees from Gila River present a very interesting problem. With the exception of only one, they were transferred to Leupp because they were officers in an organization which was believed to be strongly pro-Japanese. This organization was known as the Gila Young People's Association and was given a charter by the Project after a review of its constitution and by-laws. The organization was allowed to continue in its activities for many weeks after the evacuees above mentioned were transferred to Leupp. I believe this group, as a group, are the best boys we have at Leupp. . . . The only information we have ever received . . . [was] a letter dated June 18 from Mr. Bennett, Project Director, in which he said specific and detailed information regarding these evacuees was lacking. . . .

In nearly every case where an evacuee is transferred to Leupp, he has been told that he would be given a fair and speedy hearing. The first sixteen boys from Manzanar received a letter dated January 8 signed by the Project Director advising them, "I have been informed by Director Myer that each of you will be given a fair and speedy hearing." . . .

If a hearing is to be given these people, do you not agree with me that it should be held before transfer to Leupp? A hearing at Leupp is not only unfair to the evacuee because of his inability to present witnesses in his defense, but is of little avail to WRA due to the fact that we have no witnesses or documentary evidence to sustain a conviction. . . .

He should not be denied the right of counsel and should be permited to subpoena witnesses in his behalf. If the defendant is convicted he could then be sentenced to an indefinite period of time, his record at Leupp determining the length of his sentence. . . .[46]

Robertson's sharpened concern resulted in a number of men being released to cities in the Midwest for work opportunities; in a couple of instances, the liberation permitted the consummation of long overdue marriages. A few were permitted to be reunited with wives or families in a relocation center other than that of previous residence. To the end, the WRA maintained the "unwisdom" of permitting the men, however blameless, to rejoin their families and friends in familiar surroundings, an exception being made in the case of the mentally disturbed individual with fifteen children. It was a policy insisted upon by Gila's camp director,[47] having personally committed a number of mistaken identity blunders.

Only as an economy measure, according to Robertson, was the Leupp Isolation Center closed down on December 2, 1943. The remaining fifty-two inmates were transferred to the Tule Lake Segregation Center, where most were immediately placed in its "separate compound," the euphemism of the period for the stockade. A few of them, like Yamashiro and Kurihara, whose integrity and keen intellect had impressed key administrative bigwigs, were eventually released to the general colony area. Others were removed to alien detention camps following the voluntary (sometimes involuntary) act of renouncing their American citizenship, then deported to Japan with the coming of peace.

IV

At war's end, curiosity led Project Director Merritt to seek out possible hidden reasons behind the Manzanar riot. At Tule Lake, he managed to get at the bottom of things, including a full confession from Joe Kurihara, then making preparations to leave for Japan. The former pro-America patriot who, as a World War I volunteer, had "solemnly vowed to fight and die for the U.S." had been one of the disaffected multitude who renounced their citizenship at Tule Lake (see Chapter 12). The fifty-year-old veteran had also been the first to openly swear to "become a Jap 100 percent" following the government's flat refusal, at the time of the evacuation, to make exceptions of veterans who had already proved their loyalty to America, as he intensely felt he had: "I draw compensation for my wounds from the United States government while rotting in a United States concentration camp. . . . I spit on these scars of the United States."

The following memo to headquarters, dated January 7, 1946, was Merritt's account of his Tule Lake meeting with Kurihara. Tokie Slocum, who figures prominently in Merritt's report, was, like Kurihara, a veteran of World War I and, as a JACL activist, had led a successful fight to gain U.S. citizenship for Asian alien veterans of the war. As Slocum had headed up the special Southern California JACL committee to assist federal investigative agencies in anticipation of the war (set up by Tayama), and since he had testified before the Tolan Committee of his part in turning in intelligence information, his role as a government informer had been a matter of public knowledge.

Having in mind that there was a story in Kurihara and also that I wanted to clarify in my own mind the causes of the Manzanar "incident," I called on Kurihara in his barracks at Tule Lake on November 12th, 1945. . . . At that time in a two and a half hour talk he gave me his own story. The substance of his statement was that at the time of the evacuation a number of the Nisei leaders of JACL sold out the Issei and the Japanese cause in general. When he met those same leaders in Manzanar he made up his mind to expose them and drive them out of the Center. These men were Tayama, Tokie Slocum, Tanaka, Higashi, and Karl Yoneda. . . .

He said that, in the summer of 1942, Slocum had gotten himself a job on the police force and was working on the graveyard shift for the purpose of taking records from the administration offices to copy them and return them before daylight in order to have complete knowledge of all that was going on in the Center. Slocum was in fear of Kurihara and told him what he was doing and agreed to give Kurihara copies of all of the material which he got. I asked Kurihara for evidence of this and he showed me documents copied from the Manzanar files, particularly certain documents which he said were written by Tayama which were transmitted to the FBI through the Manzanar Police Department.

On August 8, 1942 the Kibei meeting was held in which Kurihara spoke as a representative of the citizens' group who had been mistreated by the Government. Tayama sent a report of this to the FBI. Kurihara gave me a copy of that report at Tule Lake. Because of the statement made by Tayama about Kurihara's speech, Kurihara says he decided to kill Tayama and therefore he organized the group which beat up Tayama on December 5th. Kurihara was not a member of the group and pretended to be surprised next morning when he heard the news of the beating. In the attempt to find the culprits of the beating, I, as Project Director, arrested Harry Ueno, a mess-hall worker who had been the head of the Kitchen Workers' Union.

On the morning of December 6th, a meeting was held at Kitchen 22 to demand the release of Ueno and from this meeting the Manzanar "riot" was precipitated. Kurihara was a speaker at the meeting held that day and was one of five people who composed a committee to call on the Project Director demanding Ueno's release. Because he was the most talkative, he became the leader of the group. As Project Director, I made an agreement for settlement of the disturbance on the evening of December 6th. Kurihara went before the group and spoke in what was supposed to be Japanese, telling them of the settlement. He admits and it is now generally agreed that he spoke a Hawaiian dialect of Japanese which was not understood by the crowd except when he told them that a report would be made at 6 o'clock that evening at Kitchen 22. Such a meeting was in violation of the agreement. This meeting developed the mob which later created the riot. When the mob appeared and the situation got out of control, Kurihara says he tried to prevent violence and get them to go home but that he lost control and the crowd broke up to be led in various directions by those who had particular grievances against Tayama, who was in the hospital, Slocum who was supposed to be in his barrack, Tanaka in his barrack, and others.

Kurihara took full responsibility in his talk with me for this entire matter. He said that he had spent three years in praying for forgiveness and in studying Japanese so that he in future might speak understandably. He said he was returning to Japan with the feeling that he would probably be killed but he intended to speak for America and the democratic way of living.[48]

(8)
Loyalty—Disloyalty

In reply to your letter of May ninth . . . please be assured that I am keenly aware of the anxiety that German and Italian aliens living in the United States must feel as the result of the Japanese evacuation from the West Coast.

Will you assure Mr. Antonini that no collective evacuation of German and Italian aliens is contemplated at this time? . . .

Further, in dealing with our alien problem, we shall, insofar as possible, differentiate between those who are disloyal and those who are loyal to the United States . . .

— PRESIDENT ROOSEVELT to Governor Herbert H. Lehman, June 3, 1943

I

The supreme irony of the evacuation-internment interlude was that while German and Italian aliens, blessed with more impressive political leverage than the army of tots and teen-agers that the Nisei represented, were being lavished with the reassuring solace of the President, those firmly sequestered behind barbed wire were being provoked to greater despair and alienation.

In early 1943, the vigorous sorting out of disloyals from the loyals became the new obsession of those in swivel chairs in Washington. Like a bolt out of the blue, inmates being held in the ten camps (including the citizen isolation center) were asked to declare their total undivided loyalty to America. Because of the multiple and complex reasoning behind the wholesale oath-taking—much of which was never made clear—fear, confusion, and utter chaos developed during its coercive administration, universally referred to as "registration," the wartime inquisition of Japanese Americans.

The entire proceeding, in the first place, was grievously ill-timed.

Wrenched from their homes, shorn of their property, and forced into a state of abject emasculation, the vast majority of the Issei were gripped by fears for the future and morbidly in dread of what might happen to them on the "outside." Of the young people left in the camps, most were school-age children or individuals unable to relocate because of aged or ill parents and others totally dependent upon them. Many among them had undergone the horrendous trauma of seeing wholly blameless parents led away without justification to FBI camps.[1]

Since the first shock of the Pearl Harbor attack, the Nisei, by being lumped in with aliens as "nonaliens" (to obscure the fact of their citizenship), had endured every possible humiliation. They had been bombarded by press denunciations. They had been crucified on the lie that they were more suspect than their alien parents, rejected in their efforts to volunteer for the armed services, stripped of their rights as citizens. Many of the 5,000 young men in uniform at the time of Pearl Harbor had suffered the crushing shame of becoming suspect soldiers and having their weapons taken from them. Hundreds of Kibei had been discharged and placed in camp.[2]

By July 1942, the Selective Service System had assigned a draft classification of "4C" to the Nisei and Kibei (with the exception of linguists urgently needed in intelligence work),[3] placing them in the ignominious category of enemy aliens.

Ignoring the hurts, the wounds, the injuries inflicted in pitiless succession, Washington had suddenly decided that now was the time to give all detainees in the camps (excluding children under seventeen) an opportunity to concretely register their fundamental loyalty as a group by having each swear his or her unqualified allegiance to the United States. For the WRA, such a certification of loyalty would assuredly facilitate work and resettlement leaves in the future.

The colossal folly of recording each inmate's attitude toward America in a concentration camp, *after all the damage had been done,* was to be compounded by the WRA's decision to conduct the mass registration in conjunction with an Army recruitment drive in the centers.

Roundly impressed, by now, with the superior quality of the Japanese fighting man,[4] and in light of the formidably mounting casualty list, decision makers within the military had obviously come to the conclusion that Mike Masaoka's original proposal for a Nisei suicide battalion was not all that preposterous. Normal Selective Service procedure for the Nisei had been temporarily overruled, but as an agreed "first step" in that direction, the War Department had decided, with the President's approval, that a "Japanese Combat Team" be organized, made up of Nisei volunteers from Hawaii and from the ten camps.

The interned Nisei were astounded when fast on the heels of the

President's rousing declaration, in early February, that "no loyal citizen of the United States should be denied the democratic right to exercise the responsibilities of his citizenship regardless of ancestry," teams of Army recruiters descended on the camps, accenting the momentous fact that one democratic right had been restored: the right to be shot at.

Evacuee reaction was vivid, intense, and caustic. Manzanar inmates were still reeling from the emotionalism of the December 6 riot, which had ended so tragically, and resentment remained strong against individuals and groups who had earnestly petitioned for the privilege of enlisting. Patriots who roundly cheered the development were vastly outnumbered, and in centers where feelings ran high, those who volunteered did so secretly, fleeing the camps in the dead of night.

II

As an ultimate proof of loyalty, all male and female internees aged seventeen and older were expected to give "yes" answers to two crucial questions at the end of a long questionnaire. For the draft-age Nisei, the heart of the loyalty questionnaire entitled "Statement of United States Citizenship of Japanese Ancestry" (Selective Service Form 304A) embraced questions 27 and 28, which read:

No. 27. Are you willing to serve in the armed forces of the United States on combat duty wherever ordered?
No. 28. Will you swear unqualified allegiance to the United States of America and faithfully defend the United States from any or all attack by foreign or domestic forces, and forswear any form of allegiance or obedience to the Japanese emperor, to any other foreign government, power or organization?

The questionnaires meant to be filled out by the Issei of both sexes, and all female Nisei who were seventeen years of age or older (WRA Form 126 Rev.), were identical in every detail. Many in this second category of respondents were baffled, however, by the wholly irrelevant title given the registration forms: "Application for Leave Clearance." Further indicative of how carelessly the documents had been framed by the War Department's Adjutant General's office [5] was Question 27 of the same questionnaire, which asked the Issei male along with all females: "If the opportunity presents itself and you are found qualified, would you be willing to volunteer for the Army Nurse Corps or the WAAC?"

Question 28, worded exactly alike for all registrants and considered the key loyalty question, was greeted with incredulity by the Issei as being improper, unfair, and utterly outrageous. For, in effect, it called on all Japanese nationals to categorically forswear allegiance to the country of which they were citizens and to register unqualified allegiance to America, a country which refused them citizenship. The literal-minded among the Issei population recoiled in horror at the possibility of becoming men and women without a country in giving an affirmative reply merely to please American authorities. On learning that applicants awaiting the exchange ship were wholly exempt from the oath-taking, a stampede to circumvent signing such a document by applying for repatriation gained momentum at Manzanar. But when an Issei group protesting the illegality of Question 28 threatened to call in the Spanish Consul, the offending question was quickly withdrawn by the Project Director and another substituted.

The newly framed question put to Issei residents of Manzanar proved no less disquieting, however, for the query now had to do with whether the aliens would defend the United States from attack, including attack by Japan. Few, if any, Issei could consider anything so unthinkable as taking up arms against their own motherland in the name of a country which had treated them so badly—which also left open the possibility of being punished or disowned by a victorious Japan. The furor touched off by the Issei in Manzanar was quickly felt in the upper reaches of the administration, resulting in Question 28 being reappraised and eventually changed at all centers to read: "Will you swear to abide by the laws of the United States and to take no action which would in any way interfere with the war effort of the United States?" But by the time the decision for this milder substitute question had been arrived at, the Manzanar registration had been completed.

Manzanar was the only camp in which critical dissent also developed among the Caucasian personnel, a number of them lodging a sharp protest against the diabolical twist the loyalty drive was taking. Eight Caucasian staff workers demanded in a petition to the Project Director that "the answers to the so-called loyalty question, Question 28, be thrown in the waste-basket where they belong," charging that "the answer wrung from them under the strains and perplexities with which they were faced is no more than an evidence of witchcraft."

The turmoil among the older people had a tremendous impact on the Nisei, for the decisions made by their elders were pivotal to the response of the younger generation, many Issei fearing that differing answers could result in some manner of forced separation. As a group, the Kibei were quick to read sinister meanings into Question 28 (which asked whether the registrant would "forswear any form of allegiance or obedience to the Japanese emperor"), interpreting it as a trick question, tantamount to asking citizens of German ancestry to renounce their allegiance to Hitler. Voices of dissidence cautioned of a possible "trap": "A 'yes' could well be interpreted *as an admission of prior allegiance to Japan and the Japanese Emperor;* a 'no,' an open admission of disloyalty to America." The option desired by the majority of the Nisei, to declare themselves loyal and willing to fight for America *but only after the restoration of citizenship rights,* was not available.

More than a few young men assumed that to answer both questions 27 and 28 in the affirmative was as good as volunteering—or could be so defined by the War Department—since draft-age youths were required to respond to the key loyalty questions in front of Army recruiters. In all centers, negative replies were disturbingly frequent to Question 27, which queried one's willingness "to serve in the armed forces of the United States on combat duty, wherever ordered," but such a response had less to do with disloyalty than with the gnawing repugnance felt by the Nisei to go into combat against their own brothers and cousins in Japan.

The adult Nisei, who had filled out one questionnaire after another since the evacuation for their non-English speaking parents, relatives, and for their own families, were highly incensed at being, once again, "third degreed"—in being coerced to submit to a loyalty oath like a foreigner seeking naturalization. Had not everyone already proved an extraordinary fidelity by complying without protest to the outrageous orders to evacuate?

To the once starry-eyed Nisei, highly sensitive to their citizenship obligations, registration was the ultimate insult; and heedless of what punishment was in store, many put down angry noes to give vent to their feeling of outrage, to register their repugnance at what America had done to them.

Inmates did not know that impassioned outbursts were sometimes recorded verbatim, then sent on to Washington headquarters:

Well, if you want to know, I said "no" and I'm going to stick to "no." If they want to segregate me they can do it. If they want to take my citizenship away, they can do it. If this country doesn't want me they can throw me out. What do they know about loyalty? I'm as loyal as anyone in this country. Maybe I'm as loyal as President Roosevelt. What business did they have asking me a question like that?

I was born in Hawaii. I worked most of my life on the west coast. I have never been to Japan. We would have done anything to show our loyalty. All we wanted to do was to be left alone on the coast. . . . The Japanese wouldn't have been profiteers like some people. If I made $200 a month the government could have had half of it for war purposes. That's the way we were. My wife and I lost $10,000 in that evacuation. She had a beauty parlor and had to give that up. I had a good position worked up as a gardener, and was taken away from that. We had a little home and that's gone now. . . .

What kind of Americanism do you call that? That's not democracy. That's not the American way, taking everything away from people. . . . Where are the Germans? Where are the Italians? Do they ask them questions about loyalty? . . .

Nobody had to ask us about our loyalty when we lived on the coast. You didn't find us on relief. You didn't find us in trouble and in the courts. You didn't find young people getting into trouble. We were first when there was any civic drive. We were first with the money for the Red Cross and Community Chest or whatever it was. Why didn't that kind of loyalty count? Now they're trying to push us to the east. It's always "further inland, further inland." I say, "To hell with it!" Either they let me go to the coast and prove my loyalty there or they can do what they want with me. If they don't want me in this country, they can throw me out. . . .

Evacuation was a mistake, there was no need for it. The government knows this. Why don't they have enough courage to come out and say so, so that these people won't be pushed around? . . . Why don't they think about taking care of the people and paying them for their losses?

I've tried to cooperate. Last year I went out on furlough and worked on the beet fields in Idaho. There was a contract which said that we would be brought back here at the end of the work. Instead we just sat there. I called up the W.R.A. man, Mr. Lawrence, and told him to get us back to Manzanar. He said that we would be brought back within a week. Instead it was 31 days. A week is 7 days, not 31 days. We had to spend our own money. The farmers won't do anything for you. They treat you all right while you're working hard for them but as soon as your time is up, you can starve. . . . When I got back to Manzanar, nearly all my money that I had earned was gone. . . .

They've got me on the Black List here. They call me an agitator and a troublemaker. I was living in Block 8. They had so many small children there. I took care of the food for the children. I insisted that enough nourishing things be put aside for them. This caused trouble and someone went to Mr. —— and told him I was no good at my work. Without even calling me in or asking for my side of it, he fired me. He just took their word for it. There's one white man who ought to be fired. He thinks he's a big fellow but I could handle him. The Japanese-American learns some things for his own protection. As soon as this war is over, I'm going to find him and break every bone in his body.[6]

One of the basic underlying objectives of the registration had been to speed up—on a mass basis—the clearing of loyal adults for resettlement, which probably accounted for the questionnaire being entitled: "Application for Leave Clearance." But the very use of the word "application" awakened latent fears and suspicions as to the unstated purpose of the registration: Was the government about to embark on a plan of mass eviction, the expulsion of all "yes-yes" loyals, regardless of their inability to fend for themselves? Was registration but a prelude to the reinstitution of Selective Service, a means of cataloguing all "yes-yes-ers" as potential draft bait? Were only the "no-noes"—the disloyals—to be "rewarded" with continued war-duration internment? [7]

<h1 style="text-align:center">III</h1>

Pentagon instructions had been that each relocation center provide a quota of volunteers for an all-Nisei combat regiment; that this could best be achieved through intensive propaganda bombardment within the camp communities, punctuated by mass meetings conducted by Army recruiters, where appeals could be made to the Nisei's compulsive need to restore their impugned honor. Army teams were instructed to place particular emphasis on the "golden opportunity" being opened up to the Nisei by their boosters in the War Department, who were "sticking their neck out" in order that the discredited group might be given a chance to "secure" their future as Americans.

The import of the Pentagon summons was clear: Were the Nisei going to continue accepting public accusations of disloyalty unchallenged . . . or were they men enough to go out on the field of battle and prove in a concrete and unassailable manner this patriotism which they professed? According to Mike Masaoka, who, from his Washington, D.C., vantage point, had energetically lobbied for the Nisei's right to volunteer (and was the first to do so), it was the Army's contention that "Nisei protestation of loyalty was so much hogwash . . . We had to have a demonstration in blood."

The average Nisei was dumbfounded by this extraordinary line of reasoning. Why a demonstration in blood now when hundreds of Nisei who patriotically volunteered at the beginning of the war had been summarily rejected? Why the oath-taking now when it could have been done before the evacuation? Why this need for proof, proof, and more proof? Couldn't the incessant "Jap's a Jap" propaganda, depicting them as nothing more than vile, debased descendants of monkey men, be ground to a halt? Couldn't the President simply reinstate them in the eyes of the American public by telling the nation that the Nisei and their parents have committed no wrong, that they should be treated fairly and squarely, like those of German and Italian ancestry?

And why the apartheid treatment traditionally reserved for blacks? Why a "Jap Crow" combat team, the noxious color line barring them from fighting alongside whites? In the mass orientation meetings, the agents from the Pentagon were persuasive: Only by working as a visible, segregated unit, they insisted, could the Nisei's fidelity be spectacularly dramatized!

The gut concern of Nisei everywhere was whether their volunteering would help to guarantee the security of their parents. Would their taking up arms give their folks and loved ones the choice of returning to their homes; would they, at the very least, be assured refuge for the duration of the war? Would shedding blood enable fathers being held in internment camps to return to their families? The questions hurled at the recruiting teams were often unanswerable, leaving the officers flustered, red-faced, and disconcerted, for instructions had been that they say nothing concerning matters for which they did not have prepared answers.

Terrified parents of draft-age youths immediately saw the entire proceeding as part of a plot to rob them of the only earthly possession left to them—their precious, obedient, gently brought-up sons, on whom they had pinned all their hopes and dreams. Reasoned many: Now that Washington had come to the realization that they could well exploit the same *yamato damashii* spirit which obviously was the secret weapon of the foe, the Nisei were being callously plucked from the bosoms of grieving mothers for use in segregated "suicide squads," that it was all a diabolical plot to "save white boys."

In this atmosphere of heightened tension and distrust, honor-conscious Nisei were torn by the question of what comes first: duty to country or duty to parents. Duty to their aging parents, now spent, energies gone, or to a country to whom they owed allegiance despite the betrayal. Many resisted intense parental urging to declare themselves disloyal; but numerous parents hysterically prevailed upon sons and daughters to respond similarly, and as a unit, to avoid any possibility of family dismemberment, appealing to their sense of filial loyalty. The pressure upon the young was terrific. Wrote Mary Tsukamoto: "People walked the roads, tears streaming down their troubled faces, silent and suffering. The little apartments were not big enough for the tremendous battle that waged in practically every room . . ."

Everywhere the draft-age Nisei were tormented by worries of what might happen to their parents in the event that they were killed or maimed. Once they were ejected from the safety of the camp, who would then care for them, help them get reestablished? Were their folks' dreams in America to be shattered in the bitter misery of some large unknown city ghetto where, in all likelihood, they would end up penniless, sick, despised? Would America continue treating them like lepers? What it all boiled down to was: Were the Nisei expected to lay down their lives for a country that had destroyed before their very eyes everything for which their folks had slaved and sacrificed!

For many, the pain they saw in their parents' eyes was central to the response they felt impelled to make. Obligation to shield their parents from further suffering came first in the thinking of many a tenderhearted Nisei. Hundreds of them made the decision to sacrifice their own future for parents who, unmindful of selves, had scraped and sacrificed all their lives for them. Another loyalty had become primary, as in the case of the following young Nisei:

My dad is 58 years old now. He has been here 30 years at least. He came to this country with nothing but a bed roll. He worked on the railroads and he worked in the sugar-beet fields. If I told you the hardship he had, you wouldn't believe me. I owe a lot to my father. Everything I am I owe to him. All through his life he was working for me. During these last years he was happy because he thought he was coming to the place where his son would have a good life. . . .

I tell you this because it has something to do with my answer about the draft question. We are taught that if you go out to war you should go out with the idea that you are never coming back. That's the Japanese way of looking at it. Of course, many in the Japanese armies come back after the war, just like in all armies, but the men go out prepared to die. If they live through it, that's their good luck. I listen to white American boys talk. They look at it differently. They all take the stand that they are coming back, no matter who dies. It's a different mental attitude.

In order to go out prepared and willing to die, expecting to die, you have to believe in what you are fighting for. If I am going to end the family line, if my father is going to lose his only son, it should be for some cause we respect. I believe in democracy as I was taught in school. I would have been willing to go out forever before evacuation. It's not that I'm a coward or afraid to die. My father would have been willing to see me go out at one time. But my father can't feel the same after this evacuation, and I can't either. . . .

I know my father is planning to return to Japan. I know he expects me to say "No" so there is no possibility that the family will be separated. There isn't much I can do for my father any more; I can't work for him the way I used to. But I can at least quiet his mind on this.[8]

Most Issei were convinced that a "no" answer, though insuring continued refuge in internment communities, would be punished by segregation, deportation, or both. No such announcements had been authorized, but camp officials occasionally took it upon themselves to threaten noncompliant evacuees with the possibility of such dire consequences, provoking strong criticism from a number of community analysts then studying the ferment in their respective camps. Chief Washington Analyst Embree, taking note of the registration uproar during a stopover in Topaz, wrote back to WRA headquarters:

There were statements issued which seemed to imply that the registration was to separate the loyal from the disloyal, not only segregation in regards to loyalty, but physical segregation. That such action on the basis of "yes" or "no" answers to two questions is unsound and unfair is without question.[9]

Morris E. Opler, Community Analyst at the troubled Manzanar

camp, was openly critical of the manner in which the loyalty drive had been administered there and, with similar candor, warned WRA policy makers:

> I hear rumors that the "no" answers are likely to act as a basis for repressive action against those who gave them. No policy could be more unwise. In these cases it would only increase the hopelessness of the individual and make his rehabilitation virtually impossible. Certainly a sympathetic and constructive policy is required, one which penetrates beyond the verbalisms of "yes" and "no" to basic motivations, fears, and uncertainties.[10]

Opler called for a reregistration of the Issei based on the far milder loyalty question belatedly made available by Washington. Headquarters did not always take the good advice of its social scientists, whose views were often in direct conflict with those of camp administrators; but in this case it did, resulting in an amazing 98 percent of the Manzanar Issei ending up as "yes-yes" loyals. In an ironic twist of events, however, the posing of a wholly innocuous loyalty question to the Issei a month or so later left many young people, whom parents had forced into giving "no" answers, in the category of "disloyals." [11]

Another concession eventually made by camp administrators everywhere was the permitting of conditional responses, such as "Yes, but . . ." and "No, if . . ." But the acceptability of these qualified replies could not be immediately determined. Certainly not by the battery of eleven attorneys then on the WRA payroll in the nation's capital to assure that the detention "program is carried on within constitutional and statutory limits." No one had anticipated such an extreme reaction. Burdensome red tape prevented required policy decisions, however pressing, from being arrived at in an instant, which left camp administrators and their personnel as confused as evacuees. Little did they or the evacuees realize that answers to questions such as, "What would be the consequence of answering 'no'?" could not be determined by anyone less than Secretary of War Stimson.

To the Secretary, the widespread unrest and agitation were only confirming evidence of "vicious disloyals" stirring up revolt; not that the persecution, the continued effrontery to the evacuees' self-respect was becoming intolerable. It was only *after* the registration turbulence had been forcibly—even violently—suppressed that Stimson's desire and intent were to become known: that of weeding out the "traitors" from the patriots, the physical separation of all "rotten apples."

IV

Because much was unexplainable and confusing to all concerned, the recruitment drive was to reap only 1,181 volunteers from the ten camps. The quota imposed had been 3,000. In Hawaii, where the Washington-decreed evacuation had been effectively stymied, where a "loyalty test" was not imposed, where racial harmony was being actively encouraged, parents proudly offered up their sons to do battle for the Stars and Stripes. In a spontaneous burst of gratitude, nearly 10,000 Nisei rushed to volunteer, though the Hawaii quota for the all-Nisei combat team had been set at 1,500.[12] Even among the "enemy aliens" of the many Japanese families in Hawaii, fair play and magnanimous treatment were succeeding in promoting a spirited, often surprising Americanism, as a child's essay gives moving testimony:

> Father feels that the U.S. has been most generous in distributing masks free of charge to all the population of Hawaii, aliens as well as citizens, and you may be sure he is grateful. He also feels that the U.S. has been most fair with enemy aliens here in the island as compared with other countries.
>
> Although father is an enemy alien, he believes in the democracy, liberty and justice for which he knows the U.S. stands.[13]

The freedom and "benevolence" enjoyed by enemy nationals in Hawaii made more poignant the plight of the mainland Nisei, who had been maneuvered by a luckless set of circumstances into a position where even to express abhorrence of the barbarity legalized as war was tantamount to being a traitor. Finer emotions were not to hinder the soulless missions of murder, slaughter, and incineration of fellow human beings—the "golden opportunity" now opened to the Nisei—even if against one's own kin.

Provoked by the lukewarm response to recruitment and a definite surge toward noncooperation in a number of the camps, project directors were instructed to threaten inmates with severe penalties that went with violating the Espionage Act: Dissenters and parents were ordered to promptly desist from "sabotaging" the drive by advising sons, daughters, and colleagues not to register. Or risk facing a future of twenty years in prison, a $10,000 fine, or both.

In the desert outpost of Gila, camp-wide furor had been touched off by the announcement in the center publication, the *News Courier,* that a negative answer to Question 28 not coupled with a request for repatriation was a treasonable act.[14] On February 17, FBI chief J. Edgar Hoover advised Dillon Myer of impending agency plans to stamp out the resistance:

> I have been informed that representatives of the War Department are presently at the War Relocation Center at Rivers, Arizona, endeavoring to register and enlist loyal Japanese for service in the United States Army. On February 15, 1943, approximately seventy per cent of the Japanese who were contacted refused to sign the loyalty pledge and it has been determined that for the past few days fifteen Japanese aliens in this particular camp have been discouraging these individuals to

sign the loyalty pledge and have also persuaded the parents of these individuals to threaten to commit suicide if they enlist in the United States Army.

The representatives of the War Department and the Camp Director are desirous that the registration continue and have advised that they are of the opinion that the removal of these fifteen Japanese aliens would solve the present difficulty.

These facts have been discussed with the United States Attorney at Phoenix, Arizona who has authorized an emergency apprehension of the fifteen Japanese aliens and accordingly these individuals will be taken into Federal custody on February 26, 1943 . . .[15]

In camps everywhere, the Kibei spoke their piece, no matter the consequence. In Gila, the Project Director speedily took advantage of the FBI incursion to sweep the center clean of citizen dissenters proving irksome by their brazen exercise of the freedom of speech. Documentation left by James H. Terry, Gila's Project Attorney, betrays the arbitrary nature of camp-style justice meted out during this period of turbulence:

. . . permission was secured from the Director to remove from the Center a number of citizens, largely Kibei, who had shown most active resistance and hostility to the registration program. On February 26, 1943, agents of FBI and Internal Security with some cooperation from MP units removed 28 persons, half to Moab, half to FBI camps. In this exodus it appears that there were a few persons unjustly removed, and probably at least one case of mistaken identity. Few, if any, of the removals could have been sustained by competent legal evidence. They rested, generally speaking, on no more than a reasonable basis for suspicion.[16]

In relocation centers situated farther inland, removed from the hostile racial climate of California and Arizona, registration proceeded in a far more orderly manner. In being less frequently unnerved by racially slanted media bombardment, evacuees in such camps as Minidoka, Topaz, Amache, Rohwer, and others, felt considerably less threatened about their future, resulting in more wholesome interaction between the colony and their custodians.

The personal diplomacy of the Project Director also had much to do with a smooth-running camp in time of stress. In camp Minidoka, for example, public discussion forums had been held over a period of five days in advance of the arrival of the Army recruiters. The controversial questionnaire had been studied and discussed, grievances openly aired. In an inspired move on the part of Project Director Harry Stafford, the more respected elders of the community had been persuaded into taking over the awesome task of interpreting the meaning and importance of the drive, an assignment which they fulfilled with sensitivity and splendid diplomacy:

. . . since our children were born here, they belong here. Morally speaking, they do not belong to us, but to their country. I believe our attitude towards this principle will be extremely important for the future welfare and happiness of our own race in the United States. We should look to our own moral code in this matter.[17]

Minidoka took the lead in the number of volunteers.

Tule Lake, probably the largest of the camps, made the poorest showing. Only fifty-one volunteered. Everything had gone wrong.

Attempts of residents and the Community Council to obtain prior information about the impending registration had been brushed aside by the Project Director, who, on realizing that Washington's intent was not at all clear and definable, had decided that the responsibility for explaining the joint drive be left to Army recruiters.

Only after their arrival in Tule Lake were a series of mass meetings held—on the day and evening before the registration was to begin. Residents turned out in great number, as all were profoundly alarmed over the possible consequences of the latest governmental move and were eager for a firsthand clarification of the issues. But the standardized answers with which the recruiting team had come equipped proved embarrassingly inadequate, numerous questions were left unanswered, and the meetings ended up being cut short to prevent floor debate. As a matter of desperate urgency, a special forum was requested by the Issei so that questions of intense personal importance bedeviling the community could be thrashed out, but the request was turned down by camp administrators on the grounds that the loyalty decision was a matter to be decided privately.

In utter frustration and out of boiling anger at the tactless way the whole thing was being handled, few, if any, reported for registration.

> The authorities here, after ordering us to register, refused to discuss it at all. There were some questions in the registration questionnaire which we did not understand and which we wanted explained. The War Relocation Authority refused to explain anything. That made us mad. We wanted to know whether by answering certain questions one way or another, we would be considered disloyal to the United States. All we wanted from the War Relocation Authority was an explanation.[18]

A mimeographed question-and-answer sheet was subsequently distributed by camp authorities in response to hundreds of questions gathered up and tabulated by the Community Council. But evacuees bitterly resented their being excluded from a more direct give-and-take relationship with authorities and continued to feel that explanations were vague and intentions sinister.

Since few were willing to commit themselves in writing to something they could not understand, resistance to registration mush-roomed. Whole blocks vowed noncooperation: 5, 28, 35, 46, and 48 vowing absolute noncompliance.[19] One block, No. 28, voted to sign up for mass repatriation.[20] And in blocks of heightened agitation, ruf-fians began threatening bodily harm to individuals unwilling to join in what was fast becoming a camp-wide mobilization to frustrate the drive.

As had happened in Manzanar, people rushed to sign up for repatriation as a means of circumventing the signing of a document which many suspected might be used in any way the government de-sired. Posted notices warned of the dangers, especially to the Kibei, of committing themselves in writing: WRITTEN STATEMENTS OF YOUR "YES'S" OR "NO'S" WILL BE USED AGAINST YOU. [CONGRESS] COULD DEFINE ALL OF US DISLOYAL, THEY COULD CANCEL OUR CITIZENSHIPS MAKING US ENEMY ALIENS . . . THEN CONFISCATE LEGALLY OUR PROPER-TIES.[21] To stem the repatriation stampede, the issuing of such forms was suspended temporarily on February 18. The action ignited intense anger and resentment, especially when it was learned via the *Tulean Dispatch* that, contrary to previous notices, registration was mandatory for male citizens, whether or not they had filled out repatriation or expatriation forms.

To underscore the compulsory nature of the registration, the administration issued warnings of severe penalties to dissenters under the Espionage Act and announced that certain designated blocks would have to register every day; and to further emphasize the seri-ousness of the campaign, the Project Director, accompanied by Army officers, began appearing during the noonday lunch period at key mess halls to read off names of draft-age men expected to register.[22]

When, on February 19, a group of thirty-five youthful recalci-trants from a block under compulsory registration orders marched into the administration building to present a protest letter stating that they had no intention of registering "for Selective Service," but that they would sign "any time" for repatriation,[23] a decision was made for their arrest (with Washington approval) as an object lesson for all who would persist in the defiance. Two evenings later, twenty-four troops were sent in from the nearby garrison with clear-cut orders "not to fire unless one or more were knocked down or attacked." [24]

An account of what happened has been left by a Nisei high school instructor who, until then, had been serving as a registrar for the drive, but who ended up in the Leupp Isolation Center for refusing to register in support of the arrested youths.

. . . Among memories of Tule Lake, the night of February 21st will long be remembered by the residents. The above mentioned thirty-five boys, the majority of them aged seventeen, eighteen years were taken to Alturas County Jail at the point of bayonets. They were apprehended by an army of soldiers equipped with light machine guns, tear gas bombs and fixed bayonets. The prisoners were all residents of Block 42. The Commando equipped soldiers had surrounded that block and without much resistance had captured the thirty-five boys.

When all this armed might was being displayed there, the residents of the nearby blocks all gathered around and witnessed many pathetic, tearful scenes. They observed the capture of American-citizen niseis by American soldiers. . . .

These people had evacuated from the Pacific coast peacefully and obediently because they were told by the so-called J.A.C.L. that to do so was to aid America in her war effort. All their livelihood, their treasured homes, their fortunes were sacrificed so that America might be benefited. All those men, women, and children, brothers and sisters that looked on that night of February 21st will not forget the sight. After being forced to live behind barbed wire fences for nearly a year, this act of unnecessary sword-rattling was insult upon injury. Their faith in Democracy's so labeled, "with liberty and justice for all" was beginning to wave a little before their very eyes. There is a limit to human endurance, mankind will concede that. Many cried as they waved farewells to boys that they expected never to see again. Many little kid brothers and sisters clung to their elder brothers—sobbing and hysterically screaming that they wanted to go with them. Soldiers tore them apart as they were arrayed into the awaiting trucks. Countless people shouted "Banzais" to express to the departing young boys that they will not be forgotten.

That night and the nights and days following, the once peaceful camp of Tule Lake was a bedlam of activities and commotion. Tule Lake was a scene of mob violence, convulsive meetings, and the likes of a town in Ireland after an election day.

To the Japanese mind the army's provocation was an indignity and a challenge. So they accepted the challenge and all those having conviction and courage flatly refused to register, taking the similar stand as the thirty-five young boy prisoners of Block 42.

So it came to pass that because of a blind personnel staff at the Tule Lake Relocation Center . . . the Registration at Tule Lake was a dismal frustrated failure, compared to the accomplishments of the other relocation centers.[25]

The immediate reaction had been a block-by-block breaking up of resistance as terrified evacuees began rushing to register. But an inflamed, highly organized backlash to the Army violence quickly followed, turning Tule Lake into a seething cauldron of angry, frightened, and intimidated people.

JACLers and moderates who had sought to point out the merits of the WRA-Army objectives suffered beatings or were hounded and terrorized with threats of violence. Evacuees considered "friendly to the administration" were subjected to mass ostracism and compelled to eat at special tables set aside for "dogs." Even women were threatened with shaved heads by roving "pressure boys" who attempted by threats and intimidation to shore up the movement of mass defiance.

In time, few evacuees reported for work in the administrative area for fear of being labeled an *inu,* or a collaborator; and the flow of communication between the Caucasian personnel and colonists virtually ceased. Headquarters in Washington was given a firsthand report of the surly mood of the populace:

> Tule Lake wears a grim and belligerent face. . . . Only a few weeks ago the faces of the overwhelming majority of evacuees would dissolve into smiles when these people were encountered anywhere . . . Now, on approaching a colonist, he looks intently on the ground, oblivious of everything but the ground, apparently. Young men frequently jeer at members of the Administrative personnel and teachers . . . some colonists have shaken their fists at the Project Director . . . Other members of the appointed personnel have had similar experiences.[26]

The emotional uproar precipitated by the arrest of the thirty-five youths spurred the Community Council and the Issei advisory group to urge the administration to release the youths and to postpone further registration until community sanity could be restored. Upon the Project Director's refusal to cooperate, both bodies resigned in protest.

But in stumbling from blunder to blunder, local administrators, to their shock and disbelief, were to learn belatedly that refusal to fill in the questionnaire was not a violation of the Selective Service Act; that it did not carry penalties of up to twenty years in jail, as had been threatened; and that Project Director Coverley had had no legal right to order the arrest of the thirty-five young men. In fact, agents from the FBI who arrived on the scene on February 23 were greatly vexed at the WRA's unwarranted usurpation of FBI power:

> Mr. Gleysteen and Mr. Jacoby [FBI agents] demanded to know why arrests on suspicion of violating Selective Service regulations had been made when such matters were entirely within their province. . . . It was later made clear, as Mr. Edgar Hoover pointed out, that *there was no violation of the Selective Service Act involved.*[27] [Italics mine]

On seeking additional clarification, the War Department, on February 26, also handed down its belated—equally startling—determination that registration and the answering of the loyalty questionnaire by draft-age Nisei were *not compulsory.*[28]

After grappling briefly with the dilemma, a consensus was apparently arrived at to feign official unawareness of such War Department determinations as contradicted its initial order for maximum compliance: WRA persisted without letup in applying pressure on Kibei bachelor resisters everywhere to appear for registration, extending the deadline into early March. A sharply worded ultimatum was subsequently issued which stated that failure to meet a March 10 deadline "will be considered as having violated the orders of the War Department and the War Relocation Authority and subject to such penalties as may be imposed." [29] Headquarters was also apprised:

> Mr. Cozzens [Regional WRA Director] introduced a plan whereby known kibei were ordered to the registration hall. . . . Upon refusing to register, these boys were immediately transported to the CCC Isolation Camp [operated jointly by the Army and WRA] in waiting trucks.[30]

As the WRA-Army crackdown began in earnest, a packed suitcase became the Kibei's badge of defiant pride, and in its initial stage, arrested dissenters were given rousing send-offs. But the mood quickly soured, and internal security officers ran into a near-riot situation after a few attempts had been made to arrest suspected ringleaders in their sleep, many of whom slept nightly in the home of a different friend. In blocks harboring key agitators, a system had been worked out whereby a piercing shriek activated the mad ringing of mess hall gongs, which, in turn, roused residents of neighboring barracks to run out and form a human barricade around the victim's apartment or hiding place, a tactic which eventually put a stop to midnight pickups.[31]

As the movement of intransigence threatened to make a shambles of the loyalty drive at Tule Lake, an *inu* stepped forth to volunteer information about individuals then brilliantly masterminding the obstructionist activities. On two consecutive nights, clandestine meetings with the informant were held in a rented hotel room in the nearby village of Tule Lake, after which the collaborator was dropped off in the blackened shadows of the camp. An administrative memo betrays the plan of entrapment to be subsequently sprung on fellow evacuees:

> Within the next twenty-four hours or so, an event will take place which will eclipse anything like it seen heretofore on the Tule Lake Project. Arrests will be made of most of the real subversive leaders, the names of whom have been turned in by a member of the City Council. This young man's name, for obvious reasons, is being guarded with the utmost secrecy. . . .
>
> The plan is to pick up a number of young kibei bachelors who have not registered among whom will be two or three of our young informer's friends . . . He will then come to the Project Director to ask their release, insisting that they are all "good boys." Some will be retained.
>
> Twenty-four hours later, the real ring-leaders will be taken into custody and it will be inferred that some of the issei and kibei have squealed on the second group.[32]

The carefully staged betrayal and ensnarement added more fuel to the ferment, and even after another stunning attempt to frighten the community into acquiescence, nearly 3,000 residents persisted in their refusal to register. Record of the final violence meted out to Tule Lake dissidents has been left by a *San Francisco Chronicle* reporter:

> The Army moved in, followed by the FBI. There were mass arrests, and one hundred men were thrown into nearby jails and deserted C.C.C. Camps. When the prisoners were carried off they were surrounded by howling Japanese who yelled 'Banzai!'
> "You can't imagine how close we came to machine-gunning the whole bunch of them," one official said. "The only thing that stopped us, I guess, were the effects such a shooting would have had on the Japs holding our boys in Manila and China . . ." [33]

A job which authorities had hoped would take ten days took two months in Tule Lake, where registration pressure did not cease until April 7, 1943. By then, arrests had climbed to the 140 mark. [34]

To the end, the community was never informed that threats of severe penalties had been a mistake and unwarranted. [35] This and the extraordinary ex post facto discovery that the War Department regarded the filling in of the loyalty questionnaire as a wholly voluntary matter thus became more of the egregious secrets withheld from the evacuees throughout the war—especially the Nisei, Kibei, and Issei languishing like common criminals in isolation pens, FBI camps, and various county jails throughout the land.

V

The trauma of registration had hardly time to wear off when even more relentless assaults on the loyalty and integrity of the evacuees followed. As a direct result of the registration fiasco and its alarming "confirmation" of mass disloyalty, the WRA and its captive population came under near-constant fire from regional politicians, vituperative congressional critics, and a string of investigative committees and agencies in 1943.

The most unbridled campaign aimed at discrediting not only the evacuees but also their allegedly "soft-on-Japs" keepers was the one conducted by the House Un-American Activities Committee of the U. S. Congress, with a Californian, Representative John M. Costello, heading up its subcommittee probing the WRA program. Rather than a rigorous investigation of the WRA and camp conditions which could have proved constructive, the sensationally publicized procedure turned out to be a well-orchestrated fear and hate campaign aimed at terminating the WRA resettlement policy and driving the released evacuees back into the camps. Weeks before the hearings got under way (on June 8, 1943), headline-making absurdities had been fed the press—notably that the committee had evidence pointing to the existence of an underground army on the West Coast prior to Pearl Harbor, that thousands of Imperial troops and officers were now a part of the relocation center population, which the JACL-"dictated" WRA was overfeeding, overpampering, and overreleasing into un-suspecting American communities. Rumors of invasion and of *banzai* uprisings were once again fired up, revitalized. By the committee's manipulation of inflammatory headlines achieved by its clever timing of smear-type witnesses, including psychopaths fired from WRA camp positions, Representative Costello and his cohorts succeeded emi-nently in making the racist stereotype of cunning and treachery not only a West Coast but also a national fixation.

Another sinister development unnerved the interned Issei and Nisei, particularly those who had not disposed of land holdings. Now that the Nisei in the camps and on the battlefields were in no position to protect their interests, the state of California began the seizure of evacuee-held land, enticing the cooperation of its counties by promis-ing equal division of the bounty. Forthwith declared illegal were properties purchased by the Issei in the name of their citizen children, a practice which had gone unchallenged for decades. Since these and other practices which were not entirely honorable abounded during their exile, the reluctance to see the Issei and Nisei return became widespread. Abetted by negative publicity surrounding the registration-provoked tumult, regional agitation to prevent their return reached a white heat.

As one Californian put it, it was "a question of whether the white man lives on the Pacific Coast or the brown man." From Wash-ington state, a detractor warned in a widely distributed hate sheet: ". . . with moderate advantages of education and training they have shown themselves at times capable of better things. Americans . . . who regard our Jap citizens as a permanent class of dishwashers and furniture dusters are doomed . . . we must reach a general agree-ment as to what shall be done with them." And considering that ex-clusionist forces had largely succeeded in their plan of eviction and of repossessing what once belonged to the Issei and Nisei, many were no longer taking pains to hide the real reason behind the military-necessity rationale as an area-wide lockout campaign went into high gear. "We should strike now, while the sentiment over the country is right. The feeling of the East will grow more bitter before the war is over and if we begin *now* to try to shut out the Japanese after the war, we have a chance of accomplishing something. . . . Congress . . . could easily pass an act ordering all nationals of Japan to return after the peace . . . We don't want to see the time return when we have to compete with the Japanese again in this valley." [36]

VI

From beginning to end, the subjugation of the Japanese American minority was a project which garnered spirited support of Southern lawmakers. Among them was Senator A. B. "Happy" Chandler of Kentucky, who had headed up another of the several state and congressional investigatory subcommittees which sprang up after the Manzanar riot. Chandler was perhaps the first of the lawmakers to come out strongly for a policy which would separate the disloyals from the loyals in a special camp, a decision based on his lightning "fact-finding" tour of six relocation centers, during which the Senator inspired blazing headlines by declaring that the Issei and Nisei were ready to commit "almost any act for their Emperor," that 60 percent of them were disloyal.

With mingled dismay and disgust, an evacuee reflected on the infuriatingly cursory nature of the Senator's highly publicized junket: "Senator Chandler spent about two hours . . . riding through in a car with two armed soldiers on the running board to 'protect' him. These investigations are a hoax and we laugh about them whenever they come up in our conversation. But it's a bitter laughter when we read in newspaper releases by the committee: 'After careful investigation . . .' " [37]

On-the-spot reaction to the performance of the flamboyant Senator and his wife was further captured by Project Director Merritt of Manzanar in a letter speeded to the National Director. Parts of it read:

> . . . Enroute, Mrs. Chandler took the opportunity to express her very vigorous opinion about all Japanese, which was summarized by the expression that they should be put on shipboard and dumped in the ocean when Tokyo was bombed, and to various people she spoke vigorously against the whole present WRA policy, mentioning the cost to tax-payers, the disloyalty of the Japanese as a whole, making exception only of the kids in the Children's Village [the camp orphanage], and attempting to draw the Senator away from various things which interested him. At all times she was under the personal guard of one of the Army officers, who was instructed by the Senator to remain at her side to protect her from any danger. . . .
>
> The Senator was something of "all things to all men," telling the Japanese that he believed everyone was an American regardless of color and race, who in his heart believed in America, but on the side he was critical and I believe that if there is any point which he can hold up to criticism, he will do so. . . .
>
> Senator Chandler then had a long talk with representatives of the "Manzanar Free Press," expressing his feeling that all citizens of

Japanese ancestry should be loyal to the United States on account of what the country had done for them, 110,000 people having accumulated $200,000,000 in worldly goods in the United States. "It's a good country—it has been good to you and you must be loyal to it." . . .
That's all I know about senators.[38]

For politicians anxious to capitalize on the headline-making and vote-grabbing potential of keeping the "Jap issue" alive, it was a field day. Back in California, Earl Warren, who had gone on to defeat Governor Olson, was insisting that every evacuee being released was a potential saboteur; therefore a more rigorous military clampdown on the camps was called for, as were measures to keep the relocatees from returning to California.

Not a shred of legally airtight evidence had yet materialized which could support the wild accusations of disloyalty and subversion from all sides. But it was this steady buildup of racial antagonism and mistrust which was to result in Senate Resolution 166, passed on July 6, 1943, calling for a physical weeding out in the camps of all disloyals, a move which had been strongly urged by the Western Defense Command team of DeWitt and Bendetsen, seconded by Stimson, strongly recommended before a Senate committee by John J. McCloy, and endorsed by the JACL and nervous project directors everywhere.

Tule Lake was chosen to be converted into a maximum-security segregation center for having had the largest percentage of evacuees who refused to register or who answered "no" to the loyalty question (42 percent). Announced in the centers, forthwith, were the consequences of actions taken during registration. Those who fell in the disloyal category, and family members who wished to accompany them, were ordered to pack up for another move. To the amazement of all, more U. S. citizens ended up as disloyals than aliens (at a ratio of 43 percent to 17 percent), largely as a result of Question 28 not being modified for the confused and troubled Nisei, most of whom were minors. The nearly 3,000 evacuees who signed up for repatriation or expatriation during the registration turbulence had also been placed in the disloyal column.

In the fall of 1943, the surgical separation of those lumped as disloyals took place. Again in the zeal of democracy's standard-bearers to solve a "problem"—which was once nonexistent—decency and humanity got lost in the shuffle. Recalled Carey McWilliams:

I witnessed the departure of the segregants from some of the centers for Tule Lake and it was my most fervent wish that the entire membership of the Native Sons of the Golden West might have been present to see for themselves the anguish, the grief, the bottomless sorrow that this separation occasioned. They might then have been convinced —although I doubt that even these scenes would have convinced them—that the Japanese are not an inscrutable, unemotional, stoical, or mysterious people. The evacuees realized that those who were going to Tule Lake were destined to be deported, some day, to Japan; and that this was a final separation, a fateful farewell. Parents were being separated from children and children from parents; brother from brother, sister from sister. In those scenes was the stuff of timeless tragedy and excellent documentation for the one immortal theme: man's inhumanity to man.[39]

(9)
Tule Lake

The barbed-wire stockade surrounding the 18,000 people there was like that of the prison camps of the Germans. There were the same turrets for the soldiers and the same machine guns for those who might attempt to climb the high wiring . . .

The buildings were covered with tarred paper over green and shrinking shiplap—this for the low winter temperatures of the high elevation of Tule Lake. . . . No federal penitentiary so treats its adult prisoners. Here were the children and babies as well.

. . . To reach the unheated latrines, which were in the center of the blocks of fourteen buildings, meant leaving the residential shacks and walking through the rain and snow—again a lower than penitentiary treatment, even disregarding the sick and the children.

So also was the crowding of the 18,000 people in the one-story shacks . . . In the cells of a federal penitentiary there is no such crowding.

—CHIEF JUDGE WILLIAM DENMAN,
Ninth Circuit Court of Appeals, August 26, 1949

I

The story of the relocation camps of World War II would not be complete without thrusting deeper into the dark, hushed chapter that was Tule Lake, the relocation center turned into a segregation center, ultimately ending up as a "resegregation center" for democracy's discards. As was the entire experiment with concentration camps on American soil, Tule Lake was an extraordinary monument to the high cost of racism: an incredible waste of once highly industrious human lives on the inside and shocking military might squandered on the outside. Its maximum-security paraphernalia included a half-dozen tanks patrolling its outer perimeter and a guard contingent of campaign-equipped troops at full battalion strength.[1]

Had equally impressive preparations been made in the area of housing, sanitation, mess operation, health care, and other more human considerations, those forced to undergo another uprooting and resettlement might have been spared the debacle on debacle that followed. But a situation ripe for upheaval was set up in the "benign neglect"—or woeful miscalculation—which found over 18,000 segregants of widely divergent loyalties jammed into space meant for 15,000.

To recapitulate: It was some four months *after* the trauma of the bungled loyalty registration that consequences for actions then taken were finally disclosed: the war-duration incarceration of all evacuees believed to be disloyal at Tule Lake. Disloyalty with regard to descendants of the Japanese had been defined by Washington as follows:

Those who had answered "no" to Question 28 or had *failed* to or *refused* to answer the loyalty question. (Conditional responses also failed to fulfill the stringent requirement of "unqualified allegiance.")

Those who had applied for repatriation or expatriation to Japan.

Those whose loyalty was questionable *in the opinion of the Project Director* "because of previous statements or because of other evidence."

Those who had been denied leave clearance due to some unexplained adverse information found in dossier; also parolees from alien internment camps recommended for detention.

Except for repatriates and expatriates summarily denied review privileges,[2] mitigation hearings were permitted persons who wished to change their original answers. But the reexamination procedure, to determine whether or not petitioners were still adhering to "pro-Japanese views," merely reopened wounds; and the feeling of having been tricked and violated was irreversible among many who appeared before the hastily improvised hearing boards manned by junior camp functionaries often grievously prejudiced against the Kibei and Buddhists. Impassioned outbursts against a country which had jailed them, slandered them, and stripped them of rights had little to do with the petitioners' disloyalty to America or loyalty to Japan. Though generally interpreted as a dereliction of allegiance, it was a registering of grief, disappointment, anger, and sometimes rage, against what the Nisei and Kibei considered disloyalty on a mammoth scale—America's disloyalty to them.

Numerous Issei held to disloyalty as a means of "getting back to California" (Tule Lake was still within its borders), or because of the pervasive fear that declaring themselves loyal would mean being turned loose without resources. The top-security camp for disloyals, where leaves reportedly were to be strictly prohibited, appeared to offer a wartime haven for evacuees whose economic base had been shattered and for families worried over the possible reactivation of the draft.

Many Kibei chose Tule Lake imprisonment because of an overwhelming sense of frustration generated by obvious official distrust of the group, which clouded their hopes of ever being accepted in America. Segregation opened up the possibility of reunion with loved ones in Japan and of a future in the Orient, "where I won't have to live on the wrong side of the tracks just because my face is yellow." The hearings actually resulted in an increase of inmates requesting transfer to Tule Lake.[3]

Also undergoing their third relocation within a year were individuals "who wish to accompany family members." Many who fell in this category had no choice. There were grandparents, close relatives, the old, the young, the enfeebled, who could not be left behind. There were youths resignedly accompanying elderly parents who wished to end their days in Japan. There were school-age children by the thousands. Only those over seventeen years of age were given the right to defy parental pressure and stay behind.

In the months of September and October 1943, the mass reshuffling took place. While the shipment of 9,000 "disloyals" to Tule Lake got under way, about the same number of Tulean "loyals" were ordered out and redistributed among the other centers.

This left approximately 6,000 original settlers remaining in Tule Lake, many of whom had quickly embraced the disloyalty stigma merely to avoid being evicted. Over 1,000 of them were "loyals" who simply refused to be expelled, who decided to take a stand against being forever pushed about. Some balked at subjecting the sick, the old, and infirm in their family to another grueling move to distant, unfamiliar surroundings. And at a time of sharp cutbacks in employment, individuals with fairly decent means of earning their $16 a month were unwilling to give them up. Many quickly stepped into even better jobs, which opened up with the mass eviction.

Only much later did these technically loyal residents legitimatize their "disloyalty," to placate authorities, by signing up for repatriation.[4]

II

Called in as administrator of this troubled and undoubtedly most fortified city then in the Western Hemisphere was a former Southern Californian, Raymond R. Best. Educated in Los Angeles, a veteran of the Marine Corps in World War I, and father of a son in the Air Corps, Best had had ample experience in dealing with "troublemakers" of the Japanese variety. Moab, and later Leupp, the Stalinist-style citizen isolation camps for political dissenters, had been set up by Raymond Best.[5]

Being one in whom distrust of the "Japanese" was perhaps more than slightly ingrained (in the wake of his initial evacuee involvement), Best was an unhappy choice for a position requiring infinite tact and understanding, considering that only a small minority could be considered disloyal in an ideological sense—when half the population were children under eighteen years of age.

Doubly lamentable was the fact that to Washington decision makers suffering ever-increasing pangs of a "constitutional conscience," the wretched multitude corraled at Tule Lake represented, at long last, impressive justification for the harsh preventive detention measures heretofore taken.[6] Segregation had finally resulted in the concentration of "bad apples" to be conveniently expelled at war's end from American soil.

Unaware of this pervasive bureaucratic assumption, transferee activists and center politicians had no idea of the drastic consequences which would follow attempts to organize for better conditions. In voting in so many "no-no" transferees to head the "Negotiating Committee" of the hastily formed protest faction, the *Daihyo Sha Kai*,[7] inordinate apprehension of local and Washington administrators had been aroused. Dossiers were already in Best's possession on most Kibei activists voted into office, including that of George Kunitani (pseud.), a twenty-eight-year-old transferee from Jerome chosen as head spokesman.

Kunitani's "first impressions" of deplorable center conditions and of the tactless, surprisingly testy Project Director are worth noting as a preface to events to follow. Since evacuee mail underwent lawless snooping and scrutiny at times of heightened tension, raw material for analysis (such as Kunitani's letter to a Community Analyst acquaintance back in Jerome, which follows) was often sent on surreptitiously to WRA headquarters. More than likely, Kunitani's letter had ended up back in Tule Lake—on the desk of Project Director Best.

On my second day here I went to see Mr. Raymond R. Best, the Project Director, with Rev. Kai, and Messrs. Kimura and Kobayashi. We were more than disappointed in him. Therefore a call from Dr. Opler [Tule Lake Community Analyst] coming at the heel of my unimpressive meeting with Mr. Best was certainly welcome. If I may say so, Dr. Opler seems to be just the type of a man needed in a center such as this. Of course, it is too premature for me to comment extensively about Dr. Opler as yet. My skepticism about Mr. Best lies in the fact that he does not seem to understand the Japanese at all. To understand the residents will have to be the prerequisite for Mr. Best especially when he has been bestowed with the responsibility to operate a center of this nature, the likes of which does not exist in this country. Unless he makes the right start, his task will become unnecessarily strenuous. He certainly has left us with an unforgettable *bad* impression when he started his conversation by saying, "I don't recognize any group activity, I don't care what you have done in the past, but as far as this center is concerned you shall represent no group or groups of people; I am not interested in your demands." Imagine, a project director speaking in that tone!! We went there to meet him, not to make demands or even a request! It was very rude of him to receive us in that manner, especially in view of the fact that Mr. W. O. Melton, the Assistant Project Director for Jerome who accompanied our train to Tule, was the one who introduced us to Mr. Best. I don't know the real reason for his hot-tempered behavior, but if he thinks that he can employ such high-handed methods in administering us, I'm afraid he is making a big mistake. Well, so much for Mr. Best. If you can make any suggestion to him, I deem it wise for you to do so, not only for us but also for Mr. Best so that he may have less difficulty in running this unique center.

The conditions existing at this center are a mystery to me. The facilities, the sanitations, the administration, in fact, much as I would like to appraise favorably in at least one phase . . . I can't find a thing . . . And I thought Jerome was a hell hole! Even the set-ups among the residents such as the co-op seem to be corrupted. There is a definite clean-up job to be done and I think the newcomers will do the work. The most pressing item appears to be dust control. Next should come sanitation work in showers and lavatories. It would be a disgrace for the State of California which claims such a high standard of living to let an unsanitary condition such as this exist within its own borders. The filthy condition of shower-rooms and toilets are beyond words. . . . The over-crowdedness of this center should be cared for as soon as humanly possible. It was really a crime to induct so many people without proper facilities. Every recreation hall is filled with bachelors. In some instances, two separate families are grouped up in one unit.[8]

III

It was Project Director Best's mishandling of a farm accident which had first spurred Kunitani and a number of concerned Kibei into furious activity.

A truck carrying farm hands had overturned, seriously injuring five of the twenty-eight occupants, killing a segregee from Topaz. When it was learned that an inexperienced minor had been the driver of the truck, all were quick to blame the WRA. A work stoppage ensued.

Best's first mistake was to abort, by making the public address system inoperable, a massive public funeral for which he had declined to give permission.[9] The farm group and the protest committee had, nevertheless, pressed ahead with their plans; and thousands had turned out for the ceremony to honor the memory of Mr. Kashima, whose tragic end symbolized the suffering and injustice which had befallen them all.

When it was learned during the same day that the monthly compensation for the widow of the deceased would be a scant two-thirds of the small $16-a-month salary of a farm worker, shock waves of anger and disbelief reverberated throughout a community already overwrought by what they considered a callously inhuman act on the part of the Project Director.

At this point, even the "old Tuleans"—the more conservative element in the community—fully backed the spirited young activists who sprang to the ramparts to organize and take action against the fast-accumulating abuses and injustices, unintimidated by the power arrangement which had them chronically pushed around, inured to deplorable conditions. Though it was unheard of to speak sharply or defiantly to Caucasians in demanding one's rights, most agreed that it was high time for new tactics.

The farm work stoppage was now deliberately calculated to bring matters to a crisis stage. The 2,900-acre operation supplied tons of produce to the Army and Navy, to various relocation centers and their military garrisons. The saving of the crops depended on negotiating a swift settlement.

On October 26, the *Daihyo Sha Kai* leaders squarely confronted administrators with the complaints of the community. The no-nonsense intensity of spokesman Kunitani and others comprising the Negotiating Committee caught the Project Director completely off guard. Withering under the barrage of charges—of overcrowding, deplorable sanitation, wretched living and working conditions, insufficiency of milk for children, deficiencies in the diet—the Project Director could do little but acknowledge the validity of many of the grievances, blaming Congress for the disastrous speed-up in segregation. But Best did not take kindly to being presented with "demands" which, among other things, included the WRA's recognition of a prisoner of war status (under the Geneva Convention) for all Tuleans; their accepting the responsibility for the farm accident; the confinement of farm production to only Tule Lake needs; and the "completion" of segregation by a physical separation of the loyals and "fence-sitters" in an area separate from those desiring to make their future in Japan.

As for the crucial farm impasse, hot words were exchanged over more decent compensation for the injured, safeguards against accidents, and over the ten-day work stoppage then jeopardizing some

$500,000 worth of vegetables. But even as he went through the motions of negotiations, Project Director Best had already arranged for the importation of strikebreakers.

Not until a few days later did some 800 "retroactively" terminated farm workers discover through a San Francisco newspaper the real reason behind their summary layoff: Quartered outside the camp were "loyals" from other relocation centers working for a dollar an hour, making in two days what Tuleans normally made in a month!

IV

On November 1, 1943, the National Director, Dillon Myer, visited Tule Lake. The protest group quickly organized a demonstration involving over 5,000 men, women, and children, hoping this would impress the Director with the community-wide extent of its discontent. With Kibei youths in charge, a human barricade encircled the administration building for three hours while within, Myer and administrative heads were confronted with charges of widespread neglect, incompetence, and corruption. A list of eighteen demands were made for an immediate redress of grievances, including retroactive restitution for farm workers terminated "in bad faith," the upgrading of food allowed per person from twenty-seven cents to forty-five cents per day; the establishment of an evacuee governing body, and the resignation of Best and other staff workers accused of being imperious, inept, and harboring feelings of racial superiority.[10]

As strong-arm squads prevented the Caucasian personnel from taking leave of the building, the more excitable among the staff members viewed the sudden surly and disrespectful behavior as a prelude to massacre. Troops were alerted and "tanks in the military area were warmed up" to charge in at a moment's notice.[11] But lacking sufficient provocation, the meeting had ended in orderly Japanese fashion—following a brief address by Myer—climaxed by the thousands of milling demonstrators being commanded to respectfully bow to the National Director before being allowed to disperse.

Yet, the mammoth demonstration had thrown those of uneasy conscience into a paroxysm of unreasoning terror. Some fled to a nearby town. A rash of resignations followed. Construction of a manproof fence separating the "white" quarters from the colony was immediately begun, and sweeping police powers, including the authority to call in the Army, were given WRA security officers. Macabre rumors soon had the surrounding countryside horror-struck.

Not all papers and news services sought official verification of the rumored camp insurrection, which had been immediately picked up by the media. Wildly distorted stories proliferated, some of them no doubt giving rise to the grotesquely garbled version given the President by the Attorney General:

MEMORANDUM FOR THE PRESIDENT

Serious disturbances have recently taken place at a relocation center of the War Relocation Authority at Tule Lake . . . Five hundred Japanese internees armed with knives and clubs shut up Dillon Myer and some of his administrative officers in the administration building for several days. The Army moved in to restore order.

The feeling on the West Coast is bitter against the administration for what they think is its weak policy towards the Japanese. I believe that we should make an immediate FBI investigation, and indict if any crimes have been committed. . . . Hoover, however, hesitates to make the investigation on account of the presence of the Army, and because the War Relocation Authority has heretofore made it difficult for the FBI agents to get the facts.

I suggest that it would make for better cooperation if you direct that the investigation be made. I enclose a memorandum which you may wish to send to me.[12]

V

The Army invasion of Tule Lake actually took place three nights *after* the protest demonstration, triggered by a relatively minor scuffle.

Trucks driven off by Caucasians had sent a swarm of evacuees racing toward the "white" area, determined to prevent what they suspected was the clandestine loading of food "belonging to us" for strikebreakers. In the National Director's own words: "The advance of this crowd was resisted by several WRA internal security officers, one of whom tripped, struck his head on a stone, and was then struck by evacuees with clubs. No other persons were injured." [13] Seeing the crowd then headed toward his residence, the Project Director instantly ordered in the Army—tanks, jeeps with mounted machine guns, and a swarm of campaign-equipped troops—the swift, keen precision with which it happened giving substantial indication that it might have been planned.

"Most pathetic individual in the area was a San Francisco news photographer who had not been allowed to take his camera into the premises," reported Portland's *Oregonian* of November 6, 1943. "It's just like Salerno and my box is outside," the newsman kept raving in a fit of frustration, as eighteen startled evacuees trapped by floodlights and challenged by guns and bayonets became the first prisoners —soon afterward, the first of the casualties.[14]

Among them was a baffled sixteen-year-old who later recounted the circumstances surrounding his arrest and three weeks' incommunicado detention:

> On the night of November 4, 1943, we were, as usual, in the Motor Pool for we were working from 3:00 P.M. to 11:00 P.M. on that nightshift. About 8:30 P.M., Mr. Jarrett, Mr. Zimmer, and a few other Caucasians came in with requests for farm trucks. . . . when they presented the requests, the signature of the Motor Pool head was missing. I told them that we could not issue trucks without the proper papers and signatures . . . so I turned and asked my fellow workers in Japanese what I should do. The head dispatcher came and took care of the matter.
>
> Nothing more happened until about 9:15 P.M. About that time, we noticed a commotion outside and we saw the army coming in. Everyone thought it was nothing until the soldiers began to charge. A few of the workers thought it better to leave but one of the older fellows said that we would not be in any danger for we worked in the Motor Pool and should be there. But the soldiers came in and told us to get out or suffer the consequences. We left, and as we ran towards the colony (for they were making us run), Captain Archer came up and stopped us. Without a word, we were taken into the Administrative building and lined up. We were forced to keep our hands above our heads until they took us individually for questioning. This was difficult since you couldn't link hands. Some of the fellows we saw in there were bloody.
>
> When I was being questioned, Mr. Jarrett came up and said that I was the one who spoke in Japanese and told them not to give him a truck. After my questioning, we were taken to the hospital and kept there under guard for four days. On November 8th, we were taken into the Army compound and kept there with no trial or anything until we moved into the Army Stockade. I was questioned a few times during my stay there. On November 28th, I was released.
>
> At the time of this incident and my stay in the Stockade, I was 16 years of age. But when I told the authorities they would not believe me, and insisted I must be older. . . . While I was in, some men were questioned or third-degreed and some were hurt or physically injured. I didn't know what the "politics" was all about, but it struck me as a big mistake. The only reason I was stuck in there was because I had a night-job in the Motor Pool . . .[15]

Throughout the nation, the "Jap rebellion" received spirited media coverage, wreaking havoc upon WRA relocation efforts. "For a week or so in early November, Tule Lake displaced the battlefronts in top news interest with the West Coast press," the WRA noted. Lurid accounts of the uprising, based largely on imaginings of Caucasian ex-employees, served as fodder for the racist press, inspiring such editorials as the following:

> It's something of a relief to learn that Army forces—"some of whom are veterans of the fighting in the Pacific area"—have taken over at

the Tule Lake internment center for disloyal Japanese and, presumably, "have the situation well in hand."

The War Relocation Authority policy of coddling and kidgloving these treacherous, fanatical, insolent monkey men finally has resulted in an incident which promises to clean up the whole mess.

Protecting the Nation from the thousands of disloyal Japanese rounded up after Pearl Harbor is a military policing job, not a welfare worker's tea party.[16]

VI

With the Army seizure of Tule Lake, fear, regimentation, and mass repression became the dominant theme. Effectively wiped out was the "weak policy toward the Japanese" troubling coastal patriots. The segregation center was soon an armed camp, crawling with troops, security patrols, and FBI agents.

A 7 P.M. to 6 A.M. curfew was strictly enforced, and arrest followed arrest of marked men. Tear gas was used on crowds which failed to disperse when ordered. Schools closed. Recreational activities ceased. Work crews were slashed to a minimum.

Though mute, the community response was angry and impassioned. Especially resented was the wholesale purge of suspected dissidents from work crews, a program vigorously pursued by the Commandant as a means of cutting the payroll and getting more intensive work per man. The residual work force soon found itself in the embarrassing position of being categorized as "proadministration." As time went on few, if any, reported for work for fear of being considered *inu*. Outside of hospital and mess operations, all services soon ground to a halt.

Meanwhile, the Negotiating Committee attempted to bridge the widened gap between the community and the administration, unaware that political rivals were busily making discrediting reports to the Commandant that they were a "Jerome faction" and not representative of Tule Lake residents. Attendance at a November 14 Army-WRA mass outdoor assembly had been earlier ordered by the Commandant, during which the committee, along with Army and WRA administrators, was to make its report to the community. But since a day earlier, Kunitani and his liaison team had been abruptly informed that the Army refused to recognize them as representatives of the entire community, they failed to get the people out.

Not one evacuee, in fact, showed up for the impressively staged rally, an insubordination which was to bring on staggering consequences. The zero attendance was witnessed by a lone WRA official:

Colonel Austin . . . arrived at the scene a little before the set time with a detachment of M.P.'s. Armed guards were stationed around the stage and armored cars made a cordon around the ground where an audience was supposed to gather. . . . At two o'clock, no one came and there was no sign of anyone coming to hear his speech. Like an Army man, true to his tradition, Austin began his speech. No one was there. Not a single soul! Colonel Austin spoke to the air. . . . It was a pitiful sight which I cannot forget.[17]

Suspect insurgents were speedily dealt with. Arrest orders quickly went out for all members of the Negotiating Committee, leaders of the farm group, and others suspected of having a hand in the movement of noncooperation. Word of the roundup raced through the project and many men went into hiding.

Almost immediately, martial law was declared to give the military unchecked powers of search and seizure; and in the days to follow, terroristic night raids reminiscent of the Gestapo's midnight knocks snared one suspect after another. On November 26, a camp-wide dragnet was instituted as a result of the community's refusal to betray their hidden leaders. The deployment of a vast army of soldiers enabled two teams to work from each side of the camp toward the center firebreak. Squads of MPs made a thorough search of the grounds, barracks, living quarters, and personal possessions, with WRA security officers assisting in the assault. To justify this massive intrusion of privacy, a wide variety of personal property was seized as contraband, such as wooden canes, binoculars, hatchets, short wave radios, rice, homemade sake, etc.[18]

In this all-out drive to crush the resistance, Kunitani and three of his Negotiating Committeemen proved too elusive for the Army dragnet. Ninety other men were pulled in during the sweep—mostly "no-no" Hawaiians from Jerome and Topaz, whose role as strident social critics and fist-swinging antiadministration "toughs" was no longer being tolerated.

The violent expansion of arrests led to the building of a prison setup within the fenced-in "white area." High barbed wire fencing and four guard towers impressively set apart the six detention barracks, referred to by the colony as the "stockade." Washington, however, did not recognize it as a prison within a concentration camp. Officials scrupulously referred to it as the "segregated area," "Area B," or the "separated area" in their correspondence.[19]

Within the stockade, human rights were all but stamped out in order that the community might be kept in ignorance of what was occurring within. Mail was censored and held up for long stretches at a time. As inmates were kept in strict incommunicado detention, medical attention and access to the base hospital were denied, as were visits from family and friends. Authorities eventually stopped the daily waving to wives and children when inmates were found weeping on the wire gate of the compound. A twelve-foot-high beaverboard wall was built to obstruct the view.

VII

As a protest against the Army's suppressive tactics, Tuleans were to persist for more than two months in their stubborn adherence to the *Daihyo Sha Kai* policy of *"status quo"* calling for unconditional release of stockade victims, passive noncooperation with the military, and absolute noncapitulation to official demands that they select a new set of community leaders. Even in hiding, the dissident delegation managed to keep the spirit of resistance amazingly buoyed by channeling directives through a satellite "Communications Committee," the *Renraku-iin.*

But the price of noncooperation began to take its toll on the embattled community. Along with the futility of jobless and hopeless days, young and old suffered acutely from the constant disruption in services: from sudden cutoffs in the milk supply, shortages in food, hot water, fuel, warm clothes. In the freezing cold of midwinter, according to a Tulean, "many people with children had no shoes, no money, no clothing. Some of the children were beginning to go barefooted." [20]

As the health of residents became imperiled, the Army made its first major concession: Whether suspected of antiadministration behavior or not, every worker in the coal and garbage crew was restored to employment. Jeeps and armored cars were also pressed into service to accelerate delivery of the desperately needed coal and foodstuffs.

Quiet despair within the distraught community soon erupted into fault-finding and recriminations. Although Kunitani and his fugitive colleagues had enjoyed wide approval at the outset as men with mettle enough to stand up for evacuee rights, the hardships of Army rule enabled the opposition—"old-timers" who made up the moderately inclined, administration-favored minority—to spread the seed of disaffection. They blamed the Army's regressive tactics and the misery of prisoners in the stockade on *Daihyo Sha Kai* lack of diplomacy and extremist ardor. The tension and conflict sharpened, more than ever, the differences between "loyals" and "disloyals." Even among the ranks of the once passionately loyal *Renraku-iin* retainers, growing public cynicism raised troubling doubts; and a few among the team of seven soon lost total interest and enthusiasm for their thankless—and dangerous—role as liaison for sought-after leaders in hiding.[21]

Stung by the mounting wave of criticism, and fearing a complete loss of prestige, Kunitani and others turned themselves in to FBI agents on December 1, 1943. On the assumption that the agents from Justice would grant them a fair hearing, a complete record of *Daihyo Sha Kai* activities was also handed over to the FBI. But the webwork of tyranny was absolute. The FBI men promptly marched the activist leaders over to the Commandant, who immediately incarcerated them in the "little stockade," which was made up of flimsy isolation tents devoid of heat.[22] After surviving eleven freezing days and nights under heavy guard, Kunitani and others were thrown in with the main stockade population.

The desperately awaited visit to Tule Lake on December 13 of the San Francisco-based Spanish Consul found supporters and relatives of stockade detainees in a thorough state of imbalance—many furious that the Consul had not come sooner. The high-handed treatment, the searing humiliations, the unbridled invasion of rights had heightened their emotional ties with Japan. Citizen wives and relatives hysterically implored the Consul to report the outrage without delay to Tokyo, insisting that with the total abrogation of citizenship rights at Tule Lake, they had a right to be considered "Japanese" and were entitled to the intercession of the Japanese Government.

The Consul raised grievous doubts that the Embassy would, in any way, interfere in matters involving citizens of the United States; but the emissary felt he had succeeded in urging the Commandant to permit the selection of an evacuee arbitration team to help in resolving the stockade issue. After the Consul's departure the following day, seven block representatives were selected to negotiate with the Commandant. But, without warning, these men also ended up in the stockade.

Pulled in, likewise, by order of the Commandant—now determined to make a clean sweep of all vestige of leadership—were many of the remaining block representatives. A mere handful were to escape this second dragnet.[23]

VIII

The first of three hunger strikes to be undertaken by stockade inmates in a fit of desperation was begun on New Year's Day, 1944 —a move triggered by a run-in with guards. In Kunitani's words: ". . . the detainees in the front row were asked by the soldiers to remove the foodstuffs [cakes, fruits, and cigarettes sent in over the holidays] from the barracks to the truck. Some detainees hesitated and, being slow in their actions, were kicked and prodded with bayonets. This was the direct reason which started the detainees on the hunger strike . . ."[24]

Notwithstanding Army efforts to keep news of a situation capable of triggering international repercussions from going beyond the stockade walls, rumors swiftly circulated throughout the colony.

Meetings were held at the Mess Halls almost every day to determine what to do to save the people in the stockade. Block 20 decided to send women and young girls to see if any negotiations could be made in releasing of the representatives of its block. Men did not go because they might be detained. . . . Different women went on three different days and talked with the lieutenant, but it was very definite that the block Daihyosha could not be released . . .[25]

In face of administration efforts to keep all stockade happenings confidential, daredevil Kibei youths were taking the risk of carrying on yelling conversations with inmates whenever the sentry was found not to be at his post. A letter from underground activists, dated January 5, 1944, finally reached the Spanish Embassy in Washington:

Dear Excellency,
May we be as selfish as to request your Excellency's attention concerning the incident at Tule Lake Center, Newell, California.

When your representative, Consul de Amat, was here on December 13, 1943, Lt. Colonel Austin, Commanding officer at the Tule Lake Center took a very kind attitude and requested the Japanese internees to send seven elderly persons to negotiate with him for the release of the then 169 persons confined in the army guard house. Consul de Amat was pleased with Mr. Austin's attitude, and left for Manzanar. Immediately after the Spanish Consul's departure, Mr. Austin's attitude turned icy cold and when he attempted to force the Japanese internees to accept his wishes and failed, he arrested the seven elderly persons mentioned above as well as approximately thirty more people.

At present more than 200 Japanese, including our nine representatives and delegates of the Negotiation Committee, are confined in the army barracks. Furthermore:

1. Japanese people who are detained in the stockade are being inhumanly treated from the military authority.
2. The food and coal situation of the people held in custody in the army guard house is very acute.
3. The army is ordering Japanese held in custody to forced labor at the point of a gun.
4. There have been cases where Japanese in custody received brutal beating and serious injury without any reason (as in the case of Mr. Nogawa and others, who are now confined to the hospital).

For the reasons above, all the two hundred people held in custody have gone on a hunger strike since January 1, 1944. . . .

Consequently may we request of your Excellency two favors, namely:

1. To report to the Japanese government the facts mentioned above . . .
2. [To investigate] the lives and health conditions . . .[26]

Almost immediately, a second letter reached the Spanish Ambassador. This one is significant in that the dispatch is dated January 6, 1944. The mass hunger fast had been terminated on that very afternoon—"after six days and two meals"—as tempers flared in close-packed conflict.

Dear Excellency:

Two hundred and seven Japanese leaders, including all the representatives of the Negotiation Committee, of the Japanese residents at the Tule Lake Camp held in the army prison have been on a Hunger Strike from January 1, 1944. Without food for a week, they are now weak and many cannot stand up . . . Relatives and residents are anxious about the lives of these 207 Japanese. Should they or any of them die, there may be a serious resentment on the part of the Japanese here and elsewhere toward those who were in a position to prevent but failed to prevent such deaths.

Therefore, may we humbly but urgently appeal to Your Excellency two favors:

1. Please send to Foreign Minister Shigemitsu, Tokyo, Japan, at once the following wireless message:

TO: FOREIGN MINISTER SHIGEMITSU
TOKYO, JAPAN

207 JAPANESE LEADERS, INCLUDING ALL REPRESENTATIVES, OF JAPANESE RESIDENTS AT TULE LAKE SEGREGATION CAMP HELD IN ARMY PRISON HAVE BEEN ON HUNGER STRIKE FROM JANUARY 1, 1944 STOP WITHOUT FOOD FOR A WEEK, THEY ARE NOW WEAK AND MANY OF THEM CANNOT STAND UP STOP THESE JAPANESE ARE LEADERS OF JAPANESE LOYAL TO JAPAN IN THE INCIDENT WHICH BEGAN NOVEMBER 4, 1943 STOP PLEASE MEDIATE IMMEDIATELY IN BEHALF OF JAPANESE IN TULE LAKE INCIDENT BEFORE MANY JAPANESE LEADERS DIE OF HUNGER STRIKE.
TEMPORARY TULE LAKE JAPANESE COMMITTEE

2. Please send a Spanish diplomatic representative immediately to Tule Lake . . .[27]

These and other emotion-laden communications spurred the following appeal to the State Department from the Spanish Embassy. It was delivered by hand on January 11, and read in part:

URGENT MEMORANDUM . . . TO THE STATE DEPARTMENT

For a better understanding of the complaints of these internees, the Spanish Embassy enclose herewith copy of two of the many similar letters which this Embassy has been receiving . . .

The Spanish Embassy is inclined to believe, in view of reports from its Representative, that the discontent and unrest of the internees would be greatly relieved if the "Committee for Negotiations" and the aforementioned group were to be granted their freedom. No doubt among the 204 detainees there are many Japanese who are American citizens, Second Generation who are outside the protection of the Spanish Embassy. Nevertheless, this Representation kindly asks indulgence for all in said group, entreating the Department of State, with the utmost urgency, to use its good office with the corresponding authorities that they may exert their usual benevolence and humanitarian spirit, to avert major disorders which threaten for the near future, and release not only the Japanese proper, but the Japanese American citizens . . .

The Spanish Representative in San Francisco can serve as arbiter if the American authorities should so desire, to obtain from the internees at Tule Lake their formal promise that once the release of the group in question is granted, they will return to complete normality.[28]

In a memo written and sent off the very day the appeal from the Embassy had been received, the Secretary of State alerted Stimson to the "vital nature of this problem arising from the desire of this government to keep open negotiations with the Japanese Government, looking toward future exchange operations through which Americans in Japanese hands may be repatriated and to do its utmost for the relief and protection of Americans under Japanese control . . ."[29]

Misjudging the seriousness of its international implications, the Secretary of War remained resolute in championing the Army-WRA handling of the Tule Lake malcontents. Historically known for his strong anti-Japanese prejudices, Stimson may have readily been persuaded by the local Commandant that incommunicado detention was no more than a mild form of pest control. For it was Stimson, himself, who had insisted upon a policy of rigorous precautionary confinement for all dissidents whose basic aim and purpose, the Secretary firmly believed, was "to cause U. S. authorities as much trouble as possible." He therefore advised Secretary of State Hull in the strongest of terms:

. . . the Spanish Embassy suggests the advisability of permitting the internees now held in the separate area, numbering slightly over 200, to rejoin the main body. I have already stressed the fact that this element is vicious. To restore them to the main body would only serve to bring on once more a reign of terror, under which the more peacefully inclined would be driven by threats and by force to an attitude of non-cooperation. In the interests of the majority of the residents, as well as to facilitate an orderly administration free from incident, the Spanish Embassy's proposal must be rejected. . . .[30]

Charges of abuse were categorically denied by the Secretary of War:

Japanese in the stockade, so-called, are not being inhumanely treated. They are being treated in the same manner as those in the main area, with the exception that they are more closely confined and are subject to two daily roll calls. The food and coal situation for those in the stockade is identical with that of the main area residents. No person in the stockade or elsewhere has been forced to labor at the point of a gun. . . . No internee in the stockade or elsewhere has been brutally beaten by any representative of the United States Government.[31]

The mass demonstration of November 1, involving an immense number of Tulean residents, had brought on a series of governmental probes of the local administration, much of it substantiating *Daihyo Sha Kai* charges of mismanagement and neglect—leading Stimson, himself, to advise the Secretary of State that "certain irregularities in the distribution of food were uncovered by the Federal Bureau of Investigation, and . . . curative steps were immediately instituted." A WRA memo of December 7, 1943, to headquarters recounted other instances of administrative malfeasance:

At Tule Lake there had been considerable comment regarding stealing and mishandling of property, particularly food stuffs. . . . Our investigation which was conducted by myself, the Project internal security, and members of internal security of other projects detailed for that purpose, revealed very conclusively that some stealing had been carried on. Every case, however, pointed to the activities of one individual who was killed in a railroad accident in his car prior to the conclusion of the investigation. . . .[32]

It should be noted that although several persons appointed to the head property position at Tule Lake appeared qualified on paper, they were incapable of administering the work and relieved of their duties. There had been three changes in this position within a year's time.

Mr. [Tom Nash] was requested to resign because of his unreliability as a direct result of excessive drinking of alcoholic beverages. On two different occasions within as many weeks, Mr. Nash appeared in the center in an intoxicated condition. . . . Mr. Nash further proved his inability to administer the operation of mess management particularly during the segregation program primarily because of his excessive "drinking" which resulted in his inability in handling the personnel under his direction; his inability to carry out orders and conform to established policies.

Regarding Mr. Tom Nash and others who were either requested to resign or transfer from the center because of their inability to administer their positions . . . such as, Mr. Lee in the Accounting, Mr. Weiss in Property, Mr. Kallam, Mr. Slattery and several others,

. . . changes have already been effected in addition to other proposals for changes in the staff . . .[33]

[Reparagraphed by author]

The Tule Lake "riot" had exploded into headlines at the very moment when the lives and safety of over 6,000 American detainees in Japanese prison camps hung precariously in the balance as they awaited exchange ships. In two years of war, fewer than 3,000 persons had been exchanged; and extremely delicate negotiations had been carried on by the State Department to accelerate the fullest possible repatriation of U. S. citizens and to enable food, clothing, and medical supplies to be speeded to Americans in enemy hands.

From data no doubt gleaned from the sensationalist media coverage in the coastal area, Radio Tokyo announced on November 8, 1943: "The American Army has entered the Tule Lake Center with machine guns and tanks, and is intimidating the residents." [34]

With the follow-up report from the Spanish Embassy concerning the stockade, the 200 men being held therein, and the extraordinary Army seizure of a camp full of civilian detainees, Tokyo called an abrupt halt to prisoner-exchange negotiations. The cutoff proved permanent.

Appendix 1

KNOX DEMAND FOR WHOLESALE INTERNMENT OF HAWAIIAN JAPANESE

THE SECRETARY OF THE NAVY

WASHINGTON

February 23, 1942

THE WHITE HOUSE
FEB 25 9 11 AM '42
RECEIVED

<u>MEMORANDUM FOR THE PRESIDENT</u>:

You will recall that on several occasions at Cabinet meetings, I have urged the policy of removing the 140,000 people of Japanese blood from Oahu to one of the other islands in the group. Each time the question has become bogged down because it dealt with the matter of interfering with the constitutional rights of American citizens of Japanese descent. Is not this difficulty now cleared up by your recent order covering exactly this question on the mainland?

Personally, I shall always feel dissatisfied with the situation until we get the Japanese out of Oahu and establish them on one of the other islands where they can be made to work for their living and produce much of their own food.

I know that such a movement involves considerable effort and will require some sizeable means of transportation. However, since our forces in Oahu are practically operating now in what is, in effect, enemy country--that is all of their defense of the islands is now carried out in the presence of a population predominately with enemy sympathies and affiliations. No matter what it costs or how much effort it takes, it ought to be done for the sake of the security of that most important outpost of American defense.

I have taken the matter up with the War Department, but to date have made little progress. I have in my files a long letter from General Emmons arguing against any such wholesale movement of Japanese. Since this was sent to me through military channels, I assume that it, in a general way, reflects the Army point of view.

Have you any suggestions to make on this matter?

Frank Knox

Note: Frank Knox, well-known publisher of the *Chicago Daily News* (and candidate for the Vice-Presidency in 1936 teamed with Alfred Landon), had been brought into the FDR Cabinet in 1940 with another prointerventionist Republican, Henry Stimson, as a unity move. Knox's stint as general manager of the Hearst press in the twenties may have had some bearing on his attitude toward persons of "Japanese blood."

Appendix 2

ADDENDUM, MARCH 11, 1942, TO J.C.S. 11, FEBRUARY 12, 1942, ADOPTED BY THE JOINT U. S. CHIEFS OF STAFF ON MARCH 9, 1942

SITUATION IN HAWAIIAN ISLANDS REGARDING JAPANESE POPULATION

While the present Naval local defense forces and the Army forces being sent to the Hawaiian Islands are considered adequate to cope with attacks from without, there still remains the grave threat of inimical action from within on the part of the (approximately) 100,000 residents of Japanese origin.

It is probable that eventually all Japanese residents will be concentrated in one locality and kept under continuous surveillance. It is essential that the most dangerous group, approximately 20,000 persons, should be evacuated as soon as possible. This can be effected either by

(a) Instituting a concentration camp on one of the Hawaiian Islands, such as Molokai.

(b) Transferring the Japanese population to a concentration camp located on the U.S. mainland.

Use of the method (a) above would constitute a tremendous logistics problem, since it would be necessary to transport to the Islands material to build the camp, all supplies for the continued maintenance of the Japanese, and the supplies for the additional troops allocated for their surveillance. The maximum use of the ships so used would not be attained, since they would be empty east-bound.

Transfer of the Japanese residents to the U.S. mainland would eliminate this almost prohibitive additional burden on the already over-taxed requirements of U.S. merchant shipping.

The Joint U.S. Chiefs of Staff therefore unanimously recommend that:

All Japanese residents of the Hawaiian Islands (either U.S. citizens or aliens) be transported to the U.S. mainland and placed under guard at a concentration camp in such locality as is most suitable.

DECLASSIFIED

JCS memo, 1-4-74

Note: A March 28, 1942, memo to the Assistant Secretary of War from Major General Dwight D. Eisenhower (then Assistant Chief of Staff) reveals that FDR had approved the above large-scale pan-Pacific removals to the U.S. mainland and that aliens and citizens, alike, be *"placed in a concentration camp."* On giving his approval (on March 13, 1942), however, the President specified that "for the moment, evacuation should involve such Japanese as are considered, by appropriate authority . . . to constitute a source of danger." Document No. WPD 4520-5, ASW 014.311, RG 107, National Archives.

Appendix 3

DISTRIBUTION OF JAPANESE RELIEF GOODS
RECEIVED ON EXCHANGE SHIP M. S. GRIPSHOLM
ON DECEMBER 1, 1943

	TEA	SOYA	BEAN MASH
ROHWER	40	325	13
HEART MOUNTAIN	64	480	15
AMACHE	44	310	14
MINIDOKA	50	440	18
POSTON	90	680	27
GILA	60	480	20
MANZANAR	54	425	17
TULE LAKE	100	747	30
JEROME	44	330	13
TOPAZ	46	360	14

INTERNMENT CAMPS

	TEA	SOYA	BEAN MASH
KENEDY (TEXAS)	7 *	62	2
MCCOY (WISCONSIN)	6 *	73	2
KOOSKIA (IDAHO)	6 *	50	3
SANTE FE (NEW MEXICO)	62 *	977	22
MISSOULA (MONTANA)	19 *	210	7
CRYSTAL CITY (TEXAS)	28 *	305	12
ANGEL ISLAND (CALIFORNIA)	1 *	4	1
SHARP PARK (CALIFORNIA)	1 *	4	1
EAST BOSTON (MASSACHUSETTS)	1 *	8	1
FLORENCE (ARIZONA)		4	
TUNA CANYON (CALIFORNIA)	1 *	5	1
LORDSBURG (NEW MEXICO)	2 *		
ELLIS ISLAND (NEW YORK)	2 *		

---

* An earlier distribution had been made of cases of green tea which arrived on the first exchange trip (June, 1942) of the *Gripsholm*.

As the existence of Justice Department internment centers came under wartime censorship (*Pacific Citizen,* November 6, 1943), even today, less information is available on these camps than on relocation centers. Most of the camps were considered nonpermanent. Since a complete listing of the camps was not available from the Justice Department, some idea of the number of camps in which persons of Japanese ancestry were held, their location, and the relative number of internees held in each of the camps might be gained by a comparison study of the distribution of relief goods sent by the Japanese Government through the Red Cross. See Report of Marc Peter (Red Cross delegate) to James H. Keeley, Jr. (State Department), June 28, 1944, Department of State File 740.00115 PW/6-2844, RG 59, National Archives. The number of *Japanese nationals* in each center at the time figured in the allotment per center.

OTHER MAINLAND CENTERS IN WHICH
PERSONS OF JAPANESE ANCESTRY WERE HELD

SEAGOVILLE (TEXAS)
FORT SILL (OKLAHOMA)
BISMARCK or FORT LINCOLN (NORTH DAKOTA)
STRINGTOWN (OKLAHOMA)
TULAHOMA (TENNESSEE)
FORT MEADE (MARYLAND)
ASSEMBLY INN (MONTREAT, NORTH CAROLINA)
FORT LIVINGSTON (ALEXANDRIA, LOUISIANA) According to
    Department of State File 740.00115 PW/801, National Archives,
    571 persons of Japanese ancestry were held at Fort Livingston at
    one point.
FORT RICHARDSON (ALASKA)

HAWAIIAN ISLAND DETENTION CAMPS

SAND ISLAND   This was a detention camp which had been prepared
    in advance of the war's outbreak and was located on Sand Island,
    Honolulu Harbor. All suspects were detained under *military cus-
    tody* (some in other military camps) because of the imposition of
    martial law throughout the Islands—"FBI camps" were not utilized.
    In February, 1942, a group of 170 inmates of Japanese ancestry were
    transferred from Sand Island to Camp McCoy Internment Camp
    (Wisconsin) and later dispersed to various FBI camps when McCoy
    became a training camp for the 100th Infantry Battalion. The shipment
    from Sand Island, and other camps, to Tule Lake of 67 inmates con-
    sidered "pro-Japan," in November, 1944, was the last group to be
    shipped to the mainland for detention.
HONOULIULI   This lesser known detention camp, located near Ewa on
    the Island of Oahu, was shut down soon after the exclusion of the 67
    "undesirables." So-called "desirables" were paroled and made to sign
    papers which held the U.S. blameless for the internment. (Data, cour-
    tesy of Kazuo Miyamoto, *Hawaii: End of the Rainbow*. See also the
    Honolulu Star-Bulletin of March 18, 1976, for a three-page exposé
    by Hank Sato on the Honouliuli camp.)

Note: Not mentioned above are the various internment facilities operated by the
State Department where diplomatic personnel and their families were detained pending their repatriation. Among them were The Greenbrier at White Sulphur Springs,
West Virginia, The Homestead at Hot Springs, Virginia, and Grove Park Inn at Ashe-
ville, North Carolina.

Appendix 4

SURVEILLANCE BEHIND BARBED WIRE

WAR RELOCATION AUTHORITY
Washington, D. C.

30 July 1943

From: War Relocation Authority.
To: Lieutenant Welden, Room 4740, Navy Department.

    1.   This will certify receipt of the following files as of the date shown above:

Source	Date	Subject	ONI Routing Slip Number
11ND	4-21-43	Japanese Relocation Centers, contact with	F 82972
11ND	12-14-42	Japanese School Children; attitudes of, during Poston General Strike 11, 21-23, 42	E 65096
11ND	12-7-42	Colorado River Relocation Project, Poston, Arizona (Camps #1, 2, 3)- Japanese subversive activity therein	E 58200 (copy)
11ND	9-14-42	Letter Written by Conf Informant at Poston Arizona Relocation Camp	D 95997
~~11ND~~	~~7-29-42~~	~~Japanese Evacuation Center, Poston, Arizona~~	~~D 61772~~
11ND	7-20-42	Parker Reception Center, Poston, Arizona	D 56855

    2.   It is understood that the information contained in the above files is extremely confidential in character and that its security must be preserved by carefully safeguarding its existence and source as well as the name of any informant mentioned therein. It is further understood if the report covers an investigation of an individual, that the report shall not be shown to the individual or individuals mentioned or involved nor shall copies be made of such report, nor shall the Office of Naval Intelligence be mentioned in connection with any action on the basis of such report.

    3.   Ultimate return of this correspondence is requested.

Helen C. Paul
WAR RELOCATION AUTHORITY

Note: Naval intelligence continued to carry on its counterintelligence activities in the centers with active cooperation of the WRA. Note (item 2): To indirectly probe attitudes of parents, even children's essays underwent scrutiny.

Manzanar, Calif.
Feb. 23, 1943

Secretary of War
Henry L. Stimson
Washington, D.C.

Dear Sir:

This is in connection with the
letter of Feb. 22, in which I
have listed names and addresses
of persons questioned me
prior to and after registration.
I didn't meant for you to
arrest them, I just reported
what has occured in connection
with the registration so do
not misunderstand me.
I forgot to put down two more

names. They are: Yutani Yezosaku,
10-5-3 & Kingoro Toma, isser 10-11-2
The persons who question-
was the following:

Kobigashi, Jotaro
Shimo, ? ?
? ?, ?
Yabe, Shinichi
Yutani, ?yezo — not on earlier list
Toma, Kingoro

Please do not arrest these persons. I
just wrote what occured to me because I
had volunteered into army last april 1941.
Every time something comes up regarding army
I be the target. Please take this into
consideration. I do not need any
answer.

Sincerely yours,

"During wartime there is no Democracy. If there were, a few people wouldn't control
the nation. One example is that the evacuation wouldn't have been necessary if it
were not for these small groups. . . .

"If there were Democracy in these camps these people wouldn't form a mob. The Director of the camps just order this then he orders that, well when you are ordered to do
some thing you feel more like not doing it. . . .

"Outside the people go into National Defense plants to make money not to help the country.
Well that is what is wrong with this country. Everyone wants to make money for their
own use and they think of no one else but themselves. The Nation Defense plant head are
making bullion of dollars by government order thus they raise the price and make more
money. . . . . This government does say that it is Democratic but if you sum up all the
whole thing there are too many things that seem like a dictatorship. . . .

(an excerpt from themes prepared by Poston school children)   Kyoto Kanato

179

Appendix 5

CENSORSHIP OF RELOCATION CENTER PUBLICATIONS

FILE COPY °

TRANSLATION
Japanese Section, The Manzanar Free Press
July 12, 1944

 Warns Against Over Optimism

From L. A. Times, July 11, part 1, page 2, column 3

2. Cost Of Loan 200 Billions

From L. A. Examiner, July 4, part 1, page 5, column 4

3. China, Another Year

From Time Magazine, July 10, page 38, column 1, 2 and 3

4. Japanese American Units Praised

From L. A. Times, July 11, part 1, page 4, column 6

5. Whirlwind

There is a reason for the turmoil caused by the Tule Lake people. We cannot judge about this matter as the radical group are seeking for the trouble and causing the turmoil.

The murder of the general manager of the Co-op in Tule Lake shows signs of explosion of the suppressed people, who were not satisfied with the Co-op system. Thus I anticipate after gathering the information.

There is a rumor that Tule Lake Co-op is being operated under the capital of the Caucasian people and it is not organized in a cooperative system.

We see a great difference in comparison between the Manzanar and Tule Lake Co-op. Co-op system of Manzanar is perfect and the general manager and other Co-op workers are participating to improve the the Co-op for the sake of all the residents in Manzanar. I am glad to see that no trouble has occurred.

6. Fifth War Loan Over Top Says Sec'y Morgenthau

From L. A. Examiner, July 19, part 1, page 1, column 2

7. War Costs $2387 Every Second

From L. A. Times, July 7, part 1, page 2, column 1

Note: Though censorship of camp newspapers was one accusation most project directors were quick to deny, the degree of freedom enjoyed by journalists in the relocation centers was carefully—if subtly—controlled by the local Reports Officer and the Chief of Reports, Merrill M. Tozier, at WRA headquarters.

Appendix 6

PRESIDENTIAL PROCLAMATION NO. 2655
—in part—

(which enabled removal from the U.S. of renunciants)

Signed into law by Harry S. Truman
July 14, 1945

All alien enemies now or hereafter interned within the continental limits of the United States pursuant to the aforesaid proclamations of the President of the United States who shall be deemed by the Attorney General to be dangerous to the public peace and safety of the United States because they have adhered to the aforesaid enemy governments or to the principles of government thereof shall be subject under the order of the Attorney General to removal from the United States and may be required to depart therefrom in accordance with such regulations as he may prescribe.

Note: By those adhering to "aforesaid enemy governments," it referred to alien enemies of Japan, Germany, Italy, Bulgaria, Hungary, and Rumania.

Appendix 7

SELECTED DOCUMENTS
RELATING TO HOSTAGE-RESERVE
PROJECT

"A GENERAL STAFF STUDY: THE PLAN 1. To arrest and intern certain persons of the Orange race [Japanese] who are considered most inimical to American interests, or those whom, due to their position and influence in the Orange community, it is desirable to retain as hostages."

> —GEORGE S. PATTON, JR., Chief of Military Intelligence, Hawaii, circa 1936 (RG 338, National Archives)

"It is suggested that the 'hostage idea' has not been sufficiently explored. . . . The question should be . . . whether the individual has any close relatives in the armed forces . . . in [a] hostile [nation]."

> —MAJOR KARL R. BENDETSON (aka Bendetsen) to Coloniel P. L. Hayden, G-1, January 16, 1942 (RG 389, National Archives)

7a. COMPLAINTS REGARDING TREATMENT OF PANAMANIAN JAPANESE REPATRIATES, OCTOBER 1, 1942

EMBAJADA DE ESPAÑA
WASHINGTON

Protecciones

No. 438

ECEIVED
OF STATE   **MEMORANDUM**

RE: Claim made by Japanese from Panama.

The Spanish Embassy begs to transmit to the Department of State a claim made by the Japanese Imperial Government for the treatment they said was given the Japanese from Panama upon being brought to the United States.

The text of the Japanese telegram sent to this Embassy through the Foreign Office in Madrid reads as follows:

"The Japanese diplomats and residents of Panama who recently arrived in Japan, denounce the inhuman treatment given the Japanese in Panama.

They advise that on December 7th, all Japanese residents in Panama were arrested without allowing them to take anything more with them than what they had on, and were held up to 24 hours in the jail of Panama and by the Police of Colon without any food or water.

On the 8th, they were turned over to the American Authorities and for one week were put in very unsanitary concentration camps, forced to work and given extreme punishment.

Immediately after their arrest, the homes and residences of these detainees were looted.

Upon being transferred, the American Authorities of the Canal Zone, confiscated all the money that they had. In some

740.001 5 PACIFIC WAR/7304

EMBAJADA DE ESPANA

WASHINGTON

Protecciones

.cases receipts were issued, but later these were confiscated too.

Among the Japanese detainees, there was one named Alejandro who fell ill, and neither the American or Panamanian Authorities gave him medical attention until the 2nd of May, when he was placed in a hospital and where he died the same day.

The Japanese Imperial Government presents a protest for this inhuman treatment, having in mind that the Panamanian Government in Note of May4th, solemnly advised that the Japanese internees were transferred to the United States only because there was not adequate place for them in Panama, having asked the cooperation of the United States Government with the understanding that these Japanese would be entirely and only under the orders of the Panamanian Government.

The Japanese Imperial Government understand this complaint, holding that both Governments are responsible for these serious deeds."

WASHINGTON, October 1st, 1942

FROM A MEMO TO THE STATE DEPARTMENT FROM ASSISTANT SECRETARY OF STATE BRECKINRIDGE LONG, FEBRUARY 13, 1943

I think it would be inadvisable to break up family groups of the Japanese and Germans listed for transportation to the [United States] for internment. . . . There is too great a danger that that would cause the Germans and Japanese authorities to retaliate on Peruvian and our citizens in their custody. Japan . . . has just sent us a protest against our bringing Japanese . . . from Peru. [W]e can well answer . . . by replying . . . that [they] are available for return to Japan. . . . We will hardly be in a position to make such a reply if we should bring the Japanese men here and *leave their women and children in Peru* [emphasis added]. (p. 288, fn. 22, memo in National Archives)

7b. PERPLEXED JAPANESE GOVERNMENT REGISTERS PROTEST AGAINST REMOVAL OF BOLIVIAN AND PERUVIAN JAPANESE TO THE UNITED STATES

SPANISH EMBASSY

WASHINGTON

Protections

No. 133

Ex. 119.01

MEMORANDUM

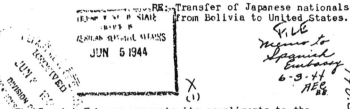

RE: Transfer of Japanese nationals from Bolivia to United States.

JUN 5 1944

The Spanish Embassy presents its compliments to the Department of State and begs to transmit a complaint received through the "Ministerio de Asuntos Exteriores" of Madrid, from the Japanese Government, which reads as follows:

MEMORANDUM - May 29th, 1944 -

"The Japanese Imperial Chancery is cognizant that the American Government has recently interested the Bolivian Government in the transference of the custody of Japanese residents of that country to the United States.

The fact of the American Government having whimsically transferred the custody of Japanese residents of a third country, namely Bolivia, to the United States, is as unjust a measure as the one taken by the American Government with the Japanese residents of Peru, a measure that the Japanese Government is still at a loss to understand.

The Japanese Government wishes to protest emphatically to the American Government, pointing out the grave responsability it will incur and reserving all rights on the matter. At the same time the Japanese Government requests that the American Government will not repeat these unjust measures in the future."

WASHINGTON, May 31st, 1944

Department of State

Washington D.C.

PREPARING OFFICE
WILL INDICATE WHETHER

Collect

Charge Department:

Charge to Department

TELEGRAM SENT

Department of State

Washington,

NOV 18 1944
3

TO BE TRANSMITTED
SECRET
CONFIDENTIAL
RESTRICTED
CLEAR

UNCLASSIFIED

This telegram must be closely paraphrased before being communicated to anyone.
SECRET

DECLASSIFIED
E.O. 11652, Sec. 3(E) and 6(D) or (E)
State Dept. Letter, Aug. 9, 1973
By _____, NARS, Date 6-17-75

AMPOLAD

CASERTA

2

FOR BERRY

In view of the state of negotiations with the Japanese
for exchanges of nationals, Department would view with disfavor any arrangement whereby the return of Japanese from
occupied areas to their homeland might be effected without
procuring some advantage to the nationals of the United
States and the other United Nations held by the Japanese.
(REURTEL 1228, November 2. 8 p.m.) The Department therefore
suggests that you propose to the Rumanian Government that the
fourteen Japanese nationals in Rumania be turned over to the
United States for custody and that they be transferred to Italy
where they may be suitably accommodated pending satisfactory
arrangements for their repatriation. You should inform your
British colleage of this proposal.

Stettinius
ACTING
(E.A.P)
S/OR
NOV 18 1944

740.00115 PW/11-844

SWP:AES:BB   11-11-44   EOR   SE   JA

Confidential File

OK

DEPARTMENT
OF
STATE

B-486

**INCOMING
TELEGRAM** Brussels

DIVISION OF
COMMUNICATIONS
AND RECORDS

This telegram must be
closely paraphrased be-
fore being communicated
to anyone. (SECRET)

Dated January 12, 1945

Rec'd 4:33 p.m., 13th.

Secretary of State

Washington.

SPECIAL WAR PROBLEMS
DIVISION

JAN 15 1945

DEPARTMENT OF STATE

37, January 12, 6 p.m.

Foreign Office welcomed suggestion that
Japanese nationals in Belgium be considered as
hostages for eventual repatriation of Belgians and
other Allied nationals detained by Japanese
Government. (Your 14, January 9, 9 p.m.) It is
obtaining from appropriate authorities a list of all
such Japanese nationals and will ascertain if appropriate steps have been taken to prevent their escape.
(Repeated to Paris for Reber as 3). The official
consulted promised to discuss matter further with us
as soon as complete information had been obtained.

SAWYER

RB

[Charles Sawyer, U.S. Ambassador to Belgium]

740.00115 PW/1-1245

MAY 20 1946

FILED

CS/MAH
Confidential File

DCR - CP-O Unit
Anal. M.A
Rev.
Cal. E.M.S.
Dist.

187

7e. DESPITE JAPAN'S DISINCLINATION, HULL PERSISTED IN HIS ATTEMPTS TO NEGOTIATE A THIRD EXCHANGE

PREPARING-OFFICE
WILL INDICATE WHETHER

Charge Department:

Charge Department

TELEGRAM SENT

Department of State

Washington.

TO BE TRANSMITTED
~~SECRET~~
~~CONFIDENTIAL~~
~~RESTRICTED~~
CLEAR

CLEAR

87

AMLEGATION

BERN

3053 FOURTH

SEP 4 1944

AMERICAN INTERESTS JAPAN - REPATRIATION

Request Swiss Government to inform Japanese that on Saipan there have been captured approximately 10,000 civilians among whom are a number of high-ranking government officials. The United States Government is willing to exchange these civilians for sick and wounded United States prisoners of war and for United States civilians captured on Guam, Wake and in the Philippine Islands, and other Japanese-occupied territories, including nationals of the other American republics and Canada.

Please submit this proposal to the Japanese Government for consideration pointing out that its views should be urgently formulated in order to preclude the adoption of measures which might make such an exchange less feasible.

If the Japanese Government is interested in this proposal one of its hospital ships could be made a repatriation ship to effect the exchange and might carry American nationals to Bikini Atoll in the Marshall Islands, Latitude 11 degrees 30 minutes North, Longitude 165 degrees 25 minutes East. It would return to Japanese-controlled areas with a representative selection from among the Japanese civilians captured on Saipan. This operation could be

repeated

TELEGRAM SENT

Department of State

Washington,

-2-

TO BE TRANSMITTED
SECRET
CONFIDENTIAL
RESTRICTED
CLEAR

88   CLEAR

repeated as long as there are nationals to be exchanged.

The Japanese might (vessel) carry a neutral observer agreed upon by the Japanese and United States Governments and the United States Government might place on Bikini Atoll a neutral observer similarly agreed upon by both parties. The function of the two observers would be that of liaison during the period of exchange and the observation of the execution of the agreement by both parties.

Hull

OaB

740.00115 PW/8-2444

SWP:ALC:BB   9-1-44   JA   FE   WRB(M. Ge Warren)

PI
P.TS.

189

Appendix 8

MEMORANDUM TO CORDELL HULL: POSTWAR DEPORTATION OF JAPANESE AMERICANS DISCUSSED IN RELATION TO POSSIBLE MEASURES TO BE PURSUED BY CANADA

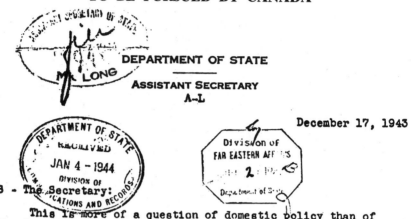

DEPARTMENT OF STATE

ASSISTANT SECRETARY
A-L

December 17, 1943

DEPARTMENT OF STATE
RECEIVED
JAN 4 - 1944
DIVISION OF
COMMUNICATIONS AND RECORDS

Division of
FAR EASTERN AFFAIRS
2

8 - The Secretary:

This is more of a question of domestic policy than of foreign policy, though the repatriation phase of it, the foreign citizenship of many of the persons concerned and the similar situation of Canada bring to it a color of foreign affairs.

The Canadian problem is similar to ours but not identical for we have (a) quite a number of these Japanese (of American nationality) serving in our Army whom we could not in justice kick out of the United States after they had fought with us; and (b) laws of citizenship different from those of Canada. However, the Canadian analysis as prepared for the Prime Minister is considered well done.

I have recently gone into this problem in several of its phases. The Department has a responsibility - because of the reciprocal treatment provision in the Geneva Convention - in connection with internment camps, relocation centers and prisoners of war camps in this country where Japanese citizens and American citizens of Japanese race are confined. I have appeared before two committees of the Senate where the subject has been discussed and I may say where an avid interest in the future of the Japanese in the United States has been considered. Legislation will be needed if any large-scale operation is desired - and a large-scale operation to get them out of the United States seems to be the hope of the members of those committees.

The problem has been complicated by our laws relating to citizenship and by the constitutional provision regarding the native born character of the citizenship of those born here. The Attorney General is reported to have said recently to one of the Committees that he had a formula under one of our statutes by which a native-born Japanese or one naturalized could be divested of his American citizenship - thus making him eligible for deportation. However, there has been no official ruling by the Attorney General on this point.

I think the far larger part of official sentiment is to do something so we can get rid of these people when the war is over -

FEB 18 1944 FILED

obviously we cannot while the war continues.

But sentiment is liable to wane if the authorization measures are not adopted before the war ends.

We have 110,000 of them in confinement here now - and that is a lot of Japs to contend with in postwar days, particularly as the west coast localities where they once lived do not desire their return.

As the problem involves both foreign and domestic policy and as detention, immigration regulations, deportation proceedings, probably authorizing legislation and appropriation of funds to defray costs as well as allocation of tonnage for transport, and as constitutional questions are involved it seems you may want to suggest to the President that he may want the Attorney General to study the question and take steps to work it out, keeping you advised as regards those matters which have a bearing abroad.

The letter of Mr. Atherton might be answered to the effect that we are studying the matter here but find it very complicated and that we will let Canada know later what we propose to do.

B. L.

attached - editorial today's Wash. Post.

[B.L.: Breckinridge Long, Assistant Secretary of State and author of *Genesis of the Constitution of the United States*]

A-L:BL:DY

Note: A document, dated January 14, 1942, sent to the State Department from the U.S. Legation in Ottawa, enumerated a series of declarations by Prime Minister Mackenzie King in which it is revealed that "Canada will continue to collaborate with Great Britain and the United States with a view to the substantial coordination of their policies in relation to persons of Japanese racial origin . . . ." Department of State File 740.00115 PW/147 RG 59, National Archives.

Appendix 9

ARMY WARNING TO GOVERNOR EARL WARREN
THAT RETURNEES
MUST BE ALLOWED SAFE RETURN

15 December 1944

Governor Earl Warren
State Capitol Building
Sacramento, California

My dear Governor Warren:

As you are well aware, the military situation on the West Coast
has considerably improved over that which existed two years ago. Although
it is still possible for the enemy to send small forces to our coast, it
is my belief that the danger of mass invasion does not exist at the present
time. The fact that the danger of mass invasion is remote in this particular area should not make any of us relax our part in the war effort and
should not be used as a basis for failure to maintain all necessary precau-
tions to prevent small enemy incursions being successful or to prevent sabotage or espionage.

The military situation which existed in 1942 required the exclusion
of all persons of Japanese ancestry from critical areas of the West Coast.
The action taken at that time was based solely on military considerations.
The authority under which the Commanding General of the Western Defense
Command acted at that time was solely operative as long as military neces-
sity required the action taken.

Not only has the military situation improved between 1942 and the
present, but it has been possible to assemble a very large amount of information concerning all those persons of Japanese ancestry who have been excluded.
This information was not available at the time the exclusion was effected.

It has been most heartening to find that the very great majority of
persons of Japanese ancestry, both among American citizens and aliens, are
Americans in thought and have completely severed their ties with Japan. On
the other hand, there are a considerable number of individuals, both among
the American citizen group as well as the alien group, who still consider
themselves as Japanese, who do not wish to be Americans and who are willing
to sacrifice themselves to further the interests of Japan. These can now be
treated on an individual basis.

In view of the improved military situation and in view of the fact
that it is now possible to make an individual determination as to whether
or not each person of Japanese ancestry is potentially dangerous, there is
no logical or proper course open to me other than to terminate mass exclusion
based solely on ancestry, and to substitute for it a system which will permit
the return of all persons of Japanese ancestry who have been cleared by the

DECLASSIFIED
DOD Dir. 5200.9 Sept. 27, 1958
NX by _____ ERC ____ Date 3-30-71

~~SECRET~~

192

Army and to continue to exclude those individuals who still remain loyal to Japan and are considered to be potentially dangerous to the military security of the West Coast. In order to accomplish this revised program, I have this date issued Proclamation #21. A copy of that Proclamation is enclosed.

I wish to make it perfectly clear that the authority of the Army covers solely those spheres which may properly be considered as military and that the original exclusion was accomplished on the basis of the military situation existing at that time. The present change in policy is likewise based solely on military considerations coupled with a consideration of the extent of the authority vested in me and a due regard for the constitutional rights of all American citizens regardless of ancestry.

It is my hope that the return of those Japanese-Americans who choose to return may be accomplished without serious incidents. Community acceptance, housing and jobs are important. It is contemplated that the return will be accomplished gradually and that the critical housing and employment situation existing in many localities will be taken into consideration in putting the program into effect.

I wish to assure you and request that you will assure the people of your state that those persons of Japanese ancestry who are permitted to return have been cleared by Army authorities and that they are entitled to every consideration that normal, law-abiding residents should be given.

I am confident that the fine Americans of your state will realize that the present is not the time to permit internal controversy. I am sure that they will also realize that among the American citizens of Japanese ancestry who are being permitted to return there are many families with sons or daughters now serving in our Armed Forces. I would also invite the attention of all our citizens to the fact that there are still a large number of American soldiers who are now held as prisoners of way by the Japanese. Any internal disturbances directed against American citizens of Japanese ancestry because of their blood will without question be used as a pretext for the mistreatment of these prisoners.

I particularly urge that our children be asked to treat the children of returning Japanese-Americans with the same fine sense of fairness with which they have treated American youngsters of German and Italian ancestry.

With cordial best wishes,

Sincerely yours,

ROBERT H. LEWIS
Major General, United States Army
Commanding

1 Incl:
    Proclamation #21.

Note: Two days later, on December 17, 1944, the War Department officially revoked West Coast exclusion orders, effective on January 7, 1945.

Appendix 10

JAY FRANKLIN'S COVERING MEMORANDUM

Confidential   WASHINGTON, D.C., *November 7, 1941*

MEMORANDUM ON C.B. MUNSON'S REPORT "JAPANESE ON THE WEST COAST"

Attached herewith is the report, with supplementary reports on Lower California and British Columbia. The report, though lengthy, is worth reading in its entirety. Salient passages are:

1) "There are still Japanese in the United States who will tie dynamite around their waists and make a human bomb out of themselves . . . but today they are few."

2) "There is no Japanese 'problem' on the coast. There will be no armed uprising of Japanese. There will be undoubtedly some sabotage financed by Japan and executed largely by imported agents. There will be the odd case of fanatical sabotage by some Japanese 'crackpot'."

3) "The dangerous part of their espionage is that they would be very effective as far as movement of supplies, movement of troops and movement of ships * * * is concerned."

4) "For the most part the local Japanese are loyal to the United States or, at worst, hope that by remaining quiet they can avoid concentration camps or irresponsible mobs."

5) "Your reporter * * * is horrified to note that dams, bridges, harbors, power stations, etc, are wholly unguarded everywhere. The harbor of San Pedro could be razed by fire completely by four men with hand grenades and a little study in one night. Dams could be blown and half of lower California might actually die of thirst. * * * One railway bridge at the exits from the mountains in some cases could tie up three or four main railroads."

J. F. C. [Jay Franklin Carter]

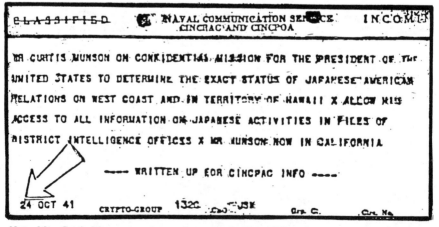

Note: Mrs. Curtis Munson sought out the author in May 1983 and revealed that her husband had found "you people to be like our Pilgrim fathers," loyal and entirely laudatory, but that FDR "did not want to hear about it."

STIMSON RECEIVED THE REPORT
WITH THE FOLLOWING MEMORANDUM

PSF Stimson Folder

THE WHITE HOUSE

WASHINGTON

~~CONFIDENTIAL~~

November 8, 1941.

MEMORANDUM FOR

THE SECRETARY OF WAR

Please read this and let me have it back. There is nothing much new in the first four paragraphs on Page #1 but paragraph five relating to the guarding of key points should be examined into.

F. D. R.

Note: On February 5, 1942, the very day when mass evacuation plans began to be drawn up in the War Department (see p. 51; also p. 290, fn. 4), Stimson returned the Report, declaring in an accompanying letter to FDR: "Since you are generally aware of the radical steps which have been taken since December 7 to control the situation on the West Coast . . . I see little need of commenting on the report I have before me. . . . I may add that our officials have consulted with Mr. Munson on the matter of the defense of the West Coast against enemy agents." PSF Stimson, Box 106, FDR Library.

Appendix 11

LEAVE CLEARANCE
INTERVIEW QUESTIONS—25 AUGUST 1943

The purpose of this interview is to provide the W.R.A. with the assurance that in permitting your leave from this center, it is doing the best thing for the United States as a whole and for you as an individual.

Before questioning you any further, we would like to ask if you have any objection to signing a Pledge of Allegiance to the United States.

Do you object to taking an oath that you will tell the truth and nothing but the truth in this interview? Will you raise your right hand? Oath:

What is your name?

Address?

Address before evacuation?

Business, Occupation, or Profession before evacuation?

Did you belong to any Japanese organizations?

Did you attend a Japanese Language School?

Where did you get your education?

Have you at any time been a resident or visitor to Japan? If so, give inclusive dates.

Have you ever asked for repatriation?

Give the names of your parents.

When did they immigrate to the United States?

What was their occupation before evacuation?

How many people are there in your family?

Do you have any relatives in Japan?

Are any relatives serving in the Japanese Army?

Are any relatives serving in the Armed forces of the United States?

Where are you planning to resettle?

Will you voluntarily remain out of the States of Arizona, Nevada, Utah until such time that public opinion makes you more welcome?

What is your plan for mixing into the community to which you will resettle?

Do you know what clubs and organizations would welcome you?

Will you assist in the general resettlement program by staying away from large groups of Japanese?

Will you avoid the use of the Japanese language except when necessary?

Will you for the duration of the war, avoid the organization of any typically Japanese clubs, associations, etc?

Will you try to develop such American habits which will cause you to be accepted readily into American social groups?

Are you willing to serve in the Armed Forces of the United States if called upon by Selective Service to do so?

Are you willing to serve in war production?

Are you willing to give information to the proper authorities regarding any subversive activity which you might note or which you might be informed about directly or indirectly, both in the relocation centers and in the communities in which you are resettling?

To whom would you report such information?

Would you consider an informer of this nature an "Inu"? (Stoolpigeon)

How long do you plan to stay on this job?

If you find a better job, how much notice will you give your employer?

Will you accept a position at a lower than standard wage? How will you find out what standard wages are?

Will you conform to the customs and dress of your new home?

Will you make every effort to represent all that is good, reliable, and honest in the Japanese Americans?

Will you report any change of residence or employment to the W.R.A. office?

What is your plan for your family?

What were your average expenses before evacuation for:
   a. Rent or housing?
   b. Food?
   c. Clothing?
   d. Misc. Expenses?

What was your income?

Do you have any of your household equipment here?

Have you planned what you need?

Have you contacted the Supervisor of Evacuee Property?

What do you consider the necessary items which you will have to purchase before you can resettle with your family?

Do you plan to take your family with you?

How many dependents do you have? Give names and ages.

Do you have any automotive equipment?

What has been your work while at the relocation center?

What part did you play in the development of any constructive organization or development at the center?

To what clubs do you belong?

Have you ever been accused and pleaded guilty to any crime of any kind within the center?

Have you been associated with any radical groups, clubs, or gangs which have been accused of anti-social conduct within the center?

Have you ever participated in any stealing, destruction, or illegal use of government property?

Give 5 references of people who can vouch for your conduct in the center other than members of your family. Include at least 2 representatives of the administration.

Can you furnish any proof that you have always been loyal to the United States?

What do you think of the Segregation of the loyal from the disloyal in the relocation centers?

What do you think of the United States in general?

What effect has the report of any Japanese *victory* in the Pacific and in the Far East upon your thinking?

Why are you requesting leave?

What would you do if you found a shortwave set, both sending and receiving or either, in your neighbor's apartment?

What is the difference between the present Japanese government and that of 10 years ago?

Does the Japanese government have a parliamentary government at the present time?

Do you think you are "losing face" by cooperating with the United States?

What does the Samurai tradition mean to you?

Do you think that the American people are generally soft and easy, both physically and mentally?

Do you believe in the divine origin of the Japanese race?

Have you ever celebrated February 11?

For what is the Ise Shrine famous?

For what is February 22 famous in Japanese history?

What does "kigensetsu" mean to you?

What would you consider a disloyal act to the United States?

What do you think loyalty to Japan would demand of a person in the centers under the present conditions?

What is your opinion of dual citizenship?

Would you under any circumstances, act contrary to the dictates of your parents?

Have you been associated with any groups whose membership is made up of those who have the majority of "No" answers on the Army Questionnaire?

What, in your opinion, did the "Yes" answer imply?

Do results at any time justify the means?

In your opinion, does the "population pressure" justify the Japanese expansion program?

Note: Evacuees given clearance were granted "indefinite leave cards" carrying their photographs and fingerprints. As the above document is from the files of the Assistant Secretary of War (ASW 014.311 WDC Segregation-Japs, RG 107, National Archives), interview questions were apparently formulated in the War Department.

Appendix 12

CONVINCED THAT PENDING HIGH COURT CASES WOULD BE LOST, BIDDLE REFUSES TO PROSECUTE ON THE BASIS OF EXECUTIVE ORDER 9066

Office of the Attorney General
Washington, D.C.
April 17, 1943.

MEMORANDUM FOR THE PRESIDENT

Re: Exclusion Orders - JULIA KRAUS and SYLVESTER ANDRIANO.

I have your memorandum of April 7th, suggesting that I talk to the Secretary of War about these cases. I shall, of course, be glad to do so, and so informed him sometime ago. Conferences have already been going on for several months; and I have talked personally to McCloy (and others) for several hours.

The Secretary's letter misses the points at issue, which are:

1. Whatever the military do, as Attorney General I should decide what criminal cases to bring and what not to bring. I shall not institute criminal proceedings on exclusion orders which seem to me unconstitutional.

2. You signed the original Executive Order permitting the exclusions so the Army could handle the Japs. It was never intended to apply to Italians and Germans. Your order was based on "protection against espionage and against sabotage." There is absolutely no evidence in the case of ANDRIANO, who has been a leading citizen of San Francisco for thirty years, that he ever had anything to do either with espionage or sabotage. He was merely pro-Mussolini before the war. He is harmless, and I understand is now living in the country outside of San Francisco.

3. KRAUS was connected before Pearl Harbor with German propaganda in this country. She turned state's evidence. The order of exclusion is so broad that I am of the opinion the courts would not sustain it. As I have said before to you, such a decision might well throw doubt on your powers as Commander in Chief.

4.   We have not approved the Army procedure, which does not permit the persons excluded - American citizens - to confront witnesses before the Military Tribunal. This is against a fundamental conception of constitutional rights.

5.   Prosecution would have little practical effect. Bail would be granted and the individuals would go on living where they chose until the cases were ultimately decided by the Supreme Court. If the Army believes that they are dangerous they have express power to exclude them under the Executive Order and do not need your approval as requested by the Secretary of War.

6.   Obviously the exclusion procedure has nothing to do with black-out or any similar powers exercised by the Army.

7.   A question involving power to exclude the Japanese has been certified to the Supreme Court and will be determined very soon by the Court. No action should be taken until this decision. The Andriano exclusion order was issued by General DeWitt, in charge of the Western Defense Command. The quality of his judgment may be gauged by his recent statement: "A Jap's a Jap. It makes no difference whether he is an American citizen or not . . ." I call your attention to the attached editorial in the Washington Post for April 15th, on the General's remarks. These are particularly unfortunate in view of the case pending in the Supreme Court.

8.   Exclusion is based on military danger. This element is entirely lacking from these cases.

Respectfully yours,

Francis Biddle
Attorney General

Encl.

Note: On March 31, 1943, Secretary of War Stimson had complained to the President that the Attorney General "flouts the intent of Congress as expressed in what was virtually a ratifying act," meaning Public Law 503, and that "the Department of Justice suggests . . . that if the individual is dangerous to national security, he be forcibly removed through the use of Federal troops. The use of bayonets when the Congress has prescribed criminal prosecution through the courts . . . is undesirable for obvious reasons." From OF 5262, FDR Library.

(10)
The Stockade

That Japan, a nonsignatory, and the United States had both agreed to honor the Geneva Convention in regard to civilian as well as military detainees was another one of the wartime realities kept discreetly suppressed, as is made apparent in the following letter to Manzanar's Project Director Merritt from Washington headquarters. The document leaves little doubt that the general applicability of Geneva Convention regulations in the relocation centers was a matter conveniently swept under the proverbial rug because American civilians held by Japanese authorities appeared to be benefiting from the Accords—sufficiently, at least, to allay Washington fears.

> The WRA has never considered that the Geneva Convention is applicable anywhere except, possibly, at Tule Lake. However, the Japanese Government, after the evacuation of the West Coast by our military authorities, instituted a somewhat similar program with respect to Americans in occupied China. They designated some of the camps "assembly centers" and explained that the program was necessary because of military considerations. Since the United States has sought to protect Americans in the Far East by the Geneva Convention, with rather moderate success, there has seemed to be no particular advantage in making an issue of the applicability of the Geneva Convention in the United States . . .
>
> Shortly after the United States became involved in the war, the United States Government stated to Japan that we propose to follow the Geneva Prisoners of War Convention in the treatment of prisoners of war and to apply applicable provisions to civilian internees. Japan replied that though it had not ratified the Convention, it would reciprocate "mutatis mutandis." [1]

However much WRA officials were privately prepared to concede the possibility of Geneva Convention applicability at Tule Lake, transferee attempts to bring it about (meaning that a standard as high as in alien internment centers would then have to be instituted) had been brushed aside as a nonnegotiable issue. Chief spokesman Kunitani of the protest faction had hoped that by having their legal status switched to that of "prisoner of war" and placing segregants under the Accords' protective mantle, basic rights guaranteed even conquered peoples might be restored. Under the Geneva articles, to cite an example, disciplinary punishment could not exceed thirty days at any one time and transfer of inmates to prisons or penitentiaries was prohibited.

But a semantic blur-out, once again, enabled Washington legal practitioners to avoid living up to commitments. The key word was "internees." The "relocated" Issei and Nisei were never referred to by officialdom as internees or prisoners.[2] As far as Washington was concerned, segregants were "segregees," segregated in a segregation center.

Only the 2,000 or more aliens held in Department of Justice detention camps were considered prisoners of war actually "interned" and Geneva Convention regulations were more closely adhered to because of their "internee" status.

In being mixed in with the citizen Nisei who had no recourse to rights due enemy prisoners as outlined in the Geneva protocols, the vast majority of Japanese nationals during the war were, thereby, notoriously short-changed.

II

Tokyo's response to the frantic appeal of those concerned for the lives of relatives and loved ones in the stockade was far from hurried. It was already late in April when Tokyo protests reached the attention of the State Department. They made no mention of the stockade hunger strike, leading one to speculate that the wire from the Tule Lake "underground" directed to Foreign Minister Shigemitsu in Tokyo had not been sent; indeed, the neutral intermediary may have been persuaded not to forward it as a direct result of the stormy reception given the Spanish Consul on his delayed visit to Tule Lake. Consul de Amat and the State Department Representative who had accompanied him had been incensed by the "arrogance and lack of tact" displayed by overwrought *Daihyo Sha Kai* extremists in angry exchanges with the emissaries.

The April 24 memorandum from the Spanish Embassy quoted a Japanese Government memorandum, dated April 18, which charged that "Japanese subjects and United States citizens of Japanese origin who had failed to swear allegiance to United States" had been transferred to the Tule Lake segregation center as "punishment." It vigorously protested atrocities in the camps in which "Japanese subjects were killed, of which at least four cases involving six deaths have come to knowledge of and have been protested against by Japanese Government." [3] It accused U. S. authorities of undue pressure tactics in the loyalty registration and of using the drive as part of a plot to exploit evacuee manpower, saying that authorities had "tried to remove Japanese subjects out of Relocation Centers and utilize their labor."

A large number of evacuees, who knew this motive actuating United States authorities and who were aware their safety after release from Relocation Centers not guaranteed, did not change their answer despite American authorities threats, and even an increased number of them applied for repatriation . . .[4]

The Tokyo declaration went on to repudiate the protective custody rationale as being a mere "pretext" for interning Japanese subjects at war's outbreak. It denounced as "unjust" the categorizing of individuals who had expressed a desire to be repatriated as being "disloyal to the United States." It protested troops being sent in during the registration "to pick up young men who were termed recalcitrant." It objected to the "dispatch of troops with tanks and machine guns" during the November 4 late-night fracas, popularly referred to as the "riot." Lastly, it called for the following remedial measures to be taken at Tule Lake:

Japanese Government deem minimum requirement in order to relieve state of anxiety prevailing at Tule Lake to be compliance with three demands presented to Department of State by Spanish representative, that is to say:
1) Withdrawal of troops from Tule Lake and restoration of control of that relocation center to non-military authorities.
2) Recognition of legitimacy of committee of fourteen.
3) Release of fourteen committeemen and over two hundred persons.[5]

Tule Lake, by April, was already in nonmilitary hands. Washington, however, persisted in its intransigency over enemy demands that the legitimacy of the committee of fourteen be recognized and that the group be released. From Secretary of War Stimson on down, the maintenance of the stockade and the separation of "troublemakers" was believed to be essential for maintaining tranquillity at Tule Lake.

Within the aggrieved, frustrated, and psychologically exhausted community, the stockade continued to be the prime source of disharmony and a symbol of galling injustice. The WRA had regained full administrative control of the center, but the Army continued to exercise dominion over the loathsome, closely guarded institution which stood in the out-of-bounds "white area," in full view of the community. Moreover, military patrols were still very much in evidence, assisting in the pickup of antiadministration belligerents. In the months following the hunger strike, the stockade population had climbed beyond the 350 mark.

Owing to the leadership vacuum brought about by the relentless Army pickups and purges, Tule Lake saw, in the spring of 1944, the temporary ascendancy of a collaborative clique. A conservative rival minority, consisting mostly of old Tulean "loyals," had had enough of the "useless display" of bravado and patriotism being stirred up by hot-brained newcomers whose preoccupation with human rights had accomplished nothing but brought on ever more repressive measures. A conciliatory team, a group of leaders from among the established settlers, approached the administration with a proposal for smashing the *Daihyo Sha Kai* deadlock, and the domination of the Kibei, by putting *status quo* to a center-wide vote. Only by the utilization of the secret ballot—by giving Tuleans the choice between *status quo* and a "return to normalcy"—could the protest leadership's uncanny hold on the transferee majority be broken, they insisted. Authorities agreed to give it a try.

On January 11, as the Army take-over entered its third month, *status quo* was put to a community-wide referendum. In a move to catch the opposition off guard, no sooner was the vote-taking announced than it was speedily carried out with troops out in full force. The expected buildup of resistance was expeditiously headed off, moreover, by the arrest of potentially disruptive elements in the early morning hours preceding the balloting.[6]

Jolted by the surprising governmental tactics, residents of one of the sixty-four blocks refused to vote. But there was little fight left in the general population: "People got wise that the longer they maintained the *status quo,* the more they were going to yank them and stick them in the stockade." Against angry charges of "bandit-like methods" used, *status quo* was overturned by a slim plurality of less than 500 votes out of the 9,000 cast.

Almost immediately the group of seven men who had come up with the referendum proposal were appointed by a coterie of camp moderates to formulate a back-to-work plan in cooperation with the Army and WRA. It was at this juncture (on January 15) that martial law was lifted and the center restored to WRA control.

The radical fringe of *status quo* advocates who were adamantly against cooperation as long as men were being held without trial in the stockade, who still considered the detained *Daihyo Sha Kai* leaders to be their duly elected representatives, were wild with anger to see the accommodationist team given immediate recognition by the

Army and WRA, provided with an office, placed on the WRA payroll, and given the use of an official car. They were not alone. Oppositionist groups were springing up in wild profusion [7] and many were quick to unleash accusations of "administration stooges" and "coop *inu*" against the seven appointees, now calling themselves the "Coordinating Committee," for a number of them were administration-favored, established old settlers influential in the Cooperative Enterprise, an institution resented by the "have-not" segment of the population, the transferees, as making money off the evacuees.

In spite of rumors of beatings and threats of violence to those who would capitulate to the latest Army-WRA manipulation, the back-to-work possibilities opened up by the new clique in power were privately welcomed by residents thoroughly disgruntled by the hardships brought on by the stubborn commitment to noncooperation. People with family responsibilities were in dire straits and desperate for their $16 a month. However incensed the declassed population continued to be over the overwhelming injustice of the stockade, the bulk of them were fed up with the self-defeating, counterproductive tumult. Many, who would never publicly admit it, were willing to swallow their pride and go along with kowtowing "loyals" and their conciliatory policy of only "justifiable" releases. Irresistible, under the circumstances, was the committee's pledge of "full employment." There was a spontaneous response to its clarion call for an all-out, back-to-work restoration of normalcy.

But little had the well-intentioned mediators realized that the employment picture at Tule Lake, never too good, had taken a dismal turn for the worse. Strong *Daihyo Sha Kai* protest against the vast Tule Lake farm supplying "loyal" centers, the Army, Navy, etc., had brought about a drastic curtailment in agricultural operations. Caucasians who had taken over jobs during the strike were not willing to be dislodged. At a time when WRA crisis managers were stressing budget cutbacks and bending over backward to counteract charges of coddling, repeated committee attempts to move camp officials to open up new job opportunities proved futile. When more than 1,000 of the unemployed could, in no way, be placed, faith in the sincerity of the committeemen rapidly deteriorated—plunging to an all-time low in late February, 1944, with the sudden intake of 2,000 more segregants from Manzanar. Sweeping job restrictions were uncompromisingly imposed by the administration, limiting employment to two jobs per household, regardless of the number of able-bodied persons in the family. And purged from the WRA payroll, by denying reinstatement, were all inmates considered antiadministration "undesirables," making a mockery of the committee's pledge of full employment.

Realizing that the seething discontent among the unemployed

could momentarily erupt into violence, the Coordinating Committee had little difficulty persuading the WRA to open up job opportunities involving the appointment of "30 men with WRA remuneration for the purpose of performing intelligence work which is to be used only for the advantage and benefit of the colony." [8] Confidential informers, euphemistically referred to as "fielders," were hired to infiltrate meetings, record incriminating opinions in boiler rooms, latrines, laundries, mess halls, and in various suspected storm centers of dissent. Dossiers were maintained on antiadministration heretics, agitators, and those suspected of underground sympathies.

From the outset, the administration chose to remain coolly indifferent, however, to the matter of stockade releases. Committee efforts to intervene on behalf of the detainees were considered meddlesome, and the conciliators were severely berated for interviewing prisoners without official sanction.

When distressingly little headway was made by the committeemen in the area of "justifiable" releases while the efficiency of fielders resulted in more and more people ending up in the stockade, charges of *inu* activity mounted in an ever-increasing tide. Since little could be done about the release of the all-important protest leaders, the Coordinating Committee was accused of freeing only friends when releases did occur. In this charged atmosphere, rival factions began consolidating their strength and goon squads were sent out to threaten violence. Reprisals were promised all who would "side with the U. S. government against the Japanese people." Fearing for their physical safety and feeling double-crossed by a capricious and untrustworthy management, the Coordinating Committee turned in their resignation on April 10.

III

With renewed probing of the State Department following the Tokyo protest of April 18, the release of stockade prisoners took on an accelerated momentum. By April 29, 276 detainees had been freed. On May 23, the Army withdrew from the stockade.

The underground was jubilant, boasting of the part they had taken in fomenting the international incident. "More extremist big talk," pooh-poohed the general population at the partisans' elated contention that the Army withdrawal and the speedup in prisoner release was due to the intercession of the Japanese Government.

For Kunitani and thirteen others who continued to be held in incommunicado detention despite Tokyo's demand that the committee of fourteen be turned loose, the months dragged on wearily, with no prospect of release. With Issei detainees in the stockade packed off to alien internment camps, their one important lever, access to the interceding power, seemed forever lost. As American citizens, they could hardly expect Japan to address the U. S. further in their behalf. In Washington's semantics of repression, moreover, the committee of fourteen had not even been arrested: They were merely undergoing "administrative separation."

In the months following the establishment of the stockade, more than fifty friends and relatives of detainees had petitioned the WRA for an opportunity to meet with an American Civil Liberties Union representative concerning their legal rights. Despite obstructionist tactics employed by camp authorities to discourage such a delegate from making an appearance, Ernest Besig, the Director of the Northern California ACLU, finally succeeded in gaining access to Tule Lake on July 10, 1944.

> As soon as I arrived, accompanied by Mrs. Adams, [his secretary] I was besieged by scores of evacuees who wanted to register complaints with me. Mrs. Murai [pseudonym] was the first woman I interviewed. She complained amid her tears that her husband had been placed in the Stockade for eight months and that she and her three children had not been permitted to visit him; that she had requested and had been denied permission to do so by the Internal Security staff, and that she had been turned away when she sought to appeal the matter to Mr. R. R. Best. . . . After hearing the complaint, I immediately prepared a written request by Mrs. Murai to visit her husband, which she signed, and I presented it to Mr. Best. Mr. Best declared he had no objection to having Mrs. Murai visit her husband but said she had never sought permission to do so. Mrs. Murai was permitted to see her husband at the Stockade that afternoon.
>
> I had no sooner settled the Murai case, however, when another woman came to complain tearfully that her husband had also been incarcerated in the Stockade for eight months, and that she had likewise never been permitted to visit him.[9]

From grief-stricken wives and relatives, Besig heard shocking tales of abusive treatment. Mrs. Murai was the first person permitted a visit since the establishment of the stockade; indeed, she was the only individual granted the privilege, despite a mound of applications Besig hastily prepared for distraught relatives. Vigorous protest on the part of the ACLU chief that even in state prisons and federal penitentiaries immediate relatives of incarcerated persons are allowed visitation rights failed to move the camp administrator, who stoutly refused to institute a system which would allow periodic visits for prisoners.

The ACLU executive was staggered by Best's insensitivity to the many grave violations of rights.

> I told him [Project Director Best] of complaints I had received that prisoners in the Stockade had not been permitted to see children born

after their incarceration, and that one young man had been denied visits from his fiancee, whom he was scheduled to marry the day after his arrest on November 13, 1943. Mr. Best acknowledged the truth of these charges, but declined to do any more than consider individual applications . . .

Until these women came to me with their complaints, I had no knowledge that there was a Stockade at Tule Lake, nor that around 400 persons had been detained there for periods varying from one month to nine months without any charges filed against them. . . . I arranged with some difficulty to interview seven or eight of those whose relatives had specifically requested me to counsel with them.

The interviews were conducted with considerable difficulty. Although Mr. Best and the project attorney Mr. Irving Lechliter assured me that the men in the Stockade were not prisoners, I was permitted no privacy in interviewing them.[10]

The first person to be interviewed was *Daihyo Sha Kai* spokesman George Kunitani:

Besig: My understanding when I came over to visit you fellows was that we were to be allowed a private conference with you. I am now informed such a private conference will not be allowed us, that the administration insists upon the presence of these boys with the guns on their hips, to which we object of course, insisting we are entitled to confer with clients privately. And I personally don't wish to participate in proceedings such as this, because I feel maybe you boys wouldn't express yourselves as freely . . . and unless you have something to say to me, O.K., otherwise, I am not going ahead.

[At this point in the interview, the project attorney, Mr. Lechliter, came into the police headquarters and wished to know what was wrong—Mr. Besig having previously telephoned to Mr. Best to protest the lack of privacy and having been told he could take it or leave it— and at Mr. Besig's insistence that he would not conduct interviews with these boys with a policeman in the room, Mr. Lechliter arranged for the two policemen to sit directly outside the doors of the small room in which the interviews were held.]

A. My name is Kunitani.

Q. And you have some parents in the Center?

A. No. I have a fiancee.

Q. Oh, you are the boy with the baby. I understand it is a good looking baby.

A. I haven't been given a chance to see it.

Q. Your fiancee was around to see us yesterday afternoon, and I don't know what I can do to help you here. I understand you are a citizen of the United States. Where were you born?

A. That's right. San Diego.

Q. And how old are you?

A. Twenty-nine, now.

Q. You're twenty-nine now. I understand that Mr. Ennis was around here the other day—he is from the Department of Justice—and that he discussed with you the possibility of renouncing your citizenship.

A. I have not consented.

Q. You appreciate of course that if you consent to renunciation of your citizenship, then you will therefore be treated as an alien and will be shipped out of here. That is the reason why they want you folks to renounce.

A. Now, I read and I have taken keen interest in what your organization has been doing in order to uphold the civil rights of the American citizens and the only thing I ask, which I wish to request, is decency. . . . I cannot see the reason of my detention, especially over such a long period of time . . . and the mail has not been coming in.

Q. You have not received any mail since about the first of July?

A. And first-class mail has always been censored and has to be opened before it comes in. . . . And then you have heard about the fact that we haven't been given an opportunity to even see anyone . . .

Q. I can't see any justification for that. Can't see what in hell basis they would have for denying that. Of course, the claim is that messages might be sent to the Center proper and cause additional difficulties. That is their story, of course.

A. That is their fear. And we cannot seem to convince them that it is going to be otherwise. . . . that the friction which is existing in the Center at the present time could be dissolved by liquidation of the Stockade . . .

Q. What sort of proposition do they come to you with?

A. They haven't come with any proposition.

Q. Except last Sunday, when Ennis was here—or when was he here? He was here very recently.

A. Three or four days ago, five days ago.

Q. Why did he come to you? Did he explain the new bill that was passed? [11]

A. That's right.

Q. Did he say he was going to send forms here?

A. That I didn't hear, but I hear someone was told to that effect.

Q. And that is apparently what they intend to do, and apparently think they have got it well set up so that the boys will request renunciation. That, of course you understand, is a personal matter with each person and you don't have to do anything you don't want to do. They won't be herded into any action. I think you boys are capable enough of deciding that issue for yourselves. It's none of my business. Anyone wants to renounce his citizenship, that's up to him. What was your relation to this situation here?

A. I was elected to be the head of this block representatives body.

Q. You were to be the head?

A. Yes, I was elected to be the head . . . of the negotiating committee, the chairman.

Q. . . . And who elected these block representatives?

A. The people at large. . . . It was the fifteenth of October, I believe, there was an accident on the farm road and in order to handle that situation the people formed the block representatives; they elected one person or an alternate from each block.

Q. Now, let me interpose a question here. Was that election held with the approval of the administration?

A. No, not at that time. The intention was that since the Center was in such a turmoil on account of this segregation . . . our intention of course was that organization was to be temporary . . . we had to get the approval of the authority in order to form a permanent one, and that formation was more or less ok'd by Mr. Myer during his visit here, November first. . . . November fourth we were in the process of electing these committees . . . for approval . . . but they evidently got the impression that the block representatives were responsible for that commotion on the night of the fourth and that was the whole mix-up, and that is what started this thing going in reverse against us . . .

Q. Where were you at the time of the commotion?

A. I was in Block Fifteen Mess Hall. We were having a meeting there. Just as I mentioned a while ago, selecting this final committee.[12]

Besig also interviewed Tom Yoshiyama, who had served as secretary of the *Daihyo Sha Kai*—reason enough, apparently, for his eight-month incommunicado detention ("because I was secretary I never said a word in a meeting"). Yoshiyama's arrest and ordeal in the "little stockade" was described to Besig as follows:

Q. You came in here November thirteenth?

A. Yes.

Q. And I suppose the military——

A. Picked me up? Oh, yes, about forty of them all around the block and about four of them came in, searched me and searched the whole room and picked me up with flash lights and bayonets. It was a sight though. They put me in the little stockade there for about four days. Oh, I had a hell of a time there, jiminy, that place——

Q. In what sense?

A. Well, in the first place you can't wash your face or anything and of course, if you want a toilet or something two police guards escorted us with the point of bayonet, even if we sat a couple of minutes on the toilet, urging us to hurry up. It was really a terrible time. And every time of eating, they brought us to the mess hall up there and about twenty soldiers, maybe more, escorted us to that mess hall and we ate and came back again. . . . When we were first in here we only had rice and carrots

> I don't know how many weeks. . . . some rice—so much—one spoon, and if lucky a carrot on top; and of course we have to eat because there is nothing else.[13]

Besig was to learn from the interviews that wanton acts of brutality had followed the arrest of the men during the November 4 incident:

> They claimed that the Internal Security officers had sworn at them and had knocked them to the floor with baseball bats and that one boy had been taken to a latrine and beaten up by the officers. Later, I also interviewed and received the same stories from two boys who had been beaten up at the same time and who had been released from the Stockade after lengthy detention without any charges or hearings of any kind. These complaints of brutal beatings were confirmed by Anne Lefkowitz and Gloria Waldron, W.R.A. employees, who told me that when they went to work in the Administration Building the morning following the incident, they found a broken baseball bat and a mess of blood and black hair on the floors and spattered on the walls, which they were compelled to clean up before they could go about their duties.[14]

Tule Lake was an object lesson on how the easy availability of power corrupts men who wield it—of righteousness sinking to ruthlessness as ordinarily decent men harnessed themselves with near-sadistic zeal to the trappings and techniques of tyranny, relieved of any sense of personal accountability by their patriotic commitment to what was clearly national policy: an inflamed chauvinism that fed on hatred and contempt for things Japanese.

Except for improvement in the diet, the transfer of the stockade from Army to WRA rule saw no step-up in concern for the rights of the accused nor in an amelioration of prison conditions, according to the eight detainees interviewed by Besig:

> Each stated he had sought unsuccessfully to ascertain the grounds of his detention from Mr. Best, Mr. Schmidt, the police chief and Mr. Lechliter. They also told me that Mr. Edward J. Ennis of the Department of Justice had talked to them at the Stockade about the new law permitting them to renounce their citizenship during war time, but had advised them against renunciation, whereas such representatives of the W.R.A. as Raymond Best, Assistant Director Harry L. Black, Project Attorney Irving Lechliter, and Messrs. Schmidt and Mahrt of the Internal Security Police had pressed such renunciations upon them while they were imprisoned in the Stockade. Indeed, in my conversations with each of those W.R.A. officials, each of them stated quite frankly that they had gotten rid of some alien Japanese by sending them to the Santa Fe, New Mexico, internment camp, and that they expected to solve their Stockade problem by getting the imprisoned men to renounce their citizenship and then send them on to Santa Fe for internment. . . .[15]

Following a Spanish Embassy protest that the WRA was violating the Geneva Accords in holding thirty-three Issei over three months, Best had shunted the men off to an FBI internment camp, without trial or hearing, for easy postwar deportation.

The wives of such men complained tearfully to me that . . . when these husbands and fathers were transferred to Santa Fe their families were not permitted to say goodbye to them. They begged me to do everything possible to permit them to rejoin their husbands. I sent written letters to the Justice Department and the W.R.A., requesting that they also be transferred to unite their families . . .

The W.R.A.'s cruel treatment of the evacuees is also exemplified by the erection of a beaver board wall on the side of the Stockade facing the colony or main camp. This wall was erected to prevent the worried women and children of the prisoners' families from waving to them a hundred yards away. Before the wall had been erected, Internal Security officers had from time to time driven these people away, and on a number of occasions had shot over their heads to frighten them away.

On August 11, 1944, several of the wives of the Stockade prisoners, who were near hysteria from the prolonged concern over their husbands, tried to get permits to see them. When permits were denied, the women refused to go home, so Internal Security officers dispersed them by dumping water on them. . . .[16]

Among WRA executive managers on the regional level, Besig's aggressive undercover work aroused consternation and alarm. Without warning the Project Director ordered an immediate halt to his activities. Before two days were up, the ACLU Director and his secretary were summarily ordered out of the camp.

Consequently, Mrs. Adams and I packed up at once and departed under the escort and surveillance of two armed Internal Security officers who followed us in an automobile. . . . I stated in my letter of July 14, 1944, to Secretary Ickes, "It is rather difficult to understand why such a procedure was necessary, but then, from our observations, we have found that an arrogant display of force is the rule rather than the exception at the Center." We drove the 500 miles to San Francisco with great difficulty, discovering after our arrival that two sacks of salt, including the paper sacks, had been dumped into the gasoline tank of my car while it was parked in the administrative section of the camp.[17]

During the two days spent within the guarded compound, Besig had learned for the first time of loyals living indiscriminately mixed in with disloyals in the supposedly segregated center. In an effort to head off what he sensed was an explosive situation in the making, Besig had urged the Project Director to quickly take remedial action:

He [Project Director Best] told me that he knew of the dangers the situation presented and of the terrific pressure the aliens who desired to be repatriated to Japan were subjecting the citizens in the camp and also subjecting the aliens there who wished to remain in the United States. I told him that I thought such a dangerous situation ought to be corrected and that the aliens who desired to be repatriated to Japan should be segregated from the residents of the Center and be placed in separate quarters where they could not intermingle with the others. He said that the Government would not undertake what he called a "forced segregation" at the Center. He told me, in substance, that such a segregation would be regarded as a confession of weakness on the part of the camp authorities' management of the Center and also that if the Government carried out such a segregation it would look as though the management had given in to the demands the aliens there who were seeking repatriation already had made . . .[18]

The administration's profound unconcern over the fast-proliferating Japanese-language schools, where the grandeur of being Japanese was being vigorously inculcated, also baffled the San Francisco lawyer:

While I was in the Center I expressed amazement to Mr. Best that Japanese language schools were allowed to be conducted in the Center. I told him that it was dangerous to allow those schools to exist and that it was wrong for the administration to stand by complacently while parents of children in the Center were being forced to send their children to such schools where they were subject to being indoctrinated with Japanese sentiment. Mr. Best told me that the maintenance of those schools was justified because "the evacuees would be sent to Japan anyway so it was desirable to have them learn about Japanese culture." [19]

In a constant jockeying for power, factionalism, intrigue, and espionage abounded among key administrative heads—as among center politicians—in the intrigue-permeated colony. Evacuee frustration, distorted by boiling indignation, had transformed the camp into an arena of intense political activity. There was open criticism among staff workers of the inept managing of the camp, some grimly predicting that the conditions under which the internees were living could only bring dire consequences. One of them reflected caustically:

Instead of being a center of disloyal Japanese, Tule Lake is really the dumping ground for misfits, anti-administration leaders, embittered youngsters and a lot of old people who just want to go back to Japan. The administration under Best is so stupid that it succeeds in uniting all these elements against itself, but that's the only point of unity in the colony.[20]

Among disgruntled camp denizens, Besig detected a smoldering resentment invoked by the undisguised race prejudice exhibited by certain minor executives and other civil servants.

> A considerable number of the administrative personnel, as was pointed out to me and as I observed, were Southerners who were outspoken in their contempt of the internees as members of a colored race . . . A minority of the camp staff were friendly to the evacuees and sought to help them as much as possible, but their friendliness merely caused further dissatisfaction and strife because they were assailed as "Jap-lovers" by a majority of the administrative staff.[21]

On his return to San Francisco, Besig enlisted the aid of attorney Wayne Collins, a longtime ACLU colleague and cofighter for the rights of the violated, then readying the Korematsu petition for a Supreme Court hearing, who had given vigorous support to the *Yasui, Hirabayashi, Endo,* and other evacuation test cases.[22] Collins immediately called the WRA office in San Francisco, demanding the release of the stockade prisoners. R. B. Cozzens, the officer in charge of the regional office, brusquely dismissed Collins' request, asserting that the WRA had every right under "military and executive orders" to segregate troublemakers in a "separate area"; and he vehemently denied that the stockade inmates were "imprisoned."

Collins' response was a blistering threat of a full-scale exposé of legal and physical atrocities perpetrated in private on native-born citizens in wanton violation of constitutional rights; and he issued a stern warning to the WRA: Unless the inmates were immediately and unconditionally released from the stockade, a habeas corpus lawsuit would be filed.

Horrified by the specter of hurtful publicity leading to additional congressional investigations, the Regional Director requested that Collins take no action until an opportunity was given Chief Solicitor Philip Glick and Tule Lake's Raymond Best to first confer with him in San Francisco. Collins agreed to the meeting, but he immediately began to lose his patience over stalling tactics which became quickly apparent. In Collins' words:

> On August 19, 1944 I telephoned to the WRA office and spoke to Cozzens and delivered an ultimatum to the WRA. He stated he would see Glick and Best immediately and arrange for a conference date. At 3:06 P.M. I telephoned to Mr. Cozzens who stated that Glick and Best wished to confer with me on Tuesday . . . I stated that I would not brook any delay following the conference date (Tuesday) but would file suits and also go to the Tule Lake Center. He stated that "no one can see anyone in the Center unless he has a written request from inmates." I informed him I had written authority to represent the persons confined in the Stockade and that no one would dare pre-

vent me from seeing my clients. I had already prepared Applications for Writ of Habeas Corpus for [George T. Kunitani] and Tom S. Yoshiyama.

On Tuesday following Aug. 19, 1944, the conference was held at the WRA office in the Sheldon Building; Best, Glick, Cozzens and I being present. I delivered another ultimatum. Then we went to another room in that office where Mr. Dillon Myer was found. He was suffering from some lameness and was tired. I was introduced to him. I delivered another ultimatum. They agreed to liberate all the persons confined in the Stockade. Mr. Best telephoned to the Center in my presence and ordered all the persons there confined released immediately. I informed Mr. Best that I intended to visit Tule and see the Stockade. He stated I would be welcomed.

I went to Tule a few days later. There was no vestige of the Stockade then discernible. Even the fence that surrounded it was gone.[23]

The sudden release of the men and the hurried demolition of the stockade left the colony baffled. It was not until August 31, 1944, that an explanation was given by the administration—the camp news-sheet, the *Newell Star,* announcing: "Conditions in the center at the present time are such that isolation of individuals is no longer considered necessary."

But attorney Collins had a footnote to the story of the hastily razed stockade: A year later it was, once again, re-established.

Arriving at the Tule Lake Center I discussed this new Stockade problem with Mr. Raymond Best, the Project Director, Mr. Lou Noyes, the Project Attorney, and other members of the WRA staff, upbraided them for having reopened the Stockade and for having incarcerated citizens therein without preferring charges against them . . . Because they came to doubt whether their actions could be justified in court and because of their fear that if the outcome of habeas corpus proceedings was unfavorable to the WRA the facts would be publicized . . . they consented to release all the persons who were held in the Stockade and to close the Stockade permanently. The imprisoned persons were released immediately and they were brought from the Stockade into the room so that I could verify the fact of their release.[24]

The prisoners turned out to be minors ranging in age from fifteen to seventeen.

Though assurances had been solemnly given that the stockade would be forevermore closed, it was employed anew as a tool of suppression following the orgy of renunciation, to be treated in one of the chapters to follow.

(11)
To Liberate
or Not to Liberate

. . . The Japanese stock with its extraordinary powers of loyalty, self-abnegation before a great ideal and endurance under danger and privation, has great values to bring to a rational world order. Japan must be crushed to earth. But when the fate of the Japanese is being decided—even more when, today, fools start empty-headed agitation against resettled Japanese American workers—one hopes that the record of the 100th Infantry Battalion [and the 442nd], U.S.A. will be remembered and pondered.

—*New York Herald Tribune* editorial, September 9, 1944

I

Despite the long-diminished justification of the military-necessity rationale, and ever louder protestations from the WRA that its purpose was not the operation of internment camps, it was at the pleasure of the President that the detention-exclusion program could be lifted. Authors Jacobus tenBroek, et al., writing in *Prejudice, War and the Constitution* (p. 331), contend that the President "personally directed that its termination be delayed until after the presidential election of 1944."

It was soon after Roosevelt's reelection to an unprecedented fourth term that the President, at a press and radio conference, made one of his rare public statements on the relocation centers. After answering a reporter's query about the West Coast exclusion by referring to the Nisei as "Japanese people from Japan who are citizens," the President made what might be construed as a Freudian slip: ". . . it is felt by a great many lawyers that under the Constitution they can't be kept locked up in concentration camps." [1]

One who was hotly pressing this very issue—of quickly liberating the camps—was Secretary of Interior Ickes, who, in the intervening period, had become the topmost man of Franklin Roosevelt's concentration camp' hierarchy.

Over a considerable span of time, the State Department, requested by the War Department, had asked the press to soft-pedal Japanese atrocity stories to enable the safe return of U. S. detainees.[2] In December 1943, the War Department finally authorized the release of the shocking data to coincide with the landing of the exchange ship, *Gripsholm,* "as this may work advantageously for our war effort even though it may jeopardize those of our nationals still imprisoned in Japan." [3] In the midst of raving West Coast and congressional furor arising from the inciting revelations, with renewed invectives hurled at the Administration's "social worker handling of U. S. Japs," the jurisdiction of the WRA had been hurriedly transferred, by Executive Order 9423, to Ickes' Interior Department on February 16, 1944.

"The bitterest witches' brew since the black days of the Reconstruction is boiling on the Pacific Coast," a January *PM* survey of coastal attitudes toward Japanese Americans had noted. "A campaign is underway to make lynching popular, and the vast majority of the press, the politicians, the profiteers, and the patrioteers have enlisted for the duration." In face of this rekindled racist uproar, the President had been advised by Attorney General Biddle on December 30: "Some of [WRA's] difficulties with the press and some elements of Congress might be lessened if, instead of being required to meet these pressures as a small new independent agency, WRA were part of a permanent department of the Government under the supervision of a member of the Cabinet and could rely on the relations of such a department with the public and Congress." In a follow-up memorandum Biddle urged the President: "If any action is to be taken, I think it should be taken promptly as the feeling on the West Coast is very strong and is extremely critical of the Administration." [4]

Ickes, the in-house critic of the whole sordid matter of "fancy-named concentration camps"—as he called them—was initially disinclined to take on so unsavory an assignment. But when it came to hostile anti-Administration cross-fire of the kind that the WRA and its National Director had been subjected to throughout 1943, no one was better qualified to run interference than the peppery "old curmudgeon." And he knew it.

On assuming his new responsibilities, Ickes stepped immediately into the line of fire by declaring to the press that even though the WRA had been criticized for not engaging in a kind of a "lynch party," under his jurisdiction "it will not be stampeded into undemocratic, bestial, inhuman action" by what he sarcastically labeled as "vindictive, bloodthirsty onslaughts of professional race-mongers." [5]

Coastal patriots bristled. The vitriolic crackpot fringe went wild with indignation at such unsubtle outbursts from a member of the

President's Cabinet. The White House was inundated forthwith with irate letters of Californians.

> I am quite disgusted with your appointment of Harold L. Ickes as War Relocation Authority chief. He is as bad as Dillon Myer. They both love Japs and should be sent back to Japan along with every Jap in this country. . . . A Jap is a Jap and they have certainly proved it in every way. Dillon Myer defends them to the point of insulting real Americans and Ickes, (who just loves Japs as he was the first to hire them for his farm) says those who are against the Japs are race mongers now isn't that an insult to Americans. You bet it is and I think he is a Jap lover and money grabber. He isn't thinking of America he is thinking of Ickes . . .
>
> 100% against Japs [6]

Though the mild-mannered National Director was not one to let his fists fly, figuratively speaking, like the blunt-spoken Interior chief, Myer also did not shrink from speaking out for just treatment of Japanese Americans. Whatever the mistakes of commission or omission of either of them in the discharge of their responsibilities as Uncle Sam's jailkeepers *extraordinaire,* the basic dedication of the two could not be challenged. Both Ickes and Myer were men of uncommon pertinacity to have put up with the scorn and venomous insults which were part and parcel of their distasteful wartime calling.

As head warden and chief troubleshooter for the interned population, Ickes was an inspired choice. Forthright with his friends as well as with his foes, Ickes showed the courage to repeatedly confront the President with humanitarian sentiments which were often stiletto-sharp criticisms of prevailing policies. In a forthright letter to Roosevelt some three months after taking on his new assignment, Ickes gave a strong, persuasive analysis of why the President should bring about an immediate revocation of West Coast exclusion orders and a quick end to the camps. Dated June 2, 1944, the letter began: "I again call your attention to the urgent necessity of arriving at a determination with respect to revocation of the orders excluding Japanese Americans from the West Coast." Ickes then proceeded to give his reasons:

> 1. I have been informally advised by officials of the War Department who are in charge of this problem that there is no substantial justification for continuation of the ban from the standpoint of military security.
> 2. The continued exclusion of American citizens of Japanese ancestry from the affected areas is clearly unconstitutional in the present circumstances. I expect that a case squarely raising this issue will reach the Supreme Court at its next term. I understand that the Department of Justice agrees that there is little doubt as to the decision which the Supreme Court will reach in a case squarely presenting the issue.

3. The continuation of the exclusion orders in the West Coast areas is adversely affecting our efforts to relocate Japanese Americans elsewhere in the country. State and local officials are saying, with some justification, that if these people are too dangerous for the West Coast, they do not want them to resettle in their localities.

4. The psychology of the Japanese Americans in the relocation centers becomes progressively worse. The difficulty which will confront these people in readjusting to ordinary life becomes greater as they spend more time in the centers.

5. The children in the centers are exposed solely to the influence of persons of Japanese ancestry. They are becoming a hopelessly maladjusted generation, apprehensive of the outside world and divorced from the possibility of associating—or even seeing to any considerable extent—Americans of other races.

6. The retention of Japanese Americans in the relocation centers impairs the efforts which are being made to secure better treatment for American prisoners-of-war and civilians who are held by the Japanese. In many localities American nationals were not interned by the Japanese government until after the West Coast evacuation; and the Japanese government has recently responded to the State Department complaints concerning treatment of American nationals by citing, among other things, the circumstances of the evacuation and detention of the West Coast Japanese Americans.

I will not comment at this time on the justification or lack thereof for the original evacuation order. But I do say that the continued retention of these innocent people in the relocation centers would be a blot upon the history of this country.[7]

By his blend of compassion, insight, and talent for "straight talk," Ickes had started the momentum for liberation. The pivot on which the evacuation had turned was "military necessity." Ickes was insisting that this was all nonsense now, that even the Army considered the argument unjustifiable.

Passing on Ickes' secret letter to State Department's E. R. Stettinius, Jr., the President inquired of the then Under Secretary: "Will you talk about this with Secretary Stimson and after that with Secretary Ickes?"

The Pacific Coast area, by then, had long ceased to be considered a "theater of operation," and not the slightest possibility of a Japanese landing existed. Though the Mayor of Los Angeles and others opposed to reabsorbing the minority were insisting that returnees would be in a position to blow up war plants and vital installations, far more war-related installations were to be found in the industrial East, where evacuees were free to go. Authorities had to think long and hard for a good military alibi for the continued exclusion. General George C. Marshall, the supreme head of the military, had advised the War Department a month earlier that "the only military objection to this move is the one presented by G-1 that the return of these people to the West Coast will result in actions of violence that will react to the disadvantage of American prisoners in the hands of the Japanese." The General, moreover, must have had the forthcoming presidential election in mind when he pointed out: "There are, of course, strong political reasons why the Japanese should not be returned to the West Coast before next November, but these do not concern the Army . . ." [8]

Satisfied that there was little controversy involved, Stettinius replied at once and without equivocation: "The Army is in accord with the views set forth by Mr. Ickes." The Under Secretary also alluded discreetly to the election year realities: "The question appears to be largely a political one, the reaction in California, on which I am sure you will probably wish to reach your own decision." [9] In other words, should the West Coast be antagonized? The Japanese issue could prove to be a political liability.

Mindful of the votes at stake, the President suggested that the Army first investigate California attitudes.

It required little research on anyone's part to realize that the media's enlargement on the atrocity revelations, often juxtaposed with distorted tales of Tule Lake "disloyals," had poisoned racial feeling to a point where it was worse than it had ever been in 1942.[10] Foremost in aggravating this anti-evacuee ill-will were the newspapers of the powerful Hearst chain, then outdoing one another in prostituting the privilege of free speech. The hue and cry were now aimed at disenfranchisement and deportation of the Nisei, for their "relocation" on some Pacific isle. Members of Congress from the coastal area were among a growing throng insisting that even loyals, regardless of their citizenship, would not be welcomed back. Some had quickly made capital of the shocking atrocity reincitement to importune the President into having "loyal citizens of Japanese ancestry" scattered about "in other parts of the United States," pleading that the "West Coast in general and California in particular have always faced a more complex problem in connection with people of Oriental extraction than have other parts of the United States." [11]

On June 12, 1944, in a memorandum directed to both Ickes and Stettinius, the President briefly outlined his own recommended course of action: "I think the whole problem, for the sake of internal quiet, should be handled gradually, i.e., I am thinking of two methods":

> (a) Seeing, with great discretion, how many Japanese families would be acceptable to public opinion in definite localities on the West Coast.
> (b) Seeking to extend greatly the distribution of other families in many parts of the United States. . . . Dissemination and distribution constitute a great method of avoiding public outcry.

Why not proceed seriously along the above line—for a while at least? [12]

Cordell Hull, Stettinius' superior, hastened to inform the President that though he fully agreed "that the matter of their resettlement in the Western Defense area should be approached discreetly," it was the Secretary of State's conviction that "the welfare of our people still in Japanese custody will be served by the release as soon as circumstances permit of all these people who are found to be loyal to the United States." The issue at hand—which had been bluntly presented by Ickes but which the President had chosen to skirt—was the "continued retention of these innocent people in the relocation centers." Hull continued:

> Moreover, the detention of these people and incidents that have occurred in our detention centers have resulted in protests from the Japanese Government and have supplied that Government with pretexts for refusing to negotiate for further repatriation of our nationals in Japanese custody or for their relief. Experience has shown that incidents involving persons in our custody attract more attention and result in more publicity unfavorable to our interests than incidents involving Japanese nationals and Japanese-American citizens at large. As long as these people remain in the custody of the Federal Government, therefore, any incidents concerning them are more likely to give rise to protests from the Japanese Government and to the possibility of retaliation and reprisals than if the people concerned are at liberty.[13]

Nothing had jolted officialdom as much as Japan's abrupt loss of enthusiasm for repatriation following the Tule Lake disturbance— a denouement which brought home to more than a few misguided politicians, and the press, the extent of the dangers implicit in their own inflammatory rhetoric.[14] In the improvident mishandling of the Japanese American minority, a singularly powerful weapon had been handed copy writers of Radio Tokyo. The wholesale racial detention of a people based on the mere accident of ancestry substantiated, as nothing else could, Japan's claim that the war in the Pacific was a crusade against the white man's arrogance and oppression; that "the Anglo-Saxon race feels superior to the Asiatics"; that "latest happenings [in the U. S.] show that their slogan, equal rights for all people, is nothing but a lie." [15]

II

The government had forced postponement of the Korematsu case, originally slated to be argued before the Supreme Court on May 1, 1944, by pleading that it was "not prepared." A companion suit, challenging the WRA's right to hold loyal U. S. citizens in detainment (*Ex parte Endo,* 323 U. S. 283), had also been conveniently pushed back beyond the presidential elections of 1944.[16]

Acutely troubling the War Department, as the day of reckoning drew closer, was the clear possibility of massive enemy retaliation on American POWs should a negative ruling smash to smithereens the camp setup, throw open the gates, and touch off race riots. With coastal bigots welled up on the idea of keeping the evacuees out by whatever means necessary—columnist Elsie Robinson threatening to "cut the throat" of any evacuee who dared to return, Los Angeles District Attorney Fred Howser warning of mass slaughter, California Congressman Clair Engle predicting "wholesale bloodshed and violence," and other hysterical absurdities making headlines—the War Department had reason for concern.

Starting in early 1944, the Army had begun quietly experimenting with a bit-by-bit return of selected evacuees to the excluded area in hopes of taking the shock out of the large-scale reentry, which they knew was inevitable. Certificates of Exemption were issued to evacuee wives of Caucasians, families of veterans of the 442nd, and other applicants considered unimpeachable in their loyalty on the basis of a careful security screening. As early as April 21, 1943, restrictions on travel within the Western Defense Command had been eased for Nisei soldiers, following the drive for volunteers in the camps.

Eventually, the War Department arrived at a system whereby evacuees desirous of returning to their rightful homes were subjected to another loyalty reexamination, administered this time by the Western Defense Command in cooperation with the Provost Marshal General's office—protested by Dillon Myer for the way "it discredits the loyalty determination of the War Relocation Authority." Myer echoed the outrage felt by evacuees: "I will not emphasize the frustrating and demoralizing effect the new processing will have upon the evacuees who already have reason to feel that they have been sorted, sifted, and classified beyond anything citizens of this country should have endured." [17]

Initially, Myer was determined to put a stop to the reprocessing, which he believed could turn into "a very vicious form of persecution"; and he sought help from Under Secretary of Interior Abe Fortas (later to become an Associate Justice of the U. S. Supreme Court), unaware that Fortas, himself, had originated the suggestion for submitting the evacuees to one last loyalty review. As early as March 1944, Fortas, while opposing a precipitous modification of coastal restrictions as sought by both Myer and Ickes, had recommended as a step in that direction the establishment of a loyalty reevaluation board, not unlike the Joint Board then clearing evacuees for outside work, which "would have final authority over releases." The Fortas proposal had been relayed in a memorandum to McCloy by a War Department aide:

Fortas does not feel that this screening by a board is necessary from a security point of view and proposes it only to promote public confidence. He believes that any substantial resettlement is impossible until a thorough public relations job has been done. . . . I think Fortas' approach is sound. Myer always went ahead on the principle that to admit the necessity of an investigation of these people cast a smirch which did not already exist, and I think the result of this policy has been exactly the opposite of that intended.[18]

Before long, the Fortas proposal for interdepartmental cooperation in the matter ended up becoming an Army move to perpetuate indefinitely its own power, whatever the Supreme Court ruling. Especially upsetting to Myer was the War Department decision to rescreen individuals already certified as loyal by the WRA and relocated to various parts of the country. Myer's displeasure and sense of exasperation over the latest Army absurdity were shared by Justice Department officials; and obviously unaware of the impetus that Fortas had initially given the reprocessing now to be initiated in the name of "protection against espionage and sabotage," Edward Ennis directed the Under Secretary's attention to the utter pointlessness of the whole procedure:

The adoption of such a procedure is not only contrary to our entire internal security experience in this war in which there has been no sabotage whatever by persons of Japanese ancestry, or espionage for that matter . . . but also it is directly in the teeth of the military authorities' own experience on the West Coast which resulted in the cancellation of most of the exclusion orders [issued against Germans and Italians]. . . . In fact the several Japanese propaganda agents whom we have caught and convicted were white, not Japanese.

In view of these considerations, the only purpose in excluding thousands of Japanese is to persuade public opinion . . . If the Government is going to act on any such basis, the least it can do is to keep such a group to an absolute minimum and not seriously accept the military security views which have been again advanced although they have been already abandoned even by the military authorities apart from this special racial application.[19]

On December 13, 1944, Secretary of War Stimson dispatched a seven-page memorandum to the President in which he reiterated the fear then being shared by many within the Administration that "serious trouble against returnees might result in retaliation against American soldiers." Since continued mass exclusion was "no longer a matter of military necessity," advised Stimson, he recommended the establishment of a carefully worked-out plan "which permits the orderly return of the bulk of the people . . . to the alternative of risking an unfavorable court decision with the confusion and disorder which would attend a sudden and unplanned return." The procedure was to include a quick switch-over from mass exclusion based on ancestry to *individual exclusion based on potential threat to military security*—against the possibility of espionage and sabotage, which, according to Stimson, was still an important consideration for the "critical" Pacific Coast area "because it is the base of our supply line to the active theaters of the Pacific War" and because, as Stimson put it, "the well-known face-saving attitude of the Japanese may provoke action of some sort against our West Coast." He referred to Tulean militants and "the possible damage which might be done if this group were permitted to be at large." The Secretary of War then briefly outlined the loyalty review procedure and subsequent governmental moves then in the planning stage:

> The determination of those who will be excluded will be made as a result of an examination and an evaluation of the information which the various agencies have accumulated . . . Persons to be excluded will be those against whom information is available showing their pro-Japanese attitude. It is expected that less than ten thousand will be excluded in this manner. . . . When the final determinations have been made, the War Relocation Authority will transfer all persons to be detained to a segregation center. It is understood that the Department of Justice will ultimately . . . take over the responsibility for such detention and for determining which individuals should be released from detention.[20]

Of key importance to the proposed procedure was that the revocation of West Coast exclusion would be accompanied by an announcement by the Commanding General that only evacuees who had passed a rigorous loyalty clearance conducted by the military would be permitted reentry. "When this is known," Stimson assured the President, "I am confident that the common sense and good citizenship of the people of the West Coast is such that the inauguration of this program will not be marred by serious incidents or disorders."

Stimson, of course, had been one of the privileged few to be privy to the Munson certification of Japanese American loyalty, making his less-than-convincing attempt to justify for the record the original evacuation order all the more noteworthy. Stimson's memorandum to the President had begun with a familiar line of reasoning long manipulated by exclusionists:

> As you know, that program was instituted at a time when an attack on the West Coast was a definite probability and an invasion on a large scale had to be considered as a real possibility. Experience in Europe had given warning of the danger of the fifth column and had shown that residents having ethnic affiliations with an invading enemy

are a greater source of danger than those of different ancestry. The vast majority of persons of Japanese descent in the United States resided in the West Coast region. Social, economic and political conditions had intensified their solidarity, strengthened their ties with Japan, and had retarded their assimilation with the rest of the population.[21]

Having weathered the crucial November elections assuring his fourth term, the President resisted no further the Stimson recommendation for rescinding the West Coast exclusion. Though only a partial revocation, the return of the vast majority of evacuees was thereby assured—the announcement coming on Sunday, December 17, 1944, just hours before the Supreme Court handed down (on December 18) the *Korematsu* and *Endo* decisions. On the same Monday, December 18, the War Relocation Authority made public its termination policy: All centers under WRA jurisdiction were to be emptied within a half year to a year's time.

The sudden government reversal stunned exclusionist forces. Only two days earlier, several chapters of the Native Sons of the Golden West had wired the President: PRESS DISPATCHES STATE THAT IT IS YOUR POLICY THAT FORMER JAPANESE RESIDENTS SHALL NOT RETURN TO THE WEST COAST. NATIVE SONS OF THE GOLDEN WEST HAVE SERIOUSLY CONSIDERED THIS MAJOR SUBJECT AND COMPLIMENT YOU UPON YOUR STAND TO KEEP ALL JAPANESE OUT OF OUR WESTERN COASTAL AREA AT LEAST UNTIL THE TERMINATION OF HOSTILITIES WITH JAPAN.[22]

To help subdue nativist passion and excesses which might inflame the enemy to retaliate on captive U. S. nationals, the Army immediately executed a remarkable about-face from their previous position, assuming thereafter the role of champion and vindicator of a wrongly humbled minority. Lavish homage was paid the Nisei fighting man—leading, in time, to the utilization of the speaking talents of front-line white officers familiar with their do-or-die battle conduct in a propaganda counteroffensive in California which eventually zeroed-in on rural racial hot spots. Long overdue praise began to be heaped on the valorous Nisei's parents (many of whom were still behind barbed wire) for their "forbearance," their "decorum and dignity," their "magnificent restrained behavior." Governors, attorney generals, mayors, and other responsible officials who had shamelessly thrown their weight behind the inciters of race hatred were sternly put on notice that rights of the Japanese minority must be restored without incident, that the lives of American detainees and POWs now, more than ever, depended on their refraining from making inflammatory statements (see Appendix 9). Tolerance and American-style fair play were the message, at long last, spread across the width and breadth of the land.

III

Administration worries over impending litigations had been for naught, thanks to the unwillingness of the FDR Supreme Court to circumscribe the war powers of the President or the military, especially in relation to a group which, in the words of the highest tribunal, harbored "disloyal members . . . whose number and strength could not be precisely and quickly ascertained" (*Korematsu v. U.S.*).

The jailed and abused population was severely faulted, moreover, for having "retained loyalties to Japan" *subsequent* to incarceration. The majority Court opinion in *Korematsu* exonerating and upholding the federal action found it unpardonable that "approximately five thousand citizens of Japanese ancestry refused to swear unqualified allegiance to the United States and to renounce allegiance to the Japanese Emperor, and several thousand evacuees requested repatriation to Japan." Over the strong protests of Justices Jackson, Murphy, and Roberts (p. 74), the military-necessity rationale—about which the President's closest advisers shared serious doubts—was firmly vindicated by a majority ruling of the Supreme Court as justifying "exclusion of the entire group" because of the "finding of the military authorities that it was impossible to bring about an immediate segregation of the disloyal from the loyal." On the basis of suppositions, assumptions, and "findings," compulsory mass evacuation, based on the mere accident of ancestral affinity, was legalized as a proper exercise of war powers.

In *Ex parte Endo,* a case of a Nisei of exemplary citizenship seeking unconditional release from a relocation center, there was unanimous agreement among the nine Justices that an American citizen whose loyalty was unquestioned should not be subjected to the harassing leave procedure (see Appendix 11); that there was no legal basis for holding blameless citizens against their will. But again, the Court found it unnecessary to pass on the constitutional issues involved; and it chose not to find the "big guns"—the military, the President, or Congress—culpable for what had been perpetrated in the intervening years. Instead, the majority opinion, delivered by Justice William O. Douglas, went on to cast total blame upon the lowly WRA for exceeding its statutory authority. "Whatever power the War Relocation Authority may have to detain other classes of citizens, it has no authority to subject citizens who are concededly loyal to its leave procedures." The avowed, ostensible purpose of Executive Orders No. 9066 (authorizing the evacuation) and No. 9102 (establishing the relocation centers) had been "protection against espionage and sabotage." The Court found both orders "silent on detention"—also in the case of the Congressional Act of March 21, 1942, the one giving "teeth" to the military. In other words, all these enabling statutes had, in no way, authorized detention as a part of the original program of evacuation, *certainly not the detention of loyal citizens.*[23] Detention of law-abiding, exemplary citizens which has no relation to "protection of the war effort from espionage and sabotage" is therefore unauthorized and illegal, concluded the learned Justices.

The Supreme Court, by using a "divide and conquer" tactic (by adjudicating each of the test cases on as narrow a ground as possible), had allowed *Hirabayashi, Korematsu,* and *Endo* to pass "through the court without at any point encountering constitutional condemnation," according to tenBroek, et al. Though *Gordon K. Hirabayashi* (see p. 291, fn. 14), a Quaker college student who refused to submit to what he believed were out-and-out racist orders had been convicted on evacuation as well as curfew violations, the Court had ruled upon the curfew order only.[24] Though the *Korematsu* challenge involved the unconstitutionality of detention as well as the evacuation, the Court chose to rule on the exclusion only. The "court divided the indivisible," maintain the authors of *Prejudice, War and the Constitution* in describing the High Court maneuvers as "a feat facilitated by the fact that the *Endo* case, purporting to deal with detention, was handed down with *Korematsu* on the same day as a sort of package."

The Court's scandalous failure to dig for the facts while indulging in "tactics of division, delay and evasion" also came under severe condemnation:

> The court declined to review the military action for bad motives or unreasonableness; declined to investigate factually whether there was a military peril, whether the measures adopted were appropriate to cope with that peril, and, if so, whether they unnecessarily invaded constitutional rights and guarantees; declined even to inquire whether the judgment made by the military was a military estimate of a military situation. Apparently all that the court required to foreclose judicial scrutiny was that the action had been taken by the military. The military thus was allowed finally to determine the scope of its own power.[25]

The more fundamental gut concern of many, that the nearly three-year moral atrocity—the imprisonment, the physical and mental abuse, of thousands of men, women, and children not accused of crime—violated and grotesquely distorted nearly every guarantee of the Bill of Rights, the Supreme Court carefully chose to sidestep. Also left open and unresolved was the question of a democracy's right to hold in detention even citizens branded disloyal in the arbitrary judgment of a handful of its functionaries.

(12)
Renunciation

. . . As a nation we began by declaring that "all men are created equal." We now practically read it "all men are created equal, except Negroes." When the Know-Nothings get control, it will read "all men are created equal, except Negroes and foreigners and Catholics." When it comes to this, I shall prefer emigrating to some country where they make no pretense of loving liberty . . . where despotism can be taken pure, and without the base alloy of hypocrisy.

—ABRAHAM LINCOLN, August 24, 1855

I

A policy affecting the Nisei more destructive of loyalty than the dogmatic oath-taking of registration was one which proceeded from the so-called "denaturalization bill" passed by the 78th Congress and signed into law on July 1, 1944. As Public Law 405, the legislation provided that an American, with the Attorney General's approval, could renounce his citizenship on American soil in time of war, a procedure generally not allowed in civilized countries due to the well-known reaction of war hysteria.

Proposed by Attorney General Biddle, Public Law 405 was a compromise measure to a number of more punitive and constitutionally doubtful bills introduced in Congress calling for the sweeping deportation of Americans of Japanese parentage. Representative Clair Engle of California, for example, had pushed for far broader legislation than the Attorney General's, declaring, "We don't want those Japs back in California and the more we can get rid of the better." Another Californian, Congressman J. Leroy Johnson, had sought to revoke the citizenship of all who had replied "no" to the ill-administered, sloppily framed loyalty question. Biddle's approach: Better to pass something which could be sustained in court than go all-out and run the risk of having the law declared unconstitutional.

The renunciation bill was primarily intended for the easy post-war disposal of troublemaking Kibei, of which there were a preponderance at Tule Lake.

Regarded with suspicion in the beginning, the denaturalization privilege had surprisingly little impact on Tulean toughs, for whom its "benefits" were intended. "Not understanding the origin of such legislation," wrote back the Community Analyst, "the mere fact that the law emanated from the old bugaboo—'the government'—meant that it was part of some elaborate plot against the individual home and hearth at Tule Lake." [1]

Keenly aware of the embittered young horde demanding to be "Japanese," the Attorney General and others had fully expected an impressive number to jump at the opportunity to accomplish this legally. But with the demolition of the bitterly resented stockade, the tumult and unrest had subsided. By the end of November, the Justice Department had received only 117 requests for applications.

Initially, the group in Tule Lake most perturbed by the Justice Department announcement that applications for voluntary removal of citizenship were now receivable were the Nisei and the Kibei of the loyal stripe. Pro-America Tuleans viewed with apprehension the preposterous rumors taking shape among repatriates and rebelled at attempts of busybody well-wishers to talk them into "renouncing" as invaluable for chalking up a "record of loyalty" to the land in which they would, in all probability, have to make their future as America's rejects.

II

With the annihilation of the short-lived collaborative movement in April 1944, the radical fringe of the *status quo* advocates surfaced from their underground activities to become the dominant power faction. The once fragmented movement was made up largely of alien repatriates and parolees from internment camps who bore the scar of bitter misfortune and mistreatment, who wished to be sent back to Japan as quickly as possible. Backing up this reactionary leadership was a fervently pro-Japan nucleus of militant Kibei expatriates, equally ardent in their loathing for a "counterfeit democracy" which had treated them badly and had vilified every ideal they held as sacred. United under the title of the "resegregationists" (*Saikakuri Seigan*), they agitated and petitioned constantly for the fulfillment of a more complete segregation which would physically separate them from those whom they suspected of stool pigeon activities, the pro-America loyals—a clear-cut separation which they insisted the government had originally intended in setting aside Tule Lake as a camp for disloyals.

[A mixture would be] the fundamental cause for disturbance and rest-lessness . . . which will add another accusation to WRA policy by Dies Committee, Race-baiting Politicians and professional patriotic organizations . . . The re-segrees [sic], if granted to live in a sepa-rately established area, will guarantee full cooperation with center officials in keeping peace and harmony within that area.[2]

There were contending official viewpoints as to the advisability of going ahead with another costly and administratively difficult segregation of the segregated in light of the High Court litigations then threatening to challenge the very concept of holding American citizens not charged with crime on the vague charge of disloyalty. It was hoped, at least by the WRA, that the problem might be re-solved by the expediting of repatriation by the State Department. The end result was bureaucratic ennui and inaction.

And in strange contrast to the WRA's uncompromising authori-tarian stance of a few months earlier, when dissidents and disruptive revolutionaries were summarily disposed of in the "separated area," the energies of the local administration, after the downfall of the accommodationist faction, were no longer directed at solving prob-lems but at ignoring them.

Events of the past two years had conspired to convince a large number of the vanquished thousands who ended up in Tule Lake that their future belonged in the Orient, where, at least, "we have the chance of being equal for having the same colored skin." Or as put by one young pessimist: "Someday there might be another war and another evacuation. Why risk such a chance and let the next genera-tion suffer? Why stay where we're not wanted?"

Ill-prepared as most residents were for a future in Japan, the resegregationists were persuaded that the first order of business for Tuleans was to more fully pursue the "Japanese way of life" given WRA sanction at the time of segregation: to cultivate the mind, body, and awaken the "Japanese spirit" in preparation for their eventual expatriation. Among thousands of frustrated, idle, and anxiety-ridden young Tuleans the resegregationists easily won recruits. The Com-munity Analyst cued his Washington superiors: "The social and cul-tural community is emerging, and discussion is turning more and more to activities of an educational and cultural nature thought to be vital to the resident's welfare. . . . Politics, says the average Joe Goto of the Center, brought losses not gains." [3] In this climate, even the staunchest loyals became caught up in the public-spirited activities of the pro-Japan clique and their rallying cry of, "Let's increase the appreciation of our racial heritage," for identification with the glories of a proud and ancient culture acted as an antidote for the feelings of inferiority and shame long imposed on them. Under the resegrega-tionist banner of unity based on their common heritage as Japanese, a powerful group solidarity emerged in a backlash movement to the collaborative epoch, manifesting itself in a resurgence of devotion to their ancestral culture, which, for the sake of acceptance in America, most Issei and Nisei had made strenuous efforts to sublimate.

The gaining-acceptance-in-Japan community action program placed stress on self-refinement and self-cultivation in hopes of speeding up their assimilation abroad and began with a series of educational lectures on Japanese history, customs, ideals, and current affairs, the latter based largely on reports of Radio Tokyo. On a more practical level, a variety of private classes sprung into operation, offering instructions on Japanese manners and etiquette, Japanese cooking and other household accomplishments, and *odori* (dancing) lessons, considered essential for imparting to young ladies the much desired mark of refinement: gracefulness of movement. For the aesthete, there were *senryu* poetry clubs, *utai* singing and classical drama societies.

Long disparaged by the Issei and their Kibei peers as being an uncultivated generation, lacking the polish of a "true Japanese," worried Nisei teen-agers flocked in droves to classes on Japanese cultural pursuits. Language ability and cultivation of Japanese-style "good manners" were prime requisites, but mastering the rudiments of the tea ceremony, flower arrangement, Japanese-style painting, calligraphy, and other disciplines were considered important for enhancing the cultural attributes of a person. Attendance of English grade schools fell off precipitously as various wards soon established their own Japanese-language schools. Faced with the dilemma of assimilating back into their own "race," the young crammed frantically in their agonizing fear of ending up in their parents' homeland being only an embarrassment and a family burden.

> When your future is washed up here, and you're just a green kid in your parents' eyes, there's plenty to learn, plenty to master. My father says I couldn't get by with what I know now. The issei have worried about our futures long enough. Now it's our turn. . . . They never had a place here, never even had citizenship. Now we're put in the same boat and we're not prepared.[4]

In Tule Lake, the grueling schedule imposed by parents and teachers made no allowance for "frivolities," such as movies or socials. Nisei dances were frowned upon as wholly inappropriate and unfeeling at a time when loved ones in Japan were undergoing extreme hardships—and roundly disparaged by the Issei and Kibei as an example of effete Americanism: "When the first dance here after segregation was broken up, there was no shocked raising of eyebrows at this act of gangsterism, but general approbation."

Considered far more worthwhile was the resegregationist program of inculcating in young minds the importance of conditioning the body to the severe discipline expected of a "true Japanese." Under the direction of Kibei drillmasters, open-air calisthenics and cold showers became a regular 6 A.M. ritual in many of the blocks.

III

Though polite language had been used by resegregationists in their numerous petitions to Washington to be permitted to live in a separately established area, their humiliating failure to achieve this aim resulted in a militant take-over and "Japanization" of all community activities. Hurt by the incessant and often vicious propaganda stigmatizing the camp as one full of faithless disloyals, the pro-Japanese group decided that there couldn't be anything illegal in turning Tule Lake into one—into their homeland in miniature—where serious preparations for a future in the real Japan could be made with all due haste. The more cynical among them fully expected the approval of the government (whose officials were, indeed, even then debating the pros and cons of allowing in the "disloyal center" the ever-increasing un-American utterances and activities).

Of far-reaching consequence to the innocent thousands trapped at Tule Lake was the feeling which ultimately prevailed among policy advisers: that since the center was, in fact, set aside as a place for persons not loyal to the United States, "it would not be consistent with our general policy to prohibit expressions of loyalty to Japan whether in school or not. If, moreover, we set out to prohibit such expressions in the school specifically, we would be involved in a monitoring program which I feel it would be impossible to carry out." [5]

It did not take long before Tule Lake's cultural revivalism entered an out-and-out patriotic phase. Under resegregationist influence, early morning calisthenics metamorphosed into militaristic marching and drilling to the fanfare of a bugle corps, with Rising Sun emblems stenciled on sweat shirts and sweat bands.

In camps for loyal denizens, evacuee papers and pamphlets underwent careful scrutiny for un-American sentiments (see Appendix 5) but at Tule Lake, the heightened fervor of ultranationalism was given free expression in publications which sought to convince residents that reports of Japanese defeats were nothing but distortions and lies, that the war would be a long one, but that Japan would emerge triumphant. Japanese-language schools were turned into propaganda outlets where pro-Nippon proselytizers exalted the doctrine of Japan's national destiny ("to free the Orient of the domination of Western nations"), where youths were daily exhorted to return to the moral and spiritual values of their Oriental heritage: to the spirit of self-denial and sacrifice. The school day in Tule Lake began with a ceremonial bow to the East.

The fear of swift reprisal and the ever-intimidating presence of marauding "pressure boys" kept the subservient majority from uttering anything in disapproval. Following the stabbing death in July of an influential "old Tulean" who had spoken out against the radicals, no one dared to criticize the fanatical clique or their extremist innovations.[6]

The increased militancy of the resegregationists was reflected in the formation of three patriotic organizations in the fall of 1944: the *Hokoku Seinen Dan* for young men; the *Hokoku Joshi Seinen Dan* for women and girls; and the powerful parent organization, the *Sokuji Kikoku Hoshi Dan* (Organization to Return Immediately to the Homeland to Serve) for older men. To the immense satisfaction of the militant leadership, officials of the WRA gave tacit approval to their overt nationalistic setup and pretensions of being a "cultural study" group by alloting administrative office space and raising no objections to the installation of the Rising Sun flag.

The Nisei viewed the increased radicalization with grave misgivings, and by feigning colds and other indispositions, many dropped out of attendance at morning drills and exercises—giving rise to unsubtle tactics on the part of zealots to swell the resegregationist membership. The pressure subsequently exerted on recalcitrant loyals by this dictatorial extremist element became intense and constant.

Since there were no moves made to stamp out the proselytizing, which a few months earlier would have been stoutly punished, the Nisei could not help but wonder: Were authorities now determined to make the people disloyal? Were total spoilage and deportation a damnation conspired at? Why, otherwise, would they allow such anti-American pressure to work itself up into such a violent frenzy?

IV

Then came the staggering, totally unexpected announcement of the lifting of exclusion and the closing of the camps. Tuleans were thunderstruck. Transferees who had counted on Tule Lake being the one "permanent camp" were downright furious. The WRA liquidation policy at a time when the war was still raging was denounced as cruel, inhumane, "another double cross," and segregation a "dirty trick": "bringing us here with so much trouble and now it doesn't mean a thing!" Was the protective custody for which so many had paid dearly with their "no-no" declarations of disloyalty all for naught?

Newspapers soon told of terroristic efforts on the Coast to stop the return: night riders intimidating families attempting to resettle;

shots fired from speeding cars into Japanese homes; war-scarred Nisei veterans being assaulted, thrown out of restaurants and barber shops. With each new incident, Tuleans became wild with fears of the "outside":

> You know, people who live for three years in a camp know nothing about the outside. They can only believe what the papers can say. On the west coast, such a paper like the Examiner speak about bullets and terrorism . . . caused by fanatics who hate even the Nisei who never did them any harm. The papers said people were shooting, dynamiting barns, burning houses.[7]

To be sure, there were resident loyals who could hardly wait to extricate themselves from the rising tide of paranoia swallowing up the fenced-in population in their total isolation from reality. But the general reaction to the prospect of going "back to America" at a time when white boys were still being killed and maimed by the Japanese in the Pacific was one of terror and revulsion: "And be pumped full of lead? Hell no, not me!"

As in camps everywhere, tactics by which the government could be forced to live up to its commitment of protective custody were fiercely debated.[8] Parents doomed for deportation were in mortal fear that in the liquidation of the special camp for disloyals, sons could easily be reclassified as loyals, made subject to the draft, and the family would be forever parted. Something drastic had to be done, and quickly!

At this time of quiet desperation, a group of twenty Army officers appeared on the scene to clear residents for reentry into the once forbidden coastal areas. To the shock and dismay of male disloyals called up for loyalty reexaminations, an alarming number—*despite protestations of disloyalty*—were receiving "individual exclusion orders," which were tantamount to eviction notices but carried severe penalties if they would attempt to return to their home communities. In other words, the vast majority of Tuleans were being reduced to the same status as residents of relocation centers, with the exception that they would have to stay clear of the West Coast and make their fearful way in some strange, unknown community. Thus an alleged query made by a number of Army examiners, "Do you want to go out or do you want to renounce your citizenship?" [9] caused residents to conclude that since authorities appeared to be intent on emptying the camps, the only possible way of avoiding the unknown consequences lying outside the gate was to "renounce."

This, in fact, was the view given widespread dissemination by the *Hokoku-Hoshidan*,[10] which, thereupon, began the manufacturing of a wholesale stampede toward renunciation, a campaign aggravated by the presence in the project of a Justice Department official, John

Burling, who proceeded to conduct hearings for the 117 embittered Kibei who had earlier sent in renunciation applications. Youthful fanatics seized upon the ongoing hearings, where citizenships were being "denounced" in no uncertain terms, to step up their campaign of intimidation, aimed at compelling all Nisei and Kibei to solidify their disloyalty. The call went out for mass action: If citizen Tuleans would act as a unit in renouncing a totally "worthless" citizenship, authorities would be forced into keeping Tule Lake open!

Unbearable psychological pressure was thereafter brought to bear on the neutral Nisei and Kibei, with appeals shrewdly calculated to play on their sense of family and community obligation: that becoming a renunciant was the only sure way that security for the whole family could be achieved while helping the camp-wide campaign to build a disloyalty bulwark against forced relocation.[11] For those consumed by fear, indecision, and hopelessness, the argument was persuasive. Why risk the chance of falling victim to Caucasian atrocities or the possibility of not finding work and starving to death on the outside? By simply declaring loyalty to the Emperor and tossing off what amounted to a mere "scrap of paper," they could cancel out forced resettlement, rule out the draft, and extend protective custody for the entire family until such time as they could depart for safer shores.

In an effort to maximize group and parental pressures, the *Hokoku-Hoshidan* also resorted to lies, exaggerations, and the dissemination of outrageous rumors. Whispered murmurings crystallized into the widespread belief that unwillingness to renounce would be reported back to Japan via the State Department, resulting in the Imperial Government's taking reprisal on sisters, brothers, and other close relatives in Japan—that citizens who refused to renounce would be punished as enemies of the state on their arrival in Japan.

V

The renunciation applications of the 117 Kibei were quickly approved by the Attorney General on the return of Burling to Washington, on December 23, 1944. Endorsed, also, was a plan for the subsequent removal to internment camps, as "undesirable enemy aliens," of seventy activists from among the 117 confirmed citizen renunciants.[12] Their zealotry as officers of the patriotic organization had resulted in a staggering 2,000 renunciation applications flooding the Justice Department in the intervening period.

Troubled by this bizarre turn of events, in which the carefully laid trap to ensnare and weed out the provocators was catching, instead, their blameless victims, Biddle, Ennis, Burling, and others in the Justice Department hierarchy had second thoughts on the wisdom of further permitting what had obviously turned into an incredible renunciation snowball. Edward Ennis was to recall later:

> When thousands of applications for renunciation were received we debated . . . whether to scrap the whole program as a mistake or go ahead with it and attempt to persuade the applicants not to renounce. There was a division of opinion but the Attorney General concluded that since the law had been enacted we could not refuse its "benefits" to applicants . . .[13]

Justice Department officials had hoped that the immediate arrest and removal of key *Hoshidan* leaders, including a clean sweep of the officers of the fanatical youth arm, the *Hokoku,* would effectively stamp out the fast-developing hysteria. But the removal (made two days after Christmas, 1944) succeeded in only exacerbating difficulties. The wanton display of brute force in the predawn assault on the sleeping victims roused the embers of community-wide rage, sweeping up the neutral majority in heightened support for the radicals. The camp attorney, in later filing a report, commented:

> The Department of Justice administrative methods employed in the handling of the removal of this group of seventy proved to be not so good. A detail of some forty Border Patrol Officers and men armed with automatic rifles and sub-machine guns took custody of the group in an atmosphere of tension caused by the apprehension of the internees in the dead of the night and the display of mass force and arms. The military unit stationed at the Center also took advantage of the occasion to stand by in a display of weapons and arms wishfully anticipating trouble. . . . That method was spectacular but harmful in that it served to make the leaders appear more important than they really were, thus making them martyrs and heroes.[14]

Police state tactics stirred sickening memories of earlier removals: of stockade detainees packed off to internment camps with nary a farewell visit with wives and children; of terroristic no-knock break-ins and Army dragnets; of bayonet-point arrests and removals during registration and other assaults on their sense of self-respect.

Within the community, the news of the predawn violence spread rapidly. Seizing the emotion-fraught occasion to enhance their power and prestige, the *Hokoku-Hoshidan* acted swiftly to dramatize their open defiance of the latest governmental savagery. Following breakfast, the cold Tule Lake air was pierced by the shrill "emergency call" of the hurriedly assembled bugle corps, bringing "*Hokoku* members in headbands, about 500 strong" racing to the Gate 3 departure point. There in hailing distance of the corralled prisoners, a dazzling farewell send-off was staged to the blare of bugles, exhibitionistic marching, and the singing of nationalistic airs:

> Wives and relatives joined with them. Although a nasty blizzard was

up, about a thousand were lined up, the *Hokoku* coming down in marching order. . . . the trucks drove off after lunch amid the usual shouts and *banzais*.[15]

The rousing, soul-stirring demonstration had an immediate chain reaction among the stricken families, evidenced in an attitude of not wishing to lower their pride to "those *ketos*." Anger and humiliation shifted to a posture approaching triumph: "My son has now become a Japanese!" exclaimed parents of transferees as they received congratulations of well-wishers. A fielder reported to his Caucasian superior: "People who went to sympathize with Mrs. Aramaki told me that she was happy about his [her husband's] internment, because it made him a real Japanese. They say every one of the wives is like that." Since it was strongly rumored that internees at the Crystal City "family camp" received far better treatment as POWs than citizen inmates of relocation centers, wives were already looking forward with euphoric certainty to having the family reunited there.[16]

Nurtured by their own wishful thinking, the *Hokoku-Hoshidan* immediately began proclaiming that the long-sought-for goal of resegregation—the process of separating the "true Japanese" from the fence-sitters—had finally begun. Extremist propaganda now took on a new twist: Join the *Hokoku* and make yourself quickly eligible for the "honor of internment." What better long-term haven could be achieved than one safe behind prison walls of Bismarck or Santa Fe, where many of our revered prewar community leaders are still being held!

In the belief that it would provide a swift, sure avenue to the "honor" of internment, there was a rush to elect new officers to replace those arrested. In the days to follow, the local administration was badgered by requests that the Justice Department be informed of the *Hokoku's* eagerness to join the first group transferred to Santa Fe. A "preferential hearing" was urgently requested, and renunciation classes were begun by Kibei leaders to instruct members in proper answers to be given, so that acceptance would be positively assured.

VI

The reappearance in Tule Lake on January 11, 1945, of John Burling and a team of Justice Department hearing officers threw the seething community into a frenzy of renunciation hysteria as the fanatic fringe broke all restraint in their campaign of fear and intimidation to bring about a wholesale disloyalty stampede. There were families living in overzealous resegregationist blocks who secretly changed living quarters, hoping to escape the influence of terrorists. Youths ran away from home to get out from under the nightmarish conflicts which often raged within a family. But behind watchtowers and fences there was no way of fleeing the intense, un-relenting, and inescapable pressure which closed in from all sides. Hundreds of Nisei and Kibei allowed themselves to be corralled into the ranks of the *Hokoku* out of fear of unknown consequences to themselves or their families if they did not comply. In terror of fron-tier-style lynchers and lamp post artists to whom the Chinese had once fallen victim, countless others joined willingly in the frenzied drilling, bugling, and goose-stepping, hoping it would achieve re-moval as a group to the safety of a Justice Department haven, free from threats of being cut adrift in a vindictive, hate-filled America.

On December 31, the Justice Department had announced that the renunciation law would be restricted to those over seventeen years of age. It was a clarification long overdue, for panicky residents had begun to pressure all of their children to renounce on the assumption that unless every one became "just another alien" like his parents, citizen members of the family would be evicted while alien members would end up on ships bound for Japan—another one of the pre-posterous rumors driving terror into youths bound by strong family ties:

One [thing] that put a scare into me was that families would be sepa-rated. To me, I just had to sign on that paper, so I piled lies upon lies at the renunciation hearing. . . . I didn't mean anything I said at the time, but fear and anxiety was too strong. I have regretted that I took such a drastic step, in fact I knew I would regret it before I went into it but I was afraid if I was torn away from the family I would never see them again in this uncertain world. I should have had more confidence in America but being torn away from my home and all made things so uncertain. I would never have renounced if . . . Administration made it clear that there would be no family separation. But the Administration could not assure us . . .[17]

Though it was generally understood that no one showing signs of coercion would be permitted to sign the renunciation document, official insensitivity in this regard moved the on-the-scene social ana-lyst to warn his Washington superiors: "This is history repeating itself again. Mass hysteria has struck again. Individual and voluntary ac-tions are rare." Concerning the 117 Kibei whose ill-timed hearings had helped to touch off the renunciation mania, the analyst had passed on the following confidential observation: "Mr. Burling as-tutely noted a patterning of response after the first few hearings."[18]

The point of greatest interest is that, except for a disclaimer inserted now and then in the *Tulean Dispatch,* neither the WRA nor Justice Department lawyers involved in the hearings made any constructive move to stamp out the absurd rumors then being given credence or to call a halt to obvious coercive tactics and pressures gathering irreversible momentum. Nor was any decent attempt made by the battery of legal specialists on the scene to provide counsel to the confused, misinformed, and fear-crazed Nisei who could no longer respond as normal human beings.

Was it indifference and apathy, or could local officials and hearing officers have been unaware of the hysterical illogic then prevailing? The later observations of John Burling, then Assistant Director of the Alien Enemy Control Unit of the War Division of the Department of Justice and in charge of the mass hearings, provide insight:

> It was a commonplace witticism among the officials of the center at the time of these hearings that the population of the center was largely mad and that the center might properly be taken from the management of the WRA and transferred to the Public Health Service to be run as a species of mental institution. . . . Rumors of the most foolish nature circulated widely and were given wide credence. Given . . . a group of 18,000 substantially idle persons, most of whom had suffered racial discrimination for years and who had just been the victims of what must have appeared to them as the most outrageous incident of racial discrimination in American history, it was foreseeable that a state of very great emotional excitability would be created. Given further a nucleus of genuinely pro-Japanese leaders, it seems, at least in the light of hindsight, also foreseeable that this group could be whipped up into a sort of hysterical frenzy of Japanese patriotism.[19]

The failure of camp authorities to institute protective measures in the interest of the large neutral majority ended up in a veritable reign of terror. To escape being considered unsympathetic to the camp insurgents, young and old men everywhere began shaving their heads to simulate the *bozu* haircut of Japanese soldiers, the badge of *Hokoku-Hoshidan* membership. (*Joshi Dan* stalwarts were identified by pigtails.) Families of citizens who refused to fall in line and do the bidding of the rebel clique were often hounded night and day with threats of violence.

> It wasn't long before everyone who had no intention at first, were coerced to become a member . . . We had no other choice for we had no way of moving out or away from terrorism in this fenced-in concentration camp. . . . We complied by clipping our hair and abiding by the regulations of that organization. I was married in February, 1945, to a girl from the same block as ours whose family were members of the organization for the same reason as we were. Then on the 12th of February, my brother was interned at Bismarck Internment Camp in North Dakota. At the time of his apprehension, he had just become a member but since he was listed on a membership list which was confiscated by WRA, he was taken. . . . He was eighteen years old then having graduated in December, 1944, from Tri-State High on the Project. Since he was only a kid, he was afraid to withdraw from the organization since the pressure placed upon him was too great. I

regret very much that I sent my brother as a member . . . but that was the only way out at the time, for he had sacrificed himself in order to protect our family. . . . Once a member of the organization, there was no way of withdrawing from that organization and of feeling safe to roam in the colony. . . . During the time hearings were conducted in this center, these organizations were permitted to display their might and power so ostentatiously as though their selfish aim was the intention of everyone in this camp. It is just disgusting to believe that the Justice Department and the WRA remained on the sideline to watch us all renounce against our wishes when we couldn't act freely and express our true feelings toward this country. . . . I've never believed that such gangsterism could ever have been tolerated by any law-enforcing body.[20]   [Reparagraphed by author]

A vast spy network apparently enabled the *Hoshidan* to know who was renouncing and who was not. At the hearings, one did not dare to utter one's true feelings for rejection of one's renunciation application would be tantamount to betrayal of the rebel leadership, whose coaching classes demanded that one not weaken in damning U. S. wrongs, in feigning devotion to the Emperor, and in claiming dual citizenship, whether one possessed it or not.

. . . the fanatical groups seemed to know everyone's act and nothing seemed confidential in this congested center. So I could not tell the Justice Department's hearing-examiner my real reason. . . . I do not believe such an absurd idea as the Emperor is God. But the fears make the answer slip out . . . When they told me to sign the paper, my heart really sank, for I could see I made a mistake and was really sick and shaking with fear. The hearing officer didn't seem to care about this, or he would have called me back and asked me [for] the true story.[21]

The vicious climate, the fears, the worries, and resultant despair proved too much for a Nisei wife who, according to the Community Analyst, ended up in a mental institution.

[H.D.], a young wife of 26, broke down completely because of pressures on her husband to join the Hokoku-Hoshidan. Of late, she had heard "voices" telling her she is "not a true Japanese," that she should leave Tule Lake. Her first crises came after the November incident, when obviously, she realized that she did not belong in Tule Lake. The real crack-up, however, came after "friends" of her husband put pressure on him to join the Hoshidan, with the same pleas and threat she now hears in frequent hallucinations.[22]

Many Nisei naïvely acted on the assumption that renunciation was not a final act, that it could later be canceled.

On that day of the hearing, I remember I was afraid to back out . . . My wife and I decided we will have to go since the eyes of that group were upon us and then later on we'll cancel our renunciation like expatriation applications. The hearing lasted for a short time. It was very simple. The questions were identical to the ones others had been asked so I answered them in the same fashion as instructed.[23]

Authorities remained strangely immobilized as thousands, out of terror and hopelessness, play-acted the part of fanatic. Internal security officers who had been ruthlessly efficient in picking up agitators and suspected troublemakers for the stockade, now curiously opted for a "hands off" policy in a discreditable breakdown of law and order—a policy which led many to believe that the *Hokoku-Hoshidan* program had the sanction of the WRA.

It was well into January, after 2,500 more renunciation applications had poured into Justice, when a letter from John Burling condemning extremist activities was made public—copies of the letter being posted in all mess halls beginning on January 23. Addressed to top *Hokoku-Hoshidan* leaders, the message read in part:

I am well aware that your two organizations have put pressure on residents of this Center to assert loyalty to Japan and that in a number of cases physicial [sic] violence was employed. There is no more right to engage in Japanese patriotic ceremonies or to publish a pro-Japanese paper in this Center, where some loyal Americans still live, than there is anywhere else in the United States. It is as treasonable to coerce others into asserting loyalty to Japan here as it would be outside. All these activities will stop.[24]

For all his expostulation, it was a gesture too weak to make any kind of an impact—it had come too late. In overt defiance of the cease and desist orders, the fired-up partisan constituency doubled in fury their noisy drilling and bugling, now conducted with a vengeance in front of the "white area." Participants in this mass delirium soon numbered in the thousands, with two mammoth-size performances given on Sundays for the benefit of their late-sleeping white overlords.

The exasperating early morning din caused authorities to momentarily awaken from their bureaucratic stupor. *Hokoku-Hoshidan* headquarters were broken into by security officers and the joint membership list was confiscated. With the *Hokoku* list as a guide, renunciation applications of over 1,000 Nisei and Kibei were automatically approved by the Attorney General. So were plans to remove them, as "enemy aliens," to internment camps.

In four spectacular transfers, carried out on January 26, February 11, March 4, and March 16, a total of 1,016 citizens were turned into "instant aliens" and hauled away amidst wildly patriotic demonstrations which accompanied the send-offs. Following each removal, wave on wave of Nisei and Kibei flocked to fill the *Hokoku*'s depleted ranks, many of them begging to be "resegregated" as talk of nonrenunciants being used as slave labor and equally devilish draft-the-rest rumors were stepped up by extremists.

Only later were authorities to learn that their summary removals involved mainly victims of the *Hokoku,* not its leaders.

Justice's inability to rid the camp of a leading agitator (one in no hurry to avail himself of "benefits" being pushed upon others) led to a drastic administrative solution which went far beyond the mere "invitation" to renounce—a priority extended to all suspect leaders of the insurgent clique. Tex Nakamura, a Nisei attorney then serving as assistant to the Project Attorney, recently recalled that in a Gestapo-style predawn raid, government officers forced themselves into the apartment of Kinzo Wakayama—a World War I veteran and embittered extremist leader—and compelled him to sign away his citizenship at gunpoint. Nakamura explains in a letter of June 25, 1973:

I interviewed him [Wakayama] during the summer of 1957 in Hakata, Japan. At which time he stated to me that he was rudely awakened about 3 or 4 in the morning. The FBI came to his quarter with a pistol brandishing, and the officer that accompanied the FBI compelled him to renounce.

Mr. Wakayama told the Justice Department official that he will only sign the renunciation document under protest. The officer stated to him that he may do so. Consequently, Kinzo Wakayama signed the renunciation document under protest. This means that the document so obtained would not be valid, and was obtained by duress.[25]

The easy availability of power made citizen Wakayama immediately removable—and deportable—as an "enemy alien," for the personal endorsement of the Attorney General in the nation's capital had been speedily secured.

Among confused and fear-crazed young citizens, the whipped-up "honor of internment" ardor made the use of such force unnecessary. The very idea of redemption from the awful insecurity of a terror-ridden Tule Lake—the promise of realizing a war-duration haven free from all of life's gut-rending uncertainties—became so irresistible, the neutral, uncommitted Nisei and Kibei were swept up in droves. The prestige of the *Hokoku-Hoshidan* reached its zenith by their being able to claim for their members "preferential treatment" by the Attorney General's office.

Beginning with the second of the mass transfers, a mere "apprehension notice" issued a day in advance to those slated for removal was sufficient to bring prisoners-to-be dutifully—and gratefully—to the police station.

APPREHENSION NOTICE

160	NOTICE	JANUARY 25, 1945
TO: _____	_____	_____
Name	Fam. No.	Address

You are hereby informed that the Attorney General of the United States has ordered that you be apprehended as an alien enemy pursuant to Section 21, Title 50, U.S. Code, and that you be transferred to a Department of Justice internment camp. Report at 9:00 AM on Friday, January 26, 1945, to:

Internal Security Building

Be sure to bring with you your identification badge and your work badge.

You may take one small bag or parcel with you on the train. Other baggage which you wish to take with you must be ready in your home before noon Thursday, January 25. A truck will call for baggage after that time and the baggage will be checked through to the internment camp.[26]

A grotesque phenomenon thus held sway on U. S. soil whereby hordes of frightened, demoralized Americans sought self-imprisonment at the price of an irreparably depreciated, seemingly worthless citizenship, so great was the fear of resettlement in America. Exploiting this general insanity, the Justice Department turned one Nisei after another into an "instant alien" on the presumption that the tie of loyalty of those possessing dual citizenship was, by then, more to Japan than the U. S. Also rounded up and removed for easy postwar disposal were 318 Issei: advisers and teachers of the "Greater East Asia School," writers for the *Fatherland* magazine, some Buddhist priests and ex-Justice Department internees suspected of having aided and abetted the nationalistic setup.[27]

On March 17, the Justice Department hearings at Tule Lake drew to a close. Only one day before—on March 16—local authorities had decisively swung into action, seeking to put an end to all the pressures and paranoia they had permitted to operate. Prohibited by WRA edict were the drilling, the bugling, the cultural activities promoting nationalistic attitudes, the wearing of clothes with Japanese emblems—now punishable by a project trial and incarceration of those found guilty in a hastily reestablished stockade. But by then, over 5,000 Americans had signed away their citizenship.

With the departure of the hated agents from Justice, the early morning exhibitionism diminished in size and fervor and the influence of the *Hokoku-Hoshidan* ebbed. The once remarkable solidarity of the fascistic leadership disintegrated into factious wrangling as a split developed between those who would abide by the WRA ultimatum and those who would persist in the early morning pattern of defiance.

Renunciation applications fell to a mere trickle and never rose beyond the 200 mark following a June statement issued by the Internal Security Chief that no forced relocation would result in withdrawing from *Hokoku-Hoshidan* membership.

On June 24 and July 3, two last transfers of voluntary and involuntary "undesirables" were carried out, this time by the WRA, bringing the total removed to Justice Department internment to 1,516 persons. But the "honor of internment" fervor had worn off—many attempting at the last minute to get names withdrawn—as the realization hit home that the disuniting of families had ended up only in increased hardships and tragedies. Bitterly resented by residents were *Hokoku-Hoshidan* stalwarts, who, after talking dozens of others into realizing the "honor" of internment, had decided against it for themselves. A marked contrast in mood to earlier removals was noted by the Tule Lake Analyst in the June 24 transfer of 374 men, including nearly 200 aliens and 190 citizen renunciants:

The sendoff crowd was mainly Manzanar Ward 8, plus a few friends and curious onlookers from other wards and blocks (B1. 32, for example, well-represented). There was a continual crowd of about 2500, small compared with Justice transfer crowds of a few months back. . . . The crowd, emotionally, was subdued; women and girls were crying and otherwise looking anxious; the men and boys looked sad and concerned. There was none of the defiant joviality and noise of earlier sendoffs. When the groups of men marched off to the Stockade, there were waves of "Good-bye, papa-sans!" and children crying. There was not a bugle toot all morning, not a sweatshirt or *hachimaki* [protest sweat band] in sight. The group #2 *taiso* [drill] we had been tipped off to was called off because of the apprehension of the 25 from their group, an apprehension of leaders which made *taiso* inappropriate under the circumstances. . . .

The age-group fitted no draft-the-rest rumors. The fact that they were family heads evinced sympathy and concern at the fact of their leaving. They marched, in a shambling old-man's gait, looking much like a prison-march, down to the Stockade. This was effective far beyond the truck-convoys of earlier transfers. They went willingly, but as if taking medicine. Walking off, a smile disappeared too soon, and the motley of costumes and small bundles seemed ridiculous.

There was one high blood-pressure case, Honda [pseud.], cleared by Drs. Hashiba, Boardman and the two public health physicians assigned to the trip . . . Honda's son, likewise concerned, was with him. The father had taken an overdose of sedative, I think to avoid the trip, and was unable to walk. The boy explained his fear that Santa Fe was "too high up for high blood pressure" . . . He said he'd advise his father, "when he woke up" to try for parole. The father had joined the Hoshidan merely to be able to "take me back to Japan after the war and see my mother; they told him unless he joined, he could never go back." [28]

VII

With the removal of key agitators coupled with the radical opening up of the gates to relocation, there occurred an easing of Tule Lake tensions. Sons and brothers fighting in Europe and the Pacific were making a spectacular showing, and War Department exploitation of their heroic feats enabled Japanese Americans to, once again, hold their heads up high.[29] Hopeful news floated back from friends who had successfully relocated. And contrary to the propaganda of insurrectionist hotheads, it was obvious that Japan was on the verge of defeat—120,000 of their kinsmen annihilated on Okinawa, her major cities ablaze from end to end.

Against this backdrop, a startling new stampede began to gain momentum in the latter part of June, 1945, as thousands of Nisei and Kibei renunciants awoke from their mass delirium and frantically sought ways to cancel their renunciations. Contributing to this new hysteria was the incredible flip-flop in status which had taken place: While countless Issei parents had been virtually transformed from disloyal to loyals and made eligible for liberation, in a cruel twist of fate their citizen offspring were being sent notices of their amended legal status: "undesirable enemy aliens." To insure their continued detention, regardless of the phasing out of the WRA, the Justice Department, in the meanwhile, agreed to have the segregation center turned over to it as a resegregation center.

Ill-considered decisions made by one or more family members now convulsed the entire family in irreconcilable torment and tragedy. Anguished letters of regret, such as the following sent to Edward Ennis, inundated the Justice Department through the summer of 1945.

I wrote you about my wife June 30, and your reply taking away all hope came yesterday. You are a man who I am sure can put yourself in my place. May I tell you something of my awful situation and please, Mr. Ennis, please do something for my little family.

I am one of the block managers and have a place of responsibility in this center. I have been block manager since September 1944. One of my duties is to stop all rumors but have you ever tried to put out a forest fire or stop the tide from coming in? We were up against a real tide when the Department of Justice hearings were on. My wife picked up all rumors and believed them. She thought if she renounced she would stay here. Otherwise she would be pushed out. We are from Hood River and that was a dangerous place. My wife was afraid to go there if we were made to leave. She felt that some way she must fix things so the family could stay here together and her "fixing" was to renounce. Night after night I pleaded with her not to do such a thing. She tried to get me to renounce also but I would not. Nothing could change her mind. She was completely hysterical and unbalanced with fear and worry. Well, she renounced in spite of all I could do.

We found the rumors false and she began to change her mind but according to your letter, it was too late. Do you know what it means in a few minutes of hysteria to throw away your happiness, your family, your future, seemingly forever? All night long she cried. When there had been hope of cancellation we had talked of going out and raising the children to be good citizens. Then your letter came. She told me to go out and take the children who are anxious to leave (we have three children, 13, 11 and 7 years of age) and she would stay behind alone and commit suicide. So now I must not go, knowing I had killed my wife, and my children must remain in this abnormal atmosphere and so must I. Don't you see what a tragedy a few minutes has made for us? And now, Mr. Ennis, isn't there some way that we can go out? Even if my wife's citizenship is gone, can't she go out as an alien? She did not renounce out of disloyalty. She would never do anything against this country. She only wants us to be together. Isn't there some way by which our little family can relocate? Don't you see how awful our situation is? Do help us if you can.[30]

A strong inference may be drawn that the arbiters of Justice remained icily contemptuous of those wallowing in the injustice of their authorship. Practically all renunciation applications were approved by the Attorney General, even in cases—it would be learned later—where evacuees sought to cancel their applications prior to approval. No conscientious effort had been made to dissuade applicants during their renunciation hearings, though the pattern of response had plainly indicated "coaching" and coercion. Approval of renunciation applications had been expeditiously bestowed by Justice even in cases involving seven renunciants known to be idiots.

With Roosevelt's death in April 1945, Tom Clark had become President Truman's Attorney General (Ennis continuing in his position as Director of Alien Enemy Affairs until 1946), but there was no easing of the hard-line approach to the dilemma of the innocent thousands caught in Justice's baited trap.[31]

The final count of renunciants at Tule Lake came to 5,461. Seven out of every ten Nisei had taken the fatal step. In the nine other camps, where project directors and commandants of nearby garrisons had taken their wartime omnipotence less seriously, hardly a ripple was evidenced over the renunciation issue. From the nine other camps combined, only 128 renunciants were reported.

At Tule Lake, the Nisei and Kibei were again made the scapegoats for bureaucratic bungling and miscalculations on a gargantuan scale. Of the egregious errors compounded by their governmental

jailors, perhaps the most corrosive was their failure to more scrupulously follow through and complete the ill-advised segregation after
dumping together a highly concentrated mixture of wholly contra-
dictory and combustible elements.

(13)
Native American Aliens

The mistreatment of these citizens is not to be attributed so much to the abnormality of the times as to the abnormality of the minds of those responsible for the outrage. Apparently these officials reposed little confidence in the Constitution and disbelieved in the Sermon on the Mount while beguiled by the Rosenberg lies on white supremacy.

—WAYNE M. COLLINS

I

For the Issei and Nisei still trapped at Tule Lake, the atomic incineration of a quarter of a million kindred fellow humans in Hiroshima ushered in the final nightmare stage in the sequence of injustices which had issued forth from the order to evacuate. One-third of the segregant population were either natives of Hiroshima or had relatives living there, hundreds of them war-stranded Nisei.

"The atomic bombing of Hiroshima City had left the center stunned on August 8 with a complicated series of reactions," Community Analyst Marvin Opler advised headquarters on filing an on-the-spot narrative account:

Issei from Hiroshima-ken were going to hold Memorial Services for relatives assumed to be obliterated; Ward VIII was leading in this, the ceremonies to be in a definite religious and traditional style. This was not surprising when one considers that the distribution of Issei population by *ken* [prefecture] shows that more than one-third of the Issei of this center come from Hiroshima. . . .

The news of the second atomic bomb on Nagasaki City (only 28 people from this *ken* here) was hardly so devastating. In general, I noted a slight amount of "hate-the-hakujin" [whites] feeling which soon died out, along with some feelings of persecution: "Maybe we'll be bombed next." . . . Generally, however, the center recognized what we noted on the 8th—that the war was over. . . .

Over the weekend, the center was distinctly well up on the news.

249

To say that the imminence of a Japanese defeat spelled gloom is to misread the picture. People were quietly at their radios; and when I visited I found every sort of reaction.

One old Issei who had been consistently misinformed by the shortwave and was totally unprepared for news of victory stood in the washroom of his block and shouted to all comers, in Japanese, "It's a rumor! It's a rumor!" A woman in another block was slightly banged up by an Issei man for announcing on the 11th that she had heard definitely of "Japanese surrender." On the other hand, I met many Nisei who were possibly as jubilant as anyone anywhere over American victory. In general, in the homes the younger generation was "confronting" the older with the news. The Issei comeback would be that the Japanese broadcast had not confirmed surrender. On the 10th, the 7:45 Japanese broadcast was said to carry news of surrender in English, though not in the Japanese version, possibly adding to the cleavage in opinion. Slowly, even with the "village elders," the persecution and blind faith factors seemed to be dropping out, as word of victory became more definite. . . .

On August 10, with excellent timing, the Project Director called together all section heads in order to bring the entire staff in line. A few members of the staff had, in a few scattered instances, given noticeable vent to their joy over victory—rubbing it in, as it were, in the presence of evacuees. . . .

On the 11th, with the war's end approaching, I heard of a good many Nisei rebukes to parents along the line of "You brought me here and into this mess." Some Issei took the initiative with "I'm sorry, I didn't know it would be this way." . . .

There was practically no hysteria in advance of the final word. (A few possible suicides were mentioned. One case which I tracked down was a fellow who had formerly served in the Japanese army and who himself vowed he would commit suicide in the event of defeat. Even by the night of the 14th, and down to the present, there have been no suicides and only one brush between two bachelor Issei in their 70's reached the hospital; a 70-year old in bachelor quarters in Block 4 slightly bruised an equally old and infirm room-mate). My own staff was poised for the event, and at 4:10 when cessation of hostilities was announced, they spontaneously suggested, "Let's celebrate victory." . . .

On the evening of the 14th, of three Nisei soldiers visiting the center, one was willing to remain inside the fenced area for the night but the other two thought it better to remain in the Administration area. . . .

One block manager, before supper on the evening of the 14th, took it upon himself to announce in the messhall the news of Japanese surrender. Apparently, the use of the word, "surrender," was too public and a half-dozen Issei, without saying a word got up and left the messhall without eating. Others, upset by this occurrence, ate a few mouthfuls and then hurried home. In fifteen minutes, the messhall was empty and the radios were blaring throughout the block.[1]

Appended to anthropologist Opler's report of August 18 were copies of letters written by Tule Lake renunciants entreating the Justice Department to withdraw and cancel their renunciations, duplicates of which had been sent by each renunciant to the Secretaries of State and Interior, Dillon Myer, and others.

After reading Marvin Opler's sympathetic assessment of each of the renunciants' purported reasons for having renounced his citizenship, John H. Provinse—a top aide to Myer—was moved to urge the National Director that the report "should be the occasion for serious consideration of attitude and stand to be taken by WRA in connection with renunciants."

By this, I do not mean we attempt to determine Department of Justice policy on deportation, etc., but that WRA, which has the fullest data and experience concerning renunciants, should carefully examine what its responsibility is in the situation, and whether or not, under the circumstances, we should make a real effort to present for the use of Justice, Congress and the State Department a full and documented account of the facts and background of renunciation.

For example, we know more than anyone else about the pressures, the confusions and the protective and devotional familial factors that influenced many of the renunciants. Should we wait until our advice is sought, which may be too late, or should we push forward our own considerable knowledge and experience while important questions are being answered with less than the available knowledge? The immediate categorical answer suggested by Representative Dickstein's "deportation within two months" is a simple solution from an administrative standpoint, but it is open to question that a problem as complex and far-reaching as this one can be satisfactorily answered so simply. The war is over, extreme urgency does not seem necessary and hasty ill-considered action can have regrettable consequences.

I do not know the answer, though personally I believe that on the basis of several definable criteria acceptable to most Americans, the country *not* being in a state of war, more than half of the renunciants could be reaccredited as good citizens. If the Army can set up clemency boards to review some 50,000 cases under sentence for infractions of military rules, why cannot Justice set up similar boards to review political misfeasance or indiscretion? The point of this memorandum, however, is simply this—Does WRA have a responsibility to bring aggressively to the attention of other agencies now concerned with our Tule Lake group its considerable background of information concerning this group? [2]

Provinse's letter takes on special significance in light of the incredibly protracted litigation to be exacted before the renunciants were to be reaccredited as good citizens.

Had the known facts been made immediately available in defense of the helpless Nisei, they would have shown that the renunciation law "disregarded social, economic and psychological realities" and was grossly "inapplicable in a concentration camp setting," as forcefully argued by Analyst Opler, who had been in the eye of the storm and who had skillfully documented and interpreted on a weekly, sometimes day-to-day basis, the microworld of mass hysteria. As early as April 23, 1945, Opler had sought, in a confidential memo to Dillon Myer, to direct Administration attention to the rank injustice of the predicament in which renunciants had been ensnared:

> According to the law, renunciation of citizenship must be an individual and voluntary action. . . . At Tule Lake, only a minor proportion of the actions taken were individual and voluntary . . . in many of the hearings, the fear of forced relocation, though phrased in protestations of disloyalty, was the real fear . . . renunciation was a way of continuing dependency on the American government until the time came to shift dependency to Japan. . . .
>
> I have found renunciants who did so in defiance of family pattern "because friends renounced," renunciants who have taken the step simply out of fear that relatives abroad would be prosecuted by the Japanese government (notification through the State Department) if they failed to make a show of disloyalty. . . .
>
> With mass pressures at work in the community, renunciations were neither individual nor voluntary. Parental pressures, the pressure of draft rumors, mass sign-ups and mass-applications were the order of the day. The hearing officers recognized that wives followed husbands, and children parental decisions. . . .
>
> Renunciation split families, immobilized a large segment of center population, and if taken seriously, will produce post-war dependency problems both here and abroad. The law cannot be applied in center life. . . . Renunciation is not real disloyalty. It is mass-hysteria of the type which has caused other and earlier upheavals in the Relocation Centers.[3]   [Reparagraphed by author]

It is doubtful that Congress or the State Department was ever presented with "a full and documented account of the facts and background of renunciation," as had been urged by Provinse. That the War Relocation Authority had "unsuccessfully" attempted to persuade Justice that the mass deportations "would result in a grave injustice to thousands of basically blameless people" is indicated in a postwar WRA publication.[4]

Considering the possibility of suits and damages which could conceivably be extracted if the course leading to deportation were not pursued, it might be assumed that the Justice Department, by then, was motivated more by anxiety than compassion. On October 8, it announced that on or after November 15, all renunciants "will be repatriated [expatriated] to Japan together with members of their families, whether citizens or aliens, who desire to accompany them." Attorney Collins recalls:

. . . a general hysterical condition developed in the Tule Lake Center and also in the Alien Internment Camps at Bismarck, North Dakota, and at Santa Fe, New Mexico, to which numbers of renunciants had been removed . . . The internees decided something must be done quickly or they would find themselves on board U. S. Army transports bound for Japan.[5]

II

It was late July, 1945, during Collins' trip to Tule Lake for the purpose of closing down the reestablished stockade, that he had been besieged by parents of renunciants desperate for legal counsel. Hearing that thousands of young people had unwittingly transformed themselves into "men without a country," Collins' first reaction was one of disbelief: "That's ridiculous. You can no more resign citizenship in time of war than you can resign from the human race." [6]

Only a fraction of the renunciants had possessed dual citizenship at the time of renunciation. No opportunity had been given them, then or subsequently, to produce evidence of a want of such dual nationality.[7] Now on Justice's presumption of their possessing an alternate Japanese citizenship, all had been informed that they were being removed to Japan.

During his July visit to Tule Lake, Collins had prepared a number of sample cancellation letters, urging that copies of them be placed in the hands of all renunciants:

I advised them that their citizen children first should write immediately to the Attorney General and inform him of the conditions under which the renunciations were made and assert that the renunciations and his orders approving the renunciations were unconstitutional and void for being the direct and proximate result of governmental duress and also for the additional reason of private coercion exerted upon them by persons and groups in the Center and to notify the Attorney General that they cancelled those renunciations. . . . Also I informed each of the parents and renunciants present that, in my opinion, each of the citizen renunciants who wished to cancel his renunciation also should seek the immediate advice of his own personal or family attorney.[8]

But not a lawyer could be found willing to take on the wretched, hopeless-seeming cases involving individuals branded "dangerous to national security" pitted against the full might of the U. S. Government. Instead, Collins' office was flooded by calls from countless attorneys, each begging the San Francisco lawyer to take on various personal clients if he had intentions of taking on any of the renunciants. Among them were attorneys who "telephoned me and advised me I'd be in for trouble if I represented such persons," Collins recalls.

The peripatetic attorney was called back, in early September, to

Tule Lake. In the intervening period, nearly 1,000 renunciants had banded together into a "Tule Lake Defense Committee," in the hope that Collins would take on the group as their sole attorney. Collins agreed. But convinced that the larger the number of attorneys representing the renunciants, the better, he had encouraged one last attempt on the part of renunciants to recruit additional lawyers:

> Mr. Tetsujiro Nakamura who was a resident of the Tule Lake Center and was the assistant legal officer of that Center was sent from that Center as an emissary of residents to enlist the aid of attorneys who might be willing to represent such internees. He visited Los Angeles, Fresno, San Francisco and elsewhere in California but was unable to find a single other lawyer willing to represent such persons. So it was that I was selected to be the sole attorney for such a large number of renunciants.[9]

Reviled as a "madman" for defending "Jap traitors," Collins was *persona non grata* to bigoted friends and colleagues as he became a full-time commuter between San Francisco and far-flung concentration camps operated by both the WRA and the Justice Department.

According to Collins, "the only group that in anywise assisted me in my endeavors was the Northern California branch of the ACLU and its director, Ernest Besig." The national office of the ACLU (New York) categorically forbade intervention in behalf of renunciants.[10] The maverick San Francisco group defied national's veto, giving energetic publicity to Collins' proceedings on the ground that inaction could result in thousands of Nisei being unjustly shipped off to Japan while the test cases were being litigated.

At a time of widespread indifference to the suffering of his clients, Collins recalls cooperation from one other source: Raymond Best. In the months preceding Tule Lake's closing, the Project Director—now shocked and disquieted by the tangled web in which thousands of young Tuleans were entrapped—allied himself foursquare with Collins and his embattled legion. Collins remembers gratefully:

> Mr. Best personally contributed several hundred dollars to enable a number of persons there confined to contribute their bit to the Defense Fund and I do not believe any portion of his money was returned to him . . . Further, Mr. Best deliberately prolonged his stay at Tule Lake Center at my request so that I would be enabled to have him served with process in the Center and thereby obtain jurisdiction over him . . . He wrote many letters on behalf of individuals and families requesting their liberation from detention at Tule and elsewhere. . . . He also along with Ivan Williams [officer in charge of Tule Lake for the Justice Department] did a great deal to convince the Justice Department that it should liberate the unfortunate renunciants and their alien parents and relatives from detention.[11]

For their "cold-blooded" indifference to the aggrieved and wretched victims of various "governmental abominations," Collins is scathingly less charitable with "oppressive Attorney Generals, their subordinates and hirelings," and can be aroused to highs of flaming indignation over insentient civil libertarians who, he maintains, were "in favor of concentration camps while they existed."

Mention the JACL and Collins erupts into unprintable epithets: "They're a bunch of jackals who did nothing to aid victims of the vicious renunciation program." He recently told journalist Bill Hosokawa: "The JACL pretended to be the spokesman for all Japanese Americans but they wouldn't stand up for their people. They didn't speak up for the Issei. They led their people like a bunch of goddam doves to the concentration camps."

The tart-tongued Irishman thinks he may be the only one left who is as incensed today as he was thirty years ago. His ex-inmate clients have forgiven Uncle Sam, but he cannot: "I still feel bitter about the evacuation. It was the foulest goddam crime the United States has ever committed against a wonderful people." [12]

III

On November 13, 1945, in the U. S. District Court, San Francisco, Collins filed two mass petitions for 987 renunciants, consisting of (1) mass proceedings in habeas corpus designed to restrain the Justice Department from carrying out its announced plan of "repatriation" and to pry the renunciants loose from internment; and (2) mass suits in equity to void the renunciations and to restore to each his U. S. citizenship. Restraining orders were also obtained prohibiting the forced removal of petitioners from the camps and to prevent authorities from closing Tule Lake without Collins' consent.

The suits charged that the renunciations were a fraud as they were not free acts, that the government had knowingly allowed a small pro-Japanese clique to carry on a campaign of violence, terrorism, and sedition calculated to force loyal Americans into repudiating their citizenship. The suits alleged, furthermore, that the U. S. Government had

> condoned the same and was responsible for, and actually aided and abetted the same . . . by failing to invoke the federal sedition and espionage laws or other criminal laws against them and by failing to segregate such criminal elements from the petitioners and other loyal internees and to isolate them.[13]

Collins contended that the evacuation order was an unlawful, racialistic, dictatorial decree. This capricious treatment of a minority, he maintained, was compounded by the extreme duress brought about by the government's "inhuman," "criminal," and unconstitutional detention of the group for three and a half years; therefore, the U. S. Government was the causative factor for the existence of insurgent organizations headed up by "Government-created fanatics" because such extreme behavior was "foreseeable and inherent in a percentage of oppressed persons." The suits accused the federal government, its agents, and hirelings of deliberately inflicting misfortune for racial reasons and for knowingly permitting frightened parents to coerce their children into signing renunciation applications. In Collins' words:

> It was my theory and argument that each renunciant was faced with an election of one of two choices the government forced them to make. The first was to renounce citizenship in order to secure liberation from a prolonged detention by being transported to Japan with alien family members . . . The second was to renounce citizenship in order to be held in the protective security of internment in order to escape being forced out of camp to face a hostile civilian community in an impoverished condition. In either event renunciation was not the product of free will but was forced upon them by the unlawful detention and the conditions prevailing at the Tule Lake Center, *for which the government alone was responsible.* In consequence every renunciation was the direct product of governmental duress.[14]

Collins' mass suits took pains to point out that renunciation, in itself, is not a criminal act, nor is it punishable. Nor did Congress, in any way, authorize detention or banishment in passing the denaturalization law. In detaining the renunciants for deportation to Japan, the suits charged, the Attorney General illegally exercised extraconstitutional power.

When a last-minute stay was handed down by the Court, the lawyer literally raced on board the ships to remove clients. Removal to Japan of approximately 4,700 Nisei and Kibei being held in Tule Lake, Bismarck, Santa Fe, and Crystal City was thus halted.

Foiled in its mass removal plan (see Appendix 8), the Justice Department was faced with the problem of holding thousands of young ex-Americans in detention for two, three, or more years—at the then estimated cost of $100,000 a month [15]—pending the outcome of the suits. Justice thereupon decided to release the bulk of the youthful internees. As a "face-saving device," in Collins' estimate, the expediency of "mitigation hearings" (which gave renunciants the opportunity to "show cause" why they should not be removed to Japan) was employed to determine who should be released.

Another compelling factor in this decision to ascertain on a more individual basis whether renunciants should be permitted to remain in the U. S. was a plea on behalf of the renunciants from Interior Secretary Ickes. His November 1 letter to Attorney General Tom Clark read in part:

> I believe that it would be unjust in the extreme to treat all renunciants as a class, without individual differentiation, and to assume that they would all be dangerous to the national security or would otherwise be undesirable aliens. . . . I understand that it is a regular procedure of the Department of Justice to make administrative investigations through the Immigration and Naturalization Service to establish the facts concerning the legality of and the need for deportation . . . Such investigations or hearings are clearly needed in the case of the renunciants, and I recommend most urgently that they be held. Unless they are held, I think that the deportation of the renunciants could in many cases be called seriously into question on the grounds of legality, justice, and plain decency.[16]

Beginning on January 7, 1946, the investigatory hearings to determine deportation or release were conducted at Tule Lake. Alien parolees from internment camps segregated at Tule Lake were also permitted to "show cause" why they should not be removed to Japan. Renunciants and parolees who failed to or did not request a hearing were summarily issued deportation orders.

Collins labels these interviews, in unequivocal terms, as "fraudulent Star Chamber proceedings." According to Ernest Besig, who, as one of four impartial observers, was permitted access to the hearings, renunciants were totally denied the right to counsel by government examiners.[17] During the several days spent in Tule Lake, the ACLU Director was astonished by the coercive influences still prevailing:

> All during my stay I saw, observed and found the evacuees to be in a state of terror. Members of the Hoshi Dan pressure groups were still in the camp and seeking to impose their will upon the evacuees generally. . . . They [the residents] said there had been no let up in the activities of the pressure groups until August, 1945 . . . and that everyone in the camp was in great fear of them until most of the pressure group leaders were repatriated from the camp to Japan in November, 1945, and that a large number were still in fear of the leaders of those groups who still were in camp but were soon to be repatriated to Japan.[18]

As deportations and removals were aggressively carried out by the Justice Department in the winter of 1945–46, a hard core contingent of "die-hards" had left on a November sailing. A sizable group of renunciants declined to fight removal orders (1,116 failed to apply for mitigation hearings) because of shame, despair, a reluctance to go through the ordeal of another grilling, and a paranoiac fear that "the government would brook no further defiance even in this legal form." [19]

The mitigation hearings proved time-consuming and costly, and the Justice Department ended up abandoning the procedure after some 2,000 cases had been heard. Of the 3,186 persons who had requested a hearing, all were released to relocate except for 449 "rejectees" held for removal to Japan "simply because they were kibei, possessed dual nationality, or some other capricious reasons," according to Collins. Since the hearings had nothing to do with the restoration of citizenship, the category of "native American aliens" had been invented to describe the renunciants' new state of statelessness.

IV

In late January, 1946, one last visit was made by Ernest Besig to Tule Lake, as an incredible mass evacuation in reverse was being forced upon the unrelocatables: the ill and impoverished; many too old and frail to hold down regular employment; some with no families to care for them; most with no place to go. The early part of February had been targeted for termination, but to the exasperation of authorities, nearly 5,000 internees still remained, many of them families and relatives of detainees reluctant to part with them.

By then, frayed nerves had thoroughly dulled compassion, resulting in an official attitude among the overworked administrative staff of "get them out, and to hell with the way it's done." Executive officers busily assured all of them of "places to stay," "good jobs," and financial aid at the end of the line, but no one believed them.

As the termination date neared, after nearly four years of treatment savagely destructive of their ability to cope, minds snapped among those whose whole impulse was to stay banded together, beginning with the hanging suicide of a seventy-seven-year-old bachelor on the day before his removal. Besig's record of his late-January visit reveals with terrifying clarity the toll in human lives and sanity the internment experience exacted: warping, mutilating, and destroying minds and lives as ruthlessly as any sadistic barbarism dreamed up by totalitarian despots.

I learned . . . that a Mrs. [F.] . . . because of her worries and fears arising from her detention, was committed by the Center authorities to a mental institution for hammering one of her children to death and injuring another. A Mr. [S.], an internee, worried over his separation from his sons, tried to commit suicide by drinking gasoline. A Mrs. [K.], an internee, took pills in an attempt at suicide because of her fear of being deported from the United States. Many mental cases were known to have been hospitalized at the Center because of their fear of the pressure groups, continued detention, deportation, separation from their families and the splitting of their families.[20]

Evacuees who refused to leave were given train fare and bodily deposited on trains which would take them back to the "point of evacuation."

In Tule Lake's closing hours, "rejectees" and the "unnotified" were subjected to brutalization of another sort. The Community Analyst witnessed and recorded the final "involuntary removal" of the hounded crew of "native American aliens" (and accompanying family members) which officially closed down the camp of infamy:

Yesterday, March 20 [1946], the intricate complex of detention and relocation ended at Tule Lake with the movement of 554 persons. The bare figures hardly convey the sense of the dramatic: 102 relocated, 60 of them released in the "eleventh hour"; 450 to the Department of Justice internment at Crystal City . . . A survey of the empty barracks left no doubt that the center residential area closed the evening of March 20. And as night fell, March 20, the perimeter lights went off.

While the night of closure-date found an empty center, the day of closure had all the dramatic touches which marked the beginning of segregation more than two and a half years ago. There were the train lists to detention center, the tearful partings and distraught people, the pall of internment hanging over the camp—this time internment in Texas, sudden changes of plan (following release), the same last minute rush for the relocation bus, and, as always at Tule, the inevitable waves of rumors. . . .

Again, anachronistically considering the time, place and what was known of the people involved, armed guards were swarming, search and seizure of "forbidden articles" were conducted, but in addition, the youthful internees were stripped and searched, quartered in the Stockade without provision for feeding women and children (lunch was missed) and marched onto trains with all the fanfare which accompanies rigid detention train-trips. Like evacuation, it was the first forced movement to internment of women and children, and like evacuation, several fathers and husbands were conspicuously absent through previous internment. . . .

[S.N.], a relocation office worker mentioned in earlier reports, was so shocked by last-minute reprieve that he came to the relocation office visibly upset, shaking, and almost dazed; the list included [K.F.] whom we described in our last as rejected, then released, then detained, and finally now "relocatable." . . .

Again, some were "unnotified" like the [N.] girls, caught just as they were leaving their apartment for what the youngest, just twenty, appropriately called "the last mile." Rejectees dropped to under 400 and fever set in near the gate where the renunciants were gathering.

As Swanson put it, "each Jap will be stripped and searched, and the process started." At 2:00 on the gate, amid final goodbyes, hungry babies and as much hysteria as could be generated in a sober, glum group of young internees, 13 more releases were announced over the loudspeaker. . . .

As the train pulled in, rumors or hysterical waves of "10 more"

or "a dozen more" releases gripped the Stockade. In search and seizure procedure, an English dictionary was taken, ironically, from a young man, who in his mitigation hearing was castigated by his hearing officer for not knowing more English and needing an interpreter. . . . I am happy to add that contraceptive devices were *verboten* for the menfolks though I have it on good authority, the women were not so deprived. A six-day old baby accompanied by her mother, Mrs. [N.], was among the "voluntary internees."
Thus ended Tule Lake.[21]

By the end of February, 1946, 4,406 Tuleans had voluntarily repatriated or expatriated to Japan, including 1,116 renunciants, 1,523 aliens, and 1,767 U. S. citizens—all minors in the latter group except for forty-nine.[22]

By the time word got back from earlier repatriates begging and imploring others at Tule Lake not to return, it was too late. According to tenBroek, et al., "some eight thousand persons of Japanese descent [including repatriates and expatriates from other camps] left for Japan between V-J Day and mid-1946."

There was grim irony in the term "voluntarily," used by officials to describe removals. Through the alchemy of intimidation, racism, duplicity, and duress, a clean sweep of 8,000 Issei and Nisei had been accomplished. This meant, of course, 8,000 fewer who could claim indemnification for wrongful imprisonment, destruction of health, sanity, livelihood, property, and lifelong savings so painfully accumulated.

V

All the while, Collins carried his fight through the courts—a long, tortuous quarter-century legal odyssey.

On June 30, 1947, U. S. District Court Judge Louis E. Goodman ordered that Collins' application for a writ of habeas corpus be granted and the petitioners be released from detention. In so doing, the Judge held that resident native-born Americans could not be converted into enemy aliens by the mere renunciation of citizenship; consequently, it was illegal to keep them imprisoned. Nor could they be forcibly removed to Japan.

Following a court order that all detained petitioners be freed, rejectees being held at Crystal City and Seabrook Farms, New Jersey,[23] against whom "repatriation" orders were still outstanding were released or paroled into Collins' custody on September 6, 1947. After five years of being shunted in and out of concentration camps, the 302 individuals involved were finally permitted to return to their West Coast homes.[24]

In the meanwhile, three years had gone by since the nightmare of renunciation. Then—incredibly—what seemed like the impossible happened. On April 29, 1948, Judge Goodman entered an interlocutory judgment in complete favor of Collins' army of youthful clients. In canceling all the renunciations and declaring each to be a citizen of the United States, the Judge scathingly rebuked the government's lawless abuse of power:

> In view of the admissions contained in affidavits in this case, I have no doubt that there was a complete lack of constitutional authority for administrative, executive, or military officers to detain or imprison American citizens not criminally charged or subject to martial law . . . even expediency cannot remove the taint of unfairness with which the renunciations subsequently executed were clothed. It is shocking to the conscience that an American citizen be confined without authority and then while so under duress and restraint for his Government to accept from him a surrender of his constitutional heritage.[25]

A May 19 issue of the *Christian Century,* one of the few publications which had taken a sympathetic pro-Nisei stand from the onset of the war, roundly hailed the judgment: "The day is steadily drawing closer when the Court will hold that the treatment accorded citizens of Japanese extraction was unconstitutional, a betrayal of American traditions, militarism out of legal control and race prejudice run wild."

Though fully persuaded that renunciants had acted abnormally because of abnormal treatment received and that none should be held individually responsible, Judge Goodman nevertheless left the way open for the government to submit evidence that certain individuals did act freely and voluntarily.

A year later (February 25, 1949), after being granted numerous extensions of time, the Attorney General finally filed "Designations," naming every one of the 4,354 plaintiffs as having acted *without* undue influence. The Designations stated that the Department of Justice would offer evidence of answers made to the loyalty questions (27 and 28); written requests for repatriations; refusals to swear unqualified allegiance to the United States; membership and/or leadership in the *Hokoku* or *Joshi Dan;* FBI and WRA dossiers relating to each renunciant; and even the fact of being a Kibei to prove the renunciations were made voluntarily. Transcribed statements made at the renunciation and mitigation hearings also were proposed as evidence against them,[26] as was a fresh-off-the-press copy of *The Spoilage* to show such "voluntariness."

A shocked and angry counsel for the defense demanded that the Designations be stricken on the grounds that they were sham ("nothing but a classified list of all the plaintiffs"), and had not been filed in good faith. The Court ordered them stricken.

On March 23, 1949, Judge Goodman handed down a final judgment. By declaring the renunciations unconstitutional and void, he restored citizenship to over 5,000 Nisei.

The government appealed the decision.

On March 1, 1950, the Ninth Circuit Court of Appeals in San Francisco heard the government's arguments. It decided that Judge Goodman had erred in "lumping the cases." Collins would now have to prove singly and individually that the renunciations were coerced. Rights of citizenship were restored to fifty-eight adults against whom no offers of proof had been made by the Designations and also to all those under twenty-one years of age, who were declared legally incapable of renouncing their citizenship.

Two factors powerfully influenced this setback. First was the vacillating attitude toward rights of citizens generated by the cold war "red hysteria," which then gripped the nation. More catastrophic, however, was that in *Murakami v. U. S.* (176 Fed. 2d 953), a case involving three renunciants which had unexpectedly preceded Collins' into the same court, undue blame had been placed on fellow evacuees. This had the effect of relieving the Justice Department and the WRA of cardinal blame. It did irreparable damage to Collins' mass proceedings.[27] And with a nationwide loyalty obsession then distorting the perception of arbiters, the more basic questions involved—such as the unconstitutionality of the renunciation statute and the causative factor of governmental duress—were deliberately ignored by the court though persuasively presented by Collins.

A plea was made to the U. S. Supreme Court following the Court of Appeals' refusal to grant rehearings. In October 1951, the Supreme Court rejected the petition.

Thus the tedious, time-consuming task of entering individual suits for his numerous clients—now totaling 5,000—was begun. But "the whole thing backfired on the Attorney General. He would be tying up his staff and court machinery for years," according to Collins:

> I informed him and his agents that it would take me considerably over thirty years or, if I engaged the services of other lawyers to assist me it would take up some ten years of constant trial and would tie up the three federal judges in San Francisco to the exclusion of any other cases since my cases would have priority in trial dates. . . .
>
> The Attorney General in Washington thereafter informed me that he was willing to proceed administratively to dispose of the cases if I would consent that each plaintiff would supply an affidavit, with copies, showing why each renounced. If he found that there was nothing in the Justice Department files that was sufficient as evidence to overcome the plaintiff's arguments, he would not oppose a court judgment being entered cancelling the renunciation . . .[28]

Before the whole regrettable episode became a closed chapter in 1968, Collins was to write and file some 10,000 affidavits in defense of, and in redefense of, his numerous clients, both in the United States and Japan.

In due time, the Justice Department announced to the press that, in order to expedite the settling of the renunciation suits, it had initiated a "liberalized" administrative review of cases; that there would be a redetermination of cases where citizenship restoration had been denied because of inadequate affirmative proof of loyalty.

But years went by with no appreciable speedup in settlement.

VI

May 20, 1959. Fourteen years after the inception of the mass suits, much fanfare and publicity attended an unusual public ceremony in the office of Attorney General William P. Rogers. Assembled newsmen and invited dignitaries were informed that the administrative review of the renunciation cases had been completed. Attorney General Rogers then made public the restoration of "precious rights of citizenship" to 4,978 Nisei, declaring: "Our country did make a mistake. We have publicly recognized it and as a free nation publicly make restoration."

Edward J. Ennis, one of the guests of honor and then general counsel to the national office of the American Civil Liberties Union (Chairman of the ACLU in 1969), stated in an address: "I think the Department of Justice has responded magnificently to the problems presented by taking practically all the 'divorced' citizens back into the family of our American country." [29]

"I would like to believe that our liberal policy of citizenship restitution has conformed to the hope and promise of sound American ideals," responded Assistant Attorney General George C. Doub,[30] who further expressed the hope that the Nisei would "have the charity to forgive their Government." Doub added:

It is a remarkable tribute to the fortitude of the Nisei that comparatively few surrendered their American citizenship under the prevailing hysteria conditions in the WRA camps. They were indeed so loyal that from them came the soldiers of the 442nd battalion whose casualty notices were delivered to parents behind the barbed wires of the camps.[31]

Media reaction throughout the nation was eulogistic. The *Christian Science Monitor* of May 22, 1959, announced editorially that "the federal Justice Department deserve gratitude from Americans for painstakingly righting a grave injustice . . ." The *Washington Post and Times Herald* of May 28, 1959, followed with lavish praise:

Today all the Nisei who suffered in this wave of hysteria have been generously compensated for their property losses and all of the renunciants against whom no other evidence of willful disloyalty could be found have now been restored to full civil status. The great credit for the completion of this program of restitution belongs to Assistant Attorney General George Cochran Doub, who heads the Civil Division of the Department of Justice.

Mr. Doub's energy in pursuing the settlement of the Nisei claims proves . . . that although we have shown ourselves "as a Nation capable of wrongs," we have also shown ourselves capable "of confessing and of seeking to expiate them." Or as a celebrated historian, describing a somewhat similar change of heart and reversal of judgment by the citizens of another democracy, put it: "The morrow brought repentance with it and reflection on the horrid cruelty of a decree which had condemned all to the fate merited only by a few." [32]

Probably the only person outraged by the whole proceeding was the fiery San Francisco attorney, for with all the self-congratulatory platitudes and rhetoric of expiation, this was no blanket amnesty, as had been demanded by him for over a decade as rightly due a group of citizens who had been abandoned so utterly. Seventeen years after they had been driven into peonage—some into insanity—and defrauded of their rights, mercy was still begrudgingly withheld from 350 renunciants. "We will vigorously defend our adverse determination of these comparatively few cases in the courts . . ." [33] the Assistant Attorney General had thrown out the challenge, as though to Collins personally.

By this time, 2,031 renunciants had gone to Japan. Of the 3,735 who remained in the United States, all but eighty-four had regained their citizenship. [34]

The discredited ex-Americans again turned to Collins in their lonely Armageddon, although a number of them abandoned their fight; some decided to remain in Japan; a few passed away. Collins: "The maintenance of the stigma of wrongdoing was consistent with Justice's obsession with face-saving. Having inflicted the gravest type of injury upon these blameless people, then criminally soliciting and taking renunciations from tormented persons, the Justice Department sought to whitewash its own reputation by persisting in blackening those of young Americans who had courage enough to stand up and fight for their rights—Americans who would not brook insults forever. Practically all the young men denied their citizenship rights were Kibei. Their mistreatment is unprecedented in American history." [35]

Contrary to the pronouncement of the Justice Department to all assembled that "this ceremony today concludes a colorful chapter of American history," the issue of citizenship restoration dragged on into the late sixties. And as aptly underscored by authors Girdner and Loftis in *The Great Betrayal:* "Wayne Collins was the agent for democracy in correcting this most disastrous of all evacuation mistakes." Not the Justice Department.

March 6, 1968. It was twenty-three years after he had brought the illegal, racially abetted deportation of the Nisei and Kibei to a screeching halt that Collins was finally able to write in the concluding renunciation proceedings (*Abo v. [Ramsay A.] Clark*) with an air of justifiable triumph:

A majority of those who had been forcibly removed to Japan were restored to their home in this country. The fundamental rights, liberties, privileges and immunities of these citizens are now honored. The discrimination practiced against them by the government has ceased. The episode which constituted an infamous chapter in our history has come to a close.[36]

(14)
Epilogue

They say the Nisei should have resisted. I say to them when you guys
were 14 years old, as I was then, what would you do—throw rocks
and bombs? . . .

When I came back from the service in 1945, people would spit at
me and push me off the road. We don't tend to tell our kids that. We
try to forget and look at how good things are now.

—MAS FUKAI in a *Newsweek* interview

I

Time, mercifully, has a way of spreading a softening patina over
the most painful of life's slights and wounds. This, coupled with the
all too often obscured fact that the overwhelming number of guiltless
victims swept into America's concentration camps were mere minors
may account today for what has been observed as a striking absence
of bitterness, for the seeming inability of ex-evacuees to nurse old
hatreds—"some of whom," notes a recent *Newsweek* article, "like to
invite the American commandants of their wartime camps to give
speeches at Nisei reunions." It is unusual to find a former evacuee
who has not forgiven the human weaknesses of his fellow white
Americans.

For this extraordinary demonstration of tolerance, no small credit
is due the steadfast, persevering Issei. After all was said and done,
remarkably few succumbed to negative influences in the camps.

Time, perspective, and justice, moreover, would dictate that the
stigma of disloyalty be removed from those whose untimely departure
from U. S. soil had less to do with disloyalty than a retreat from an
annihilating defeat in their struggle to achieve the American Dream
—an escape to a country "where they make no pretense of loving
liberty . . . where despotism can be taken pure and without the base
alloy of hypocrisy."

266

After all was said and done, the Nisei would readily concede that it was the residual dignity of their elders which prevented disaster from becoming a catastrophe; that it was the hardy, enduring Issei who made possible the reversal of a crushing humiliation into an ultimate demonstration of triumph. How? By their awesome loyalty, in the face of overwhelming immoralities, to their own rigid moral code. By continuing to stress patience, obedience, and duty more than rights. By demanding of one another the subordination of self to the larger interest. By urging in their children unstinting allegiance to their country—their "master"—right or wrong.

The innate moral fiber of the Issei, their resilience, their quiet poise under pressure, helped to soften the impact for the Nisei.

Noting that given the same set of circumstances, white Americans with their low boiling point would have gone on a rampage within a week, Wayne Collins (himself a symbol of lonely courage at a time of lawless violence) maintains: "No other nationality would have taken with such forbearance treatment so dastardly. Under our American democracy, even alien enemies, to my concept of constitutional interpretation, should have been entitled to basic constitutional immunities. Despoiled of rights and presumptions granted even common criminals, the Issei and Nisei suffered in silence, hoping that acquiescence would prove their loyalty and improve their lot. They did not know the government."

The damage done to these innocent people without cause was utterly evil. It was a war crime from which our nation proceeded to divert attention by harassing and mercilessly executing individuals like General Yamashita for allegedly condoning crimes of subordinate officers of which he probably knew nothing.[1] What is then to be said of our own Generals and civilian officials who not only condoned governmental crimes against our native-born citizens but systematically aided and abetted them?

Hundreds of the ill, the halt and aged infirm paid with their lives in the three years of physical moves forced upon them. But this was conveniently forgotten. Atrocities were committed in those camps, but sentries and security officers went unpunished. Not one cent went towards indemnifying these wrongs.

Compared to the past venality of scums, bums and rascals who shamelessly destroyed reputations and exploited the misery of a people for personal notoriety and gain, and compared to the indecent and lawless connivance which then transpired between the executive and the judiciary—when even judges wore epaulets under their robes— today's Watergate shenanigans are just fun and games. That the unconstitutionality of so many of the illegalities perpetrated were never conceded by the High Bench is scandalous—leaving us only a moment of passion removed from the destruction, once again, of our liberties. Given another manufactured hysteria over "national security" or some such expediency to justify ends, citizens can again be carted off at the point of bayonets. That is America's evacuation legacy.[2]

In his inexhaustible outrage, Collins is inclined to believe that the Nisei can forgive because they have only a vague, fragmentary knowledge of what really went on in the war years: "They were too young, and the adults too traumatized to fathom all that was happening to them when so damn much happened and only one side had the "facts." They were victims of a sham, a cruel deception. They were lied to from beginning to end. And if you go by our literary apologists and chauvinist court historians, they are still being lied to."

As it turned out, the real spies and subversives during the war proved to be individuals of Anglo-Saxon descent. Observes Carey McWilliams in *Witch Hunt:* "To compare these moral derelicts with a proud Japanese-conscious Issei, aware of his loyalties, sensitive to his moral obligations, is to learn why loyalty is a positive good in itself and why the loyal are brethren."

II

However great the cost and sacrifice, there is no question that unexpected good things also came out of the Japanese Americans' wartime travail. It pushed the Issei and Nisei out of the framework of teeming Lil Tokyos. It forced them to discover the rest of America and, in so doing, opened up opportunities for them that would never have been possible on the Coast.

Even before the war's termination, an evacuee wrote back with wonderment from New York City:

. . . the color of my skin and the slant of my eyes do not close doors upon me . . . Draftsmen are working as draftsmen, engineers as engineers, teachers as teachers. Fruit stands are no longer the ultimate end of every college graduate.[3]

The status of being perpetual aliens came to an end for the Issei when the right to become American citizens was granted them in their twilight years with the passage of the Walter-McCarran Immigration and Naturalization Act of 1952—a veritable tour de force for the Japanese American Citizens League for that time, achieved largely through the intensive lobbying efforts of its Washington representative, Mike Masaoka. By virtue of this omnibus legislation, the Issei's bête noire, the "ineligibility for citizenship" clause, was made forever void; it nullified, in turn, hundreds of discriminatory laws and ordinances throughout the country historically designed to keep people of Asian origin "in their place." The 1952 Act (Public Law 414) canceled out, as well, the notorious Oriental Exclusion Act of 1924, which, three decades earlier, had literally slammed the door on immigration from

Japan—often cited as one of the root causes of the deterioration in U.S.-Japanese relations leading to Pearl Harbor. The yearly entry of 185 immigrants from Japan (and a number of other Asian nations) was thereafter permitted, with spouse and children of American citizens allowed on a nonquota basis. Immigration on the same basis as Europeans finally came about in 1965.

There were other changes. Only a quarter of a century after they were looked down upon as spies and subversives, and caricatured as a horde of monkey men "unfit for the human race," a dramatic switch of stereotype was also evidenced: to that of "America's model minority." Noted sociologist William Petersen set the updated image in motion by arriving at the following exuberant conclusion in a *New York Times Magazine* article, "Success Story: Japanese-American Style":

> By any criterion of good citizenship that we choose, the Japanese Americans are better than any other group in our society, including native-born whites. They have established this remarkable record, moreover, by their own almost totally unaided effort. Every attempt to hamper their progress resulted only in enhancing their determination to succeed. Even in a country whose patron saint is the Horatio Alger hero, there is no parallel to this success story.[4]

"Petersen's claim does not seem inflated," was the hearty concurrence of scholars, educators, and the nation's media—*Newsweek*, for one. An article entitled, "Success Story: Outwhiting the Whites," cited dazzling supportive data:

> On nearly all levels of conventional success, the Japanese-Americans not only have outshone other minority groups but . . . have "outwhited the whites." . . . More than 15 per cent of Japanese-Americans now hold professional jobs, a far higher percentage than all other non-white minority groups, and one that puts them on a par with whites. In Los Angeles County, which has the largest Japanese-American population on the mainland, school authorities report that children of Japanese descent outstrip all others in IQ.[5]

And from wartime charges of "clannishness" and "unassimilability," the consensus today is that the Japanese American's power of assimilation and accommodation is not only phenomenal, it is "rarely equaled."

Such accolades, which began to be lavished on Japanese Americans at the very height of the civil rights convulsion of the sixties, was disconcerting to Nisei and Sansei of keen sensitivity to social inequities. There were individuals who began to wonder if a foxy brand of racism wasn't being perpetrated by whites, a pitting of minority against minorities in the Nikkei (persons of Japanese ancestry) being held up to blacks and others as an example of rags-to-riches triumph over adversity through adaptation, not confrontation. The subtlety of the message: "Why can't you be like them?" As if to obscure the more odious reasons why the black man and other oppressed minorities were, at long last, lashing out in reckless, uncontrollable fury.

Among the Nisei, it triggered a searching self-examination. Are we "good" in the eyes of whites, they began to ask, merely because we "know our place," bend over backward not to offend, work hard, and "don't make waves"? Are we America's "good niggers"? Some challenged the validity of a "success story" achieved at the price of such rigid conformity and accommodation: one that has stifled spontaniety, stunted and underdeveloped their creativity, undermined a people's impulse for compassion—such as concern for and involvement in the troubles of other minorities—because of their own need for security.

One might guess, with a degree of accuracy, that even their uneasiness over praise is rooted in an urge to invisibility. For the Japanese Americans' anguish is the inescapable feeling that success and acceptance are at best tenuous as long as their dilemma in America remains essentially unchanged: the still exasperating inability of the American populace to differentiate between the citizenry of Japan and Americans who happen to look Japanese. Thirty years after being held accountable for what Japan had done, and paying an agonizingly high price for the right to be called Americans, the Japanese Americans realize that, like it or not, they are still looked upon as "foreigners" in the land of their birth—linked inextricably with Japan.

This is not to deny that the Nikkei, on occasion, have benefited mightily from a spin-off which has not always been bad. For example, the often complimentary stereotyping bestowed on the Japanese people in the postwar years was a bonanza for Americans of Japanese ancestry. Since Americans, in a radical about-face, believed the Japanese to be relentlessly hard-working, deathlessly loyal, polite, conscientious, intelligent, resourceful, neat, precise, artistic, serene, etc., the Nisei ended up having the lowest unemployment rate of any of America's minority groups; their children grew up in an atmosphere of relative racial amity. The Nisei's comeback from penury was immeasurably accelerated by this historic turnabout of American public opinion toward Japan and the Japanese. The Nisei, moreover, luxuriated in a vicarious pride of achievement in seeing their tiny ancestral homeland rise from smoldering ruins to catapult herself into a position of awesome international prestige: to the position of "second-largest economic power in the world, outranking the Soviet Union," according to a mid-1973 pronouncement of former Ambassador to Japan Edwin O. Reischauer, albeit an assessment precipitously altered since then by the global energy emergency.

It had seemed for a while that the Nisei could finally admit to

being "Japanese" without self-consciousness or fear of majority criticism as Irish Americans, Italian Americans and others do about their
ancestral roots with unabashed pride.

But as relations once again become chilled between Tokyo and
Washington, as Japan moves into an increasingly independent posture
in international relations and in economic and trade matters, there is
reason for disquiet among an all too visible group whose popularity
soars or topples with the American citizenry's attitude toward Japan.
From lavish praise of the reconciliation years, there are hints of resentment tinged with jealousy now that millions of Americans are being
laid off (much too often because U. S. mills and factories cannot
compete with made-in-Japan imports), while the relentlessly energetic
Japanese, who possess to an excess the enterprise and dedication ad-
mired by whites, enjoy a far greater degree of job security than their
Western counterparts, notwithstanding the recession and roaring inflation which has eroded the island nation's once phenomenal afflu-
ence. Misunderstandings, recriminations, and bruised feelings over
protectionist policies adopted by both powers have impaired once
warm relations—resulting, predictably, in an impaired image of Japan,
the Japanese people, and in turn, the Japanese Americans.

In the United States, the use of the emotionally charged epithet,
"Jap," and the stereotype of Oriental supercunning and inscrutability
so firmly emblazoned on the public mind during World War II are
beginning to resurface in hurtful slurs, slogans, and don't-buy-Japa-
nese advertising, leading one to imagine that anything like a "Tokyo-
Peking axis" could bring on a new wave of "yellow peril" paranoia
and fanatical intolerance against Asian Americans.

Already, a "boycott the Japanese" campaign launched by con-
servationist and environmental groups to force Japan to honor the
whaling moratorium has unleashed a sudden surge of anti-Japanese
feelings that finds Japanese Americans, once again, on the receiving
end of the often racially oriented harassment. "The most insidious
aspect of the well-intentioned 'Save the Whale' campaign [which has
chosen Japan as its primary target though Russia, Peru, Iceland, and
a few Scandinavian countries number among the offending nations]
is the so-called 'children's crusade,' the mobilization of the nation's
grade school children in the massive protest movement calling for the
boycott of all goods and services 'Japanese,' which has created an intolerable situation for our Japanese American children," declares
David Ushio, National Executive Director of the JACL. "Intentionally
or not, anti-Japanese bias is being sown in the classroom, and America's children are being taught that a whole race of people are cruel,
barbaric, and hold disrespect for the law. In their zeal to save the
whales, impressionable youngsters are beginning to turn their energy
toward the only visible symbol of Japan, their innocent little Japanese

American classmates. More and more, we are hearing from parents that their children are the recipients of angry racist taunts and even physical abuse by their peer groups."

On the international scene, Japan's aggressive drive for foreign markets to buttress her hard-hit but still robust economy is generating bias on a global scale—to the extent that her overseas salesmen are being scolded for working too hard and making themselves conspicuous by their tendency to cluster. Keep a low profile and strive in every possible way to enhance one's moral and ethical behavior, they are admonished. Increasingly, individuals and corporations are being urged to play a more constructive part in the affairs of their host communities.

Observers, like *New York Times* correspondent James Sterba, are inclined to believe that the sudden sprouting of anti-Japanese myths and slurs boils down to spoil-sport jealousy and antagonistic stratagems among competitors unable to keep pace with the early-to-bed-early-to-rise work ethic of the Japanese; that what Japan does, essentially, "is not just good business, but better business." Notes Sterba in *The New York Times Magazine* of October 29, 1972: "It is interesting to watch the sour grapes turn into fear, threats and bullying. . . . Americans have added a new weapon, one that other Asians have been using for years—the whispering campaign. The image of the "sneaky" and "ugly" Japanese is being spread round the world . . ."

For people of Japanese lineage, acutely sensitive to anything involving dishonor to their name, such wanton defamation and rekindling of racist attitudes are cause for alarm on both sides of the Pacific.

In Tokyo, a high-level study committee set up by the prestigious Japan Economic Research Institute, after considerable soul-searching, announced that the undertaking of a wide-ranging public relations effort was crucial if Japan is to avoid getting on an international hate list. And reminiscent of a time when the first immigrants to America had been admonished not to behave in a manner which might bring shame to the mother country, the report of the study committee included a stern denunciation of the behavior of both Japanese citizens and corporate entities abroad and recommendations on ways to correct acknowledged failings in this area.

Two other conclusions reached by the special committee, that much of the negative criticism "stems from misunderstanding and a sheer lack of knowledge, indicating that communication is not functioning as well as we would hope," and that the "Japanese people are by and large unskilled in expressing their thoughts and presenting their positions," registered an ominously familiar ring for the Nisei. For defined with near-pinpoint precision were the very weaknesses which had once made the Nisei and their Issei parents easy victims of unscrupulous jingoistic fear and hate manipulators at a critical moment in their lives. Rather heartening, therefore, to those who recall how inaccessibility to the media made monstrous untruths about them hold sway in the public mind is the committee's strong recommendation that "we develop an international media of our own that will extend to a wide range of nations and people outside of Japan," perhaps a news-disseminating agency on the scale of the Associated Press or United Press International, though specific plans were not then available.[6]

Reflecting a parallel degree of anxiety over the noticeable upsurge in anti-Japanese feelings is the Japanese American Citizens League, now a respected veteran organization, national in scope, with a full-time lobbyist installed in the nation's capital. Its rueful retrospective assessment, that "the tragedy of the 1942 Evacuation was due in considerable part to the failure of the Issei-Nisei community to project the kind of public relations image that would have made such an action unthinkable," has their top experts poring over ways and means of gaining access to the nation's opinion molders before the scapegoat hunt begins in earnest. JACL leaders do not believe they are exaggerating the threat. Knowing how easily minds fed on racist fears and economic chauvinism can inflame others or be inflamed, a special Public Relations Commission has been charged with mapping out ways to "act on the problems at this time rather than reacting belatedly in a crisis situation." [7]

III

Though to all outward appearance the recovery of Japanese Americans has been good to remarkable, the rejection and social isolation of the war years have left scars which have not entirely disappeared. A bitter evacuation legacy shared by ex-inmates in varying degrees is a psychic damage which the Nisei describes as "castration": a deep consciousness of personal inferiority, a proclivity to noncommunication and inarticulateness, evidenced in a shying away from exposure which might subject them to further hurt. A behaviorism summed up by Nisei activist Edison Uno: "We were like the victims of rape. We felt shamed. We could not bear to speak of the assault."

It is little wonder that after being released back into society like a pack of ex-convicts, Japanese Americans sought with a vengeance to restore their demeaned honor and extricate themselves from the pariah status imposed—to "make it" by becoming "better Americans than the regular ones because that's the way it has to be when one looks Japanese." [8] The sense of *giri* handed down to them by their parents, to clear their name of insult and shame, became the Nisei's driving force.

Perhaps nothing had influenced the Nisei so profoundly as wartime accusations of their "unassimilability," innuendoes that it was their clannishness and propensity to cluster which had helped to bring on the calamity. "I would try very hard not to have too many in the same place because I think that has been one of the mistakes of the past," was the admonition of the First Lady, Eleanor Roosevelt, on a camp inspection tour of Gila. In centers everywhere, a new purpose and direction were vigorously inculcated: Dispersion. Diffusion. A blending into the melting pot.

The Nisei took such advice to heart. The goal of jettisoning their Japaneseness and of assimilating themselves into the larger society became a near obsession for them in the early postwar years. Many forced themselves into resettling in unknown parts of the country, cutting themselves adrift from the tight-knit society in which they and their parents had once found security. A few vowed never "to return"; for a small segment of the scorned population, it was a matter of pride and principle. But as the hurt wore off and West Coast bias and barriers began to disappear, a large percentage were to eventually make their way back to their former communities.

"People in the East and Midwest are good, opportunities for career advancement there are perhaps better, but no state can beat the California climate," say returnees. Out of 350,000 Nikkei living on the U. S. mainland (250,000 in Hawaii), 225,000 have once again made California their home.

IV

By war's end, the Japanese American's reticence, restraint, and desire to be inoffensive (often referred to as the "enryo syndrome") had become known to officialdom, and Washington was not above taking advantage of it in its program to compensate for an avowed "mistake." An Evacuation Claims Act was enacted into law on July 2, 1948; and though eminently successful in reaping media praise as "another instance of democracy correcting its own mistake," the postwar restitution program turned out to be uncharitable in the extreme. Claims were stringently limited to so-called "tangible" losses—"damages to or loss of real or personal property." These were settled on the basis of 1942 prices, without interest, minus 10 percent for lawyer's fee. Litigation relating to the Claims Act lasted over a seventeen-year period.

Surprisingly, not one lawsuit had been filed against the government for mental suffering, physical hardships, personal injury, or death in the years following the closing of the camps. The 1948 claims law expeditiously relegated such grievances to the area of "noncompensables." Typical of the logic then prevailing, the loss of farm animals was recognized as a "tangible loss" and compensated, but no claim could be made for the loss of loved ones.

"We were had," is the candid opinion of Edison Uno, who had aided numerous claimants in arriving at a settlement. "There was a total disregard of prevailing market value or the irreplaceable nature of items lost. Settlement had to be made on the basis of prices paid at the time of purchase, or 1942 prices, at best. Immense losses were incurred through sheer ignorance of government arbiters on such items as *bonsai* plants, for example—sometimes worth thousands of dollars—since examiners insisted that appraisal by other Japanese *bonsai* experts would only be self-serving. Practically all families posed the question: 'Can you put a sentimental value on old irreplaceable photos, or would you have to settle for the film value?' The government always took the latter view. Petitioners were totally at their mercy since the Justice Department attitude was 'take it or leave it.' "

The timing had been unfortunate. The camps had been a quarter-of-a-billion-dollar fiscal embarrassment, and Congress and the Justice Department were in no mood to compound the extravaganza by a full and retroactive compensation to evacuees, as had been urged for years by Norman Thomas.

The political realities of the time were also such that the dis-loyalty factor entered into the settlement of claims, according to Uno: "If you were a 'no-no' or one labeled a 'troublemaker,' you as an individual had little choice but to accept what the government offered." Uno explains in rueful retrospect: "The Claims Law was an example of tokenism which we took, hook, line and sinker. At a time when families were reeling from destitution, going without medical atten-tion, and the Issei fast dying off, the general attitude was: 'Better a bird in hand than two in the bush,' " as in the case of a ninety-two-year-old man who settled for the $2,500 "compromise" payment. His original claim had been $75,000.

It was in 1951 that Congress gave authorization for a compro-mise settlement program to speed up payments to claimants, many of them only a few years from their grave. Only 137 claims had been settled in all of 1950. More shocking, it was costing U. S. taxpayers $1,400 for the government to decide that a payment of $450 be made.[9] Subsequently, the Attorney General was empowered to pay up to $2,500, or up to three-quarters of the original claim, "which-ever was less," minus the exhaustive investigation heretofore required. But this did not deter arbiters from remorselessly imposing larger cuts in exchange for roseate promises of instant payment. "The Claims Division drove a hard bargain, almost as hard as the unscrupulous second-hand dealers who had bought family possessions for a song," charges Anne Fisher in *Exile of a Race*. It is worth noting that each family involved was generally limited to filing a *single* claim against the government; yet a sizable majority of the 24,064 petitioners ended up agreeing to "compromise" their wartime claims for a scant $2,500, however severe their losses had been.

At the time of the enforced exodus, the material loss to the Japanese community had been put at $400 million. The restitution requested by the dispossessed—strictly limited to provable losses— had come to $132 million. Less than $40 million was returned. When the last claim had been adjudicated in 1965,[10] the total restoration amounted to less than ten cents on the 1942 dollar.

In the opinion of economist Kenneth Hansen, the $400 million loss, estimated by the Federal Reserve Bank of San Francisco, is far from a realistic figure. Hansen points to the often overlooked but unblinkable fact that "the bill gets bigger every day. . . . Losses are still being compounded because of constantly increasing evaluations of often valuable lands they were forced to let go." [11]

No estimate has ever been made of "anticipated profits" and "anticipated earnings"—salaries and incomes lost during the two, three, or more years of incarceration. The 1948 claims law forbade the right to file for such "intangibles."

Faring exceedingly better in terms of reparation are surviving victims of Nazi tyranny, at least the more fortunate ones residing outside the Iron Curtain. Indemnification (indicated parenthetically below) was made by the Federal Republic of Germany for a wide range of grievances, including:

- • loss of life (lifelong annuities to spouse, also to minor children up to their reaching majority)
- • damage to health (lifelong annuities computed in relation to the destruction of working capacity, also payment of medical treatments)
- • incarceration in concentration camps and ghettos (DM 5 per day or DM 150 per month)
- • damage to property (one-time settlement)
- • damage to profession (one-time payment not to exceed DM 40,000, or lifelong annuities)
- • repatriation (a DM 6,000 settlement is still being awarded to all citizen returnees)
- • interruption of education (one-time payment).[12]

For losses involving real estate, savings, securities, household furnishings, jewelry, and other movable and identifiable property, additional reparation was provided by the Federal Restitution Law of 1957. Regardless of where they may be living in the world, a sizable number of former victims of Nazism continue to collect lifelong annuities. It has been estimated that, by 1985, West Germany's payments in the field of restitution and indemnification may go well beyond the $35 billion mark.

Survivors of Nazi oppression also fared a good deal better than stateside evacuees in cases where substantiation by means of documentary proof was an absolute impossibility. In such instances, the West German government permitted a sworn affidavit accompanied by a sworn affidavit of a second or third party as validation of claims. It was an altogether different story for Japanese Americans. For the purpose of proving evacuee losses, the production of records was crucial. Or in the exact phraseology of the law, "documentary evidence, attendance of witnesses [an impossibility for most victims of the dispersal], and production of books, papers and documents" was mandatory to back up claims. These could be subpoenaed by the Justice Department, at any time, with a $10,000 fine and up to five years' imprisonment for misrepresentation. So rigidly unyielding had been the requirement of proof that the once bereft, still terrified victims felt disinclined to risk another incarceration. Numerous Issei did not file a claim.

In no case could a claim be filed by (or for) anyone who had "voluntarily or involuntarily" repatriated or expatriated to Japan. Not a modicum of consolation was forthcoming, in other words, for victims who had suffered the most from America's "mistake."

More recently, at a JACL national convention held in June 1970, a proposal that Congress be memorialized to provide compensation for the misdeed of "wrongful internment" was introduced by Edison Uno of San Francisco,[13] with its subsequent adoption by the body as a matter to be seriously pursued. Two of several options presently being studied are measures which would (1) grant ex-inmates (or heirs) a flat restitution payment of five dollars a day, the current prisoner of war pay, for each day spent in confinement, or (2) establish a fund which would be used to meet specific needs of the Japanese American community.

Notwithstanding the claims act legalism which rules out the right to petition for so-called "intangibles" (as salaries and incomes lost during the years of incarceration), remedial legislation to rectify such pitiless illiberalism of the past seems incredibly overdue—if only in behalf of the Issei, the fast-dwindling survivors of the sorry episode whose chance for income and security in their old age had been wiped out by it, many of whom are known to be living at a poverty level.[14] Totally shunted aside and neglected, for example, are the needs of impoverished single men, the familyless Issei pioneers whose pursuit of the American Dream has ended in the loneliness of a dingy one-room flat in some wretched Lil Tokyo rooming house, "the after-effects of racist immigration laws which produced whole generations of single men among Asian immigrants," in the words of Warren Furutani, spiritual head of a growing number of Sansei and Yonsei (fourth generation) activists intensely resentful of society's inequities, past and present.

V

In recent years, Sansei activism aimed at alleviating the plight of the neglected elderly has helped to counteract the impaired image of the Japanese American youth generation now reaching maturity, a group whose dramatic departure from the paths of their forefathers is becoming a matter of deepening concern for the ethnic community. Still highly motivated as a group and *otonashii* (subdued) in comparison to their white peers, the progeny of the Nisei are all-American in their speech, outlook, individualistic behavior, and greater involvement in the larger society; but, as pointed out by William Petersen in *Japanese-Americans: Oppression and Success,* an excellent study of both the mainland and Hawaiian Nikkei, "part of their full acculturation to the general pattern is that they are beginning to show some of the faults of American society that were almost totally lacking in their parent generation."

Drug abuse and delinquency count among problems perceptibly on the rise, notably among youths whose Nisei parents have little or no sense of race pride, according to a study within the community. Yet, considering the enormity of woes afflicting other ethnic groups, authorities are still far from alarmed; thus governmental funding for urgently desired self-help projects are hard to come by for larger urban communities groping for ways to combat the creeping blight. Contributing in no small way to the problem are traditionalists encrusted with hidebound attitudes of group "disgrace," who continue to insist: "Why spoil the community's 'good image' by begging for help?"

The assertive young reject the sweep-it-under-the-rug *enryo* approach. Indeed, the more militant, usually younger, Nisei agree that it's high time to get out from under the debilitating "quiet American" label if their needs are to be taken seriously. From all sides, there is growing anger at what the ethnic community considers a chronic governmental shirking of responsibility to a less demanding minority. In communities like Los Angeles and San Francisco, younger constituents are pressing for an Asian-American coalition, a banding together of various Asian ethnics in a common effort to keep authorities from taking advantage of their historical passivity. Says activist Furutani: "They slam the door in our faces, saying, 'Asians have no problems,' or, 'Asians take care of their own.' But we say, 'Look, kids are dying off of Reds, the old people have nowhere to go, we need socialized medicine because inflation is moving too fast,' but our cries fall on deaf ears because everyone knows 'to Asians life is cheap.' "

The divisive Vietnam years that scarred the national spirit—the cruel destructive bombing of Southeast Asia, in particular—have had a profound effect on the Sansei, who show a greater responsiveness to conditions of injustice and human inequities than their forebears. They were quick to read racist overtones into a war which would pound a tiny distant country into a pulp because its people are Oriental. (Would America do the same against a tiny European nation?) They identified themselves, their sisters and brothers, with the napalmed Vietnamese. They saw their own frail grandparents in the fleeing figures of terrified Cambodian civilians, their life possessions reduced to a knapsack. Thus a generation tenderly sheltered by the Issei and Nisei from the raw realities of overt racism became more attuned to its subtleties than their parents ever were, with the result that a growing number of Sansei seek to identify themselves with fellow Americans and fellow world citizens suffering racial oppression, whatever their color.

The tension, the turmoil, the bitter racial upheavals of the sixties may well have been a factor in turning many Sansei into a more vocal, articulate, and action-oriented generation: a far cry from the Nisei, for whom silence and noninvolvement are almost a conditioned response from years of putting up with biased accusations and assaults calling for emotional control on a colossal scale.

But if the young have succeeded in retrieving for themselves an emasculated part of the Nikkei psyche, and if they have benefited positively from a troubled time, it has come at a cost. For them, the glowing American image, the sure conviction of their nation's majesty and nobility, so closely hugged by the guileless Nisei, has been badly tarnished. The alienation bequeathed by an agonizing decade has been profoundly unsettling and will take time to heal, as with millions of the angry, hurt, and disillusioned fellow Americans across a grievously troubled nation.

VI

Within the community, the silence over the camps reflects continuing deep divisions, wounds that still fester. A cleavage, even now, divides the proestablishment patriots of the period and those stigmatized as "troublemakers"—the reckless, hard-driving camp dissidents who failed to live up to the standard of being "good" and "respectable" members of their ethnic group. One senses, also, a lingering resentment against the JACL, though it is rarely given violent expression by old-timers. Rather, it is the young who attack the organization's static accommodationist role, past and present, who prefer to make folk heroes of men who led the camp rebellions, and who would change the now ninety-chapter-strong bastion of Americanism—if they were to have their way—into an Asian-American coalition for maximum political clout. Only with power can they hope to deal effectively with the nation's manipulators of power, insist Sansei activists.

Like other American minorities caught up in the pride-of-heritage contagion, the Sansei are eagerly reembracing a cultural identity once threatened by liquidation in their parents' zeal for assimilation. Their determination to rediscover for themselves their historical roots, to gain in the culture of their ancestral homeland a sense of "belonging," has resulted in the proliferation of Asian-American courses and study centers on West Coast campuses.

Camps were rarely talked about in the homes, and whenever they were, "we would argue," says Sansei Kevin Kendo. "I couldn't understand why they just packed up and went without resistance." The more militant insist that never again will there be the *shikataganai* ("it can't be helped") subservience to the white man's caprice. "If it happens again," says Stanford lecturer Pat Sumi, "we would resist. We would fight it through legal and illegal means."

If little or no lingering bitterness over their humiliation can be detected among the Issei and Nisei, the Sansei freely admit to their boiling anger. Some bitterly denounce the camps, along with My Lai and Hiroshima, as out-and-out racist atrocities.

For parents of Sansei activist Alan Nishio, the camp experience simply "didn't exist"—but was totally banished, as it were, to the darker recesses of their consciousness. Only when asked to interview his mother and father as a part of a school assignment did young Nishio begin to understand why:

> In my case I discovered that my father had owned a grocery store before the war and ended up being a gardener after it and hating it. Before the war he took mother out once a week to the movies. Since the war, my mother has only seen one movie. Before the war my father didn't drink. But he died two years ago of alcoholism. And I was never really aware of the causes until I started asking about the camp.[15]

Pilgrimages to view the remains of the desert jails in which their parents were confined are becoming ever more frequent. At such events, the Nisei are conspicuous by their absence, except for a sprinkling of their activist element. Reflecting on the phenomenon of a whole generation clubbed into timidity and silence, Furutani claims "the camps dehumanized and psychologically murdered people without laying a hand on them."

In the beginning, disquiet approaching resentment was evidenced over the singular intensity with which the Sansei proceeded to dredge up what they referred to as the "forgotten chapter" in their lives. The Issei feared that it would offend whites. The Nisei importuned: Let bygones be bygones. Why unnecessarily imperil their hard-won "acceptance?" Why risk exposure to the often startling bigotry that lies below the façade of tolerance? Especially resented by the Nisei was their having to finally face up to the full extent of America's betrayal of their adolescent dreams and idealism.

But after the initial pain of wounds reopened, it was as though a terrible burden had been lifted. Furutani: "You talk to people and they start sitting down and tears start trickling down their cheeks —that's how important that thing was." [16] The older generation began to recognize, however reluctantly, the merit of the Sansei's determination that the story be remembered, studied, and talked about so that people will be forever reminded that concentration camps and wholesale contempt for individual rights and lawful procedure are not the exclusive province of corrupt tyrannies and maniacal dictatorships.

Redress Update

The quest for redress culminated in 1988, after some nine redress bills had been introduced in Congress, after diverse peoples, even veterans groups, had joined in support; but sadly too late for most Issei. During the ten-year crusade, remarkable facts came to light. Surely a defining moment was when John J. McCloy, top supervisor of the WRA camps, declared in his commission testimony that mass internment was "retribution" for the Pearl Harbor attack.

In response to Edison Uno's 1970 call for the JACL to act expeditiously, a redress committee of the Seattle chapter of the JACL had been activated in 1973. By December 1975 redress advocates (the team of Shosuke Sasaki, Henry Miyatake, and Mike Nakata) had formulated and distributed an "Appeal for Action" to all JACL chapters. On September 16, 1975, the team of Paul Tsuneishi and Phil Shigekuni formed Los Angeles–based "E.O. 9066" to "pressure JACL to act." Under President Clifford Uyeda, the JACL finally launched a national redress campaign by passing a resolution (July 28, 1978) seeking $25,000 per detainee. But on March 3, 1979, the federal investigatory commission route, urged by Senator Daniel Inouye, became the strategy embraced by the JACL. Preferring to pursue direct legislation, the NCJAR (National Council for Japanese American Redress), formed in Seattle in May 1979 (later Chicago-based), withdrew support of national strategy. On November 28, 1979, Representative Mike Lowry introduced HR 5977, the first direct compensation bill, which provided $15,000 plus $15 per diem in detention. In November 1980 California-based activist groups merged to form the National Coalition for Redress/Reparation (NCRR) to join in galvanizing grassroots support for redress and to lay the groundwork for massive letter-writing campaigns and media-focused rallies for public education.

Following the establishment of the Commission on Wartime Relocation and

Internment of Civilians (CWRIC), twenty days of nationwide hearings were held between July and December 1981. The initial report of the CWRIC, *Personal Justice Denied*, issued to Congress on February 24, 1983, admitted "grave injustices." The NCJAR immediately filed a $27.5 billion class action suit *(Hohri et al. v. United States)* on March 16,1983, on behalf of 125,000 victims. On June 16, 1983, the CWRIC issued its final report, *Personal Justice Denied*, recommending appropriation of $1.5 billion for payment of $20,000 to survivors, creation of an education trust fund, and formal national apology. On October 6, 1983, Representative Jim Wright introduced HR 4110 based on CWRIC suggestions. On November 16, 1983, Senator Spark Matsunaga introduced SR 2116 as a companion bill to HR 4110.

On January 3, 1985, Representative Wright introduced HR 442 to memorialize a Nisei combat team. Senator Matsunaga followed on May 2, 1985, with SR 1053. In fall 1985 the JACL empowered the LEC (Legislative Education Committee), with Grayce Uyehara as executive director and Grant Ujifusa as strategy chair, to maximize networking of letter-writing grassroots support with personal lobbying efforts and to push formal legislative strategy. Final redress bills HR 442 and SR 1009 were introduced respectively by new majority leader Representative Tom Foley on January 6, 1987, and by Senator Matsunaga on April 10, 1987. On April 20, 1987, after a successful appeal in the District of Columbia Circuit Court, *Hohri* was heard in oral argument by the Supreme Court, which ruled on a narrow technical issue, rather than the merits. From July 25 to 29, 1987, a NCRR-organized Asian American contingent, the largest in U.S. history, converged on Capitol Hill to lobby for final enactment of redress legislation. On August 4, 1987, the Senate Committee on Governmental Affairs passed SR 1009, and on September 17, 1987, the House passed HR 442, for which Congresspersons Norman Mineta, Robert Matsui, and others had struggled tenaciously for years. Finally, on July 27, 1988, the Senate approved the conference committee's reconciled version of HR 442; on August 4, 1988, SR 1009 was approved by the House. President Reagan signed it into law as the Civil Liberties Act of 1988 on August 10, 1988.

On October 31, 1988, the Supreme Court refused to hear a second appeal of *Hohri*, thus terminating suit. After President Bush signed the bill (November 21, 1989), which changed redress expenditures from discretionary to mandatory, payments began in October 1990. Despite a law that urges review of applications with liberality, the government's rebuff of numerous applicants has resulted in various exemptions, such as Hawaii residents who were forcibly excluded from their homes; Nisei soldiers who were denied the privilege of visiting families in the camps; and some Japanese Peruvians, all of whom were excluded from eligibility in the 1988 Act. Victory in *Consolo v. United States* (July 10, 1995, U.S. Court of Appeals for the Federal Circuit) granted eligibility to children of "voluntary evacuees" (those who had moved inland before internment began, who earlier had been given the right to redress). The struggle for justice continues—until the provisions of the Civil Liberties Act end on August 10, 1998.

SOURCES: Leslie T. Hamiya, *Righting a Wrong; Pacific Citizan; Rafu Shimpo;* NCJAR newsletters.

Notes for Chapter 1

1   For documentation of key enemy messages decoded in the weeks and months preceding the attack, see Admiral Robert A. Theobald's *The Final Secret of Pearl Harbor* (New York: The Devin-Adair Co., 1954). The book's Foreword, written by Admiral William F. Halsey, hero of the Pacific War, reads in part: "Had we known of Japan's minute and continued interest in the exact location and movement of our ships in Pearl Harbor, as indicated in the 'Magic Messages,' it is only logical that we would have concentrated our thought on meeting the practical certainty of an attack on Pearl Harbor. . . . I have always considered Admiral Kimmel and General Short [commanders at Pearl Harbor] to be splendid officers who were thrown to the wolves as scapegoats . . . They had to work with what they were given, both in equipment and information. They are our outstanding military martyrs." Works of historians William L. Langer, Roberta Wohlstetter, and Thomas A. Bailey might be consulted for a defense of Roosevelt's conduct of foreign policy leading up to the attack.

2   According to the findings of the Army Pearl Harbor Board investigating the attack: ". . . Washington was in possession of essential facts as to the enemy's intentions and proposals. This information showed clearly that war was inevitable and late in November absolutely imminent. . . . It would have been possible to have sent safely, information ample for the purpose of orienting the commanders in Hawaii, or positive directives for an all-out alert." U.S. Army. The Army Pearl Harbor Board. *Report to the Secretary of War,* October 20, 1944, Vol. 39, pp. 103–4 of the *Hearings before the Joint Committee on the Investigation of the Pearl Harbor Attack.*

3   ". . . the State Department and the President were not satisfied with intelligence of the Army and the Navy and the FBI and they sent out their own intelligence agents to get certain information in relation to the Japanese both in Hawaii and the Japanese on the west coast," declared Senator Homer Ferguson on making the Munson document public for the first time as Chairman of the Congressional Investigation into the Pearl

Harbor Attack (November 15, 1945, to May 31, 1946). The operation had been set up by John Franklin Carter (Jay Franklin), a journalist-radio-commentator-friend of FDR. See Appendix 10 for Carter's covering memorandum on the report.

4 Confidential investigative assignments for the State Department were taken on by Curtis Burton Munson whenever called upon. Examples: Assignments in 1941 included "Investigation into German interests of Anaconda and of General Motors" and, in September, a report on the "Attitude of French-Canadians toward the European War." From July 1942 to November 1943, Lieutenant Commander Munson served as Assistant Naval Attaché and Assistant Naval Attaché for Air to the Embassy in London. See name card index, 1940–44, of the Department of State.

5 The General Staff had also received about this time a copy of a ten-page report of Commander K. D. Ringle—intelligence chief of the Southern California naval district—strongly opposing the evacuation as "unwarranted," as the problem had been "magnified out of its true proportion because of the physical characteristics of the people." (All three West Coast naval districts had received copies of the Munson Report.) Ringle declared, moreover, that he "heartily agrees with the reports submitted by Mr. Munson." Report, Lieutenant Commander K. D. Ringle to the Chief of Naval Operations, undated (submitted "around February 1, 1942," according to Army historian Conn), Records of the Office of the Secretary of War (hereafter cited as "ASW," denoting the "Assistant Secretary of War," who then had been given charge of all matters relating to the Japanese problem), ASW 014.311 WDC, RG 107, National Archives.

6 J. Edgar Hoover believed that the demand for evacuation was "based primarily upon public political pressure rather than upon factual data" and that the FBI was fully capable of handling the small number of suspects then under surveillance. Naval authorities favored the use of hearing boards and the policy of selective internment.

7 "Issei" means "first generation"; "Nisei" means "second generation"; and "Sansei" is "third generation" in the Japanese language. As is done with other nationalities in the U.S., author will use the term "Japanese" to refer to the Japanese American minority whenever there is no possibility of confusion. Also, author will tread lightly on areas treated exhaustively in other evacuation works.

8 For a listing of pressure groups and organizations strongly anti-Japanese American, see Allan R. Bosworth's *America's Concentration Camps* (New York: W. W. Norton, 1967) pp. 30–32 in paperback edition.

9 Statements attributed to Earl Warren are taken from *Hearings,* 77th Congress, 2nd sess. Select Committee Investigating National Defense Migration (Washington: Government Printing Office, 1942). The Tolan Committee hearings (conducted from February 21 through March 7, 1942) were a sham. Executive Order of February 19 had already given the evacuation go-ahead to the Army, yet the "road show," with stops in San Francisco, Los Angeles, Portland, and Seattle, was allowed to go on—with exclusionist groups well in control of all the hearings. Assistant War Secretary McCloy had instructed General John L. DeWitt to "cooperate" with the Tolan Committee "insofar as it was compatible with military interests. . . . You might therefore suggest to Mr. Tolan that he should quietly conduct his investigations . . . into the dislocations which would be caused by the removal of these elements and into the best methods of dealing with the problem of their resettlement. There is no need for any investigation of the military aspect of the problem." Memorandum, John J. McCloy to General DeWitt, February 18, 1942, ASW 014.311 *Aliens,* Enemy Aliens on WC, RG 107, National Archives.

10   James MacGregor Burns, *Roosevelt: The Soldier of Freedom* (New York: Harcourt Brace Jovanovich, Inc., 1970), p. 215.

11   Daisuke Kitagawa, *Issei and Nisei, The Internment Years* (New York: Seabury Press, 1967), pp. 32–33. Copyright © 1967 by The Seabury Press, Inc. Used by permission.

12   Betty E. Mitson, "Looking Back in Anguish: Oral History and Japanese-American Evacuation" (New York: The Oral History Association, Inc., 1974) p. 31.

13   *Ibid.,* see fn. 19.

14   Stetson Conn, Rose C. Engelman, and Byron Fairchild, *The United States Army in World War II: The Western Hemisphere: Guarding the United States and Its Outposts* (Washington: Government Printing Office, 1964), p. 207 (hereafter cited as, *Guarding the United States and Its Outposts*).

15   Memorandum, Roosevelt to Frank Knox, February 26, 1942, OF 18, Franklin D. Roosevelt Library, Hyde Park, New York (hereafter cited as "FDR Library"). Knox was then advocating the removal of 140,000 from Oahu. See Appendix 1.

16   Conn, Engelman, and Fairchild, *op. cit.,* p. 210. See Appendix 2 for the Joint Chiefs of Staff directive of March 11, 1942.

17   Letter, Frank Knox to John H. Tolan, March 24, 1942. House of Representatives, *Fourth Interim Report of the Select Committee Investigating National Defense Migration,* 77th Congress, 2nd sess. (Washington: Government Printing Office, 1942), pp. 48–49.

Notes for Chapter 2

1   Letter, John D. Dingell to Roosevelt, August 18, 1941, OF 197, FDR Library. Dingell was grossly mistaken in claiming that there were 150,000 "additional alien Japanese in the United States." The 1940 census shows 126,947 Japanese Americans in the continental U.S., *only 47,305 of them aliens.* Two-thirds of the minority (79,642) were native-born U.S. citizens.

2   Three rough drafts (all dated "2/5/42") recommending "steps to be taken in connection with the alien enemy-potential saboteur" problem provide evidence of being precursors to the document, Executive Order 9066, which would authorize the West Coast and other mass evacuations on U.S. soil. An early draft reads: "Initially, exclusions to be essentially by class, viz. on the Pacific Coast all Japanese (except, perhaps, for a few token Japs to sustain the legality)." The drafts' opening sentences vary somewhat: 1) "Colonel Bendetsen recommends . . ."; 2) "I recommend . . ."; 3) "The War Department recommends . . ." Unnumbered documents from records of the Office of Assistant Secretary of War, RG 107, National Archives. See also pp. 69, 94 and 95.

3   Letter, Henry L. Stimson to Cordell Hull, February 5, 1942, Department of State File 740.00115 Pacific War/153, RG 59, National Archives.

4   Letter, Frank Knox to Roosevelt, August 16, 1943, PSF: War Department, FDR Library. Hull had asked for the go-ahead which would have authorized repatriation of 266 U.S. citizens in return for approximately 750 German nationals being held in the U.S.

5   Wartime Civil Control Administration Form R-104. The State Department's Repatriation Section of the Special War Problems Division maintained a list of 100,000 names of "individuals of the Japanese race in the United States" along with "their correct addresses, and with the necessary information concerning their identification, whereabouts, and repatriability" (*Department of State Bulletin,* August 6, 1944, p. 142). Tokyo was explicit as to persons to be exchanged, therefore much misunderstanding resulted among detainees from the department's desire to fulfill the Japanese Government's "priority list."

6   "New Day For Nisei Canadians," *Pacific Citizen,* February 12, 1949. Canada had refused to induct the Nisei during wartime, and only in 1947 were citizens of Japanese descent given the right to vote. See also Appendix 8.

7   Letter, M. H. to Hon. Ernest Gruening, October 20, 1942, RG 210, National Archives, in which a Nisei youth implores Governor Gruening of Alaska to help alleviate the plight of the Alaskan Nisei separated from fathers: "You no doubt already know that there are more than 120 Alaskans in this camp . . . Of this number about 50 are children under the age of 18 years. The problem arises from the fact that the Alaskan children . . are without their paternal guidance. Not a single normal family head is with his respective families."

8   Letter, Edwin C. Wilson to Sumner Welles, October 20, 1941, Department of State File 740.00115 Pacific War/1 1/3, RG 59, National Archives.

9   Wire, Cordell Hull to Ambassador (Wilson), December 12, 1941, Department of State File 740.00115 Pacific War/6. RG 59, National Archives. The U. S. Ambassador to Panama was instructed by Hull to see that the Commanding General "furnish the necessary military guard and medical services until such time as the Panamanian officials assume full control of the camp."

10   Letter, George Marshall to Sumner Welles, October 28, 1941, Department of State File 740.00115 Pacific War/1 2/3, RG 59, National Archives.

11   Telegram #375, Lane to State Department, December 8, 1941, Department of State File 740.00115 Pacific War/9, RG 59, National Archives.

12 *Department of State Bulletin,* August 6, 1944, p. 146. The Emergency Committee for Political Defense served to augment removal pressure being applied by the State Department. "It is hoped that pressure from this Committee . . . may increase the effectiveness of Mexican cooperation in the relatively near future," stated a dispatch to Cordell Hull which criticized the government's "apathy." Memorandum, Harold D. Finley (First Secretary to Embassy) to the Secretary of State, January 19, 1942, Department of State File 740.00115 Pacific War/53, RG 59, National Archives.

13 *Ibid.,* p. 147. The Special War Problems Division of the Department of State handled all shipping arrangements. In most instances, Army transports were utilized to bring up detainees.

14 See Edward N. Barnhart's "Japanese Internees from Peru," *Pacific Historical Review,* Vol. 31, May 1962, p. 172, fn. 13. Though not mentioned by Barnhart, Mexico and Venezuela were also participants. Barnhart claims that, in all, "over 600 German nationals and a few men of Italian and other nationality" were also removed to U. S. detention facilities from these countries.

15 *Department of State Bulletin, op. cit.,* p. 147. Alien deportees were still considered to be under the "jurisdiction" of the donor state, which meant that prior approval was required as to the disposition of each case.

16 Wire, Ambassador Wilson to Secretary of State, May 16, 1942, Department of State File 740.00115 Pacific War/548, RG 59, National Archives. Also see Appendix 7a.

17 *State Department Bulletin, op. cit.,* p. 146. The legislative branch of the government was apparently kept in the dark. As for the President, Warren Page Rucker in his well-documented unpublished M.A. thesis ("United States-Peruvian Policy Toward Peruvian-Japanese Persons During World War II," University of Virginia, 1970) maintains: ". . . there seems little doubt . . . that he [FDR] was aware of the internment of the Peruvian-Japanese and that it met with his approval."

18 Letter, Henry Norweb to Sumner Welles, July 20, 1942, Department of State File 740.00115 Pacific War/1002 2/6, RG 59, National Archives. The Japanese colony in Peru was then estimated to number between 25,000 and 30,000.

19 Taken from Enclosure 1 (Memorandum to Ambassador Norweb from John K. Emmerson, Third Secretary of Embassy, April 18, 1942) to dispatch No. 3422 to State Department, April 21, 1942, Department of State File 894.20223/124, RG 59, National Archives. Norweb, in the accompanying dispatch to Hull, endorsed the recommendations as "sound and well presented."

20 Memorandum, Philip W. Bonsal to Selden Chapin, September 26, 1942, Department of State File 740.00115 Pacific War/1002 5/6, RG 59, National Archives.

21 Letter, V.K.T. to Spanish Ambassador, June 30, 1944, unnumbered document from Department of State File, RG 59, National Archives. Charges of abusive treatment were filed by a number of deportees over the years. See Appendix 7a for complaint filed by a deportee from Panama.

22   Tokyo protests had stressed the inhumanity of the removals, which left families "abandoned and without resources." There is reason to believe that, as a direct result of Tokyo threats of "adequate counter measures," the family reunion program had been instituted. Tokyo was subsequently informed that initially "the facilities used for the transportation . . . were not adapted to the transportation of women and children" but that the U. S. intended to bring them over "at the earliest practicable opportunity." Memorandum, State Department to Spanish Embassy, April 19, 1943, Department of State File 740.00115 Pacific War/1549, RG 59, National Archives. Interestingly, commercial airlines and steamship lines were used in the transport of family members. See Appendix 7b for sample of protest letters sent by Tokyo.

23   Letter, Cordell Hull to Roosevelt, August 27, 1942, OF 20, FDR Library. At the time, mail, medicine, and other relief supplies could be sent to civilians and American POWs in Japanese hands only by way of the exchange vessels.

24   Letter, Francis Biddle to Secretary of State, January 11, 1943, Department of State File 740.00115 Pacific War/1276, RG 59, National Archives. The Alien Enemies Act (of 1798) provides that whenever there is a declared war between the U. S. and any foreign nation, "all natives, citizens, denizens, or subjects of the hostile nation," fourteen years or older, can be "apprehended, restrained, secured, and removed as alien enemies."

25   As quoted in a memorandum to the Secretary of State from Frank P. Corrigan of the U. S. Embassy in Caracas, August 21, 1943, Department of State File 740.00115 Pacific War/1845, RG 59, National Archives.

26   The drastic U.S. removal policy gained impetus from a resolution adopted at an Inter-American Conference in the spring of 1945. The resolution had recommended the adoption of measures "to prevent any person whose deportation was necessary for reasons of security of the continent from further residing in this hemisphere, if such residence would be prejudicial to the future security or welfare of the Americas." A Presidential Proclamation (Truman) of September 8, 1945, implemented the resolution by directing the Justice Department to assist the Secretary of State (Byrnes) in effectuating removal of all enemy aliens to lands belonging to the enemy governments "to which or to the principles of which they had adhered" and of others then in the U.S. "without admission under the immigration laws." See Department of State File 711.62115 AR/8-3145, RG 59, National Archives.

27   The impossibility of a case-by-case review may also have led to the decision for summary removals. According to a State Department memo: ". . . unless we can get Peru to take the Japanese back, we shall be forced to repatriate all of them to Japan, since we have no information which would enable us to make a case-by-case review. In the very great majority of the cases, the Japanese were sent here only on the say-so of the Peruvian Government." Memorandum, J. B. Bingham to Braden and Acheson, December 13, 1945, Department of State File FW 711.62115 AR/12-1345, RG 59, National Archives.

28   Alfred Steinberg, " 'Blunder' Maroons Peruvian Japanese in the U.S.," *Washington Post,* September 26, 1948. Author Barnhart ("Japanese

Internees From Peru") maintains that the group removed during this period totaled 1,700, which is at variance with a State Department claim of 1,440 who "voluntarily returned to Japan." Letter to author from Georgia D. Hill, Office of the Chief of Military History, December 19, 1972. There had been 476 Peruvian-Japanese included in the second exchange of prisoners with Japan (September, 1943). See "Japanese in Peru" by John K. Emmerson, October 9, 1943, Department of State File 894.20223/196, National Archives.

29 Memorandum, Wayne Collins to author, postmarked June 28, 1973. Aliens among the residual group of 365 had been informed on March 26, 1946: ". . . deportation proceedings are to be instituted immediately in the cases of all who do not file applications for voluntary repatriation. Require all to make their intentions known within twenty-four hours." (Wire to officer in charge of Crystal City from the Immigration and Naturalization Service, excerpted from the Rucker study.) Collins maintains that the earlier removal of 1,700 deportees had been in no way voluntary "even if each was asked and signified his or her desire to be transported to Japan. They were being held as alien enemies under the Alien Enemies Act and couldn't escape the internment unless they agreed to be sent to Japan. That is a perfect picture of duress and lacks every essential of voluntariness."

30 Ickes wrote in his *New York Post* column (as reported in the *Pacific Citizen,* June 29, 1946) that the record of Japanese aliens in the United States during the war as "loyal Americans" is "unblemished," and that "the immediate problem is one of halting the brutal deportation of alien Japanese who have suffered so much at the hands of 'free and democratic' America." Collins successfully halted deportation of 163 longtime residents of fine standing found to be illegal entrants and of numerous Japanese nationals who had lost their admission status as a result of the war.

31 "Town Meeting of the Air" broadcast of December 2, 1947, in *The Town Hall,* XIII, No. 32 (December 12, 1947).

32 The deportees became eligible for naturalization under Public Law 751 (68 Stat., 1044), of August 31, 1954, which entitled the Peruvian Japanese to a certification of "authorized entry" into the United States (Barnhart, *op. cit.,* p. 176). The Peruvian-Japanese were "specifically denied restitution for damages by a House bill [H.R. 3999 *Adjudication of Certain Claims of Persons of Japanese Ancestry,* 80th Congress, 1st sess.] passed in July of 1947." (Rucker, *op. cit.,* p. 65.)

Notes for Chapter 3

1 Memorandum, Francis Biddle to Roosevelt, February 17, 1942, OF 18, FDR Library.

2 Francis Biddle, *In Brief Authority* (New York: Doubleday & Co., 1962), pp. 212–13. Copyright © 1962 by Francis Biddle © by American

Heritage Publishing Co., reprinted by permission of Doubleday & Company, Inc.

3 Former Chief Military Historian Stetson Conn points to Bendetsen (currently a board member of the N. Y. Stock Exchange and Chairman of Executive Board, Champion International) as being "the most industrious advocate of mass evacuation" (see *Guarding the United States and Its Outposts*, Chapter 5). In Chapter 3 of *Concentration Camps USA* (New York: Holt, Rinehart and Winston, Inc., 1971), Professor Daniels strongly backs up the indictment by recounting in detail how Bendetsen and his superior, Provost Marshal General A. W. Gullion, succeeded in "bending the civilian heads of the War Department to their will."

4 See p. 94. See also Conn, Engelman, and Fairchild, *Guarding the United States and Its Outposts, op. cit.,* p. 128. On a few key points, Bendetsen's formula parallels remarkably Canada's exclusion decree, namely: "The Minister of National Defence . . . may, if it appears necessary or expedient so to do in the public interest . . . make, in respect to any area in Canada, an order declaring that . . . such areas shall be a protected area [coastal strip about 100 miles wide]. The Minister of Justice may, with respect to a protected area, make orders . . . a) To require any or all persons to leave such protected area b) To prohibit any or all persons from entering, leaving or returning to such protected area except as permitted pursuant to such order." Defence of Canada Regulations relating to the evacuation, relocation or internment of enemy aliens or other persons (as amended by P.C. 365, dated January 16, 1942), 39.040 Canada, RG 210, National Archives.

5 Biddle, *op. cit.,* p. 218. After receiving carte blanche powers to proceed, Bendetsen had "prepared Franklin Roosevelt's executive order that . . . started the evacuation program," according to *Time* magazine, November 30, 1942.

6 It was at a meeting attended by officials from both the Justice and War departments, held on the evening of February 17 at Biddle's home, that Gullion had produced a draft of 9066, which would expedite removal of citizens. Biddle's aides were amazed that he gave in without a fight. Assistant Attorney General Rowe's post-mortem "excuses" for his chief were that "Biddle was in such a precarious position as far as his job was concerned" and that "public opinion was so strong that the Army would probably have received its way a month later than it did, anyway." Report #15, Interview with James Rowe, Jr., by Morton Grodzins, October 15, 1942. Japanese-American Evacuation and Relocation Records, Manuscript Division, Bancroft Library, University of California, Berkeley, California (hereafter cited as Bancroft Library, University of California, Berkeley).

7 Memorandum, Francis Biddle to Roosevelt, February 20, 1942, OF 4805, FDR Library.

8 *Congressional Record,* Vol. 88, Part 2 (1942), p. 2726. Public Law 503 provided a penalty of $5,000 or one year's imprisonment, or both, for individuals disobeying military orders "in any military area or military zone . . . if it appears that he knew or should have known of the existence and extent of the restrictions or order . . ."

9   Memorandum, Henry Stimson to Roosevelt, March 31, 1943, OF 10 1943 (Justice), FDR Library.

10   Memorandum, Francis Biddle to Roosevelt, April 17, 1943, OF 10 1943 (Justice), FDR Library. Obviously unaware that Order 9066 was "never intended to apply to Italians and Germans," DeWitt doggedly kept insisting on a follow-up evacuation of other "alien enemies" as "an essential war measure" until Assistant War Secretary McCloy squarely presented DeWitt with the facts: "I want to explain to you personally that in approving this program, both the President and the Secretary of War did so with the expectation that the exclusions would not reach such numbers . . . We want, if at all possible, to avoid the necessity of establishing additional relocation settlements . . ." Letter, McCloy to DeWitt, May 20, 1942, ASW 014.311 WC Exclusion Orders, RG 107, National Archives. Earlier, in a memo of May 11, 1942, Bendetsen had urged McCloy to "direct the Commanding General . . . to rescind his curfew against German and Italian aliens as soon as Japanese evacuation is complete . . ." See also Appendix 12.

11   *Pacific Citizen,* March 18, 1944.

12   Fred T. Korematsu, who posed as a Spanish Hawaiian after undergoing plastic surgery, was convicted and prosecuted under Public Law 503 (see p. 227). The Korematsu appeal, taken to the Supreme Court by Wayne Collins, backed by the Northern California ACLU, challenged the constitutionality of an evacuation based solely on national ancestry which denied due process and the equal protection of the law.

13   From "The Day They Penned Up Their Yellow Neighbors," by Nelson Algren, *Los Angeles Times, February 27, 1972.*

14   In his article, "The Man Behind a Famous Court Case," (*Pacific Citizen,* February 13, 1970), Ray Okamura wrote: "Gordon [Hirabayashi] had a grim and thought-provoking footnote: 'The Nazi defendants at the Nuremberg Tribunal cited the *Hirabayashi* and *Korematsu* decisions as a defense. The Nazi defendants claimed "military necessity" in the "evacuation" of the Jews.' " (In *Hirabayashi v. U.S.,* 320 U.S. 81 [1943], the Supreme Court upheld a curfew violation conviction as valid, "based upon the recognition of facts and circumstances which indicate that a group of one national extraction may menace the safety more than others . . .")

Notes for Chapter 4

1   Letter, Father Hugh T. Lavery to President Harry S. Truman (sent in protest previous to Bendetsen's confirmation as Under Secretary of Army in 1949), *Pacific Citizen,* September 24, 1949. Bendetsen's official title throughout much of the war period was "Assistant Chief of Staff in Charge of Civilian Affairs of the Western Defense Command." Today, his biographical credit reads: "He served in the Army as an artillery officer

292

(1940–1945)." See program for Distinguished Service Award Banquet held in his honor, April 3, 1975, Hotel St. Regis, New York City.

2 Exemptions made, from time to time, included the totally deaf, dumb, and blind, if institutionalized; certain Japanese' wives of Caucasian husbands with mixed-blood children "whose environment has been non-Japanese"; individuals one-half Japanese or less "whose backgrounds have been Caucasian."

3 "Suicide During Evacuation," Manzanar Community Analysis Report No. 104, December 14, 1943, RG 210, National Archives.

4 Carey McWilliams, *Prejudice: Japanese Americans: Symbol of Racial Intolerance* (Boston: Little, Brown & Co., 1944), p. 133.

5 *Seattle Times,* December 7, 1969.

6 The Army was in full control of the evacuation propaganda, according to a State Department memo: "Colonel Bendetson [sic] . . . has developed a publicity organization that Mr. McCloy thinks is doing a good job . . . He receives each day large quantities of clippings from West Coast papers giving publicity to statements that are issued by Colonel Bendetson's office." Memorandum, Harold B. Hoskins to Adolph Berle, April 6, 1942, Department of State File 740.00115 Pacific War/445 PS/MNP, RG 59, National Archives.

7 Assembly center data, including per-person daily cost estimate, taken from "Summary of Available Data on Assembly Centers," by Ann Freed, Community Analysis Report No. 69, July 14, 1943, RG 210, National Archives. Further insight into the speed and thrift factor might be gleaned from McCloy's report to Stimson on March 6 (Manzanar opened on March 22): ". . . the areas are being surveyed in which the Japs are to be placed. In the first instance, we will probably put them in tents, though the shortage of canvas may affect this." Memorandum, McCloy to Stimson, March 6, 1942. ASW 014.311 *Aliens:* Enemy Aliens on WC, RG 107, National Archives.

8 A Heart Mountain report also noted the gross overcrowding: "The breakdown of persons assigned to units showed wide discrepancies; to relate an extreme case, the same size unit is being quartered by from one to thirteen persons. It is noted that there was leniency in housing families at first; as the camp began to fill, overcrowded assignments began." Heart Mountain Reports Division, May 1943, Heart Mountain Documents, Box 50, RG 210, National Archives.

9 "Santa Anita Project Report," (undated), Japanese American Relocation Records, Department of Special Collections, University Research Library, University of California, Los Angeles (hereafter cited as University Research Library, UCLA).

10 "Tanforan Hospital Report," May 18, 1942, University Research Library, UCLA. There is one recorded case of an evacuee who did manage to "get out." According to the *San Francisco News* of May 13, 1942, a twenty-one-year-old Nisei, Clarence Sadamune, whose two brothers were then in the Army, escaped from Tanforan and then attempted suicide.

11 Undated document, University Research Library, UCLA.

12 From "Wartime Diary," by Hatsuye Egami, published in *All Aboard* (Topaz), spring edition, 1944.

13 Paul Jacobs, Saul Landau, and Eve Pell, *To Serve the Devil:* Vol. 2 (New York: Random House, 1971), p. 185.

14 For example, Eisenhower, in describing the Poston campsite in his testimony before a Senate appropriations committee, referred to it as "valueless land—worthless since it is undeveloped, but for which water is available from the Colorado River—that land, after it is put into cultivation, is going to be worth from $100 to $200 an acre."

15 "I know almost every available project in the West both public and private," Campbell boasted to FDR. "I have worked for twenty-five years with the Department of the Interior which has many projects available, extending from Montana to Mexico . . ." Letter, Campbell to Roosevelt, March 12, 1942, OF 133, FDR Library.

16 Letter, Thomas D. Campbell to McCloy, February 25, 1942, ASW 014.311 *Aliens:* Enemy Aliens on WC, RG 107, National Archives.

17 Letter, John J. McCloy to author, January 6, 1975.

18 Memorandum, Thomas D. Campbell to McCloy, February 25, 1942, OF 133, FDR Library.

19 Letter, Thomas D. Campbell to Roosevelt, March 12, 1942, *op. cit.*

20 From memorandum, Thomas D. Campbell to McCloy, February 25, 1942, *op. cit.* Campbell had sent along this memorandum (which he had earlier sent to McCloy) with his March 12 letter to the President.

21 Memorandum, John J. McCloy to General Watson, March 22, 1942, OF 133, FDR Library.

22 From "Typescript of Unpublished Autobiography" of Dillon Myer (which is part of interviews conducted from 1968 to 1970), FDR Library. Hereafter cited as "Unpublished Autobiography."

23 "Memorandum For Record." See Article 3: Radio No. 1182 CM IN 0177 (7/1/42), ASW 014.311 Hawaii, RG 107, National Archives.

24 Jacobus tenBroek, Edward N. Barnhart, and Floyd W. Matson, *Prejudice, War and the Constitution* (Berkeley and Los Angeles: University of California Press, 1954), p. 136.

25 Memorandum, Ernest J. King (Commander in Chief, U. S. Fleet) and George C. Marshall to Roosevelt, July 15, 1942, PSF (S) FDR Library.

26 Conn, Engelman, and Fairchild, *Guarding the United States and Its Outposts, op. cit.,* p. 211.

27 *Ibid.,* p. 212. One "alternative evacuation plan" devised by General Emmons (then Commanding Officer of the Hawaii Department and Military Governor) involved the secret evacuation, on June 5, 1942, of twenty-one Nisei officers and 1,277 enlisted men of the Hawaiian National Guard who later, as an all-Nisei combat unit, became the highly decorated 100th Infantry Battalion, which served on the European front.

28 General selection procedure: "Voluntary (or non-voluntary, as you wish) relocation of citizen internees and their families has been, in most cases, after a conference between the internee and his wife resulting in their joint decision to be evacuated. . . . There are a few families, mostly of low income, whose evacuation has been considered appropriate aside from the wishes of one member." Memorandum For The Officer in Charge, by Frank O. Blake (Captain, Infantry), December 1, 1942 (attached to memo to Director, WRA, 12/16/42), Headquarters Security Classified Files (hereafter cited as Washington Central File), RG 210, National Archives.

29 Phone conversation, Lieutenant Colonel W. F. Durbin and Colonel Fielding, November 9, 1942, Hawaii File of Washington Central File, RG 210, National Archives. The military also found it expedient to hold numerous Hawaiian Japanese in wartime military custody (many in military camps) with little or no justification. The War Department was informed: "The review board during the period June through February 3rd 1944 has reviewed 440 internment cases of which 265 were United States citizens. In carrying out the parole policy the release of large numbers at any one time is avoided so as not to create an inference that the military authorities are relaxing their vigilance. Likewise the release of prominent Japanese leaders of known Japanese tendencies is avoided although in the record of many of these cases it appears that no overt acts have been committed by them." Richardson (Ft. Shafter) to McCloy, February 11, 1944, ASW 014.311 Hawaii, RG 107, National Archives.

30 "Interview with a Hawaiian Kibei," by Edgar C. McVoy, Jerome Community Analyst Report No. 113, September 8, 1943, RG 210, National Archives. The 1,037 Hawaiian Japanese were deported to relocation centers between November 23, 1942, and March 14, 1943. According to Analyst Frank Sweetser (Jerome Community Analysis Report 27, March 1943), deportees first had to sign a paper waiving any claims of damages or indemnity against the FBI, Army, and Navy. "Then after the ship was two or three days at sea the men who had been interned were presented with a formal 'release from internment.' This would, if given them prior to their departure from Hawaii, have entitled them to return to their homes." A final contingent of sixty-seven "excludees" (mostly Kibei) from Hawaii were placed in the Tule Lake Segregation Center Army stockade on November 17, 1944.

31 Community analysts were involved, additionally, in the collection of information helpful to the U.S. war effort. A proposed memorandum for project directors, dated August 20, 1943, by chief of analysts John Embree, made clear: "It is believed that various evacuees in the Japanese relocation centers possess information regarding Japanese social, political, economic and labor conditions which can be of great value in the prosecution of the war." DeWitt had early been in favor of "the development of a technique and plan of operation to acquire maximum data about the Japanese as a race with a view to furthering the conduct of actual and psychological warfare against the enemy." Memorandum, J. L. DeWitt to Chief of Staff, October 5, 1942, ASW 014.311 WDC Segregation—Japs, RG 107, National Archives.

32 "The Fence at Minidoka," by John de Young, Project Analysis Series No. 4, April 1943, RG 210, National Archives.

33 "Report of Investigation at Manzanar Relocation Center," by Philip Webster, August 31 to September 2, 1942, University Research Library, UCLA. On May 16, 1942, Hikoji Takeuchi had been shot by Private Phillips, Co. B747 MP Battalion.

34 Norman Thomas, *Democracy and Japanese Americans* (New York: The Post War World Council, 1942). Thomas wrote: "Two or three times children playing about near the fences have been shot at. Once a child who had crawled into some bushes was wounded." See also "Fukai tells of atrocities in relocation camps" (*Kashu Mainichi,* November 7, 1974) and "The Failure of Democracy in a Time of Crisis," by Isao Fujimoto (*Gidra,* September 1969).

35 Jacobs, Landau, and Pell, *To Serve the Devil, op. cit.,* p. 259. Reprinted by permission of Random House, Inc. Copyright © 1971.

Notes for Chapter 5

1 Letter, Henry L. Stimson to Roosevelt, July 7, 1942, OF 25, FDR Library. See also ASW 014.311 WDC General Corresp., RG 107, National Archives.

2 Only one day before, DeWitt had assured Bendetsen: "Hell, it would be no job . . . to move 100,000 people." Phone conversation, General DeWitt, General Gullion, and Major Bendetsen, February 1, 1942, Office of the Provost Marshal General (hereafter cited as PMG), 384.4 WDC Box 1399, RG 389, National Archives. Author Forrest C. Pogue (*George C. Marshall: Organizer of Victory—1943–45.* New York: Viking Press, 1973) characterizes DeWitt as having been "susceptible to pressures exerted by frantic civic leaders or anyone in authority and near at hand"; and says that the General was aided "in dealing with Washington in the early months of the war" because of his considerable "background." According to Pogue, "DeWitt was one of [George C.] Marshall's oldest friends in the service" and, in fact, "one of the two men senior to Marshall who were considered serious contenders for the Chief of Staff position in the spring of 1939."

3 Conn, Engelman, and Fairchild, *Guarding the United States and Its Outposts, op. cit.,* p. 128.

4 Memorandum, Allen W. Gullion to John J. McCloy, February 5, 1942, ASW 014.311 *Aliens:* Enemy Aliens on WC, RG 107, National Archives. Gullion's proposal and others which emanated from his office refute the assertions of apologists that only *after* the failure of voluntary evacuation did the Army and WRA find it necessary to build assembly and relocation centers.

5 Memorandum, Karl Bendetsen to Allen W. Gullion, February 4, 1942, PMG 014.311 Gen. A/E, RG 389, National Archives. Though Bosworth (*America's Concentration Camps USA,* p. 92) asserts that Bendetsen "did not instigate the Evacuation. He merely set it up, under orders," WRA Director Myer holds a contrary view, which the Bendetsen memorandum tends to strongly substantiate: ". . . some people feel that Bendetsen had little responsibility for recommending evacuation, I do not agree. I think that he was a prime mover . . ." See "Unpublished Autobiography," *op. cit.*, p. 186.

6 Phone conversation, McCloy with DeWitt, ASW 014.311 *Aliens: Enemy Aliens on WC*, RG 107, National Archives. In an interview on October 15, 1942, McCloy asserted to author Grodzins: "We civilians in the War Department posed the problem to General DeWitt on the West Coast, he consulted his staff, and they, the military men, made the decision. It was a military decision." (But a hell of a way to run a war in a democracy, was my immediate thought [Grodzins' notation].) Grodzins Interview A702, quoted by permission of the Director of the Manuscript Division, Bancroft Library, University of California, Berkeley.

7 John Boettiger, then an executive of the Hearst-owned *Seattle Post-Intelligencer* (also a son-in-law of FDR through marriage to Anna Roosevelt), remarked to an Administration official, Lawrence I. Hewes, that "he felt that DeWitt had caved in to California hysteria and had far exceeded the President's intentions." See Hewes' *Boxcar in the Sand* (New York: Alfred Knopf, 1957), p. 172.

8 Wire, Culbert Olson to Roosevelt, July 10, 1942, OF 197-A, FDR Library; also letter, W. M. Emerson (Director, FDR Library) to author, February 7, 1975.

9 Wire, North Montana Beet Growers Association to Senator B. K. Wheeler, May 6, 1942, OF 197-A, FDR Library.

10 Letter, Senator James Murray to M. H. McIntyre, September 24, 1942, OF 197-A, FDR Library.

11 tenBroek, et al., *Prejudice, War and the Constitution, op. cit.*, pp. 143–44.

12 Letter of S. J. Boyer, March 8, 1943. Reprinted in U.S. Congress, Senate, Report of the Subcommittee on Japanese War Relocation Centers to the Committee on Military Affairs, 78th Congress, 1st sess., May 7, 1943, p. 91.

13 Letter, Robert P. Patterson to Roosevelt, March 1, 1943, OF 197-A, FDR Library. The alteration of the boundaries by DeWitt's Public Proclamation No. 12 of March 2, 1943, solved another dilemma. Stimson had wired FDR on February 16, 1943: THE NEAREST AVAILABLE TROOPS ARE COLORED UNITS . . . [from Ft. Huachuca] THEIR USE MAY RESULT IN VIGOROUS PROTEST FROM THE COLORED RACE. PSF Stimson Folder, FDR Library.

14 Letter, Ralph P. Merritt to Robert B. Cozzens (undated), Manzanar Records 1942–46, University Research Library, UCLA.

15 Togo Tanaka and Joe Masaoka, "Effect of Furlough on Evacuee Attitudes Toward Permanent 'Outside' Relocation," a report delivered at JACL Special Emergency National Conference, November 17–24, 1942, Salt Lake City, Utah, November 19, 1942.

16 At the time, Myer's efforts to replace racist propaganda with truth was working at cross-purposes with the Army campaign. Early in 1942, JACL wartime president Saburo Kido had been told by "a man in charge of the public relations office" of the WCCA that "an intensive

campaign to hate anything 'Japanese' was being prepared for the Armed Forces to sustain a fighting mood. He predicted that it might take at least 15 years before the American people . . . would forget this hatred." "After Pearl Harbor," by Saburo Kido, *Pacific Citizen,* December 22, 1961.

17 See *Prejudice, War and the Constitution* (pp. 151–58) for a well-researched study of the demanding leave requirements. Capricious factors, such as alleged "disloyal statements" and strong economic ties with Japan (property ownership, bank accounts), could contribute to an adverse ruling, but as pointed out by the authors: ". . . one board member, for example, might feel that ownership of large sums of money in Japan was a certain indication of disloyalty while others would place no weight on it at all." A great deal would depend on answers to a loyalty questionnaire (see Chapter 8).

18 Letter, J. L. DeWitt to John J. McCloy, October 5, 1942, *op. cit.*

19 Dillon S. Myer, *Uprooted Americans: The Japanese Americans and the War Relocation Authority* (Tucson, Arizona: University of Arizona Press, 1971), pp. 242–44.

Notes for Chapter 6

1 Letter, Milton Eisenhower to Marvin H. McIntyre, May 15, 1942, OF 4849, FDR Library.

2 Biddle, *In Brief Authority, op. cit.,* p. 226.

3 Letter, H.D.N. to Stephen Early, August 2, 1943, OF 197-A, FDR Library.

4 "Preliminary Results of Nation-Wide Survey of Public Opinion on Japanese Evacuation" (undated, but covering letter of John A. Bird to McCloy is dated April 22, 1942) showed that 64 percent of the respondents believed that the "Japanese" should be "kept under strict guard as prisoners of war." However, German aliens (47 percent) came in ahead of Japanese aliens (36 percent) as the "most dangerous." Office of Facts and Figures Report, ASW 014.311 General, RG 107, National Archives.

5 Wire, E. B. MacNaughton to Roosevelt, June 8, 1943, Alphabetical File 41–45, FDR Library.

6 "Summary of Available Data on Assembly Centers" by Ann Freed, *op. cit.* Freed's frank report of the WCCA phase of the evacuation, and center conditions, was to remain "restricted," according to an attached memo by WRA Chief Analyst Spicer because of "implications for internees and prisoners in Japan."

7 *Ibid.,* p. 18. The Quakers (American Friends Service Committee) received the Nobel Peace Prize in 1947.

8 *Ibid.*

9 Letter, Roosevelt to Culbert L. Olson, May 18, 1942, OF 197-A, FDR Library. The letter had been drafted by Commissioner of Education John W. Studebaker, according to the Commissioner's covering letter to FDR, dated May 12, 1942.

10 Hoping for the allocation of federal money, Olson had suggested to Roosevelt: ". . . if any financial payment is to be made to individuals who are to be moved [evacuated], would it not be possible, and wise, to allow the payment of like amounts to students of college and university standing who wish to enter institutions who will accept them? It would seem to me also that help might be granted to such students through the National Youth Administration." Letter, Olson to Roosevelt, April 25, 1942, OF 197-A, FDR Library.

11 Robert W. O'Brien, *The College Nisei* (Palo Alto, California: Pacific Books, 1949).

12 Roger Daniels, *Concentration Camps USA, op. cit.,* p. 99.

13 O'Brien, *op. cit.,* p. 58.

14 Memorandum, Lauchlin Currie to Roosevelt, May 27, 1942, OF 197-A, FDR Library.

15 Memorandum, Monroe E. Deutsch to Roosevelt (undated), OF 197-A, FDR Library.

16 That key officials (either the President or Vice-President) act decisively in the correction of public attitudes had been stressed by Munson. Ringle of naval intelligence had also recommended acceptance and absorption of Japanese Americans "as an integral part of the United States population." Moreover, Ringle had urged that "measures should be instituted to restrain agitators of both radio and press who are attempting to arouse sentiment . . . against these people on the basis of race alone . . ." Report, Lieutenant Commander K. D. Ringle to the Chief of Naval Operations, ASW 014.311 WDC RG 107, National Archives.

Notes for Chapter 7

1 *The Call,* March 7, 1942. For several decades, Thomas was referred to as "America's conscience."

2 Letter, Ernest Besig to author, November 17, 1969. Initially, Executive Board members of the Northern California ACLU had also voted *against* challenging the evacuation orders. Attorney Collins recalls that it had taken some fast arm-twisting to obtain from members a written notice of "change of negative votes."

3 Letter, William Petersen to author, October 24, 1972. Dr. Petersen's thesis is more fully expounded in "The Incarceration of the Japanese-Americans," *National Review,* December 8, 1972. No less searing in his condemnation is William Manchester (*The Glory and the Dream*): ". . . the racist repression did not come from the right, where according to liberal dogma it always lurks; it was advocated and administered by men celebrated for their freedom from bigotry—Earl Warren, Walter Lippmann, Henry L. Stimson, Abe Fortas, Milton Eisenhower, Hugo Black, and John J. McCloy."

4 A State Department memo is particularly revealing: "Mr. McCloy advised that every effort is being made to handle this problem as a 'regional' one, and is anxious to have as little publicity or instructions emanate from this end as possible." Memorandum, Harold B. Hoskins to Adolph Berle, April 6, 1942, Department of State File 740.00115 Pacific War/445, RG 59, National Archives. At another time, McCloy asserted in a call to Bendetsen on the West Coast: "I want to give you another strong warning. . . . I certainly don't want to have the Chief's [President's] name in any way tied up with this whole business out there." Phone conversation, McCloy and Bendetsen, July 10, 1943, ASW 014.311 WDC General, RG 59, National Archives.

5 Norman Thomas, "Dark Day for Liberty," *Christian Century,* Vol. 59, July 29, 1942. In reply to a Tokyo protest, the State Department also denied that the centers were concentration camps, ". . . but are on the contrary areas where communities are being established in which the Japanese may organize their social and economic life in safety and security under the protection of the central authorities of the United States." Memorandum, State Department to the Spanish Embassy, August 3, 1942, Department of State File 740.00115 Pacific War/844, RG 59, National Archives.

6 Carey McWilliams, "Moving Out the Japanese Americans," *Harper's Magazine,* Vol. 185, September 1942. For more on McWilliams' early attitude toward evacuation, see William Petersen's *Japanese Americans: Oppression and Success,* pp. 75–77; see also his article in the *National Review,* December 8, 1972, op. cit.

7 *The Open Forum* (ACLU publication, Los Angeles), September 23, 1944. In a letter to the author (July 21, 1973), Wayne Collins revealed that McCloy also "realized that what this government had done . . . was an outrage" and that he had vowed "to devote the rest of his life making it up to our Issei and Nisei who had been mistreated so terribly." Collins adds that "perhaps McCloy has merely postponed making it up to those so cruelly pauperized," explaining that he has not done "one damn thing for our Issei, Nisei or Sansei and has been silent on the subject ever since."

8 *San Diego Union* (California), July 10, 1966. Unlike Clark, the late Chief Justice Earl Warren never openly expressed regret for the considerable part he played in stirring up anti-Japanese American sentiment. Warren resisted an eight-year one-man campaign by Nisei activist Edison Uno to obtain a retraction of alleged libelous statements made by Warren impugning the loyalty of the Nisei and Issei.

9 Letter, Harold L. Ickes to Roosevelt, June 15, 1942, OF 4849a, FDR Library. In his "Unpublished Autobiography" (p. 184), Dillon Myer states that Eisenhower "was practically ill," and had confessed to Myer at the time he succeeded him as WRA Director: "I can't sleep and do this job. I had to get out of it." See also Eisenhower's *The President Is Calling* (p. 125), in which he declares: "How could such a tragedy have occurred in a democratic society that prides itself on individual rights and freedoms? . . . I have brooded about this whole episode on and off for the past three decades . . . ."

10 Letter, Milton Eisenhower to Roosevelt, June 18, 1942, PPF 4849, FDR Library.

11 A cry immediately went up that "the Japanese are being treated

too well." A State Department memo explains that "a press release has been issued on the West Coast explaining that the $70 or $80 a month does of course not include clothing or subsistence and that the net per family is therefore far less than the $21 a month given our soldiers." Memorandum, Harold B. Hoskins to Adolph Berle, April 6, 1942, Department of State File 740.00115 Pacific War/445, RG 59, National Archives.

12 Letter, Milton Eisenhower to Roosevelt, June 18, 1942, *op. cit.* WRA wage policy was a part of Tokyo's first official protest lodged against the evacuation: ". . . the policy of the United States is apparently designed to eradicate all Japanese communities, under pretense of instituting military zones covering vast areas . . . the employment of these Japanese nationals in the reclamation and cultivation of wild lands, with a meager monthly salary of from $50.00 to $90.00 after they had been deprived of their means of subsistence is tantamount to compulsory labor since they have no choice but to engage in the prescribed work." Memorandum, Spanish Embassy to State Department, August 3, 1942, Department of State File 740.00115 Pacific War/844, RG 59, National Archives.

13 Letter, Colonel M. P. Fusco (Director, Compensation Administration) to author, November 17, 1969.

14 James MacGregor Burns, *Roosevelt: The Soldier of Freedom* (New York: Harcourt Brace Jovanovich, 1970). p. 267. Used by permission.

15 Alexander H. Leighton, *The Governing of Men: General Principles and Recommendations Based on Experience at a Japanese Relocation Camp* (Princeton University Press, 1945), p. 279.

16 Letter, Harold L. Ickes to Roosevelt, April 13, 1943, OF 4849, FDR Library.

17 Daniels' critique in *Concentration Camps USA* is noteworthy: "By the stern standards of the Nuremburg Tribunal then, Eisenhower, who acquiesced in an atrocity and who helped to execute it, was as guilty as Gullion the Provost Marshal General, Bendetsen, DeWitt, McCloy, Stimson, Roosevelt, and all the other prime architects of policy."

18 Letter, Milton Eisenhower to Roosevelt, April 22, 1943, OF 4849, FDR Library. After a brief stint with the OWI, Milton Eisenhower went on to serve as President of the following institutions: Kansas State College, 1943–50; Pennsylvania State University, 1950–56; Johns Hopkins University, 1956–67.

19 Preferential treatment was especially pronounced at Manzanar, where nearly a thousand volunteers, JACLers among them, had come early to assist the WCCA in opening the camp. Bendetsen noted after a visit that "there seems to be thrown throughout the center an attitude of favoritism and politics," and he referred to "politicians" who had come early "so that they might worm their way into the confidence of the center management." Memorandum, Bendetsen to Director, WRA, June 5, 1942, RG 210, National Archives.

Arthur A. Hansen and David A. Hacker in their superbly documented study, "The Manzanar 'Riot': An Ethnic Perspective," maintain that the Administration allowed JACLers a voice in shaping camp policy and, because they had volunteered, had "rewarded" them "by granting them the white-collar, supervisory, and generally favored jobs" while the Issei and Kibei were consigned to "subordinate and menial jobs."

20 Memorandum, Dillon S. Myer to "All Project Directors," December 9, 1942, Manzanar Records, 1942–46, University Research Library, UCLA. While U. S. interests in Tokyo were represented by the Swiss Government, Spain as a neutral power during World War II then represented Japan's interest in the United States, with the embassies of both governments serving as a channel of communications between the two warring nations.

21 Soliciting the intervention of the neutral power occasionally stigmatized petitioners as being "pro-Axis" (with consequent closer surveillance), as was the case in Poston, where it was suspected that the "trouble in the relocation camps is part of a well organized scheme directed from Tokyo, and that the Spanish Consulates are acting as mediums for the exchange of information," in the words of an informant. Letter, Commander Wallace S. Wharton to E. M. Rowalt (WRA Deputy Director), undated, RG 210, National Archives (see also Appendix 4).

22 Petition, Topaz Nationals (signatures) to Spanish Consul, January 19, 1943, WRA File 36.329, RG 210, National Archives.

23 WRA regulations gave project directors "sweeping powers to act as lawmakers, prosecutors, and judges" (*Prejudice, War and the Constitution,* p. 164). They could punish misdemeanor cases by deprivation of pay, clothing allowance (around $3.00 a month per inmate), or by a term in jail not to exceed ninety days. Policy of having more serious crimes punished under state and federal laws often evoked intense community ill-will, as trials held on the "outside" were believed to be grossly prejudiced against inmates.

24 Document, date unknown, Manzanar Records, 1942–46, University Research Library, UCLA.

25 The Communist Party in America shifted from "vociferous isolationism to all-out support of the war" after Germany's invasion of Soviet territory, according to William Petersen, who contends that "except for demanding that the Western Powers open a second front on the European continent in order to relieve the pressure on the Red Army . . . the Party was superpatriotic" (*Japanese American, op. cit.,* p. 73). Accordingly, evacuee left-wingers embraced a superpatriotic posture and openly endorsed the evacuation—the official Party position—though their driving concern for a second front "stemmed from their internationalist convictions," according to authors Hansen and Hacker.

26 Dorothy Swaine Thomas and Richard S. Nishimoto, *The Spoilage* (Berkeley: University of California Press, 1946), p. 367. Terminal Islanders had the ill fortune of living close to a naval base. Both citizens and aliens—most of them fishermen—had suffered an immediate work stoppage following Pearl Harbor, and community leaders had been arrested. In another FBI raid on February 1, practically all family heads had been apprehended. The Navy then ordered a twenty-four-hour evacuation of the island, but protests from Caucasian church groups resulted in a twenty-four-hour extension of the evacuation deadline.

27 *Ibid,* p. 368. Author has drawn heavily on Thomas and Nishimoto's *The Spoilage* for Kurihara quotes and background data. See Appendix of *The Spoilage* for "Kurihara Manuscript."

28 The day before, Tayama had returned from a JACL convention held in Salt Lake City, where he had proposed that the Nisei be inducted into the armed services. As he had also helped to form within the Southern California unit of the JACL (of which he was chairman) an Anti-Axis Committee which had helped the FBI and naval intelligence in evaluating the "potentially dangerous" in the event of the war, he had been the object of considerable community scorn even before the evacuation.

29 Memorandum, Harold L. Ickes to Cordell Hull, June 16, 1944, WRA File 36.239, RG 210, National Archives. Ickes' report of the incident was in response to State Department query. "A great many complex and not altogether related factors led to this unrest," wrote Ickes. "The abnormal and restrictive environment of the relocation center intensified their resentment and accentuated frictions between various groups of the evacuees. The charge of misappropriation of sugar was so widespread," according to Ickes, that evacuees generally believed that "Campbell [Assistant Project Director] caused a number of evacuees participating in the incident to be arrested being of personal animosity."

30 The Army-WRA report, jointly issued, describes the incident as a "disturbance," and it is the only account in which the claim is made that the soldiers *had been given the order to fire:* ". . . tear gas was first used in an effort to stop and disperse the members; when this failed (on account of the high wind) the order was given to halt or fire would be opened. When the crowd again ignored these instructions, the order to fire was given. One volley was fired, following which the mob dispersed." "Manzanar" (undated document), Manzanar Records, 1942–46, University Research Library, UCLA.

31 Manzanar hospital record, Manzanar Records, 1942–46, University Research Library, UCLA.

32 Contrary to the WRA claim that "the incident cleared the air," Myer was subsequently informed by Merritt of the "urgent necessity for an efficient intelligence system within the center . . . Such a system could be a part of the regular office of reports, augmented by the social welfare section and the internal police . . . Pertinent information needed for the segregation of disturbing elements could then be obtained . . ." Ralph P. Merritt to Dillon Myer, January 7, 1943, Manzanar Records, 1942–46, University Research Library, UCLA.

33 *WRA: A Story of Human Conservation* (Washington: Government Printing Office, 1946), p. 50.

34 Memorandum, Spanish Embassy to State Department, March 13, 1944, WRA File 36.239, RG 210, National Archives. Because of Tokyo protests, the State Department was told that "a thorough investigation," held on December 15, 1942, "found that Captain Hall and the officers of the Escort Guard Company, in suppressing the mob and its violence, acted with promptness, patience and determination, and employed only so much force as appeared necessary after all other measures had failed. The board further found that the soldier or soldiers who fired the shots acted in obedience to the standing order given by the company commander to fire only when ordered to do so or when rushed, and that the soldier or soldiers who fired the shots did so because members of the mob were closing in and surging toward them." The troops were to "be absolved from all blame whatever . . ." Letter, Colonel Francis E. Howard (Director, Prisoner of War Division, PMG) to Bernard Gufler (State Department), June 2, 1944, Department of State File 740.00115 Pacific War/2462, RG 59, National Archives.

35 Memorandum, W. W. Williamson (Director of Internal Security) to Leroy Bennett, June 18, 1943, WRA File 39.055, RG 210, National Archives.

36 Instances of mistaken identity: A Masuo Kanno was sent to Leupp, "DUE TO CONFUSION WITH MINORU KANNO" (confidential teletype, August 19, 1943, Myer to L. H. Bennett). A Minoru Tsuji was sent to Leupp: "THIS MAY BE A CASE OF MISTAKEN IDENTITY" (teletype from E. M. Rowalt to L. H. Bennett, August 16, 1943). "Possibility of mistaken identity in Mr. Genji George Yamaguchi's case" (letter, Robert W. Frase, Assistant Project Director, to Myer, May 24, 1943). See WRA File 39.055, RG 210, National Archives. Moab and Leupp correspondence are, in the main, still classified, and photo documentations of isolation centers appear to have been destroyed.

37 Over 200 youths were indicted and tried for violation of the Selective Service Act, and most were given sentences of two to three years. However, Federal Judge Dave Ling (Arizona) dismissed 101 Poston youths after collecting a one-cent fine from each, declaring that detention in a concentration camp was punishment enough (*Pacfic Citizen,* October 12, 1946). A presidential pardon was granted to all on December 23, 1947.

38 Letter (writer's name withheld), to block leader of Block 17, May 14, 1943, Manzanar Records, 1942–46, Box 16, University Research Library, UCLA.

39 Letter (writer's name withheld) to ——, April 22, 1943, Manzanar Records, 1942–46, Box 16, University Research Library, UCLA. The following memorandum suggests that these punitive camps may have been a WRA move to appease Army hawks calling for a drastic segregation: "The establishment of the Moab Center has had some good effects. However, the removal of some 13 from Rivers where there are over 13,000, 15 from Tule Lake where there are over 14,000, and 26 from Manzanar where there are over 9,500, hasn't gone a long way toward segregation. The establishment of the Leupp . . . Center which will be completed and ready to receive Japanese by April 25, is a step toward segregation. However, present plans of WRA now contemplate placing only some 300 single male Japanese in this Center. This will still fall short of attaining any proper segregation." Memorandum, Lieutenant Colonel Frank E. Meek (Head, Aliens Section, Internal Security Division of Headquarters Ninth Service Command) to War Department, ASW 014.311 WDC JA Segregation, RG 107, National Archives.

40 Hacker and Hansen maintain in "The Manzanar 'Riot' " that ". . . seen through the ethnic perspective, the beating of Tayama was both necessary and good," and that "there is strong reason to believe that the overwhelming majority of internees fully endorsed this beating." The authors also believe that "most accounts minimize or ignore the massive participation of internees."

41 Letter, Paul G. Robertson to author, September 4, 1969.

42 Memorandum, Dillon S. Myer to "All Field Assistant Directors and Project Directors," June 5, 1943, WRA File 39.055, RG 210, National Archives.

43 Memorandum, Lewis A. Sigler to Philip Glick, August 14, 1943, WRA File 39.055, RG 210, National Archives.

44 To protect the identity of persons involved, the author has taken the liberty of replacing actual names with pseudonyms.

45 Robertson's allegation is substantiated by a report to the War Department of a conversation with Colonel Bendetsen: "Information he [Bendetsen] has from the military authorities at Manzanar is that 13 trouble-makers are now in the hands of the military authorities. No charges against them and no specific case. They are held on information given by the informer group and partly on observations of the military police. Questionable as to sufficient evidence to take action against them." Memorandum, W.P.S. (Scobey) to War Department, December 10, 1942, ASW 014.311 WDC Segregation of Japs, RG 107, National Archives.

46 Letter, Paul G. Robertson to Myer and Leupp Review Board, WRA File 39.055, RG 210, National Archives. The WRA Administrative Instruction, February 16, 1943, defines candidates for isolation as being "addicted to troublemaking and beyond the capacity of regular processes within the relocation center to keep under control."

47 Letter, Leroy H. Bennett to Elmer M. Rowalt, August 16, 1943, WRA File 39.055, RG 210, National Archives.

48 Letter, Ralph Merritt to Merrill M. Tozier (Chief, Reports Division), January 7, 1946, Manzanar Records, 1942–46, University Research Library, UCLA. Karl Yoneda wrote the author on August 23, 1974, that though his name appears in the Merritt Report as one of the JACLers blacklisted by Kurihara, he had never been a member of the JACL and had met up with Kurihara for the first time in Manzanar. Yoneda places considerable blame for the riot on the "no-see" attitude taken by the administration in respect to the destructive activities of the Kurihara clique, even when requests were made that these be checked. Campbell had told Yoneda: "You are all Japanese, whether citizens or Black Dragons." Yoneda adds that "there are many contradictions in the 'full confession' which I can document if need be . . .'"

Notes for Chapter 8

1 Issei mothers (wives of church leaders and many language-school instructors, etc.) were not exempt from FBI arrests and war-duration separation from their families. Fifty women were incarcerated at the Seagoville women's penitentiary near Dallas, Texas. See Herbert V. Nicholson's *Treasure in Earthen Vessels.*

2 In the WRA report "Army Registration at Granada" (WRA Project Analysis Series No. 2, March 19, 1943, RG 210, National Archives), the assertion is made that "the Army discharged Kibei soldiers immediately following Pearl Harbor, a fact which was of particular importance during the registration."

3 Beginning in September 1942, WRA centers were scoured by the Army intelligence service for Nisei volunteers to be trained at the Military Intelligence Language School established at Camp Savage, later moved to Fort Snelling, Minnesota. Dillon Myer thought it "ironical that most of those who could qualify were Kibei . . . who were considered by Commander Ringle and other experts to be generally the most disaffected element within the Japanese American population." See *Uprooted Americans,* p. 145.

4 Intelligence reports from the Pacific regarding the skill, tenacity, and stoic "cool" of the Japanese fighting man had authorities agog. At the same time, the War Department was beginning to receive excellent reports on the "Japanese" in training at Camp McCoy, Wisconsin—the all-Nisei Hawaii National Guard group "evacuated" from Hawaii.

5 "The handling of the registration and the loyalty questionnaires," according to Myer (*Uprooted Americans,* p. 243) "was planned by the adjutant general's office, and the plans were completed and put into execution before the WRA was consulted." See also p. 281.

6 "Interview with . . . an Older Nisei," by Morris E. Opler, Manzanar Community Analysis Report No. 36, July 26, 1943, RG 210, National Archives.

7 Some highly placed people were already beginning to advocate much of what the inmates were fearing; and evacuee resistance to registration only served to toughen official attitudes, as seen in the following recommendation of one Army official: "Loyal Americans of military age to be inducted into the Armed Forces based upon existing induction laws. . . . Relocation of all other loyal Nisei as rapidly as possible on the principle of 'work or starve.'. . . The pro-Axis elements to be interned as enemy aliens in true internment camps under strict supervision to be deported or exchanged at the first available opportunity." Memorandum, Lieutenant Colonel Karl T. Gould to Colonel Kai E. Rasmussen (Commandant, MISLS) May 17, 1943, WRA Washington Central File, RG 210, National Archives.

8 "From a Nisei Who Said 'No,'" by Morris E. Opler, Manzanar Community Analysis Report No. 53, January 15, 1944, RG 210, National Archives.

9 "Registration at Central Utah: 14–17, February, 1943," by John F. Embree, Project Analysis Series No. 1, February 1943, RG 210, National Archives. By December 1942—at McCloy's request—Bendetsen and DeWitt had already worked out a plan calling for instant segregation on a designated day to be carried out after a military take-over of each of the centers "to insure against probable rioting and consequent bloodshed," with segregants to be eventually concentrated in Poston. "A list of

some 5600 undesirables who might form the nucleus of the initial segregation" had been provided by McCloy when the plan was presented to the
WRA (subsequently rejected by Myer as being too "cold-blooded"). Letter, McCloy to Dillon Myer, December 30, 1942 (with enclosure: "Plan
of Segregation"), WRA Washington Central File, RG 210, National
Archives.

10 "Registration at Manzanar," by Morris E. Opler, Project Analysis Series No. 3, April 3, 1943, RG 210, National Archives.

11 Thomas and Nishimoto, *The Spoilage,* p. 71.

12 From among the 10,000 Hawaii Nisei who volunteered, 2,600
were sent to the mainland to join, in combat training, the Nisei volunteers
from the camps. The group was eventually shipped overseas, landing in
Salerno, Italy, on September 22, 1943, to join forces with the decimated
100th Infantry Battalion (the first "evacuees" from Hawaii), who, in being
tried out as a "guinea pig battalion," had won swift fame for their daredevil style of fighting. The 100th Infantry Battalion thus became the nucleus of the 442nd Regimental Combat Team, whose stop-at-nothing
exploits in Italy and France were to win them the distinction of being
the most decorated Army unit in U. S. history for its size.

13 Blake Clark, "Some Japanese in Hawaii," *Asia and the Americas,* Vol. 42, No. 12, December 4, 1942, p. 724.

14 Letter, Philip M. Glick to James H. Terry, March 27, 1943,
Manuscript Division, Bancroft Library, University of California, Berkeley.
Solicitor Glick advised: "We find that this conclusion is doubtful, since
the crime of treason requires an *overt act* of levying war against the United
States or adhering to our enemies, giving them aid and comfort. Mere
attitudes or expressions of sympathy with the enemies' cause are not
sufficient to support a conviction."

15 Letter, J. Edgar Hoover to Dillon Myer, February 17, 1943,
Manuscript Division, Bancroft Library, University of California, Berkeley.
By late February, peremptory powers were given project directors in the
removal of aliens considered "disturbing factors in the community." Solicitor Glick (quoting from a James H. Terry report) advised Myer "that
the judgment of the Project Directors in such case would be accepted
without question by the Department of Justice and that persons so recommended for internment would be interned without a hearing . . . and
would not be returned to the projects for the duration." Memo, Philip M.
Glick to the Director, March 6, 1943, WRA File 39.038, RG 210, National Archives.

16 Narrative Report of Project Attorney James H. Terry, Gila
Community Analysis Section Final Report, June 1945, RG 210, National
Archives. On February 19, 1943, a similar removal took place in Manza-
nar involving ten Kibei.

17 Edward H. Spicer, Asael T. Hansen, Katherine Luomala, and
Marvin K. Opler, *Impounded People: Japanese-Americans in the Relocation Centers* (Tucson: University of Arizona Press, 1969), p. 146. In a
few centers, "no" respondents were given an opportunity to reregister
following a public meeting for the purpose of clarifying the issues. For
capsule summaries of how registration proceeded in Topaz, Minidoka,

Poston, Gila, Manzanar, Jerome, and for excellent coverage of the re-sistance which developed in Tule Lake, see Chapter 3 of *The Spoilage.*

18   As quoted in memorandum to Dillon Myer from John F. Embree, May 18, 1943, RG 210, National Archives.

19   Memorandum, John D. Cook (Reports Officer) to John C. Baker (Chief of Reports), April 13, 1943, WRA File 39.038, RG 210, National Archives.

20   *Ibid.*

21   Thomas and Nishimoto, *The Spoilage,* p. 80. Kibei fears and suspicions had some basis in fact. With Kibei possessing dual citizenship in mind, DeWitt and Bendetsen had begun in the latter part of 1942 to campaign for "the forfeiture through appropriate legal processes . . . [of] the U. S. citizenship of all such Kibei, to be undertaken in collaboration with the Department of Justice, and their internment for the duration of the war with a view to their repatriation as rapidly as opportunity affords." Memorandum, J. L. DeWitt to Chief of Staff, August 23, 1942, ASW 014.311 WDC Segregation—Japs, RG 107, National Archives. See also Memorandum, WPS [Scobey] to War Department, December 10, 1942, *op. cit.*

22   Memorandum, John D. Cook to John C. Baker, April 13, 1943, *op. cit.*

23   *Ibid.*

24   *Ibid.*

25   "The Factual Causes and Reasons Why I Refused to Register," Tule Lake Community Analysis Report No. 69, March 31, 1944, RG 210, National Archives.

26   Memorandum, John D. Cook to John C. Baker, March 12, 1943, File 39.038, RG 210, National Archives.

27   Memorandum, John D. Cook to John C. Baker, April 13, 1943, *op. cit.*

28   Thomas and Nishimoto, *The Spoilage,* p. 81.

29   *Ibid.,* p. 82.

30   Memorandum, John D. Cook to John C. Baker, April 13, 1943, *op. cit.* In a recent interview Cozzens admitted that "there was absolutely no need for it [registration] in my estimation. We had enough information on everybody in the centers at that time. The military could have picked out anyone they didn't want without any problem." Girdner and Loftis' *The Great Betrayal: The Evacuation of the Japanese-Americans During World War II* (New York: Macmillan, 1969), p. 285.

31   Memorandum, John D. Cook to John C. Baker, April 13, 1943, *op. cit.* See also "Registration at Tule Lake: By a Nisei Who was a Resident of Tule Lake during the February, 1943 Registration," Manzanar Community Analysis Report 103, December 14, 1943, RG 210, National Archives.

32   Memorandum, John D. Cook to John C. Baker, March 16, 1943, WRA File 39.055, RG 210, National Archives.

33   "Defiance at Tule Lake," *San Francisco Chronicle,* May 27, 1943. The estimate of "one hundred men" being "carried off" appears to be an exaggeration on the part of the reporter.

34 Memorandum, John D. Cook to John C. Baker, April 29, 1943, *op. cit.* The Ápril 13, 1943, report filed by Cook indicates that April 7 was the last day of registration at Tule Lake.

35 Thomas and Nishimoto, *The Spoilage,* pp. 81–82. The authors maintain that evacuees "were allowed to continue in the belief that they were violating the Espionage Act by failing to register," and that the WRA "sought legal refuge in the fact that nonregistrants were disobeying WRA administrative instructions." No announcement was ever made that the WRA had decided on February 27 that registration of aliens of both sexes and female citizens was not compulsory, according to Thomas and Nishimoto.

36 Statement of C. L. Preisker, Chairman of the Board of Supervisors, Santa Barbara County, California. *Pacific Citizen,* February 18, 1943.

37 Audrie Girdner and Anne Loftis. *The Great Betrayal,* p. 291.

38 Letter, Ralph R. Merritt to Dillon Myer, March 4, 1943, Manzanar Records, 1942–46, University Research Library, UCLA.

39 Carey McWilliams, *Prejudice,* pp. 188–89. Used with permission of author.

Notes for Chapter 9

1 Diary entry of a Tulean for September 8, 1943, reads: "Brought in 6 tanks for use against colonists in Tule just in case. Damn those guys anyway. What the hell can we do against two battalions armed with machine guns. As it goes we're prisoners of war and no doubt about it. Double fence, guard towers, soldiers, tanks, armored cars, jeeps, electrically charged fence, etc. Damn their hide!" "Diary of a Nisei," Tule Lake Community Analysis Report No. 41, November 3, 1943, RG 210, National Archives. "One battalion of military police" (899 men, 31 officers) made up the "exterior police" according to: Letter, McCloy to Dillon Myer, July 25, 1943, ASW 014.311 WDC JA Segregation, RG 107, National Archives.

2 War Department presumption that evacuees who signed for repatriation or expatriation were pro-Japan in loyalty did a grave injustice to thousands of essentially blameless people. For example, Carey McWilliams notes that 80 percent of Manzanar segregants who had requested repatriation "had actually answered the loyalty question in the affirmative. Of this same group, *35 percent of those going to Tule Lake are minors.*" (*Prejudice,* p. 188.)

3 Anne Reeploeg Fisher, *Exile of a Race* (Seattle: F & T Publishers, 1965), p. 150. One reason for the increase was that many who declared themselves disloyal did not consider it final, and they were right *to a degree.* Eventually, Tuleans who could meet the stringent qualifications for indefinite leave were allowed to relocate by first being transferred to another center.

4 Thomas and Nishimoto, *The Spoilage,* p. 104, fn. 48. After segregation, the composition of Tule Lake, according to Daniels, was roughly one-third old Tuleans, one-third segregants, and one-third family members.

5 *Denson Tribune,* August 6, 1943.

6 The report of a State Department official after two visits to Tule Lake makes the sweeping assumption that disloyals ("about 16,000 evacuees who had declared their allegiance to Japan") were concentrated in Tule Lake and that "among these 16,000 there is . . . a great number, perhaps over fifty percent, [who] are American citizens by birth, and as such cannot be treated as aliens despite their allegiance to Japan." "Visits to Tule Lake Relocation Center," by H. M. Benninghoff, November 25, 1943, Department of State File 740.00115 PW/11-2543, RG 59, National Archives.

7 The *Daihyo Sha Kai,* meaning "representative body," was made up of one block representative from each of the sixty-four Tule Lake residential blocks. This main body had elected, in turn, the seven men who made up the Negotiating Committee. With the addition of seven more members, it eventually became known as the "committee of fourteen."

8 "Letter from a Jerome evacuee newly arrived in Tule Lake," Tule Lake Community Analysis Report No. 34, October 15, 1943, RG 210, National Archives. The report, "Visits to Tule Lake Relocation Center," *op. cit.,* notes, interestingly enough, that the Spanish Consul had "referred a number of times to his conviction that Mr. Best was not suited for the position of manager of the Project, and compared him unfavorably with others whom he had met."

9 Best had resented being asked to send the widow a letter of condolence and to attend the funeral besides. In the opinion of Rosalie H. Wax ("The Destruction of a Democratic Impulse," *Human Organization* 12 (1953):15), "Mr. Best's refusal was . . . motivated by the fact that these committees stated their requests boldly. They did not supplicate; they demanded. This attitude challenged the power of the WRA which saw its proper role as that of a paternalistic authority, granting or withholding boons from the evacuees."

10 Demanded also was the removal of the entire Caucasian medical staff at the center hospital. An attack by evacuees had been perpetrated on the chief medical officer at the hospital while the meeting was taking place (a matter greatly blown up, subsequently, by the West Coast media), but it had been quickly determined that the incident had no connection with the negotiating protest committee.

11 A WRA Semi-Annual Report (July 1–December 13, 1943) noted: "A project official kept in close touch by telephone with the commanding officer of the Military Police, who stood by, ready to rush in soldiers at a moment's notice. Early in the afternoon the tanks in the military area were warmed up to be in readiness for emergency."

12 Memorandum, Francis Biddle to Roosevelt, November 10, 1943, PSF (Justice Department) 1941–44, Box 76, FDR Library.

13 Press Release of Dillon S. Myer issued through the Office of War Information, November 13, 1943, OWI-2712, FDR Library.

14 The WRA Semi-Annual Report (July 1–December 13, 1943) reads: "In all, 18 prisoners were taken on that night, all of whom needed first aid for injuries received during their capture. They were hospitalized under guard after questioning . . ." ACLU chief Ernest Besig claims injuries were received *after* their capture, as does Wayne Collins, who maintains that "the evacuees were taken by members of the internal security police to the police squad room where they were severely beaten with clubs."

15 "F.K.'s Account of the Stockade Experience—November 4th," Tule Lake Community Analysis Report No. 216, November 1943, RG 210, National Archives.

16 Editorial, *Herald-Dispatch* (Huntington, West Virginia), November 8, 1943, OF 4245-G (Tule Lake), FDR Library. Myer maintains that "the Tule Lake incident was just the kind of thing that the American Legion and the Hearst Press and all of the people who had been harassing the evacuees and the WRA were looking for in order to keep things stirred up" ("Unpublished Autobiography").

17 Thomas and Nishimoto, *The Spoilage,* pp. 155–56. Author has found *The Spoilage* (based on day-to-day records of participating Tule Lake informants, under the direction of a research staff from the University of California, headed up by Dr. Thomas) invaluable in the preparation of this chapter and a few others that follow.

18 *Ibid.,* p. 162. A few caught with contraband were later tried on the outside. Three Tuleans caught operating a sake still received jail terms of one year. Another caught with a radio transmission set "capable of sending messages only a radius of 17 miles" was sentenced to two years in a federal penitentiary. For "theft of government property" consisting of cereal, condensed milk, eggs and graham crackers, another evacuee who insisted he had accumulated it from weekly WRA allotments for his child was sentenced to a year in jail. University Research Library, UCLA.

19 Thomas and Nishimoto, *The Spoilage,* p. 287. Chapter 6 ("Incarceration") is especially revelatory of camp and stockade conditions during this period.

20 *Ibid.,* p. 176.

21 *Ibid.,* pp. 161, 163.

22 *Ibid.,* p. 165.

23 *Ibid.,* p. 174. The mass arrests may have been retaliation for a petition sent by the sixty-four block representatives to Cordell Hull (December 7, 1943, WRA File 36.239, RG 210, National Archives), which read in part: "Because of the refusal of the military authorities to recognize the said negotiating committee the local residents of the said center have signed resolutions twice thereupon signifying that the said negotiating committee is a true and entrusted delegate of the said residents of the said center." Many of the sixty-four signers were found to be repatriates, expatriates, and "no-no" disloyals. Spared incarceration were a few old Tuleans on the list.

24 Thomas and Nishimoto, *op. cit.,* p. 175.

25 "Tule Lake Under Army Control," Tule Lake Community Analysis Report No. 52, February 2, 1944, RG 210, National Archives.

26 Letter with several signatures to Minister-Counsellor Juan G. de Molina, January 5, 1944, WRA File 36.239, RG 210, National Archives.

27 Letter with several signatures to Spanish Ambassador, January 6, 1944, WRA File 36.239, RG 210, National Archives. After the war, Foreign Minister Shigemitsu deplored the "many wrongful acts involving inhumanity" of which the Japanese were found guilty. Much of it he attributed to the hatred whipped up by wartime propaganda dealing with the "inhuman handling . . . of Japanese in the United States."

28 Memorandum, Spanish Consul to State Department, January 11, 1944, WRA File 36.239, RG 210, National Archives.

29 Memorandum, Cordell Hull to Henry L. Stimson, January 11, 1944, WRA File 36.239, RG 210, National Archives.

30 Memorandum, Henry L. Stimson to Cordell Hull, January 18, 1944, WRA File 36.239, RG 210, National Archives.

31 *Ibid.* Dillon Myer, in a letter to Hull on April 3, 1944, reinforced Stimson's claim of decent stockade treatment: "Although housed separately, the conditions provided to them were substantially the same as those afforded to the residents of the Center generally."

32 The wrecked automobile of a WRA employee was found to be loaded with ill-gotten meat from the evacuee warehouse destined for the black market.

33 Memorandum, Seymour Cahn to Merrill Tozier, December 7, 1943, WRA File 36.239, RG 210, National Archives. A State Department report also corroborated evacuee complaints: "In my opinion, the evacuees at Tule Lake have many genuine grievances. The food situation, now improving, was bad, and the possibility exists that Japanese allegations of leakages are correct . . . I also feel that the beating up may have occurred and should be investigated" ("Visits to Tule Lake Relocation Center," *op. cit.*).

34 *Tulean Dispatch,* Japanese section, November 9, 1943. Thomas and Nishimoto, p. 152.

Notes for Chapter 10

1 Letter, B. R. Stauber (Chief, Statistical Division) to Ralph P. Merritt, March 16, 1945, Manzanar Records, 1942–46, University Research Library, UCLA. Tokyo had responded to the proposed reciprocal arrangement by stating: "The Japanese Government did not ratify the Prisoners of War Treaty of Geneva signed on July 27th, 1929, for which reason they state they have no obligations under same, although they will apply the corresponding similar stipulations of the Treaty to civil, as well as military prisoners, who find themselves under the Japanese jurisdiction." Memorandum, Spanish Embassy to State Department, February 24, 1942, Department of State File 740.00115 Pacific War/298, RG 59, National Archives.

2 Though the Issei internees were not considered "prisoners," the death certificates of even those "whose deaths occur at the Relocation Centers," were forwarded to the War Department's Prisoner of War Information Bureau, Office of the Provost Marshal General. Letter, Ickes to Hull, June 13, 1944, WRA File 36.239, RG 210, National Archives. A continuing vexation to the State Department, however, was the fact that relocation centers "still appear, in the eyes of the Protecting Power for Japanese interests . . . to be internment camps . . . in view especially of the tendency of Americans to describe them as concentration camps." "Memorandum of Conversation" (involving McCloy, Myer, Stauber, Keeley, Gufler, Lieutenant Hall), October 31, 1942, State Department File 740.00115 Pacific War/1088 ½, RG 59, National Archives.

3 Nisei and Issei slain by sentries during the war years included: Shoichi James Okamoto, on May 24, 1944, at Tule Lake Segregation Center by Private Bernard Goe (acquitted after being fined a dollar "for the unauthorized use of government property" [a bullet], according to former Tulean, Los Angeles Superior Court Judge Robert Takasugi); two young evacuees, Ito and Kanagawa of Manzanar, during riot of December 6, 1942 (acquittal statement: p. 302, fn. 34); James Hatsuaki Wakasa, on April 11, 1943, in Topaz Relocation Center by sentry Gerald B. Philpott; two critically ill internees, Toshiro Kobata and Hirota Isomura, on July 27, 1942, during transfer to Lordsburg Internment Camp; Kanesaburo Oshima, on May 12, 1942, in Fort Sill Internment Camp. On the basis of "attempted escapes," *acquittals* probably were handed down in all cases since State Department memorandum by James H. Keeley, Jr. (August 1, 1942, 740.00115 PW/550) states: "examination of the Army's reports on the shootings gives the impression that the Army's shooting rule comes close to making death, rather than up to 30 days arrest as provided in Article 54 of the Geneva Convention, the penalty for attempted escape." See also letter, Stimson to Secretary of State, August 21, 1944, Department of State File 740.00115 PW/2-2144 RG 59, National Archives.

4 Memorandum, Spanish Embassy to State Department, April 24, 1944, WRA File 36.239, RG 210, National Archives.

5 *Ibid.*

6 Thomas and Nishimoto, *The Spoilage,* p. 182.

7 These were, in the main, close relatives of stockade detainees who had allegedly been "third degreed" and beaten by security officers.

8 Thomas and Nishimoto, p. 205. Following the November 4 incident, FBI investigators had stressed the need for counterintelligence: ". . . it is recommended that the 'Community Analyst' be assigned to and be made a part of the Internal Security Division . . . or, that this position be eliminated and that the Internal Security Division be charged with the duty of collecting such information for the Project Director." As quoted in Memorandum, John H. Provinse to E. H. Spicer, February 11, 1944, RG 210, National Archives. See also Appendix 4.

9 "Affidavit of Ernest Besig," November 8, 1946, courtesy of Ernest Besig.

10 *Ibid.*

11 Public Law 405, permitting renunciation of citizenship during wartime, had become law on July 1, 1944 (see Chapter 12). The motivation behind it was made brazenly apparent when the Chairman of the House Immigration and Naturalization Committee (Representative Dickstein), reported that a bill was about to be passed whereby "notices will appear in every relocation center calling for volunteers to go to Japan in trade for Americans." Research Division Memorandum, February 21, 1944, OWI-4245-G (Box 12), FDR Library.

12 "Interview with George [Kunitani]," July 11, 1944, Tule Lake Stockade, courtesy of Wayne Collins. Kunitani and camp activists had "kept doggedly in session until 2:30 A.M.," as they had "no idea of WRA fear," nor did they realize that the military had assumed control of the center, according to Rosalie H. Wax ("The Destruction of a Democratic Impulse," *op. cit.*). Anthropologist Wax (who, as Rosalie Hankey, had been the Caucasian observer at Tule Lake for Dr. Thomas) maintains that the avowed "ideology of the administration was one of the factors that encouraged the revolt" and that "many of the characteristics of the revolt appear strikingly democratic and libertarian."

13 "Interview with Tom Yoshiyama," July 11, 1944, Tule Lake Stockade, courtesy of Wayne Collins.

14 "Affidavit of Ernest Besig," *op. cit.*

15 *Ibid.*

16 *Ibid.* Wives and children of men removed to alien internment camps were, in some cases, permitted to be reunited at the Crystal City (Texas) "family camp."

17 *Ibid.* See also "Tyranny Reigns at Tule Lake," *American Civil Liberties Union-News* (San Francisco), August 1944.

18 "Affidavit of Ernest Besig," *op. cit.*

19 *Ibid.*

20 *American Civil Liberties Union-News,* August, 1944, *op. cit.*

21 "Affidavit of Ernest Besig," *op. cit.* Conscientious objectors—who came under the category of "Jap-lovers"—fell into Administrative disfavor following the riot, according to the Reverend Kitagawa *(Issei and Nisei).*

22 On behalf of the ACLU of Northern California, Collins had filed *amicus curiae* briefs in support of *Hirabayashi* (see p. 291, fn. 14); in support of *Endo,* a case of a young Nisei woman who claimed unlawful detention (see pp. 223, 227–8); and *Yasui,* a case of a Nisei lawyer who had deliberately violated, as a test, the discriminatory curfew order affecting alien enemies and citizens of Japanese ancestry. The Supreme Court decided against *Yasui.*

23 Letter, Wayne Collins to author, June 13, 1968. In the same letter Collins explained: "Practically all of the final 13 persons confined to the Stockade in 1944 were removed to Japan at the end of 1945 and in early 1946. George [Kunitani] died a short time after his release from detention."

24 "Statement of Wayne Collins," *op. cit.*

Notes for Chapter 11

1 Press and Radio Conference #982, November 21, 1944, FDR Library.

2 Office of War Information Research Division, December 8, 1943, 4245-G Race (Box 12), FDR Library.

3 *Ibid.* The OWI Bulletin states: "Now, it seems that with the *Gripsholm* scheduled to dock on December 2, it may prove expedient for the War Department to allow release of Japanese atrocity stories . . ." But the strategy apparently backfired. A *Department of State Bulletin,* August 6, 1944, reads: ". . . long delays resulted before second exchange because the Japanese resented the publication of atrocity stories."

4 Memorandums, Biddle to Roosevelt, dated December 30 and December 31, 1943. Both are from PSF-Biddle, FDR Library. Obviously, Biddle was, by then, no longer in a "precarious position" jobwise, as on December 30, he had forthrightly recommended to FDR: "The present procedure of keeping loyal American citizens in concentration camps on the basis of race for longer than is absolutely necessary is dangerous and repugnant to the principles of our Government. It is also necessary to act now so that the agitation against these citizens does not continue after the war."

5 From article "Justice for Japanese Americans," *Pacific Citizen,* December 21, 1962.

6 Letter, Mrs. —— to Roosevelt, April 18, 1944, OF-4849 (misc.), FDR Library.

7 Letter, Harold L. Ickes to Roosevelt, June 2, 1944, OF-4849, FDR Library. There had been a total *lack of justification* for the evacuation order, says Dillon Myer, who claims that, once the uprooting began, the Army did an "all out job trying to justify the move." Myer adds: "I found out very quickly after I became Director that most of the reasons [given for the evacuation] were phony . . ." ("Unpublished Autobiography," pp. 185–86). James Rowe, Jr., former aide to Biddle, agrees that "there was no good military reason for it" and that "the whole story lies in the single fact that the Army folded under pressure." Report #15, "Interview with James Rowe, Jr." *op. cit.*

8 Memorandum, Chief of Staff to McCloy, May 13, 1944, ASW 014.311 WDC Permits to Enter and Live, RG 107, National Archives.

9 Memorandum, Edward R. Stettinius, Jr., to Roosevelt, June 9, 1944, OF-4849, FDR Library.

10 Biddle had advised the President in his letter of December 30, 1943 *(op. cit.),* that "a poll recently conducted by a Los Angeles paper indicated that Californians would vote ten to one against permitting the . . . citizens of Japanese ancestry ever to return." In contrast, a confidential preevacuation poll, dated March 9, 1942, had shown only 14 percent of Californians favoring the internment of the Nisei (*In Brief Authority,* p. 224).

11 Letter, dated January 28, 1944, to Roosevelt from Representatives George E. Outland, Jerry Voorhis, John M. Coffee, Chet Holifield, Will Rogers, Jr., Edouard V. M. Izac, Thomas P. Ford, OF-4849, FDR Library. Manzanar attorney J. B. Saks's letter to Solicitor Glick (January 14, 1944, University Research Library, UCLA) added another dimension to the atrocity furor: "I should like to take this opportunity . . . to point out the discrepancies in the general stories relating to how Caucasians have fared in the hands of the Japanese. While the atrocity story was reaching its zenith we had with us one of the people who returned recently from Japan . . . His account of the treatment accorded him and the others interned with him was truly a revelation. His picture was one of not only adequate meals but extravagant ones—meat every day, greens, milk, cake, etc.—this while the populace was living under the most stringent rationing conditions. He stated that plenty of reading material was made available, that there was ample recreational facilities and . . . the sole difficulty experienced was a scarcity of fuel and accordingly, at times, it was quite cold."

12 Memorandum, Roosevelt to E. R. Stettinius, Jr., and Harold L. Ickes, June 12, 1944, OF-4849, FDR Library.

13 Memorandum, Cordell Hull to Roosevelt, June 16, 1944, OF-4849, FDR Library.

14 On February 19, 1944, Representative Tom Ford of California charged that continued publicity and criticism regarding problems concerning persons of Japanese ancestry were endangering the lives of thousands of American prisoners held in Japan and that "Tule Lake was responsible for Japanese refusal to accede to recent Red Cross efforts to assist our prisoners abroad." *Pacific Citizen,* February 26, 1944.

15 Official Japanese broadcast of July 7, 1943. See *Human Conservation, op. cit.,* p. 16.

16 Though Dillon Myer also concedes that "someone in the office of the President decided that it [adjudication] should not be done before the November elections" (*Uprooted Americans,* p. 183), the WRA Director reveals that Solicitor Charles Fahey, too, was determined to delay the cases; and with *Endo,* he repeatedly sought to have WRA "mute the case" as Fahey "was sure that he was going to lose this one." Myer adds: "We argued with him time and again and he finally agreed to take it to the court . . ." ("Unpublished Autobiography," pp. 220–21). *Ex parte Endo* had been initiated in July 1942 by attorney James Purcell, who challenged the government's right to detain and to subject concededly loyal inmates to WRA leave procedures. The *Korematsu* case had been initiated a month earlier by Collins. Collins and Purcell spent a small personal fortune fighting for the rights of the interned.

17 Memorandum, June 8, 1944, Myer to Abe Fortas. From *Uprooted Americans, op. cit.,* p. 180. Interestingly, it was just about this time that nearly one thousand European refugees of Nazism (including 916 Jews) were also being scrupulously sorted, sifted and processed after the U. S. had agreed to permit the entry of a limited number of professional people outside immigration quotas. Executive Order 9417 had provided for the "establishment of havens of temporary refuge for such victims," and all were placed for the duration in Fort Oswego, New York under WRA management—a wartime haven some of these former inmates of concentration camps considered "just another concentration camp." It was largely through the efforts of Jewish agencies in the U. S. that these refugees were not forced to return to their countries of origin after the war.

18 Memorandum, John Hall to John J. McCloy, March 2, 1944, ASW 014.311 WDC Segregation, RG 107, National Archives. McCloy believed that the issuance of another Executive Order would help give "legal authority" to the perpetuation of the Army's right "to detain potentially dangerous citizens . . . who are not charged with any crime" (as a result of the rescreening), considering that "there is a substantial group [in Tule Lake] which is actively disloyal to the country," a "large proportion" of whom "are citizens of the United States." See Memorandum, McCloy to Stimson, November 28, 1944, ASW 014.311 WDC Permits to Enter and Live, RG 107, National Archives.

19 Letter, Edward J. Ennis to Abe Fortas, November 14, 1944, Washington Central File, RG 201, National Archives. Myer claims that the Army, which ended up reevaluating the loyalty status of every Japanese American living on the U. S. mainland, had "a problem of saving face" and was determined to have from 8,000 to 10,000 excludees detained, which would "tie up 20,000 to 30,000 people because of family affiliations." "After much argument," Myer explains in *Uprooted Americans* (p. 184), he succeeded in having the Army reduce the number of excludees to 5,000.

20 Memorandum, Henry L. Stimson to Roosevelt, December 13, 1944, PSF: Stimson Folder, FDR Library. For an astute study of the Western Defense Command's criteria of "potential dangerousness" as applied to Japanese Americans in the last months of the war, see Edward N. Barnhart's "The Individual Exclusion of Japanese Americans in World War II" (*Pacific Historic Review,* May 1960). In Barnhart's view, the Army's sudden policy switch to *individual* exclusion was a move to make the Army "less assailable legally."

21 Far more candid is Ickes' explanation of the evacuation genesis: "As a member of President Roosevelt's administration, I saw the United States Army give way to mass hysteria over the Japanese . . . it lost its self-control and, egged on by public clamor, some of it from greedy Americans who sought an opportunity to possess themselves of Japanese rights and property, it began to round up indiscriminately the Japanese who had been born in Japan, as well as those born here. Crowded into cars like cattle, these hapless people were hurried away to hastily constructed and thoroughly inadequate concentration camps, with soldiers with nervous muskets on guard, in the great American desert. We gave the fancy name of "relocation centers" to these dust bowls, but they were concentration camps nonetheless . . ." *Washington Evening Star,* September 23, 1946.

22 Wire, T. J. O'Brien (Secretary of Marysville Parlor #6 N.S.G.W.) to Roosevelt, December 15, 1944, OF-4849, FDR Library. Identical wires were received from San Francisco Parlor #1 on December 16, 1944, and Los Angeles Parlor #45 on December 13, 1944.

23 Solicitor Glick, who helped to draft Executive Order 9102, admits that the WRA "wished to avoid a specific reference to detention so that no one could insist that it was ordered to detain the Japanese yet it wanted a phrase with an interpretation allowing for detention if WRA needed or wished to do so." The phrase "supervision of activities" was adopted so that the agency could "jump either way." *Prejudice, War and the Constitution,* p. 364, fn. 207.

24 Hirabayashi was sentenced to three months in jail on each count, sentences to run concurrently. "Taking advantage of the concurrent sentences, the Supreme Court sustained the sentences on the curfew violation and found it unnecessary to rule on exclusion," according to the authors of *Prejudice, War and the Constitution* (p. 212), who add that "the concurring opinions strongly suggested that unanimity was possible only on the narrow grounds of curfew and that evacuation and detention were deliberately being held open for a later day and another case."

25 *Ibid.,* p. 221. The appalling breakdown of High Court standards in the evacuation decisions gives pause for thought in regard to former editor of *The Nation* Oswald Garrison Villard's accusation (on the eve of America's entry into the war) that "the Supreme Court is now packed, not with 'nine old men' out of step with the times, but with seven men appointed in the confident belief that they will do exactly what the President expects of them." The *Christian Century,* August 27, 1941.

Notes for Chapter 12

1 See p. 307, fn. 21. See also Appendix 8.

2 Petition, Resegregation Committee to Harold Ickes and Dillon Myer, May 30, 1944, WRA File 36.239, RG 210, National Archives. Petitions were invariably accompanied by thousands of signatures: 6,500 signatures were affixed to the petition of May 30; a September petition garnered 10,000 names. Many signed out of fear of being stigmatized as an anti-resegregationist. Others had been led to believe that it was the only way to obtain exchange-boat priorities.

3 "A New Slant on Education at Tule Lake," Tule Lake Community Analysis Report No. 95, June 7, 1944, RG 210, National Archives.

4 *Ibid.* The perceptive reports filed during this period by Dr. Marvin Opler (Community Analyst), the Affidavits of Hankey, Burling, and Ray, also *The Spoilage,* have provided helpful data in the preparation of this chapter.

5 Memorandum ("Subject: Secretary Ickes' Questions in Regard to School Policy at Tule Lake Center"), Edward H. Spicer to John Provinse, Community Analysis Report No. 140, May 5, 1944, RG 210, National Archives. Since the assumption was that Tuleans would all be sent to Japan, language schools had the sanction of the State Department. Myer had advised Hull on January 21, 1944: "The use of buildings and the scheduling of classes in order to avoid conflicts between the English and Japanese type schools will be arranged through the administrative staff and the responsible evacuee representatives." (WRA File 36.239, RG 210, National Archives.)

6   The fear of being considered an *inu* reached panic proportion following the murder of the head of the Coop, after brutal assaults had been made on four other alleged informers. The entire evacuee police force resigned soon thereafter; some sought refuge in the MP compound. Radicals were able to inhibit opposition to their extremist policies because anyone who dared to disagree was quickly labeled *inu,* and perpetrators of acts of vengeance were never apprehended. The Kunitani faction, as moderates, waned in influence following their release from the stockade. They were labeled "little inu," and lost out to extremists.

7   Letter, S.Y. to Edward J. Ennis, August 9, 1945 (appended to Tule Lake Community Analysis Report No. T-31 of August 18, 1945), RG 210, National Archives. The aggressive emptying of the centers in the face of West Coast terrorism was condemned by numerous humanitarian groups, who sought unsuccessfully to have at least two or three centers kept open for welfare cases. The WRA stood firm in its belief that in reestablishing the evacuees while the wartime boom was still on, Japanese Americans stood to have a far less difficult time than after the war, when the competition for jobs would be keener.

8   A WRA policy statement of May 29, 1942 (under Eisenhower), had assured evacuees that "the objective of the program is to provide for the duration of the war, and as nearly as wartime exigencies permit, an equitable substitute for the life, work, and homes given up . . ." Not one evacuee challenged the termination on the basis of a technicality which had authorities worried: "Those who signed the Work Corps pledge cards agreeing to work until 14 days after the end of the war may use this against WRA."

9   Rosalie Hankey, on whose Tule Lake observations a great deal of *The Spoilage* is based, asserts in her "Affidavit" (p. 376) that "when [Project Director] Best inquired about the significance of asking if the evacuees had applied for renunciation . . . they [the Army officers] answered that it was instructions from the Presidio." See also *The Spoilage,* p. 338, fn. 19.

10   "Hokoku-Hoshidan" is a contraction of *Hokoku Seinen Dan* (the young men's faction of the Resegregationist group) and *Sokuji Kikoku Hoshi Dan* (the parent group). The youth faction had initially been organized as a cultural study group under the title of *Sokoku Kenkyu Seinen Dan* (the "Sokoku"), meaning the "Young Men's Association for the Study of the Mother Country."

11   See Chapter 8 ("Renunciation: Mass Relinquishment of American Citizenship") in *The Spoilage.*

12   The theory of the Justice Department, according to attorney Collins, was: "If a citizen renounced U. S. citizenship and asserted loyalty to Japan it would presume he was a dual citizen who, thereupon, became solely a Japanese citizen and, therefore, automatically an alien enemy and, as such, to be interned in an alien internment camp and be removable to Japan under the provisions of the Alien Enemy Act."

13   Girdner and Loftis, *The Great Betrayal,* p. 443. Dillon Myer,

who has characterized the renunciation statute as "one of the worst pieces of legislation ever passed by the United States Congress" ("Unpublished Autobiography," p. 216), faults Justice Department insensitivity for the "snowballing" of renunciations: "We did our best to persuade the Department of Justice staff . . . that this was the worst possible time [when evacuees were faced with eviction] to conduct hearings."

14 "Narrative Report of Louis M. Noyes," Tule Lake Final Report, May 4, 1946, RG 210, National Archives.

15 "Initial Center Reaction to the Transfer of 70 Residents to an Alien Detention Center," Tule Lake Community Analysis Report No. 132, December 27, 1944, RG 210, National Archives.

16 "The living quarters were much better at Crystal City . . ." recalls Dr. Izumi Taniguchi. "Living space was allotted, X number of square feet to a person . . . family units were equipped with a kitchenette consisting of 3 burner kerosene cooking stove with oven, running cold water and sink, and an ice box. There was one lavatory and toilet in the building shared by two or three families. Food was much better than in the relocation centers because utensils were issued and each family prepared their own meals—raw food was obtained at the commissary. Each family was issued token money to be spent at the commissary, canteen, barbershop, and beauty shop." On the other hand, "housing accommodations for the Crystal City 'overflow' were awful," claims Edison Uno. "Hundreds of families lived in 'Victory Huts' which were no larger than 15' x 15' made of plywood with no insulation whatsoever. In the summer they were like ovens and in the winter they were drafty and uncomfortable. Sometimes the winds got so bad that the roofs, windows and doors would fly off. A whole family lived in one hut."

17 Thomas and Nishimoto, p. 352.

18 "Renunciation of Citizenship and Resegregationist Youth Groups —Tule Lake," Community Analysis Report No. 133, January 1, 1945, RG 210, National Archives. Since the first 117 renunciants were residents of a single ward, their applications had obviously been made as a group. Analyst Opler had been permitted to attend at least twenty of the hearings.

19 "Affidavit of John L. Burling," November 8, 1946.

20 Thomas and Nishimoto, pp. 354–55. Reprinted from *The Spoilage* by permission of the Regents of the University of California. Originally published by the University of California Press.

21 Letter, S.Y. to Edward J. Ennis, August 9, 1945, *op. cit.* Burling had instructed hearing officers to watch for signs of coercion, and if detected, to dictate a memo on the record so that the case might be further studied in Washington. Authors Spicer, Hansen, Luomala, and Opler would maintain in their final report on the camps, however, that "hysterical or coerced renunciations had been accepted by the Attorney General, in many cases, contrary to the recommendation on the scene of the Justice Department's own hearing officer." *Impounded People,* p. 273.

22 "Confidential: The 5th and 6th Transfers of Tuleans to Justice Department Centers," Tule Lake Community Analysis Report No. 163, June 30, 1945, RG 210, National Archives.

23 Letter, J.I.T. to Edward J. Ennis, August 13, 1945 (appended to Community Analysis Report No. T-31 of August 18, 1945), RG 210, National Archives. Collins contends that "not one person was informed that renunciation was irrevocable or that it could or might result in removal to Japan." Many believed that authorities would later permit them to change their minds, as they had done for registration and segregation.

24 Letter, John L. Burling to Chairmen T.H. of *Hokoku* and M.S. of *Hoshidan,* January 19, 1945, WRA File 36.239, RG 210, National Archives.

25 Letter, Tetsujiro Nakamura to author, June 25, 1973.

26 WRA form (mimeographed), WRA File 36.239, RG 210, National Archives.

27 "Statement of Wayne Collins," *op. cit.;* see also Burling "Affidavit," p. 183.

28 "Confidential: The 5th and 6th Transfers of Tuleans to Justice Department Centers," *op. cit.*

29 The exploits of Japanese Americans in the Pacific-Asia Theater —in Military Intelligence Service—did not begin to receive public attention until the last few months of the war. This was because most were involved in highly secret work as "eyes and ears" of the armed forces of the U.S. and her allies.

30 Letter from —— to Edward J. Ennis, courtesy of ACLU of Northern California.

31 Biddle had departed from the Justice Department prior to the disposition of a considerable number of cases, particularly those which hearing officers had earmarked for further review, as it was believed that "the renunciant was in fact Americanized and was acting solely out of resentment at evacuation . . ." according to Burling's "Affidavit." A "disagreement" over the cases had arisen among responsible officials, and in the cases being set aside, the new Attorney General inherited the cases.

Notes for Chapter 13

1 "The Final Impact of War and The News of Peace at Tule Lake," by Marvin Opler, Community Analysis Report No. T-31, August 18, 1945, RG 210, National Archives. Bomb had been dropped on August 6, 1945.

2 Memorandum, John H. Provinse to Dillon S. Myer (attached to Report No. T-31, *op. cit.*), August 28, 1945, RG 210, National Archives. Anthropologist Provinse (Chief, Community Management Division) had recommended the stationing of anthropologically trained social analysts at each center.

3 Memorandum, "Renunciation of Citizenship: A Program of Mass Hysteria at Tule Lake," Marvin Opler to Dillon Myer, Community Analysis Report No. 146, April 23, 1945, RG 210, National Archives. One lawmaker, Representative Herman P. Eberharter of Pennsylvania, had opposed the passage of the renunciation statute, declaring that he believed it to be unconstitutional. At the same hearing, Provinse had asserted his belief that 90 percent of the citizens of Japanese ancestry were loyal. See report on "Meetings of the Committee on Immigration and Naturalization, House of Representatives, January 25 and 26, 1944," R. W. Flournoy (legal adviser) to Berle, Hackworth, Long, January 26, 1944, Department of State File 740.00115 PW/8409, RG 59, National Archives.

4 *WRA, A Story of Human Conservation, op. cit.,* p. 74. In Collins' opinion, "the WRA and Justice were then more concerned about preserving their own reputation and preventing adverse criticism of their wartime blunders. A cloud of secrecy had been maintained over the whole terrible renunciation program, and the abominations of Nazi camps were then shocking the world community. Both agencies were disinclined to have their own scandalous deeds come to light by making them known to Congress or anyone else." (Personal communication.)

5 "The dictatorship of the WRA," in Collins' words, "was transformed into a dictatorship of the Attorney General." The Justice Department assumed jurisdiction over Tule Lake in October 1945, and MPs were replaced by border patrol guards of the Immigration and Naturalization Service. At the time, Attorney General Clark announced that he intended to deport every renunciant who had acted under Public Law 405. Letter, Ralph P. Merritt to Galen Fisher, November 27, 1945, Manzanar Records, 1942–46, Justice Department folder, Box 12, University Research Library, UCLA.

6 Girdner and Loftis, *The Great Betrayal,* p. 447. Until that time, it had been impossible for a U.S. citizen to renounce his citizenship unless he was residing in a foreign country. (Framed to procure renunciations solely from Japanese Americans, the renunciation statute was voided after the war, on July 25, 1947, by a Joint Resolution of Congress.)

7 "Statement of Wayne Collins," *op. cit.* Under the organic law of Japan (*jus sanguinis*), which provided that all descendants of Japanese were Japanese nationals, wherever born, the Nisei were automatically "dual nationals" if born before December 1, 1924. After that date, they were dual nationals if births had been registered with a Japanese diplomatic or consular officer within fourteen days of their births. Claims of dual citizenship, usually falsely asserted by persons under twenty-one years of age, had been accepted at face value by hearing officers, according to Collins.

8 *Ibid.*

9 *Ibid.* Actually, there had been one law firm willing to take on some cases, but its service was not welcomed by the renunciants or by Collins because of its ties with the JACL, which had declined to get involved with "disloyals" on the basis that the same amount of effort ought to be put into protecting the interests of returning loyals. Documents of the period, courtesy of Wayne Collins.

10 The national office of the ACLU took a position similar to that of the JACL: that aiding "disloyals" would only add to existing prejudices on the West Coast and that priority ought to be given to protecting the rights of loyals and to checking the immense pressure for deportations. Only belatedly did it give moral backing to some well-screened renuncia-

tion cases after favorable publicity had been generated by Collins' mass suits. Lawyers, in time, began openly soliciting cases in Tule Lake and successfully wooed a number of clients away from the mass suits. Documents of the period, courtesy of Wayne Collins.

11 Letter, Wayne Collins to author, June 13, 1968. "Troublemaker" Kurihara, who opted for noninvolvement in Tule Lake politics, also held Best in high regard.

12 Remarks attributed to Collins are from Chapter 24 ("Two Angry Irishmen") in Bill Hosokawa's *Nisei: The Quiet Americans* (New York: William Morrow, 1969). Wayne Collins passed away suddenly on July 16, 1974, yet he lives on in the memory of thousands who were the beneficiaries of his fierce dedication to justice. For this reason the author has taken the liberty of leaving text references to this remarkable American in the present tense—as he had last seen and OK'd them. With unfailing courtesy, Mr. Collins responded by letter or by phone to every query put to him; he generously made available heretofore unpublished documents, photos; he contributed much in the way of suggestions and criticisms after a reading of the manuscript.

13 *Pacific Citizen,* December 17, 1945. Collins' allegation that government agents had been fully aware of the campaign of intimidation being carried on by insurgent groups found confirmation in a letter Abe Fortas had sent to Ernest Besig on August 6, 1945, which stated: "It was primarily due to the pressure of these organizations that over 80 per cent of the citizens eligible to do so applied for renunciation of citizenship . . . Undoubtedly many of the applicants were in the grip of the emotional hysteria created by these organizations, or actually acting under fear of violence . . . The general uniformity of the answers given indicate the applicants were well coached." But according to Burling's "Affidavit" (p. 194), Fortas had "no recollection or knowledge" of sending such a letter.

14 Confidential letter to renunciant clients (mimeographed), Wayne Collins to K.M., March 19, 1951. While Burling contended in his "Affidavit" (pp. 187, 195) that the beatings and threats of violence had nothing to do with the renunciation, but had been "related to struggles for political leadership," Collins charged that it was *"governmental duress primarily and private duress secondarily"* which had caused the renunciations.

15 See "The Segregation Center Closes: Final Trend Report for Tule Lake Center," Community Analysis Report E 16-Tule Lake T-46 (61.319A), March 21, 1946, RG 210, National Archives.

16 *WRA, A Story of Human Conservation, op. cit.,* p. 74. After V-J (Victory over Japan) Day, all individual exclusion orders against the "potentially dangerous" were revoked, beginning on September 4, 1945; but in order to justify the mass removals, charges Collins, "the Attorney General kept up the pretense that renunciants might be a danger to our security."

17 See Besig "Affidavit" (p. 287); see also Collins brief in *McGrath v. Abo* Nos. 12251 and 12252 in the Court of Appeals for the Ninth Circuit, pp. 100–1. Ann Ray, one of the four observers, was denied access to certain hearings and found renunciants trembling and incoherent in hearings she witnessed: "All appeared intimidated . . . The gruff method, the harsh tones and the sarcastic statements made by a majority of the government examiners . . . in their questioning of renunciants clearly indicated that they looked upon the internees as mere 'Japs.' " "Affidavit of Ann Ray," December 4, 1946.

18 "Affidavit of Ernest Besig," *op. cit.*

19 Spicer, Hansen, Luomala, and Opler, *Impounded People,* p. 276.

20 "Affidavit of Ernest Besig," *op. cit.*

21 "The Segregation Center Closes . . ." *op. cit.* Releases of so-called "unnotified" kept coming through even after the group was placed in internment at Crystal City.

22 tenBroek, Barnhart, and Matson, *Prejudice, War and the Constitution,* p. 180.

23 Transfer of most of the rejectees to Seabrook Farms, New Jersey, had occurred in November 1946, after Collins had learned of work opportunities there and persuaded Justice to arrange for "relaxed internment."

24 Removal orders nevertheless continued to hang over the group until canceled in 1952.

25 77 F. Supp. 806. After the interlocutory judgment was entered, Collins kept the cases open for a year, enabling some 1,800 in Japan and others in the U.S. to join as plaintiffs to secure benefits of a final judgment.

26 See *McGrath v. Abo, op. cit.* In anticipation of lawsuits, the War Department had early sent out the following instructions: "The importance of keeping an accurate and complete record, stenographic if possible, of all that transpires at the hearing [i.e., for leave clearance, also for segregants prior to segregation], and of information secured from other witnesses and by means of other investigation cannot be over-emphasized. This record, together with material in the files concerning the individual applicant, will have to be the basis of the Government's defense in habeas corpus proceedings . . ." See "Proposed Questions [to ask segregants]" and "Leave Clearance Interviews: Suggested Topics for Questioning," both documents dated August 25, 1943, ASW 014.311 WDC Segregation—Japs, RG 107, National Archives. See also Appendix 11.

27 Collins charges "connivance on the part of the ACLU of New York and Southern California [who were backing petitioners] with Justice Department and WRA officials . . . The entering of judgment in the *Murakami* case first—by by-passing mine—set up conditions which enabled the same court to order the mass suits re-opened to allow the Justice Department to introduce additional evidence." In Collins' opinion, Judge Goodman's March 1949 decision would have established, for all time, the unconstitutionality of the renunciations had discretion been exercised: "The National ACLU and the Southern California branch proceeded recklessly in a manner which regrettably disregarded the danger such actions presented to the mass suits." June 28, 1973, memorandum to author, paraphrased in part. See also "Confidential letter to renunciant clients," *op. cit.*

28 *Ibid.* (paraphrased in part).

29 *Pacific Citizen,* May 22, 1959. In private practice, Ennis, in 1952, became a special Washington counsel for the JACL's Anti-Discrimination Committee and the Washington JACL office. He assisted in JACL efforts to obtain wartime reparation for evacuees, as well as naturalization privileges for the Issei.

30 "There was no 'liberal' policy of citizenship restitution inaugurated or pursued at any time as Doub well knew," claims Collins. "Renunciations were cancelled by court judgments and not by the Department of Justice. The court ordered restoration in individual cases, one by one, and every case was contested by the Attorney General and his *Department of Injustice* to the bitter end." Notes to author, June 28, 1973.

31 *Pacific Citizen,* May 22, 1959.

32 *Washington Post and Times Herald,* May 28, 1959.

33 *Pacific Citizen,* May 22, 1959.

34 *Ibid.*

35 Personal communication, Wayne Collins to author. In his multi-decade fight on behalf of renunciants, Collins had been a "pin in the side" of Attorney Generals Tom Clark, J. Howard McGrath, James F. McGranery, Herbert Brownell, Jr., William P. Rogers, Robert F. Kennedy, and Nicholas deB. Katzenbach. See William Petersen's *Japanese Americans,* p. 99, fn. 32. Edison Uno has called for the JACL "to actively and aggressively seek Presidential pardons for all . . . who have not regained their citizenship renounced under governmental duress . . ." See *Pacific Citizen,* September 27, 1974.

36 Wayne Collins, "Withdrawal and Dismissal of Last of Parties-Plaintiff Without Prejudice and Court Order Thereon and Statement of Counsel for Plaintiffs Concluding Cases," August 6, 1968. The case had been dismissed when the last of the renunciant plaintiffs withdrew. Outright cancellation of renunciations as of no legal validity was opposed by the Justice Department to the end. Point of interest: Suits initiated in November 1945 had been filed against Attorney General Tom Clark. Twenty-three years later, the concluding case had been filed against Ramsay A. Clark, son of Tom Clark, who, after serving eighteen years as an Associate Justice of the Supreme Court, resigned in June 1967, when his son became Attorney General.

Notes for Chapter 14

1 General Tomoyuki Yamashita, who led the invasion of Malaya, conquest of Singapore, and later commanded Japanese forces in the Philippines, was condemned as a war criminal and sentenced to death by hanging on December 7, 1945 (the fourth anniversary of the Pearl Harbor attack), by what two U. S. Supreme Court Justices, Rutledge and Murphy, called "legalized lynching." Justice Murphy wrote in his dissenting judgment: "He was not charged with personally participating in acts of atrocity or with ordering or condoning their commission. Not even knowledge of the crimes was attributed to him. . . . Today the life of General Yama-

shita . . . is to be taken without regard to due process of law. There will be few to protest. But tomorrow the precedent here established can be turned against others."

2 Memorandum, Wayne Collins to author, July 21, 1973; see also brief (12,251 and 12,252) in *Abo v. McGrath,* paraphrased. The sanctioning of the mass evacuation as a "military necessity" (*Korematsu v. U.S.*) remains irreversible since the Constitution restricts the Court to actual cases, in the opinion of Joseph L. Rauh, counsel for the Leadership Conference on Civil Rights. *Pacific Citizen,* July 7, 1972.

3 Taken from Miwako Oana's column, "Mo's Scratch Pad," *Heart Mountain Sentinel,* date unknown.

4 William Petersen, "Success Story, Japanese-American Style," *The New York Times Magazine,* January 9, 1966.

5 "Success Story: Outwhiting the Whites," *Newsweek,* Vol. 77, June 21, 1971. The article correctly points to the job bias which continues to exist on the executive level of employment.

6 Richard Halloran, "Tokyo is Urged to Fight Image of 'Ugly Japanese,' " *New York Times,* April 1, 1973.

7 Dr. Otto Furuta, "By the Board," *Pacific Citizen,* July 6, 1973. The possibility of setting up a Tokyo office for a coordinated communication program is currently being studied by the JACL Public Relations Commission.

8 From *No-No Boy,* by John Okada (Rutland, Vermont, and Tokyo: Charles E. Tuttle, 1957).

9 Hosokawa, *Nisei: The Quiet Americans,* p. 446.

10 The last claim was that of the "rice king," Keisaburo Koda, who had given power of attorney mandate over his 5,000 acres to a trusted white attorney friend and others, who, upon his incarceration, proceeded to sell off everything. Koda's claim was for $2,497,500. The settlement of $362,500 barely covered fifteen years of litigation cost. Koda did not live to collect a cent of it.

11 Girdner and Loftis, *The Great Betrayal,* pp. 436–37.

12 After a review of the text, the office of Conference on Jewish Material Claims Against Germany, Inc. (New York), was careful to point out that in every one of the seven categories mentioned by the author, there were frequent exceptions to the rule. See the Western German government's Federal Indemnification Law and the Federal Restitution Law. Interestingly, the U.S., on establishing diplomatic relations with Eastern Germany, has insisted that the East German government give highest priority to "the question of claims by United States citizens for restitution as victims of Nazism," and that "a refusal even to consider it as a problem would not wash" with the American people. *New York Times,* September 5, 1974.

13 See Uno's "Minority One" column, *Pacific Citizen* (February 14, 1975), for a discussion, vis-a-vis evacuee reparation, of the $12 million in damages awarded to 1,200 antiwar protestors illegally arrested in May 1971: $7,500 for violation of rights to free speech and assembly; $180 to $1,800 for violation of Fourth Amendment protection against unreasonable arrest, and $300 to $1,200 for false imprisonment, depending on length of detention, etc. Uno, recipient of the Hearst award as outstanding

civil libertarian, cochaired, with Ray Okamura, the JACL campaign, which, in 1971, brought about the repeal of Title II of the 1950 Internal Security Act, which allowed for the establishment of camps for detaining persons purely on the basis of suspicion.

14 The idea of receiving charity remains repugnant to the Nikkei, and fear of risking community censure and ostracism deters poverty-level Issei from applying for welfare. The "life-and-death struggles" being engaged in by the Issei aged poor remains a less publicized aspect of the Nikkei "success story." See Jeffrey Matsui's exposé in *Pacific Citizen,* May 24, 1968.

15 From the unabridged text of Paul Brinkley-Rogers' perceptive *Newsweek* article, "Outwhiting the Whites" (*op. cit.*), as reproduced in the *Pacific Citizen,* December 22–29, 1972.

16 From CBS telecast, "Guilty by Reason of Race," aired on September 19, 1972.

SUPPLEMENT TO THE NOTES

Landmark legal victories were achieved through discoveries by researcher Aiko Herzig-Yoshinaga and Professor Peter Irons of documents revealing the government's fraudulent concealment of evidence from the Supreme Court in the wartime cases of *Korematsu, Hirabayashi,* and *Yasui.* Beginning in 1983 teams of lawyers working pro bono were able to reopen the cases under the principle of *coram nobis,* which allows the reversal of a conviction if there is evidence of prosecutorial impropriety that has resulted in a complete miscarriage of justice. The vacating of the three convictions some forty years after defendants had served their terms swept away "military necessity" as justification for the internment and had a powerful impact on the drive for redress.

During the existence of the Commission on Wartime Relocation and Internment of Civilians (CWRIC), thousands of primary and secondary documents (including those on numerous lesser-known temporary camps) were gathered from diverse repositories—individual, academic, and governmental. Libraries, researchers, and individuals who wish to purchase a complete microfilmed compilation of these (under the title *Papers of the U.S. Commission on Wartime Relocation and Internment of Civilians, Part 1: Numerical Files Archives*; 35 microfilm reels) may write to: University Publications of America, Inc., 44 N. Market St., Frederick, MD, 21701.

Dramatis Personae

Acheson, Dean, Undersecretary of State under Truman
Atherton, Ray, U. S. Ambassador to Canada
Austin, Lieutenant Colonel Verne, Commanding Officer of Tule Lake garrison
Baker, John C., Chief, Reports Division of WRA, 1942–43
Bendetsen, Colonel Karl R., Chief of Aliens Division of the War Department, then Assistant Chief of Staff in charge of Civilian Affairs of the Western Defense Command
Bennett, Leroy, Project Director (Gila)
Benninghoff, Harry Merrell, Executive Officer, Office of Far Eastern Affairs, State Department
Berle, Adolf, Assistant Secretary of State
Besig, Ernest, Executive Director of the Northern California ACLU
Best, Raymond R., Project Director (Tule Lake Segregation Center)
Biddle, Francis, Attorney General of the United States
Bingham, Jonathan B., Chief Alien Enemy Control Section, State Department
Black, Justice Hugo L., handed down *Korematsu* decision
Bonsal, Philip W., Chief, Division of American Republics
Braden, Spruille, Assistant Secretary of State under Truman
Bridges, Harry, Australian-born labor leader of West Coast Longshoreman; for years the U. S. attempted unsuccessfully to deport him and revoke his citizenship on charges that he was a Communist.
Buckner, General S. B., Jr., Commanding General of Alaska Department
Burling, John L., Assistant Director of the Alien Enemy Control Unit of the Justice Department
Byrnes, James, Secretary of State (under Truman)
Cahn, Seymour, WRA Finance Section officer
Campbell, Ned, Assistant Project Director (Manzanar)
Campbell, Thomas D., expert on available farm lands, privately and federally owned
Carter, John Franklin ("Jay Franklin"), columnist and NBC commentator

327

Chandler, A. B. "Happy," Senator (Kentucky)

Clark, Ramsay A., Attorney General of the United States (under L. B. Johnson)

Clark, Tom, Justice Department's Coordinator of Alien Enemy Control

Collins, Wayne M., Attorney at Law and social crusader

Conn, Stetson, Chief Historian, U. S. Army (now retired)

Cook, John D., Reports Officer (Tule Lake)

Corrigan, Frank P., Minister Plenipotentiary to Venezuela

Costello, John M., Congressman (California)

Coverley, Harvey M., Project Director (Tule Lake Relocation Center)

Cozzens, Robert B., West Coast Regional Director of WRA

Currie, Lauchlin, Administrative Assistant to President Roosevelt

Daniels, Professor Roger, author of *Concentration Camps*

De Amat, Francisco, Spanish Consul (San Francisco)

Deutsch, Dr. Monroe, Provost of the University of California, Berkeley

DeWitt, Lieutenant General John L., Commanding General of Western Defense Commnd

Douglas, Justice William O., handed down *Endo* decision

Early, Stephen T., Secretary to President Roosevelt

Eisenhower, Milton S., first National Director of WRA

Embree, John, head of WRA Community Analysts

Emmons, General Delos C., Commanding Officer of the Hawaii Department and Military Governor of Hawaii

Endo, Mitsuye, a Nisei who challenged right of the government to subject a loyal citizen to WRA leave regulations

Engle, Clair, Congressman (California)

Ennis, Edward J., Director of Enemy Alien Control of the Justice Department

Fahy, Charles, U. S. Solicitor General

Fielding (Fielder, Colonel Kendall J. [?]), Assistant Chief of Staff for Military Intelligence (Hawaiian Islands)

Flournoy, R. W., State Department legal adviser

Forrestal, James, Secretary of Navy (succeeded Knox, who died on April 28, 1944)

Fortas, Abe, Under Secretary of Interior

Franklin, Jay (John Franklin Carter), columnist and NBC commentator

Fujita, Dr. Eugenia, Nisei physician and surgeon

Furutani, Warren, Yonsei activist

Glick, Philip M., WRA Chief Solicitor

Goodman, Judge Louis E., U. S. District Court (for Northern California)

Grodzins, Professor Morton, author of *Americans Betrayed*

Gruening, Honorable Ernest, Governor of Alaska

Gufler, Bernard, Assistant Chief of the Special Division, State Department

Gullion, Major General Allen W., Provost Marshal General

Hall, Captain John M., Secretary of the Japanese American Joint Board (War Department) and Executive Assistant to McCloy

Hankey, Rosalie, anthropologist—observer at Tule Lake for the Evacuation and Resettlement Study under the direction of Dr. Dorothy S. Thomas

Hirabayashi, Gordon K., University of Washington senior who defied curfew and evacuation orders

Hoskins, Harold B., Department of State Foreign Activity Correlation officer

Hull, Cordell, Secretary of State

Ickes, Harold, Secretary of Interior

Jackson, Justice Robert, dissented in *Korematsu*

Jones, Bishop E. Stanley (Methodist)

Kagawa, Toyohiko, internationally acclaimed Christian pacifist

Keeley, James H., Jr., Chief, Special War Problems Division of State Department

Knox, Frank, Secretary of Navy

Korematsu, Fred T., Nisei who defied curfew and evacuation orders

(Kunitani), George, chairman of the Negotiating Committee of the *Daihyo Sha Kai*

Kurihara, Joseph, World War I veteran and dissident leader

Lane, Arthur Bliss, minister to Costa Rica

Lavery, Father Hugh T., Maryknoll priest

Lechliter, Irving, Project Attorney (Tule Lake)

Lippmann, Walter, syndicated columnist

McCloy, John J., Assistant Secretary of War

McGrath, Howard J., Attorney General of the U. S. (succeeding Tom Clark)

McIntyre, Marvin H., Secretary to President Roosevelt

McWilliams, Carey, author of *Prejudice*

Marshall, George C., U. S. Chief of Staff

Masaoka, Mike, National Secretary of the Japanese American Citizens League and its Washington representative

Merritt, Ralph, Project Director (Manzanar)

Munson, Curtis B., "Special Representative of State Department," a title given him during his counterintelligence work among Japanese Americans

Murphy, Justice Frank, dissented in *Korematsu*

Myer, Dillon, second National Director of WRA

Nakamura, Tetsujiro "Tex," Assistant legal officer (Tule Lake)

Nicholson, Herbert V., former Quaker missionary

Nomura, Kichisaburo, Japanese Ambassador to U. S.

Norweb, Henry, U. S. Ambassador to Peru

Noyes, Lou, Project Attorney (Tule Lake), succeeded Attorney Lechliter

O'Brien, Robert W., Assistant Dean of Arts and Sciences (University of Washington)

Olson, Culbert L., Governor of California

Opler, Dr. Marvin, Community Analyst (Tule Lake)

Opler, Morris E., Community Analyst (Manzanar)

Patterson, Robert, Under Secretary of War

Petersen, Professor William, author of *Japanese Americans*

Pickett, Clarence E., Executive Secretary, American Friends Service Committee

Prado, Manuel, President of Peru

Provinse, John H., Chief, Community Management Division

Rankin, John, Congressman (Mississippi)

Rasmussen, Colonel Kai E., Commandant of Military Intelligence Service Language School (MISLS)

Ringle, K. D., Lieutenant Commander, U. S. Navy Intelligence officer

Roberts, Justice Owen J., dissented in *Korematsu*

Robertson, Paul G., Project Director (Leupp Isolation Center)

Rogers, William P., Attorney General of the United States (under Eisenhower)

Rowalt, Elmer M., WRA Deputy Director

Rowe, James, Jr., assistant to Attorney General Biddle

Sawyer, Charles, U. S. Ambassador to Belgium

Scobey, Colonel William P., executive administrative assistant to John J. McCloy

Shigemitsu, Mamoru, Foreign Minister of Japan

Sigler, Lewis A., Assistant Solicitor of WRA

Spicer, Dr. Edward H., head of WRA Community Analysts (succeeded John Embree)

Sproul, Dr. Robert Gordon, President of University of California, Berkeley

Stafford, Harry, Project Director (Minidoka)

Stauber, B. R., Chief, Statistical Division of WRA

Stettinius, Edward R., Jr., Under Secretary of State, later became Secretary of State on Hull's retirement in November, 1944

Stimson, Henry L., Secretary of War

Tayama, Fred, former Chairman of the Southern California chapter of the JACL

Terry, James H., Project Attorney (Gila)

Thomas, Norman, Socialist leader and reformer

Tolan, John H., Congressman (California)

Tozier, Merrill M., Chief, Reports Division, 1944–46

Ueno, Harry, organizer of Manzanar Kitchen Workers' Union

Uno, Edison, Nisei educator and activist

Warren, Earl, Attorney General and, later, Governor of California

Watson, Brigadier General Edwin ("Pa"), Secretary to Roosevelt

Welles, Sumner, Under Secretary of State

Wharton, Commander Wallace S., Office of the Chief of Naval Operations, Washington

Wilson, Edwin C., U. S. Ambassador to Panama

Yasui, Minoru, Nisei attorney who defied Army curfew orders

Yoshiyama, Tom, secretary of the *Daihyo Sha Kai*

Bibliography

American Friends Service Committee, Southern California Branch. *Information Bulletin* No. 12–17, 1944.

Barnes, Henry Elmer, ed. *Perpetual War for Perpetual Peace.* Caldwell, Idaho: Caxton Printers, 1953.

Barnhart, Edward N. "The Individual Exclusion of Japanese Americans in World War II." *Pacific Historical Review* 29 (1960): 111–30.

———. "Japanese Internees from Peru." *Pacific Historical Review* 31 (1962): 169–78.

Besig, Ernest. "Affidavit of Ernest Besig." Submitted to District Court Judge Louis E. Goodman of the Federal District Court of Northern California in renunciation suits. December 6, 1946. Transcript of Record, *Abo v. Clark.*

Biddle, Francis. *In Brief Authority.* Garden City, New York: Doubleday, 1962.

Bloom [Broom], Leonard, and Reimer, Ruth. *Removal and Return: The Socio-Economic Effects of the War on Japanese Americans.* Berkeley and Los Angeles: University of California Press, 1949.

Bosworth, Allan R. *America's Concentration Camps.* New York: W. W. Norton, 1967.

Brinkley-Rogers, Paul. "Outwhiting the Whites." *Pacific Citizen,* December 22–29, 1972.

Brown, G. Gordon. "WRA, Gila River Project, Rivers, Arizona; Community Analysis Section, May 12 to July 7, 1945—Final Report." *Applied Anthropology 4* (1945): 1–49.

Burling, John. "Affidavit of John Burling." Submitted to District Court Judge A. F. St. Sure of the Federal District Court for Northern California in renunciation suits. November 8, 1946. Transcript of Record, *Abo v. Clark.*

Burns, James MacGregor. *Roosevelt: The Soldier of Freedom.* New York: Harcourt Brace Jovanovich, Inc., 1970.

Chamberlin, William Henry. *America's Second Crusade.* Chicago: Henry Regnery, 1950.

Collins, Wayne M. Brief for Appellees, *Tadayasu Abo v. Ivan Williams and Genshyo Ambo et al. v. Ivan Williams,* Nos. 25,296 and 25,297, U. S. District Court, N.D. of California, 1945.

———. Brief for Appellees, *Tadayasu Abo et al. v. Tom Clark and Genshyo Ambo et al. v. Tom Clark,* Nos. 25,294 and 25,295, U.S. District Court, N.D. of California, 1945.

———. Brief of Appellees, *J. Howard McGrath v. Tadayasu Abo et al. and J. Howard McGrath v. Mary Kaname Furuya et al,* Nos. 12,251 and 12,252, United States Court of Appeals for the Ninth Circuit, 1950.

———. "Statement of Wayne Collins." Undated manuscript.

Conn, Stetson; Engelman, Rose C.; and Fairchild, Byron. *The United States Army in World War II: The Western Hemisphere: Guarding the United States and Its Outposts.* Washington, D.C.: Department of the Army, 1964.

Conrat, Maisie and Richard. *Executive Order 9066: The Internment of 110,000 Japanese Americans.* MIT Press, 1971.

Daniels, Roger. *Concentration Camps USA: Japanese Americans and World War II.* New York: Holt, Rinehart and Winston, 1970.

DeWitt, Lieutenant General J. L. *Final Report. Japanese Evacuation from the West Coast, 1942.* Washington, D.C.: Government Printing Office, 1943.

Fisher, Anne Reeploeg. *Exile of a Race.* Seattle: F. & T. Publishers, 1965.

Flynn, John T. *The Final Secret of Pearl Harbor.* New York, 1945.

Fujimoto, Isao. "The Failure of Democracy in a Time of Crisis: The War-Time Internment of the Japanese Americans and Its Relevance Today." Mimeographed. Also in *Gidra,* September 1969.

Girdner, Audrie, and Loftis, Anne. *The Great Betrayal: The Evacuation of the Japanese-Americans during World War II.* New York: Macmillan, 1969.

Grodzins, Morton. *Americans Betrayed: Politics and the Japanese Evacuation.* Chicago: University of Chicago Press, 1949.

———. "Making Un-Americans." *The American Journal of Sociology,* Vol. IX, No. 6, May 1955.

Hankey, Rosalie. "Affidavit of Rosalie Hankey." Submitted to District Court Judge Louis E. Goodman of the Federal District Court for Northern California in renunciation suits. January 8, 1947. Transcript of Record, *Abo v. Clark.*

Hansen, Arthur A., and Hacker, David A. "The Manzanar 'Riot': An Ethnic Perspective." *Amerasia Journal,* Vol. 2, No. 2, Fall, 1974.

Hansen, Arthur A., and Mitson, Betty E., ed. *Voices Long Silent: An Oral Inquiry into the Japanese American Evacuation.* Fullerton, California: California University, 1974.

Hosokawa, Bill. *Nisei: The Quiet Americans.* New York: William Morrow, 1969.

Houston, Jeanne Wakatsuki and James D. *Farewell to Manzanar.* Boston: Houghton Mifflin, 1973.

Inouye, Daniel K., with Elliot, Lawrence. *Journey to Washington.* Englewood Cliffs, New Jersey: Prentice-Hall, 1967.

Ishigo, Estelle. *Lone Heart Mountain*. Los Angeles: Anderson, Ritchie & Simon, 1972.

"Issei, Nisei, Kibei." *Fortune, XXIX*, No. 4 (April, 1944).

Jackman, Norman R. "Collective Protest in Relocation Centers." *The American Journal of Sociology* 63 (1957): 264–72.

Jacobs, Paul; Landau, Saul; with Pell, Eve. *To Serve the Devil: Volume 2*. New York: Random House, 1971.

Japanese American Citizens League, Anti-Discrimination Committee, Inc. "Information Concerning Claims Under the Evacuation Claims Law." Mimeographed.

Japanese American Citizens League, *Minutes: Special Emergency National Conference of November 17–24, 1942, Salt Lake City, Utah*.

Japanese American Evacuation Claims. *Hearings before Subcommittee No. 5 of the Committee on the Judiciary, House of Representatives, 83rd Congress*. Washington: Government Printing Office, 1954.

Kitagawa, Daisuke. *Issei and Nisei: The Internment Years*. New York: The Seabury Press, 1967.

Kitano, Harry H. L. *Japanese Americans: The Evolution of a Subculture*. Englewood Cliffs, N.J.: Prentice-Hall, 1969.

Leighton, Alexander H. *The Governing of Men: General Principles and Recommendations Based on Experience at a Japanese Relocation Camp*. Princeton: Princeton University Press, 1945.

Lind, Andrew W. *Hawaii's Japanese: An Experiment in Democracy*. Princeton: Princeton University Press, 1946.

Manchester, William, *The Glory and the Dream*. Boston: Little, Brown, 1974.

Martin, James J. *Revisionist Viewpoints: Essays in a Dissident Historical Tradition*. Colorado Springs: Ralph Myles, 1971.

McWilliams, Carey. "Moving the West-Coast Japanese." *Harper's* magazine 185 (1942): 359–69.

————. *Prejudice: Japanese Americans: Symbol of Racial Intolerance*. Boston: Little, Brown, 1944.

————. *Witch Hunt; The Revival of Heresy*. Boston: Little, Brown, 1950.

Mitson, Betty E., *Looking Back in Anguish: Oral History and Japanese-American Evacuation*. New York: The Oral History Association, Inc., 1974.

Miyamoto, Kazuo. *Hawaii, End of the Rainbow*. Rutland, Vermont, and Tokyo: Charles E. Tuttle Co., 1964.

Munson, Curtis B. "Report on Japanese on the West Coast of the United States," in *Hearings, 79th Congress, 1st sess.*, Joint Committee on the Investigation of the Pearl Harbor Attack. Washington, D.C.: Government Printing Office, 1946.

Murphy, Thomas D. *Ambassador in Arms: The Story of Hawaii's 100th Battalion*. Honolulu: University of Hawaii Press, 1954.

Myer, Dillon S. *Uprooted Americans: The Japanese Americans and the War Relocation Authority During World War II*. Tucson: University of Arizona Press, 1970.

————. "1942–46: Typescript of Unpublished Autobiography." FDR Library.

Nicholson, Herbert V. *Treasure in Earthen Vessels.* Whittier, California: Penn Lithographics Inc., 1974.

O'Brien, Robert W. *The College Nisei.* Palo Alto, California: Pacific Books, 1949.

Okada, John. *No-No Boy.* Rutland, Vermont, and Tokyo: Charles E. Tuttle, 1957.

Okimoto, Daniel. *American in Disguise.* New York and Tokyo: John Weatherhill, 1971.

Okubo, Mine, *Citizen 13660.* New York: Columbia University Press, 1946.

Petersen, William. *Japanese Americans: Oppression and Success.* New York: Random House, 1971.

———. "Success Story, Japanese-American Style." *New York Times Magazine,* January 9, 1966.

———. "The Incarceration of the Japanese-Americans." *National Review,* December 8, 1972.

Ray, Ann. "Affidavit of Ann Ray." Submitted to District Court Judge Louis E. Goodman of the Federal District Court for Northern California in renunciation suits. December 4, 1946. Transcript of Record, *Abo v. Clark.*

Renne, Louis Obed. *Our Day of Empire: War and the Exile of Japanese Americans.* Glasgow, Scotland: The Strickland Press, 1954.

Rostow, Eugene V. "Our Worst Wartime Mistake." *Harper's* 191 (1945): 193–201.

Rucker, Warren Page, "United States—Peruvian Policy Toward Peruvian-Japanese Persons During World War II." Unpublished M. A. thesis, University of Virginia, 1970.

Schuyler, Lambert. *The Japs Must Not Come Back.* Winslow, Washington: Heron House, 1944.

"Segregation of Persons of Japanese Ancestry in Relocation Centers." Washington, D.C.: War Relocation Authority, August 1943.

Smith, Bradford. *Americans from Japan.* Philadelphia: J. B. Lippincott, 1948.

Sone, Monica. *Nisei Daughter.* Boston: Little, Brown, 1953.

Spicer, Edward H.; Hansen, Asael T.; Luomala, Katherine; and Opler, Marvin K. *Impounded People: Japanese-Americans in the Relocation Centers.* Tucson, Arizona: University of Arizona Press, 1969.

Sterba, James. "Japanese Businessmen: The Yen is Mightier Than the Sword." *New York Times Magazine,* October 29, 1972.

Taniguchi, Alan. "Wartime Evacuation—Personal Memoir." Unpublished manuscript.

tenBroek, Jacobus; Barnhart, Edward N.; and Matson, Floyd W. *Prejudice, War and the Constitution.* Berkeley and Los Angeles: University of California Press, 1954.

Theobald, Robert A. *The Final Secret of Pearl Harbor.* New York: Devin-Adair, 1954.

Thomas, Dorothy Swaine, and Nishimoto, Richard S. *The Spoilage.* Berkeley and Los Angeles: University of California Press, 1946.

Thomas, Norman. "Dark Day for Liberty." *Christian Century* 59 (1942): 929–31.

————. *Democracy and Japanese Americans.* New York: Post War World Council, 1942.

Tolan Hearings. *Select Committee Investigating National Defense Migration.* 77th Congress, 2nd Session. Washington, D.C.: Government Printing Office, 1942.

U. S. Department of the Interior. *WRA, A Story of Human Conservation.* Washington, D.C.: Government Printing Office, 1946.

Wax, Rosalie Hankey. "The Destruction of a Democratic Impulse." *Human Organization* 12 (1953): 11–21.

————. "The Development of Authoritarianism, a Comparison of the Japanese-American Relocation Centers and Germany." Unpublished Ph.D. thesis, University of Chicago, 1951.

PERIODICALS AND NEWSPAPERS

Among publications most useful as source material include the *Pacific Citizen,** the *San Francisco Examiner,* the *San Francisco Chronicle,* the *Los Angeles Times, The New York Times,* the *Washington Post,* the *American Civil Liberties Union-News* (Northern California), *The Open Forum* (Los Angeles ACLU), *The Nation,* the *Christian Century,* the *New Republic, Harper's, Time, Life, Newsweek, Gidra* and the *Amerasia Journal.* Back issues of *Gidra* (an iconoclastic Sansei newspaper, now discontinued) and *Amerasia Journal* are available from the Amerasia Bookstore, 338 East Second Street, Los Angeles, California 90012. Send for catalogue of Asian-American publications.

Camp publications examined at the National Archives include *Gila News Courier, Rohwer Outpost, Heart Mountain Sentinel, Newell Star* (Tule Lake), *Tulean Dispatch, Poston Chronicle,* and the *Denson Tribune* (Jerome).

Camp newspapers and periodicals examined at the New York Public Library (main branch) include *All Aboard* (Topaz), *Santa Anita Pacemaker, Manzanar Free Press, Trek* (Topaz), *Communiqué* (Jerome).

Most of the existing records of the War Relocation Authority may be found in Record Group 210, held at the Social and Economic Records Division of the National Archives. According to the Archives' *Preliminary Inventories* (1955) of WRA records, however, "a large part of the records accumulated by the Authority were disposed of under Congressional authorization by the agency itself during its lifetime and by the Interior Department in subsequent years." Records of the Department of State, the Provost Marshal General's office, the Adjutant General's office, Western Defense Command, Secretary of War, Assistant Secretary of War, Office of the Chief of Naval Operations, and the Office of the Chief of Staff also contain information on the evacuation, all of which are held at the National Archives. A certain amount of this material is still restricted, though the

* For microfilms of the *Pacific Citizen* write Library Microfilms, 737 Loma Verde Ave., Palo Alto, California 94303. Most year-end holiday issues contain special stories on the evacuation. The 1967 and 1968 holiday issues feature stories on the Korematsu case; the 1965 one is devoted to Japanese immigration. Write *Pacific Citizen,* 2 Coral Circle, Suite 204, Monterey Park, CA 91755 for back issues.

wartime records of Secretary of War Stimson are now fully open for research, as declassification was completed in January 1975.

Special collections dealing with the wartime evacuation may be found at the Bancroft Library of the University of California at Berkeley, and at the Hoover Institution, Stanford University. The Bancroft Library will be the repository for the wartime papers of Wayne Collins, and duplicate copies of WRA Community Analysis Reports found at the National Archives, also WRA newspapers, photographs, internee letters and diaries, are permanently filed there.

By far, the most extensive collection of documents on Manzanar may be found at the University Research Library, University of California at Los Angeles, California 90024. The Research Library is also the headquarters for the Japanese American Research Project (JARP), whose large accumulation of documents relating to Japanese Americans includes old photographs, wartime camp records (WRA and Justice Department), oral histories, personal papers, diaries, artworks, Japanese-language publications, and a number of other categories. Back copies of the *Rafu Shimpo* (1914–70) and the *Kashu Mainichi* (1931–68) may be examined at the Research Library or purchased in microfilm from Asian-American Studies, c/o University Research Library.

Administrative records of the Wartime Civil Control Administration are maintained at the St. Louis, Missouri, Federal Records Center; and 625 rolls of microfilm on the assembly centers are held at the National Archives. But much of it is still classified information—a request for declassification review must describe a specific document. Other WCCA documents, as well as Western Defense Command materials, may be found at the Department of the Army Records Center; and material relating to DeWitt, the WRA, and the Western Defense Command may also be found at the General George C. Marshall Research Foundation, Lexington, Virginia 24450.

Data on persons held in alien detention camps are on file at the Records Center of the Justice Department and in World War II Internment Files of the Immigration and Naturalization Service, to be found at the National Archives repository located in Suitland, Maryland.

The fifty-two volumes of *The Diaries of Henry Lewis Stimson* are available on microfilm ($175.00 for the full set of nine reels or $20.00 per reel). Write to: Manuscripts and Archives, Yale University Library, New Haven, Conn. 06520.

Documents dealing with evacuation, relocation, and resettlement matters may be found scattered throughout Roosevelt's wartime papers at the Franklin D. Roosevelt Library, Hyde Park, New York.

FILMS

"Guilty By Reason of Race" (55 min.), an NBC-TV documentary, recalls the internment era through interviews, still photographs, newsreel footage. For rental information, contact any of the following university film libraries: Alaska, Arizona State, Arizona, Colorado, Florida State, South Florida, Georgia, Iowa, Illinois, Indiana, Kent State, Michigan, Minnesota, Nebraska, New Hampshire, North Carolina, Oregon State, Pennsylvania, South Carolina, South Dakota State, Utah, Central Washington State, Wisconsin.

"Nisei: The Pride and the Shame" (55 min.), a CBS-TV documentary from its "20th Century" series, narrated by Walter Cronkite, aired January 31, 1965. A print of this broadcast is available for rental through the national JACL, 1765 Sutter Street, San Francisco, California 94115. For purchase, write Associated Films, Inc., 600 Grand Avenue, Ridgefield, New Jersey 07657.

"Manzanar" (16 min.), an award-winning 16-mm. color documentary by Robert Nakamura. A young Nisei's memories of boyhood years spent in camp through the use of live action footage of the present and stills of the past. Available for purchase or rental from Visual Communications, 125 Weller Street, Room 312, Los Angeles, California 90012. (Write for a complete listing of films available; traveling photo exhibits on the evacuation may also be obtained from this source.)

"Subversion" (30 min.), a photo history of the Nikkei, revealing the effects of racism through interviews with young Japanese Americans. For rental, contact Film Department of KQED-TV, 1011 Bryant Street, San Francisco, California 94103.

"Constitution and Military Power," dealing with the Supreme Court validation of the evacuation in *Korematsu v. U.S.*, produced by Mass Communication Section of the Columbia University Press. Available for rental from the Berkeley Unified Schools, c/o Asian American Studies Task Force, 2600 Eighth Street, Berkeley, California 94710.

"Fence at Minidoka" (30 min.), an internment documentary written and narrated by Barbara Tanabe of KOMO-TV. No charge for borrowing film. For purchase, contact Production Manager, KOMO-TV, 100 Fourth Avenue North, Seattle, Washington 98109.

"Watari-Dori: A Bird of Passage," a CBS-TV documentary by Jesse Nishihata, aired on February 6, 1973. Story of the Canadian-Japanese experience from prewar days to the present. For possibility of purchase or rental, write the Canadian Broadcasting Corporation, 245 Park Avenue, New York 10017.

"Concentration Camp, USA" (60 min.), a documentary produced by Cory Shiozaki for the Theatre Arts Department, California State University, Long Beach. Interviews with three Nisei regarding their internment experiences. Hosted by Warren Furutani. Write to the university, 6101 East Seventh Street, Long Beach, California.

"Kokufuku" (The Return), a 16-mm. (30 min.) documentary produced by KRON-TV of San Francisco in 1967, dealing with the evacuation, the anti-Oriental bias leading up to it, and the Nikkei comeback. Available from the national JACL lending library.

"Topaz," a home movie filmed in secret at the Topaz Relocation Center, Utah, by Mr. Tatsuno of San Jose, California. Direct inquiry to Manzanar Committee, 1566 Curran Street, Los Angeles, California 90026.

AUDIOVISUALS ON JAPANESE AMERICANS

"Prejudice in America: The Japanese Americans" (produced by the Japanese American Curriculum Project and Multi Media Productions, Stanford) examines bias in the Nikkei experience. Included are two recordings (or cassettes), four film strips, a teacher's manual and reading list for use in secondary schools. Won 1971 award of the American Library Association Preview. For purchase, write to JACP, 414 East Third Avenue, San Mateo, California. Send for their catalogue on Asian-American publications.

"Japanese American Relocation, 1942," written by Rachel Sady and Victor Leviatin. Recordings, film strips, and a teaching manual for class distribution. A complete multimedia unit for social studies classes in secondary schools. Available through Educational Audio Visual, Pleasantville, New York 10570.

"Workshop I: The Japanese in America." Includes slide presentation, a Japanese American history outline, an annotated bibliography, and advice on how to conduct further research. Both "Workshop I" and "Workshop II" (see below) may be obtained on a purchase or rental basis through the national JACL, 1765 Sutter Street, San Francisco, California 94115.

"Workshop II: Evacuation and Camp Experience." Includes slide presentation; a chronology of events leading up to the evacuation, including events of the internment period; an annotated bibliography; a map showing location of the camps, and information as to their accessibility.

For a more complete listing, send for *Catalogue of Available Audio-Visual Materials For Asian American Studies* (which includes information on availability of commercial films on Asians and Asian Americans, also documentaries on Asia and U.S. foreign policy toward Asia), compiled by Don Nakanishi and Sue Embrey. Send 50¢ to Asian American Studies Center, 3232 Campbell Hall, UCLA, Los Angeles, California 90024. An illustrated brochure of films prepared by Asian university students may also be obtained from the same source.

FILMS RELATING TO JAPANESE AMERICANS
DURING WORLD WAR II
HELD BY THE NATIONAL ARCHIVES

"Go For Broke," 16-mm., produced by the WRA.

"The Way Ahead," 16-mm., produced by the WRA.

"A Challenge to Democracy," 16-mm., produced by the WRA.

"Japanese Relocation," 16-mm., produced by the Office of War Information (OWI).

"Nisei Soldier Newsreel," 16-mm., produced by the Army Signal Corps.

"The Wrong Ancestors," 35-mm. film strip (typed narrative), produced by the WRA.

Reference prints of above films are available for viewing and study at the National Archives (Washington, D.C. 20408), but write first for permission. Reproductions of the films may be purchased.

SOUND RECORDINGS FROM RG 210
OF RADIO BROADCASTS (1944–45) RELATING TO
JAPANESE AMERICANS

		No.
210-1	"Japanese-American Soldiers"—*March of Time* (August 17, 1944)	2-2S
210-3	"WOR (New York) Newsreel" (September 14, 1944)	2-2S
210-4	"They Call Me Joe" (October 7, 1944)	3-6S
210-5	"D. S. Myer Speech"—Gila River—(March 3, 1945)	8-16S
210-6	"Correspondents Abroad" (May 15, 1945)	1-1S
210-7	"Wings for Tomorrow: Ben Kuroki" (undated)	4-6S
210-9	"Gila River D.S.C. Presentation Program" (March 10, 1945)	2-4S
210-11	"The Family Nagashi," from "Arch Obler Plays" (September 27, 1945)	2-2S
210-12	"Dillon S. Myer interviewed by an NBC newsman," ca. 1943.	1-1S

Tape copies of recordings may be purchased from the Audiovisual Archives Division, National Archives, Washington, D.C. 20408. Researchers may visit the National Archives and record items using their own tape reproducing equipment. No charge, but write first for permission, specifying the use to be made of recordings.

ORAL HISTORY COLLECTIONS

The following is a sampling of the kinds of taped reminiscences of the evacuation-internment experience being collected and made available by the Japanese American Oral History Program at California State University, Fullerton. A complete bibliography of the collection (which includes interviews with former internees, camp administrators and employees, and residents of communities neighboring the relocation centers) may be found in *Voices Long Silent: An Oral Inquiry into the Japanese American Evacuation,* edited by Arthur A. Hansen and Betty E. Mitson.

ODANAKA, Woodrow   Nisei   O.H. 1382
High school student whose family ran retail produce business was evacuated to Santa Anita Assembly Center, where he witnessed a riot. Later graduated in Granada camp and relocated to college in Minnesota. Drafted with camp group and served with Army military intelligence in Philippines and in occupation of Japan.
Interviewer: Patrick H. West
Date: July 16, 1973   30 pp.

FUKASAWA, George T.   Nisei   O.H. 1336
Communications professor at Cal State Fullerton examines prewar Ventura County Japanese-American community, intelligence activities in post-Pearl Harbor roundup of Issei leaders in Los Angeles, evacuation role of JACL, personal role as evacuee policeman relative

to Manzanar Riot, Manzanar factions and personalities, and internment policy.

Interviewer: Arthur A. Hansen
Date: August 12, 1974   3 hours

ANONYMOUS   Nisei   O.H. 11
With father detained by FBI, one brother in Army, and other brothers relocated inland during voluntary evacuation period, interviewee was caught in the mass evacuation. Describes Poston, resettlement out of camp, and hostility toward former internees upon return to California.

Interviewer: Richard D. Curtiss
Date: March 4, 1966   24 pp.

ANONYMOUS   O.H. 1344
Matron whose husband worked on internal security force at both Manzanar and Tule Lake recalls experiences. On Manzanar: Inyo County treatment of Native Americans; economic impact of camp; and treatment of internees. On Tule Lake: pro-Japan activities; internee killing; riot and aftermath; social, cultural, and economic life of camp; and reaction of nearby community.

Interviewer: David J. Bertagnoli
Date: July 14, 1973   10 pp.

YONEDA, Elaine Black   O.H. 1377b
Former internee of Manzanar, by choice, treats impact of Pearl Harbor on San Francisco Japanese-American community, response of Japanese-American Left to evacuation, husband's illegal arrest by FBI and his voluntary evacuation, conditions in camp, work in camp library and camouflage net factory, factions and personalities, Manzanar Riot, and removal to Death Valley with "pro-American" group.

Interviewer: Arthur A. Hansen
Date: March 3, 1974   7 hours

TANAKA, Togo W.   Nisei   O.H. 1271b
In-depth analysis of discontent erupting into "Manzanar Riot" of December 6, 1942. Having been one who was subjected to harassment, he discusses camp factions and personalities in relation to some contemporaneous writing on the subject done by him in capacity of War Relocation Authority documentary historian.

Interviewer: Arthur A. Hansen
Date: August 30, 1973   42 pp.
Excerpted from *Voices Long Silent,* by permission.

Direct all inquiries regarding the CSUF Japanese American Oral History Project to Dr. Arthur A. Hansen, Department of History, California State University, Fullerton, California 92634. Transcripts of interviews are being made available in Xerox form at five cents per page.

The Bancroft Library's oral history collection is particularly noteworthy in that it includes interviews with a number of important policy makers of the period. Typescripts of some of these interviews have been bound in *The Japanese-American Relocation Reviewed* (Volume I: Decision and Exodus; Volume II: The Internment) as part of the Earl Warren Oral History Project and are being made available to manuscript libraries. Direct all inquiries to: Regional Oral History Office, the Bancroft Library, University of California, Berkeley, California 94720.

Two other extensive oral history collections on the Japanese American experience are those held by the Japanese American Research Project (University Research Library, University of California, Los Angeles, 90024) and the Asian American Research Project at California State College, Dominguez Hills (Dominguez Hills, California 90747) under the direction of Dr. Donald Teruo Hata, Jr.

SUPPLEMENT TO THE BIBLIOGRAPHY

Books on Japanese Americans and the internment now abound, and readers will find *Amerasia Journal* an invaluable source of periodic bibliographies. Among the publications that deserve reading are:

Commission on Wartime Relocation and Internment of Civilians. *Personal Justice Denied.* Washington, D.C.: Government Printing Office, 1982.

Crost, Lyn. *Honor by Fire: Japanese Americans at War in Europe and the Pacific.* Novato, Calif.: Presidio Press, 1994.

Daniels, Roger, Sandra C. Taylor, and Harry H. L. Kitano, eds. *Japanese Americans: From Relocation to Redress.* Seattle: University of Washington Press, 1991.

Duus, Masayo Umezawa. *Unlikely Liberators: The Men of the 100th and 442nd.* Honolulu: University of Hawaii Press, 1987.

Drinnon, Richard. *Keeper of Concentration Camps: Dillon S. Myer and American Racism.* Berkeley: University of California Press, 1987.

Gardiner, C. Harvey. *Pawns in a Triangle of Hate: The Peruvian Japanese and the United States.* Seattle: University of Washington Press, 1981.

Gee, Joy Nozaki, ed. *Crystal City 50th Anniversary Reunion Album.* Sacramento: Crystal City Album Committee, 1993.

Hansen, Arthur A., ed. *Resisters.* Part 4 of *Japanese American World War II Evacuation Oral History Project.* Munich: A. K. Saur, 1995.

Hatamiya, Leslie T. *Righting a Wrong: Japanese Americans and the Passage of the Civil Liberties Act of 1988.* Stanford: Stanford University Press, 1993.

Higashide, Seiichi. *Adios to Tears: The Memoirs of a Japanese-Peruvian Internee in U.S. Concentration Camps.* Honolulu: E & E Kudo, 1994.

Hohri, William Minoru. *Repairing America: An Account of the Movement for Japanese-American Redress.* Pullman, Wash.: Washington State University Press, 1988.

Houston, Jeanne Wakatsuki, and James D. Houston. *Farewell to Manzanar.* Boston: Houghton Mifflin, 1973.

Ichioka, Yuji. *The Issei: The World of the First Generation Japanese Immigrants, 1885-1924.* New York: Free Press, 1988.

342

Irons, Peter. *Justice at War: The Story of the Japanese American Internment Cases.* New York: Oxford University Press, 1983.

————, ed. *Justice Delayed: The Record of the Japanese American Internment Cases.* Middletown, Conn.: Wesleyan University Press, 1989.

Ito, Kazuo. *Issei: A History of Japanese Immigrants in North America.* Seattle: Executive Committee for Publications, 1973.

Kogawa, Joy. *Obasan.* Toronto: Penguin, 1981.

Levine, Ellen. *A Fence Away from Freedom: Japanese Americans and World War II.* New York: G. P. Putnam's Sons, 1995.

Nakano, Mei T. *Japanese American Woman: Three Generations, 1890-1990.* Berkeley: Mina Press; and San Francisco: Japanese American Historical Society, 1990.

Nelson, Douglas W. *Heart Mountain: The History of an American Concentration Camp.* Madison, Wis.: Wisconsin State Historical Society, 1976.

Tateishi, John. *And Justice for All: An Oral History of the Japanese American Detention Camps.* New York: Random House, 1984.

Uchida, Yoshiko. *Desert Exile: The Uprooting of a Japanese American Family.* Seattle: University of Washington Press, 1982.

Yamada, Mitsuye. *Camp Notes and Other Poems.* San Lorenzo, Calif.: Shameless Hussy Press, 1976.

Yamamoto, Hisaye. *Seven Syllables and Other Stories.* Latham, N.Y.: Woman of Color Press, 1988.

Yamauchi, Wakako. *Songs My Mother Taught Me: Stories, Plays, and Memoir.* New York: City University of New York, 1991.

On the proliferation of oral history projects, oral history–based books, and film documentaries related to the internment experience, see Arthur A. Hansen, "Oral History and the Japanese American Evacuation," *Journal of American History* 82 (September 1995): 625-39.

Opposition to the drafting of interned men, which became an organized civil disobedience movement in Heart Mountain, is documented in Daniels, *Concentration Camps USA*; Daniels, Taylor, and Kitano, *Japanese Americans*; Hansen, *Resisters*; Hohri, *Repairing America*; Levine, *A Fence Away from Freedom*; and

Index

Abo v. (Ramsay A.) Clark, 265
ACLU (American Civil Liberties Union), of Northern California, 65, 111-12, 208, 291n, 298n, 310n, 313n; of Southern California, 262, 323n; of the National (N.Y.), 65, 87, 111, 254, 321n, 323n
Adams, Mrs. Philip, 208, 213
Adjutant General, Office of, 136, 305n
Agriculture Department, U.S., 97, 119
Alaska, 54, 56-57; all Issei held as detainees, 286n
Alexander, Kenneth, 74
Alien Enemies Act, 63, 288-89n, 318n
Amache (Granada) Relocation Center (Colorado), 86, 130, 145, 176
Anaconda, 284n
Angel Island (California), 176
Angell, Sir Norman (Nobel Peace Prize recipient, 1933), 52
Argentina, 59
Arizona, 76, 79, 84, 86, 89, 99-100, 106, 145
Arkansas, 83, 86
Army, U.S., 28, 33, 38, 40, 48, 50, 62, 67, 69, 71, 73, 76-78, 81, 83-90, 93, 98, 105, 107, 113, 119, 138, 140, 145-53, 161-68, 171, 173, 192-93, 200-1, 205-7, 212, 220-21, 223-26, 234-35, 251, 283-84n, 290-92n, 294-95n, 302n, 305n, 314n, 316n
Army Intelligence, 40, 47, 101, 283n, 305n
Army (U.S.) units (Nisei), 442nd Infantry Battalion, 217, 246, 263, 305-6n; 100th Infantry Battalion, 217, 246, 293n, 305n; Nisei in prewar service, 48-49; in Pacific Theater, 320n; *see also* Military Intelligence Service Language School
Assembly Inn Internment Camp (North Carolina), 177
Assembly centers (reception centers), established, 79-80; food in, 81-82;

health in, 81, 89; housing in, 79-81, 93, 97; per diem cost, 79, 292n; supervision of, 79
Atherton, Ray, 191
Atrocities (in camps), 91, 124-25, 204, 212, 215, 295n, 310n, 312n
Atrocity stories, 218, 221, 314n
Austin, Verne, 165-66, 168-69

Bailey, Thomas A., 283n
Bainbridge Island (Washington), 78-79, 104
Baldwin, Roger, 111
Barnhart, Edward N., 287-89n, 316n
Belgium, 187
Bendetsen, Karl Robin, 28, 43, 56, 69, 72, 77-78, 86, 94-96, 105, 154, 290-92n, 295-96n, 299-300n, 304n; current activities, 290n; formulates detention plan, 69-70, 101, 286n; also segregation plan, 305n; urges denaturalizing Kibei, 307n; distrust of Nisei, 95
Besig, Ernest, 111-12, 254, 257, 310n, 322n; on closing of Tule Lake, 258; on stockade, 208-15
Best, Raymond R., 128, 158-63, 208-9, 212-16, 309n, 318n; aids renunciants, 254
Biddle, Francis, 63, 67-71, 73-74, 163, 190-91, 200-1, 236-37, 242-44, 290n, 314n, 320n; on "denaturalization bill," 190-91, 229-30; deplores mass removals, 67-68, 114; on the press, 68, 218
Bill of Rights, 67, 70, 228
Bismarck Internment Camp (or Fort Lincoln in North Dakota), 177, 238, 240, 253, 256
Black, Harry L., 212
Black, Hugo, 29, 74-75, 298n
Blacks, 38, 94, 113, 140, 229, 269-70, 296n
Boettiger, John, 296n
Bolivia, 59, 185
Bosworth, Allan R., 295n

343

Brazil, 58-59
Bridges, Harry, 46
Brownell, Herbert, Jr., 324n
Buddhists, 157, 244
Bulgaria, 181
Burling, John, 235-40, 242, 317n, 319-20n, 322n
Burns, James MacGregor, 68, 116
Butte ("Camp II," Gila), 126
Byrnes, James, 288n

Cabinet (White House), 27, 29, 30, 50, 73, 117, 174, 218-19
California, 27-31, 37-38, 50, 77, 79-80, 85-86, 91, 93-97, 112-14, 145, 157, 160, 169, 194, 254, 274; Japanese American population (1941), 36; return of evacuees opposed, 218-21, 223, 226, 229, 314n; seizure of evacuee-held land, 152; work camp plan, 93-97
California, University of (at Berkeley), 108, 310n, 315n
Cambodia, 279
Camp McCoy (Wisconsin), 176, 305n
Camp Savage (Minnesota), 305n
Campbell, Ned, 302n, 304n
Campbell, Thomas D., 84-86, 293n
Canada, 56-57, 188; exclusion decree of, 290n; U.S. (Ottawa) Legation in, 191
Canadian Japanese, 56-57, 190-91, 286n
Canal ("Camp I," Gila), 126
Carter, John Franklin, 194, 284n
CCC, see Civilian Conservation Corps
Central America, 56-58
Chandler, A. B. "Happy," 124, 153-54; Mrs. Chandler, 153
Chicago, 102, 106, 111
Chicago Daily News, 29, 174
Chicanos (Mexican Americans), 94, 97, 113
Chile, 59
China, 62, 108, 127, 151; "assembly centers" in, 202
Chinese Americans, 36-37, 113, 127, 239
Christian Century, 92, 112, 261
Christian Science Monitor, 263
Church groups (anti-evacuation), Brethren, 105; Fellowship of Reconciliation, 105; Maryknoll, 76; Mennonites, 105; Methodists, 92; Society of Friends, 46, 104-5, 228
Churchill, Sir Winston, 109
Civilian Conservation Corps (CCC) camps, 85, 125-26, 150-51; Cow Creek Camp, 125
Clark, Ramsay A., 265, 324n
Clark, Tom, 31, 64-65, 114, 247, 257, 262, 291n, 298-99n, 310n, 313n, 315n, 318n, 320-21n, 324n
Collier's, 70
Collins, Wayne M., 64-66, 215-16, 267-68, 298-99n, 310n, 313n, 318n, 320-24n; aids renunciants, 252-57, 260, 264-65; on Korematsu, 291n, 315n
Colombia, 59
Committee of fourteen (or Negotiating Committee), 204, 208, 309n

Communists, 46, 264, 301n; aka, 121
Concentration camps, Biddle refers to, 314n; Black (Justice) refers to, 74; Clark (Tom) refers to, 114; Eisenhower (D. D.) refers to, 175; Ickes refers to, 316n; Joint Chiefs of Staff refer to, 175; Opler (Marvin) refers to, 252; Rankin refers to, 54; Roberts (Justice) refers to, 74; Roosevelt refers to, 217; see Appendix 3 for partial listing of
Conference of Foreign Ministers of the American Republics (1942), 58
Congress, U.S., 71-73, 75, 112, 118, 161, 190, 218, 221, 227, 229, 251-52, 275, 319n; House Un-American Activities Committee, 151-52; voids renunciation statute, 321n
Conn, Stetson, 290n
Constitution, U.S., 68, 74, 96, 201, 217
Coordinating Committee (Tule Lake), 206-7, 230
Costa Rica, 58-59
Costello, John M., 151-52
Coverley, Harvey M., 149
Cozzens, Robert B., 100, 150, 215-16, 307n
Crystal City Internment Camp (Texas), 61-62, 176, 238, 256, 260, 289n, 313n; compared to relocation centers, 319n, 323n
Currie, Lauchlin, 108

Daihyo Sha Kai, 159, 161, 166, 167-69, 172, 203-6, 209-11; defined, 309n; Renraku-iin, 167; see also Negotiating Committee
Daniels, Roger, 43-44, 290n, 300n, 309n
De Amat, Francisco, 120, 137, 168-69, 203, 309n
Denman, William, 156
Deutsch, Monroe E., 108-9
DeWitt, John L., 28, 69-71, 88, 94-96, 101, 115, 154, 201, 284n, 294n-96n, 303n, 307n; instant-segregation plan of, 305n; intimate of Marshall, 295n; ordered to limit removals to Nikkei, 291n; urges denaturalizing Kibei, 307n
Dickstein, Samuel, 251, 313n
Dies Committee, 251
Dingell, John D., 55, 285n
Dominican Republic, 56, 59
Doub, George C., 263-64, 324n
Douglas, William O., 227

East Boston Internment Camp (Massachusetts), 176
Eberharter, Herman P., 320n
Ecuador, 59
Eisenhower, Dwight D., 175
Eisenhower, Milton S., 29, 84-86, 103, 106, 114-19, 293n, 298-300n, 318n; appointed head of WRA, 86, 114; recommendations to FDR, 115-16, 118-19; resigns from WRA, 115, 299n
El Salvador, 59

current situation, 269-73; loyalty rescreening by Army, 223-24; prewar population, 36-37; poll on evacuation, 297n; terrorism against returnees, 234-35; *see also* Issei, Nisei, Kibei, Sansei, Yonsei

Nisei, average age, 41; considered trade bait, 56; current situation, 269-74; defined, 35, 41, 284n; deportation of urged, 221, 229; draft classification, 135; in European Theater of war, *see* Army units (Nisei); in Pacific War, 320n; *see also* Military Intelligence Service Language School; Munson Report on, 39-47, 51-52; reaction to Hiroshima bombing, 249-50; reject work camp proposal, 97; *see also* Nikkei .

Nishio, Alan, 280

Nomura, Kichisaburo, 33

Norway, Fifth Column in, 49

Norweb, Henry, 60, 287n

Noyes, Lou, 216

Nuremberg Tribunal, 75, 114, 291n, 300n

Obata, Chiura, 120

O'Brien, Robert W., 106

Ohio State University, 112

Okamoto, Shoichi James, 312n

Okamura, Ray, 291n, 326n

Okubo, Mine, 80

Olson, Culbert L., 93-97, 106, 154, 298n

Omura, James M., 67

Opler, Marvin, 159, 239, 241, 245, 249-52, 259, 317n, 319n

Opler, Morris E., 142-43

Oregon, 36, 38, 79, 97

Oriental Exclusion Act (1924), 268-69

Oshima, Kanesaburo, 312n

OWI (Office of War Information), 115, 123, 300n, 314n

Ozawa v. United States, 41

Pacific Citizen, 177, 289n

Panama, 58, 183-84, 286-87n; concentration camp, 61, 183; Panama Canal, 59; treatment of Japanese residents, 183-84

Paraguay, 59

Patterson, Robert, 99, 296

Paul, Helen C., 178

Pearl Harbor, attack on, 26-27, 30, 36-37, 40, 46, 49, 52, 55, 94, 135; "Magic Messages," 283n; Pearl Harbor hearings (1946), 34, 39; Roberts Commission Report on, 49, 94

Pennsylvania State University, 300n

Pentagon Papers, 52

Peru, 59-66, 185, 271, 287-89n; internees sent to U.S. camps on say-so of Peru, 288n; Peruvian Japanese population, 287n; postwar deportations to Japan, 288n, 289n; "voluntary detainees," 62

Petersen, William, 42, 112, 269, 278, 298n, 301n

Philippines, 55-56, 62, 108, 188, 324n

Philpott, Gerald B., 312n

Pickett, Clarence E., 106

PM (N.Y. newspaper, defunct), 218

Pogue, Forrest C., 295n

Pomona Assembly Center (California), 113

Portland (Oregon), 90, 284n; *Oregonian,* 163

Portland (Livestock Pavilion) Assembly Center (Oregon), 79, 97

Poston (Colorado River Project) Relocation Center (Arizona), 86, 89, 99, 176, 178-79, 307n; called "valueless" land, 84, 293n, 301n; counterintelligence in, 178-79; penny fine for Postonites defying induction, 303n

Prado, Manuel, 60-61

Presidential Proclamation No. 2525 (gave Justice authority to detain suspect enemy aliens), 46

Presidential Proclamation No. 2655 (authorized deportation of renunciants), 181

Presidio (California), headquarters of the Western Defense Command, 79

Princeton University, 106

Prisoners of War (POW, civilian and military, U.S.), atrocity stories and, 218, 314n; in China, 62; in Japan, 62; in occupied territories, 173, 220, 222-24, 226, 288n; in Philippines, 56, 62

Pressure groups (anti-Japanese American), 35, 67, 284n; American Legion, 104, 118, 310n; Associated Farmers, 104; Grange, 104; *see also* Native Sons of the Golden West

Provine, John H., 129, 251-52, 320-21n

Provost Marshal General (office of), 69, 101, 223, 312n

Public Health Service, U.S., 80-81, 240

Public Law 405 (denaturalization bill), 229-30, 321n, 313n

Public Law 414 (Immigration and Naturalization Act, 1952), 268-69

Public Law 503 (provided penalties for defying Army orders), 72-73, 98, 201n, 290-91n

Public Law 751 ("authorized entry" permitted Peruvian Japanese), 289n

Public Proclamation No. 12 (altered military area boundaries), 296n

Public Proclamation No. 21 (authorized Army loyalty rescreening), 192-93

Purcell, James, 315n

Puyallup (Camp Harmony) Assembly Center (Washington), 57, 79-80

Quakers (Society of Friends), 46, 104-5, 228, 297n

Rankin, John, 54

Rauh, Joseph L., 325n

Ray, Ann, 317n, 322n

Red Cross (Nobel Peace Prize recipient, 1917, 1944), 51, 176, 315n

Reischauer, Edwin O., 270

Relocation, clearance required for, 101-2, 196-99; halt of voluntary moves, 39;

38; withheld apology for wartime racism, 299n
Wartime Civil Control Administration (WCCA), 72, 105, 286n, 296-97n, 300n
Washington (state of), 36, 38, 57, 78-79, 152, 201
Washington Post and Times Herald, 201, 263-64
Wax, Rosalie, 309n, 313n
WCCA, *see* Wartime Civil Control Administration
Weddell, Marion R., 103
Welles, Sumner, 58
Western Defense Command (WDC), 86, 101-2, 154, 192, 201, 223, 291n, 316n
Wheeler, Burton K., 98
Wickard, Claude, 114

Williams, Ivan, 254
Wilson, Edwin C., 58, 286n
Wohlstetter, Roberta, 283n
WPA (Works Projects Administration), 79, 115
WRA, *see* War Relocation Authority
Wyoming, 86, 98

Yamaguchi, Genji George, 303n
Yamashiro, George, 129, 132
Yamashita, Tomoyuki, 267; executed on anniversary of Pearl Harbor attack, 324-45n
Yamato damashii, 141; defined, 128
Yasui v. United States, 215, 313n
Yoneda, Karl, 132, 304n
Yonsei, 278
Yoshiyama, Tom S., 211-12, 216

Photo by Corky Lee

Michi Nishiura Weglyn grew up in Brentwood, California (Contra Costa County), before being incarcerated as a teenager in a desert prison, a 16,000 acre section of the Pima Indian Reservation in Arizona, then called Gila "Relocation Center." After graduating from the camp high school in 1944, she gained her freedom when Mount Holyoke College in South Hadley, Massachusetts, offered her a full scholarship. Prior to the writing of this book, she was—as Michi—a highly acclaimed theatrical costume designer in theater and television, including eight years on the Perry Como Show.

In recognition of her work on this seminal volume, Ms. Weglyn is the recipient of honorary degrees from Hunter College, New York City; California State Polytechnic University, Pomona, California; and Mount Holyoke College.

Royalties from the sale of *Years of Infamy* will be donated to the Endowed Chair for Multicultural Studies, which was established by California State Polytechnic University, Pomona, in the name of Michi Nishiura Weglyn and Walter Weglyn, her late husband, a Holocaust survivor. The [chair] seeks to implement an academic program to draw nationally and internationally known scholars to the University to promote [understanding of] peoples within our society and [the world].